DATA ANALYSIS FOR
SOCIAL WORKERS

DATA ANALYSIS FOR SOCIAL WORKERS

DENISE MONTCALM
University of Nevada, Reno

DAVID ROYSE
University of Kentucky

Allyn and Bacon

Boston ▪ London ▪ Toronto ▪ Sydney ▪ Tokyo ▪ Singapore

Series Editor: *Patricia Quinlin*
Editor-in-Chief, Social Sciences: *Karen Hanson*
Series Editorial Assistant: *Alyssa Pratt*
Marketing Manager: *Jacqueline Aaron*
Production Editor: *Christopher H. Rawlings*
Editorial-Production Service: *Omegatype Typography, Inc.*
Composition and Prepress Buyer: *Linda Cox*
Manufacturing Manager: *Suzanne Lareau*
Cover Administrator: *Kristina Mose-Libon*
Electronic Composition: *Omegatype Typography, Inc.*

Library of Congress Cataloging-in-Publication Data

Montcalm, Denise.
    Data analysis for social workers / Denise Montcalm, David Royse.
        p.   cm.
    Includes bibliographical references and index.
    ISBN 0-205-28903-7 (alk. paper)
    1. Social service—Statistical methods.   2. Statistics.   I. Royse, David D. (David Daniel)
II. Title.

HV29 .M66 2002
519.5'024'362—dc21

00-065048

Printed in the United States of America
10 9 8 7 6 5 4 3 2 1   06 05 04 03 02 01

CONTENTS

CHAPTER FIVE

Preparing and Interpreting Graphical Representations   60

CHAPTER SIX

Computing and Interpreting Measures of Central Tendency   80

CHAPTER SEVEN

Computing and Interpreting Measures of Dispersion   102

CHAPTER EIGHT

The Normal Distribution   117

CHAPTER NINE

**Inferential Statistics: Understanding
Probability and Sampling   139**

CHAPTER TEN

Hypothesis Testing   172

CHAPTER ELEVEN

Bivariate Analysis   190

CHAPTER TWELVE

Understanding and Interpreting Correlation   208

CHAPTER THIRTEEN

t-Tests and ANOVA: Testing Hypotheses about Means   230

CHAPTER FOURTEEN

A Glimpse into Multivariate Analyses 253

There appear to be three basic opinions about statistics. In the first group are those individuals who had good experiences with math all through their schooling, who believe that mathematical operations are logical and trustworthy, and that numbers are swell—perhaps even fun to compute. A second opinion group seems to consist of people who are somewhat indifferent to numbers and mathematical concepts. They are open to the value and power of statistical tools, but just not overly fond of and perhaps less certain of their footing when numbers are involved. A third group of individuals is composed of math-avoiders. These are individuals who may have had a difficult time with their multiplication tables and long division, who never "got" algebra or trigonometry. This group has likely postponed, delayed, or tried to find ways around taking required math and statistics courses. These men and women have little interest in working with numbers, are probably suspicious of them (statistics misrepresent and lie—don't they?), and are likely to identify with the phrase "the tyranny of numbers."

The good news for the readers of *Data Analysis for Social Workers* is that we have tried to present our material in such a way as to be very sympathetic to those in groups two and three who may have chosen social work because they currently aren't fond of or comfortable working with numbers. We understand that social work students don't often see the need for statistics or envision themselves as future researchers or evaluators. But then, neither of us knew when we were undergraduates that we would end up acquiring Ph.D.'s and teaching this very subject. In fact, when I (D. R.) was an undergraduate I was so afraid that I didn't understand what I needed to learn in a required statistics course that I dropped the class just before mid-term out of fear that I would get an unacceptable grade. I then shopped around in another department until I found a statistics course that I thought I could pass. I had absolutely no sense of the importance or the need for learning statistics. Rather, I viewed it only as an obstacle that was keeping me from graduating.

Poor instructors in elementary or high school can prevent students from getting started on the right foot and can contribute to much fear and loathing of statistical concepts. We acknowledge that—we've been there, experienced these instructors ourselves. As a result, we have drawn on our own life experiences and years of classroom teaching to design a book that removes much of the complexity and befuddlement that can accompany statistical texts. But make no mistake, this text is not a "Statistics for Dummies." Rather, it will cover all of the primary statistical procedures that are commonly found in introductory statistical texts.

Although we strive to remove much of the enigma and mystery about the use and computation of statistics, the topic is much broader than can be adequately covered in one academic term. After this course, you may want to acquire more depth by taking an intermediate or specialized course, such as one in multiple regression. We also want to make clear that as social work practitioners, you have a responsibility to learn statistics. You do not have the option *not* to learn. Statistics are a means for helping us solve problems, whether we are examining the average length of stay in a residential center for adults addicted to crack or trying to figure out why the number of high school dropouts has increased. As social workers, we are passionate about helping others and statistics are powerful tools available to us. Not using these tools is like not doing a complete psychosocial assessment or devising a treatment plan without interviewing the client. You *must* learn and feel comfortable about using most of the statistical procedures introduced in this text. To focus only on learning the material until you pass your last test could mean that you won't be as competent a social worker as you ought to be. The profession of social work needs competent, skilled individuals who can understand the results of and be able to conduct program evaluations and research efforts. We need to be able to demonstrate which interventions are working and which are not to discern if there are groupings of people and potential clients who are not being served by our agencies in representation to their numbers in the community.

OUR AUDIENCE

Data Analysis for Social Workers has been written for undergraduate and graduate social work students. Practitioners who need a refresher or who completed their educations without a statistical course requirement will likely find this book to be a helpful guide for helping them understand many of the key concepts and procedures necessary for interpreting and analyzing data. Our goal has been to make this text as reader-friendly as possible, knowing that many students can be expected to be less than enthusiastic about the prospect of having to learn statistical analysis. And to those of you who are excited about acquiring statistical tools, we hope that you, too, will find that the text keeps you interested and motivated to learn even more in a subsequent statistics course.

Instructors of research methodology courses will find that *Data Analysis for Social Workers* can be used as a companion or supplementary text. Educators will also find that the text provides many options for teaching. Students can, for instance, be encouraged to get the feel of computing a chi square or other procedures by hand—making use of the "Formula Alerts" found in most chapters. Or instructors can emphasize calculation using computer applications. On another level, instructors can also encourage students to seek out and bring professional journal articles to class, which relate to topics found in the micro and macro level examples found in this book. It is possible to use this text as a springboard that will propel the class into program evaluation and research literature—to stress the interpretation of reported statistics and what is statistically significant. However, we suspect that most instructors of introductory statistics courses will feel, as we do, that it is important for students to have some understanding of how statistics are derived, what they mean, and how they are to be interpreted.

ACKNOWLEDGMENTS

We would like to extend a special note of thanks to William A. Keeler for the input and technical assistance he provided in preparing earlier versions of this text. We would also like to thank the following reviewers: Fred Childers, California State University—Fresno; William Cloud, University of Denver; Michel Coconis, Grand Valley State University; Steve Kapp, University of Kansas; Stephen Marson, University of North Carolina Pembroke; Ogden Rogers, University of Wisconsin, River Falls; James Stafford, University of Mississippi; and Carole Upshur, University of Massachusetts, Boston.

DATA ANALYSIS FOR SOCIAL WORKERS

CHAPTER ONE

INTRODUCTION

DEVELOPING THE RIGHT MINDSET

Data surround us. Sometimes they are loosely stacked in cluttered piles, for example, in mounds of client intake forms heaped on a desk. That's an obvious form of data, but where else do they exist? Data may be almost invisible until we tap a few keys on our computer, log onto the Internet, or slide our credit card through some electronic apparatus. And what about the data that reside in a journal or photocopied article that we want to read? Or in the envelope the mail carrier brings with last semester's grades? These are just a few forms of data that come to mind.

As you have undoubtedly discovered, information (a synonym for data) can be like good advice—informative and helpful—or it can be like receiving bad directions when you are lost—confusing and misleading. The problem is that often we can't recognize and separate good information from bad. And when the data are unanalyzed, existing only as piles of intake sheets or clients' records, they are not very useful for making decisions.

Although statistics have been much maligned and vilified by generation after generation of students, we can say at least one good thing about them—statistics usually help us evaluate the quality of the information that they provide. Statistics are like computers that are programmed, before answering any question, to send a message that appraises you of the certainty of their answers. One computer may transmit, "Place very little confidence in what I'm about to say; I don't have enough information." In response to another question, the computer may communicate more confidently, "This is important; I'm 95% sure of what I'm about to say."

Once you begin to understand what's going on, then you will discover that although some statistical symbols may look like hieroglyphics, you don't have to learn 40,000 new characters. You'll need only to add a few new words and phrases to your vocabulary. These will be necessary to help you to navigate your way when various observations and experiences of the world are transformed into numerical values—the language of statistics. Admittedly, this requires some new learning on your part, but that's what an education is all about!

THE ROLE OF DATA IN EFFECTIVE
DAY-TO-DAY PRACTICE

Social work practice involves decision making at various levels: macro policy making and planning; administration of agencies (great and small); and direct service intervention with individuals, families, and groups. Agencies, whether operating on a national, state, or local level, need to know if their programs and interventions are effective. Are clients better or worse off? As social workers, we are required by our professional ethics to evaluate our interventions. The following statement is a passage taken from the National Association of Social Workers (NASW) Code of Ethics (1999):

> Social workers should monitor and evaluate policies, the implementation of programs, and practice interventions (sec. 5.02).

Increasingly, there is an expectation that we social workers should employ empirically validated treatments with our clients (Myers & Thyer, 1997) and that we must evaluate these efforts. In the past, social workers could defend their choice of interventions based on "practice wisdom" and not worry about gathering evidence to demonstrate whether they succeeded or not with their individual cases. But today our society is a litigious one—individuals are quick to seek legal remedies when they feel their rights (e.g., to competent treatment) have been neglected. Indeed, taxpayers and funding sources want to know that what they are paying for is money well spent. Can the intervention, whether at a community or societal level (e.g., welfare benefits) show good results? If not, then alternatives that can be supported by empirical data will be sought.

Besides the evaluation role, social workers are also researchers. At times we must conduct needs assessments to learn what new programs are needed, to determine the characteristics of the clients using our services, and to answer such questions as, "Has the number of crack babies being born in Metropolitan Hospital decreased in the last three years?" Social workers also conduct basic research and might want to look into, for instance, whether children who have been in foster care are at increased risk for encounters with the criminal justice system. Or we might want to investigate the extent of mental illness among incarcerated youth, or the prior use of methadone within a homeless population.

Good decision making requires that judgments be formed on the basis of reliable information. To this end, research methodology—that is, the systematic collection, analysis, and interpretation of data—is a tool used by social workers to investigate the various questions encountered in their practice. Statistics deal with the analysis of data created by social workers' investigations. We'll learn several different statistical procedures because the "correct" procedure is influenced by the type of data you have and what you want to know.

Knowledge of statistics will help you design better research projects and make better decisions when choosing from the various methodologies and approaches available. And you *will* be involved in research if you stay in a social work career. You might someday look at the effectiveness of a new intervention with Alzheimer's patients, compare the costs of various treatment approaches for depressed clients, examine the recidivism rates of clients placed on home incarceration, gather survey data from foster parents, or conduct a needs assessment for a new program for children with autism.

THE FOCUS OF THIS BOOK

Most social work students come into this field because they want to *do* something about our social problems, as opposed to merely observing, theorizing, or writing about them. Hence the focus of this book is on teaching the kind of practical statistics that you need to help solve problems for your agency and your clientele. We want you to be able to identify and make sense of the various types of data social workers create and encounter, as well as interpret and understand the statistics you will be reading in professional journals and reports. Finally, we hope that you will become enough of an "expert" to be able to use statistical procedures to evaluate the programs where you are employed.

You'll note if you look ahead that we feel it is important to show you how statistics are calculated—it is not a magical process, but a very rational one. Yet almost no one computes statistics by hand anymore; computers almost always do the number crunching for social work researchers. Still, we encourage you to get involved with the material by trying out a formula every once in a while—making your own calculations—in order to get a sense of the way statistics are produced and how they summarize data. Statistics is one of those topics best learned by doing. Knowing how numbers are condensed and statistical values are produced can be helpful in interpretation—in time, you may develop an intuition about when a certain value doesn't "look right."

Don't be concerned if you do not have access to the statistical software, SPSS, commonly found on college and university campuses. Although we like this popular program and use it in several computer applications illustrated in this text, there is an astonishing amount of free statistical software on the Internet. Like SPSS, these programs are menu-driven and quite simple to use. You may want to browse some of the features and abilities of the statistical computations that have been compiled on a web site maintained by John Pezzullo from Georgetown University. This amazing collection of interactive statistical pages can be found at http://members.aol.com/johnp71/javastat.html#Power. This site is so complete that you may find it unnecessary to purchase statistical software for data analysis.

Another alternative is Microsoft Excel, already installed on many new office and home computers. Excel can perform a long list of statistical functions and may, in fact, be all that you require in order to conduct all but the most sophisticated data analyses. Excel is not quite as user-friendly as SPSS, but the trade-off is that Excel is most likely to be available in the agencies where you are working or doing your internships. SPSS, on the other hand, is found on most college and university campuses, but not in many social services agencies. If you decide to learn how to use Excel for statistical analysis, you may want to consult one of the guides listed in the references at the end of this chapter. (See, for example, Albright, Winston, & Zappe, 1999; Brightman, 1999; Harnett & Horrell, 1998; and Middleton, 2000.)

The goal of this text is to help you comprehend statistical terms and procedures commonly used in the social sciences. If, by the end of the academic term you can recognize, for example, when it is appropriate to apply a *t*-test and when to use a chi-square as well as how to understand the information they provide, then our goal will have been achieved—whether or not you like math or ever thought of yourself as a "number cruncher."

If you have already taken a research course, you probably learned some terms that will appear in this text. That's great, even if you have not thought about them for a while or forgotten a few of them—a quick review will aid your recall. If you are taking a statistics course simultaneously with a research course, or even if you have not yet taken your first research course, we'll give you a brief definition of key terms. Our text does not assume that you have had a prior course in research methodology; it can be used as a primary text for introductory statistics or as a supplement for a research methods text.

DIFFERENT TYPES OF ANALYSES

Although the major portion of this text deals with **quantitative data** (i.e., things, objects, events, characteristics, attitudes that can be counted or measured), our text is somewhat unique in that it also introduces you to the concepts necessary for analyzing qualitative data. Quantitative data analysis usually involves responses from hundreds of clients or individuals who participated in a survey or program evaluation, whereas **qualitative data** analysis is concerned with discoveries that could not have been anticipated or expected, such as the experience of several single mothers on welfare, or the stories that children in foster care told themselves when they were not adopted. Qualitative researchers often employ small samples or numbers of research subjects and prefer depth and quality of information over counting or quantifying.

For instance, once a social worker in clinical practice encountered a patient with multiple personalities. The patient was an extremely talented artist, but very lonely because few people could understand what they perceived to be her mercurial mood swings and idiosyncrasies. By coincidence, the social worker also had another patient with the same diagnosis, artistic interests, and the same profound loneliness. With their permission, he introduced the two patients to each other, and the strategy seemed to work—they each gained a new friend. Qualitative researchers would want to know how these two lives changed and in what ways. To discover this, qualitative researchers might use personal interviews or possibly analyze diaries, journals, or letters written by the two patients. This particular intervention by the social worker could be evaluated only by qualitative methods. A quantitatively oriented researcher would find it extremely difficult to obtain a large sample of individuals with Dissociative Identity Disorder who had been brought together by their therapists so that the use of the friendship strategy tried by the social worker could be evaluated.

Quantitative researchers are always concerned with numbers, and use numerical values to measure attitudes, knowledge, and behaviors. Qualitative researchers put much more emphasis on trying to discover the meaning of an event, and the thoughts and feelings of the participants in their own words. Qualitative researchers usually do not use prepared questionnaires or standardized instruments, but let their questions emerge naturally from the give-and-take of their interviews or observations.

As you can imagine, quantitative researchers and qualitative researchers rely on different data analysis techniques. Social workers need to understand both perspectives—we will teach you how to find the patterns and significant differences in data, whether these data are in the form of numbers or words.

SYNCHRONIZING OUR EFFORTS

Social work programs, as well as their host colleges or universities, differ in many ways, including the manner in which particular courses are structured and sequenced. In some programs, a statistics course might be required before a research methods course can be taken, and in other programs the opposite might be true. If you have not yet completed a research methods course, then you need to learn some terms that are relevant for the analysis of data. If you *have* completed a research methods course, you will find this section a helpful review.

The following are some terms that you will need to learn, if you don't already know them:

A **population** (sometimes used synonymously with *universe*) represents all of the elements or individuals who meet certain defined criteria. Thus, a population can refer to all the recent high school graduates within a county, all the households in Reno with a phone, all people over the age of 70 who are legally registered to drive a car in the state of Delaware, or all of the clients who received services from a sheltered workshop during a specific calendar year. A population can also refer to all the inhabitants of a particular geographic location (e.g., the population of Los Angeles). A **sample** is a small group or subset of the larger population pool. If you are looking at the whole group of clients who received services during the calendar year 2000–2001, that group is the population. However, if there are too many clients for you to look at all of them (say, there are 2,500 clients), then you might draw a random sample of 300 or so to represent the client population for that year.

Social work researchers often use **descriptive statistics** to summarize data coming from either a sample or a population. For instance, you might find that the average age of the sample was 27.5 years, that 80% were female, two-thirds were high school graduates, and 15% were African American. Do you see how this works? Even though you haven't seen the data, you already have some idea about who would and who wouldn't be the typical client. You would have an entirely different concept if the average age were 70.2 years and two-thirds had earned a Ph.D. Descriptive statistics provide "snapshots" that allow us to form mental pictures of the patterns that characterize our data.

Inferential statistics are employed when data gathered from samples are used to make estimates about certain characteristics of a population. For instance, suppose you are a staff member paid to advise a U.S. senator from Ohio on social service issues. Further, the senator is planning to propose some changes in Medicare legislation but first wants to learn what her constituents think. She asks you to interview some voters back home. Your sample (whether it involves 5, 50, or 500 individuals) and how it is selected (e.g., drawn randomly from a list of voters, or a convenience sample taken at a political rally) has important implications for how well it can represent all the population of eligible voters in Ohio. From the sample, you want to be able to infer, to know with some accuracy, the sentiments of the voters. Inferential statistics allow you to determine how well the sample represents the population by understanding the sampling error. Inferential statistics permit comparisons among groups so that you can check whether males hold different opinions from females, or whether younger voters differ from older voters.

The actual interviews or surveys you make constitute the **raw data**—the unprocessed information that is tabulated or entered into the computer. When you are directly involved in conducting interviews or distributing surveys, it is possible to get a feel for the data. Imagine a scenario in which 8 out of the first 10 voters you talk with happily endorse the changes being advocated by the senator. If that pattern continues as you talk with additional voters, you could easily predict how the survey would turn out. Maybe you also get the impression that Republican voters oppose the changes, whereas Democrats favor them. Statistics allow you to check your impressions against reality.

Inferential statistics are often used when you are concerned with the probability of being in error, and when there are formal hypotheses to test. By way of review, a **hypothesis** is a statement about a presumed relationship. For instance, you might jot down the following hypothesis:

> The proposed Medicare amendments will be more popular with younger than with older voters.

Thus, you would be interested in any association between age and attitudes about the Medicare amendments. Your project director, however, might be more concerned with another hypothesis:

> Registered Democrats are more likely to support the Medicare amendment than registered Republicans.

Notice that in the first hypothesis, we would have to determine (possibly from a survey) or secure (from the local election board) a list of persons who voted. For the second hypothesis, our data would come from a list of those who were registered to vote. Are those who are registered to vote and those who voted the same group of people? Actually, there are many more individuals who are registered to vote than who make it to the polls on election day. Researchers must concern themselves with such fine distinctions. In fact, we **operationalize** our terms so that others will know exactly how we defined things and arrived at our conclusions. For instance, Jasmine might operationalize *voters* as Ohio residents who had voted in the last presidential election (since national elections tend to attract more voters than statewide ones)—even if the listing of voters was 3 years old. Wanda, on the other hand, might want a more recent list and might operationalize *voters* as those who voted in the last election—whatever the issue. For another study, Martha might operationalize *voters* as anyone who says he or she is registered to vote.

Researchers have a lot of freedom to operationalize their concepts. Even so, the availability or format of the data often has a strong effect on the way terms are defined. For instance, you might decide to operationalize *repeat abuser* as those with new reports of abuse within the last 12 months because that's as far back as the database goes. Although going back 3, 5, or 10 years might produce stronger research, there are always pragmatic decisions about what data are available to us and at what cost. The amount of time we have or the urgency with which we must submit a report or evaluation can also be a factor affecting the data that we decide to use or collect. Each time we operationalize, we are by necessity determining what gets included and what is excluded from our study.

Whenever researchers quantify, measure, or categorize observations about our research subjects—whether it be examining subjects' physical characteristics, unconscious attitudes, past behaviors, or knowledge about a particular topic—we create **variables.** Age, gender, and height are variables, and so are attitudes about marijuana smoking and abortion. The number of alcoholic beverages consumed in the past month is a variable, as is the number of candy bars eaten in the past 6 weeks, and the amount of money donated to charitable causes in the past year.

Independent variables are those that help us to analyze the data by sorting and categorizing. We might use age as a variable to examine the question, "Do older respondents have different attitudes about corporal punishment than younger ones?" The variable of race might be used to investigate the concern, "Are African American adolescents more fatalistic than Native American teens?" In this question, fatalism is the topic of investigation and, therefore, is the **dependent variable.** Our dependent variable is the thing we are trying to understand or predict—the subject of our hypothesis or research question. We would use statistical techniques to see if there were significant differences between Native American and African American youths in the extent of their fatalistic thinking, or to see if attitudes about corporal punishment varied by age group.

These are some of the basic terms you need to know. At the end of each chapter, we list the new vocabulary terms introduced in that chapter, so you can study and test yourself without seeing any accompanying definitions. Make sure you learn these terms!

TERMS TO KNOW

Dependent variable (p. 7)   Population (p. 5)
Descriptive statistics (p. 5)   Qualitative data (p. 4)
Hypothesis (p. 6)   Quantitative data (p. 4)
Independent variable (p. 7)   Raw data (p. 6)
Inferential statistics (p. 6)   Sample (p. 5)
Operationalize (p. 7)   Variable (p. 7)

REVIEW PROBLEMS

The situation: Bob has read the case records of 50 adolescents admitted to the outpatient treatment center. He has randomly selected these cases from approximately 900 persons 13 to 18 years of age admitted in the past year. He observes that 18% of the clients have dropped out of school, that most are female, and that on average the clients are 15.3 years old.

1. Has Bob operationalized "adolescent"?

2. Are the 50 case records he selected a sample or a population?

3. Bob has a hunch that a diagnosis of depression is more likely to be made for clients who have dropped out of school than for those who are regularly attending school. Is this a hypothesis?

4. If Bob is trying to understand depression—who is depressed and why—is the variable of school attendance a dependent or an independent variable?

5. Bob and his friend Sam get into a discussion. Bob maintains that the raw data for his study came from the 50 case files he read, but Sam argues that all 900 case files represent the raw data. Who is right?

6. What are the three variables mentioned in the preceding situation?

7. How might Bob operationalize the variable *juvenile delinquent*?

8. Bob is trying to construct only a quick client profile, not to say that the 50 cases he selected accurately represented all of the agency's clients. Is Bob using descriptive statistics or inferential statistics?

REFERENCES

Albright, S. C., Winston, W. L., & Zappe, C. (1999). *Data analysis and decision-making with Microsoft Excel.* Pacific Grove, CA: Duxbury Press.

Brightman, H. (1999). *Data analysis in plain English with Microsoft Excel.* Pacific Grove, CA: Duxbury Press.

Harnett, D. L., & Horrell, J. F. (1998). *Data analysis and decision models with Excel.* New York: John Wiley & Sons.

Middleton, M. (2000). *Data analysis using Microsoft Excel: Updated for Office 97 and 98.* Pacific Grove, CA: Duxbury Press.

Myers, L. L., & Thyer, B. A. (1997). Should social work clients have the right to effective treatment? *Social Work, 42,* 288–298.

National Association of Social Workers. (1999). *Code of ethics* (sec. 5.02). Washington, DC: Author.

CHAPTER TWO

ETHICAL CONSIDERATIONS

Because social work is a profession and not just a job, social workers are called to follow a code of ethics. The *Code of Ethics* developed by the National Association of Social Work (NASW) makes it very clear that social workers should "monitor and evaluate policies, the implementation of programs, and practice interventions" and further, that we should "promote and facilitate evaluation and research to contribute to the development of knowledge" (1999). Whether social workers should be conducting research and evaluation of their practice is *not* a controversial issue. The *Code of Ethics* makes it abundantly evident that social workers must examine what they do to and with clients, as well as stay current with emerging knowledge as it affects their interventions. To say this a slightly different way, social workers have a responsibility to ensure that current practices can be supported by research.

The *Code of Ethics* also requires that we follow ethical guidelines in our research of interventions designed to improve the quality of clients' lives. Additional sections of the *Code of Ethics* state that social workers engaged in evaluation or research should obtain the consent of their research subjects, and that those who refuse to participate cannot be denied any services or privileges as a punishment. There can be no coercion of clients. Research participants must be informed of all possible risks and benefits, and they cannot be harmed in any way.

Because the ethical conduct of research and evaluation activities is so important for social workers, we are going to briefly discuss some of the key concepts involved, even before we begin to discuss statistical procedures. Knowledge of the right statistics to use will not help the researcher if there is possible injury to research subjects or if litigation could result from unethically acquiring information for a study. In fact, conducting an unethical study could possibly ruin one's reputation. In short, an enormous amount of time, energy, and resources could be wasted all because generally accepted procedures were not followed in seeking approval to conduct the study, advising the research subjects of their rights and risks of participation, securing their consent, and ensuring they are not harmed in any way.

PROTECTING RESEARCH SUBJECTS

To protect research participants when sensitive information is being collected, data are gathered anonymously whenever possible. When that is not practical, confidentiality protects their information. **Sensitive information** might include such variables as age, income, number of arrests, drug and alcohol use, sexual practices, previous jobs or firings, opinions about one's boss or coworkers, and so on.

Providing **anonymity** means that clients or research subjects cannot be identified by the researcher or by anyone else assisting with the data collection. Typically, this requires that no personal identifying information is collected (e.g., no names, addresses, phone numbers, social security numbers, and so forth). Anonymity is violated even if you don't ask for an individual's name but you recognize or happen to know the person from whom you are directly collecting data. When it is important to track research subjects for, say, a pretest and a posttest, anonymity can be protected by asking subjects to create a unique code that only they would know (e.g., the last four digits of their social security number in reverse order, followed by the first three letters of their favorite food).

Maintaining **confidentiality** refers to protecting and not revealing information. Confidential data are often kept in locked cabinets, and to offer even greater protection, questionnaires may be numbered so that names or other personally identifying information are not disclosed. The listing of names or social security numbers is then kept securely in a separate place so that it is difficult for casual observers or persons not connected with the project to know what any one specific research subject reported. Social workers try to safeguard clients' and research subjects' confidentiality unless there is compelling need to violate it to prevent someone from being harmed. For example, a client may let it slip that she is planning to kill herself and her child. In this situation, you should contact the proper authorities. Researchers view confidentiality as something close to a sacred vow, and would not violate an oral promise or a written statement guaranteeing confidentiality unless drastic measures were called for. The protection of confidential data can, however, be challenged by prosecutors and criminal justice authorities. Researchers have occasionally been subpoenaed for information that may have been collected from a particular individual accused of criminal acts.

Informed consent is a process whereby research subjects are provided with full information about their participation in the project. They must understand that they may freely choose to not participate without losing any benefits or services (if they are about to be, or already are, clients). Typically, informed consent also includes a written, 1- to 2-page document that details the subjects' rights, risks, and what they can expect by participating in the research project. Oral explanations may also be provided, and staff may meet with potential participants in order to answer questions that could arise. Signatures are usually required to show that research subjects have read the explanation and understood it.

When the research subjects are children or people with diminished capacity, additional procedures are required. Minors and members of certain other special populations (e.g., persons with mental retardation, dementia, and psychosis) cannot give informed consent. Rather, parents, guardians, or persons with the power of attorney must be contacted. Even with that approval, children and other special populations must still be given the opportunity to refuse or to **assent** (agree to participation).

Informed consent commonly includes such information as

- Who is conducting the study and answering questions about it?
- What is the purpose of the study?
- Where will the study take place and over what period of time?
- What are the possible risks to subjects?
- What will research subjects be asked to do (or what procedures will be performed)?
- What payment or incentives are there (if any)?
- What happens if one stops or drops out of the project? (Usually a statement is provided that says research subjects are entitled to drop out of the study at any time without any loss of benefits or privileges.)
- Is there any possible risk or harm, and if so, what actions can the researcher take to mitigate it?
- All research subjects must be volunteers. Absolutely no implied or subtle coercion can be used to recruit subjects.

Universities, hospitals, and other large agencies that receive federal funds are required to establish **Institutional Review Boards** (sometimes known as IRBs, or human subjects committees) to approve research efforts proposed by their faculty, students, staff, and physicians. These committees review research proposals—including the research objectives, the means by which subjects will be recruited, the actual research methodology (What will the researcher do? What will the subjects do?), the instrumentation, the informed consent, and so forth. Institutional review boards can approve projects, ask for revisions of planned procedures, or simply refuse to approve research proposals that have too great a risk of harm. They also might not approve of research that seems trivial or insignificant.

Social workers involved in interdisciplinary teams will likely encounter other professionals who have their own codes of ethics (e.g., psychologists and the American Psychological Association). It's unlikely that there will be a clash of interests because of ethical codes. However, disagreements can arise easily over the "best" way to obtain data. (See the next section.) The following is a brief list of guidelines for ethical research:

- Research participants must freely volunteer (they cannot be coerced, and there can be no implied threat of loss of services).
- Sufficient information about the study must be provided.
- No harm shall result as a consequence of participation.
- Sensitive information must be protected.

ETHICAL DILEMMAS

An **ethical dilemma** exists when there is a choice between two or more equally balanced paths. For instance, lying to research subjects would generally be considered unethical. And yet at times some slight deception might be necessary in order to carry out a study. For instance, Esmail, Everington, and Doyle (1993) were interested in investigating possible racial discrimination in the hiring of physicians with Asian names. They prepared a curriculum vitae and used either one of three English names or one of three Asian names. All fictitious applicants were male, of the same age, and with a similar length of experience. They changed the description of medical schools and secondary education randomly. Similar English and Asian vitae were mailed to 23 advertised posts in England. The authors discovered that there was discrimination against ethnic minorities. Applicants with English names were twice as likely to be selected, and the difference might have been even more dramatic but the investigation was stopped prematurely when charges of committing fraud were brought against the authors for conducting this study. (However, they weren't prosecuted.)

Could the authors have investigated their hypothesis simply by asking those persons who were hiring physicians if they were prejudiced? To change the example slightly, could an instructor who was concerned that several members of her social work practice class were prejudiced administer a questionnaire and get back valid data? Or might these students respond in a socially desirable manner because they knew what they were expected to think or believe? Getting at the real attitudes, as opposed to the politically correct or public attitudes, can be a challenge for the researcher. For this reason, IRBs will allow deception of research subjects if the deception is of crucial importance to the conduct of the study, and if the research subjects are debriefed afterwards and allowed to express their anger or irritation at being misled. One consideration the review boards must weigh is whether anyone is hurt by proposed deception.

Deception is a fairly common practice in some areas. Epley and Huff (1998) have reported that 42% of studies appearing in the 1996 volume of the *Journal of Personality and Social Psychology* involved deception. Social workers, however, are probably less likely than social psychologists to conduct a study involving deception.

Another potential ethical dilemma concerns whether to compensate research subjects. On one hand, there can be a concern that paying research subjects might induce them to respond in a way they think the researcher wants. So if they know the researcher is interested in, for example, persons with chronic drug addiction, subjects and potential subjects might embellish their information somewhat to make sure that they will receive the monetary benefits resulting from participation. On the other hand, asking individuals to travel to a location on a certain day to be given a psychological battery of tests seems somewhat of a burden unless there is a little remuneration.

Reimbursing participants for their costs (travel, baby-sitting, loss of hourly income) is a well-accepted practice. Researchers, however, try to avoid giving such large incentives that this could be viewed as "undue inducement," or result in persons fabricating information in order to be eligible to participate in the study. Sometimes small incentives are needed to keep participants involved—particularly when clients have already received services and may not be interested in cooperating with a posttest, or when the testing procedure is long and complicated or requires something typically viewed as undesirable, such as drawing a blood sample.

Denial of treatment in order to obtain a control group is another possible ethical dilemma. It would be unethical to deny a group of clients service simply because someone was planning on conducting some research. Fortunately, most of the research and evaluation activities conducted on social services do not require a control group that receives no services at all. Instead, it often makes sense to employ natural comparison groups composed of persons on a waiting list for service, persons who have started treatment and dropped out, "no-shows," persons who have chosen an alternative treatment (perhaps even jail or community service), and prior clients who received the old intervention. Many times, there's also the possibility of going to another agency in the community or state and obtaining client data from those receiving similar services. Another variation is to provide the control group with the old, standard intervention, while the experimental group receives the standard intervention in addition to the new, untested intervention.

When faced with an ethical dilemma, it is often helpful to write down the problem. Writing helps to focus and clarify the specific conflicts. Sometimes, solutions then become apparent. Another useful action is to discuss with a colleague the alternatives and ramifications of each decision. That step can be done either before or after reviewing the literature to see how other researchers have handled this particular problem. By all means, read the *Code of Ethics* and try to apply appropriate principles. If there is a university in your area, you might want to contact the IRB there to see if it can provide some consultation. Be sure to talk with your supervisor or other persons above you in the chain of command who might need to know about the dilemma. Finally, there are a number of books on ethical decision making that might be helpful. See, for example, Congress (1999); Linzer (1999); Steinman, Richardson, and McEnroe (1998); and Loewenberg and Dolgoff (1996).

TELLING THE TRUTH WITH STATISTICS

In 1954, Darrell Huff wrote a popular little book entitled *How to Lie with Statistics.* This catchy title seemed to strike a vital chord in the American public, and although not many people can tell you what points Mr. Huff actually made (he wasn't interested in training people how to misrepresent the truth, but in teaching them how to avoid misleading with numbers), many people seem to believe that statistics are only good for lying and double-dealing. Huff cites a quote attributed to Disraeli which typifies this attitude: "There are three kinds of lies—lies, damned lies, and statistics" (p. i). And then there's the quote attributed to Andrew Lang that ought to concern every lover of the truth: "He used statistics as a drunken man uses lampposts: for support rather than illumination" (Phillips & Cole, 1996).

In this section, our goal is to help prepare you for ethical social work and research practice by pointing out uses of statistics that would deceive. Ethical social workers do not deliberately misrepresent findings. Although careless presentation of data can occur, we think mistakes will be less likely if readers note the following potential pitfalls.

Misguiding by Reporting Only Percentages

A clinician who writes a report claiming a 66% success rate with her clients is likely to attract a good deal of attention. Eager readers will leap to her discussion of the intervention and pore over it and notice the themes and activities, how often the therapist and clients met together, the characteristics of the clients, and so forth. However, what may be more important is whether the success rate was based on 2 of 3 clients improving or on the improvement of 374 out of 561 clients. While the success rate is of interest, it should not be viewed without consideration of the sample size.

Note: The credibility of an outcome study depends, in large part, on the sample size.

Similarly, percentages can deceive when the basis for comparing is not a fair comparison. Quick loan companies that lend several hundred dollars to individuals who need cash until payday or until their Social Security checks arrive may claim low rates of interest, say, 5% compared to the 18% annual rate charged by credit card companies. However, their 5% rate is a weekly rate—not a yearly rate. The advertised 5% rate becomes a 500% or more yearly rate.

Distortions can also occur when other factors are not considered. For instance, suppose one found some data showing that housing costs have risen by 200% over the past 20 years. Although that certainly sounds alarming, it shouldn't be viewed without considering how much inflation has also caused income levels to rise as well. Upon closer inspection, it might turn out that housing costs still constitute only about 20% of the average person's income. Thus, the proportion of one's income spent for housing might be a more accurate reflection of actual cost than dollar amounts, which have risen due to inflationary effects.

Note: When making comparisons, all elements must be as similar as possible.

When One Is More Than One

Huff mentions a concept that has been popularized by many keynote speakers and unknown wags: To understand when one is more than one, think about the recipe for horse and rabbit stew. Now think about adding to a mixture of carrots and celery simmering on a hot stove, one rabbit, and then one horse. Whether you are a vegetarian or not, the obvious differences in the amount of volume created by one horse compared to one rabbit is apparent. Sometimes a 1:1 ratio requires greater specification. What might make for a better stew might be one part rabbit—meaning one standardized measure (e.g., 8 ounces)—to 8 ounces of horse meat.

Another version of this theme is to dismiss one of something and to present it as not being important—after all, one is a very small number. For instance, maybe there's been only one case of cholera in the county in the past 6 months. That seems okay unless that one case was you. One disaster, be it an earthquake or tornado or flood, can affect thousands of lives and require millions of dollars in postdisaster aid to help the victims rebuild.

Note: Some events can be moving and impressive, regardless of sample size.

Presumption of Similarity

Percentages lull us into thinking that, for instance, a 10% funding loss in one agency is the same as a 10% funding loss in another. But richer agencies might be better able to absorb a 10% cut than a small agency because of economies of scale. Imagine a scenario in which a small program (perhaps a Big Brothers/Big Sisters agency in a rural area) has only a director and a single staff person. If their annual budget is roughly $60,000 a year, then a 10% cut means they have to save $6,000. That might be hard to do because their combined office supply, mailing, phone, and other miscellaneous expenses might not sum to anything close to that amount. And they can't do without a phone, anyway. The reduction in funding might require laying off or at least cutting back on the number of hours of one of the employees—which could have very real repercussions not only on the amount of Big Brother/Big Sister matches that could be made, but also for the person affected—particularly if he or she was a single parent with a mortgage and a car payment.

To take another example of presumed similarity, imagine being informed that the agency where you work will be getting 4% annual raises. That sounds fair, initially. Case workers earning $25,000 get a $1,000 increase in pay. However, let's say the CEO gets the same percent raise, and her salary is $150,000. Her 4% raise amounts to $6,000, or 6 times what the direct service workers are getting. Might it be more fair if the CEO got a $1,000 raise—the same as most of the other employees?

Personal Biases

Our personal biases can get in the way of our presenting true and accurate pictures. Let's say that Joe Gofast has been active in removing legislation that required riders on motorcycles to wear helmets. He points with pride to the fact that there were fewer head injuries last year. Helmets, he thinks, cause accidents because riders can't hear as well while wearing them. However, perhaps Joe shouldn't consider the number of motorcycle accidents without considering the number of motorcycles registered and perhaps even the number of riders under the age of 25. What might have happened was a serendipitous drop in accidents because there were fewer young bike riders. Another possibility is that there were fewer head injuries requiring hospitalization because there were more fatalities pronounced dead on arrival. A third possibility is that, because of our medical technology, even fewer head injuries from bike accidents might actually have cost taxpayers more in hospitalization expenses because heroic efforts can keep persons with severe head injuries alive who would not have lived even 10 years ago.

Persons who love to handle poisonous snakes might justify their actions by pointing out that fewer persons die of snake bites each year than of lightning strikes. However, the justification of their activities does not address the statistical probability of persons who handle snakes *frequently*—it only refers to accidental encounters. The more times we do something dangerous, the more we increase the odds of doing harm to ourselves. When trying to determine if a statistic or a conclusion is being fairly presented, don't forget to ask yourself if it makes sense.

Persons with particularly strong feelings about a program or intervention or certain activity should not choose a biased sample (persons known to support their position) and present statistics from that group unless the audience or reader is fully informed about who the sample is and how it was composed. Further, if there are statistical data available (for example, the number of motorcycle accidents involving those with and without helmets, the number of motorcycle fatalities, the number of young persons having accidents on motorcycles, and the public's expenditures on motorcycle-related accidents for persons without medical insurance), the ethical researcher must present for discussion all of the relevant statistics. One should not pick and choose among statistics, portraying only those that agree with one's own personal biases.

Along this line, it is also possible to mislead one's audience if it is not made clear that a convenience sample was used rather than one randomly selected. To the general public, findings drawn from a convenience sample of 10 or 12 clients might sound equally as impressive as those derived from a carefully planned, random sample of 120. It's not just sample size, however, that's important. The quality of the sample is a key factor in how much confidence can be placed in the findings. Sometimes only the researcher knows how poor a quality or unrepresentative the sample really is. Don't mislead by glossing over samples that are unrepresentative and unscientific and minimizing their flaws.

Note: The quality of a sample is just as important as its size.

Misrepresentation in Graphics

In Chapter 5 we caution against making graphs look larger than the actual amount of increase. This is easy to do with figures that represent numerical concepts. In

Figure 2.1, the graphics distort a small (only 15%) increase in the actual growth of the social action fund.

Additionally, the way we present data in tables may be misleading. Suppose you are conducting a community needs assessment, and 47% of the respondents indicate that they want to find solutions to the recent rash of traffic accidents by young people. On the Internet, you seek national data on rates of motor vehicle accidents by age group, and this is what you find:

Motor Vehicle Accident Rates per 100,000

Ages 15 to 24	5.4%
Ages 25 to 44	17.5%
Ages 45 to 64	14.2%
Age 65 and older	22.7%

One thing that strikes you immediately is that the youngest age bracket has proportionately fewer accidents than any of the other age groups. But is this accurate? Ask any parent who has a 17-year-old driver in the house and relatives of 65 years of age or older or so who they would rather have drive their new car. These actual statistics are somewhat misleading for a couple of reasons. First, 15-year-olds in many states can't drive, and 16-year-olds in other states may not begin driving immediately, but instead take weeks of driver education classes and may be closely supervised. They may not own cars and thus have to rely on parents or others for a vehicle. In short, teens probably are not driving as much or as many miles as other drivers who own cars. Second, notice that the age group 15 to 24 is the narrowest of the four age brackets. For instance, the 25 to 44 group spans 20 years, as

Social Action Fund 2000

Social Action Fund 2002

FIGURE 2.1   **Example of Misrepresentation in Graphics**

does the group 45 to 64, but the group 15 to 24 spans only 10 years—the age intervals are unequal. What would make for more accurate data, although it is probably harder to obtain, would be the number of accidents per miles driven in the past 6 months by drivers' actual ages. So, while these 1995 data were obtained from a very legitimate source (*Monthly Vital Statistics Report,* Centers for Disease Control and Prevention, 1997), we have learned enough about statistics to know that at times the reader has to question the data—not simply accept them at face value because they appear in an official publication.

Note: Apply equal intervals whenever constructing categories for presentation of tabular data.

To take another example: In higher education, universities compare average salaries of assistant, associate, and full professors in various fields. Often these salaries are a lot higher than assistant professors in social work are actually earning, but these averages lead the public to think that social work professors are extremely well paid. Would it make a difference if professors from medical schools and law schools were averaged in to compute a university's "average" salaries?

Social workers living close to state lines sometimes find a situation in which an agency director proclaims, "Our salaries are the highest in the state." Yet salaries in that state might be, on average, $2,500 less than those just across the state line. Although the director's statement is technically true, it could be misleading in a metropolitan area where residents routinely live in one state but commute to the bordering state for employment.

In sum, there are many ways that statistics can be used to mislead and distort. However, the ethical social worker never tries to deceive his or her audience while presenting statistical data or analysis. When in doubt, check out troubling statements with knowledgeable colleagues. Try to take a perspective opposite to the view you hold, and at all times try to keep an open mind. If you try to be as objective as possible, you're on your way to being an ethical researcher!

TERMS TO KNOW

Anonymity (p. 10)
Assent (p. 11)
Confidentiality (p. 10)
Ethical dilemma (p. 12)

Informed consent (p. 10)
Institutional review board (IRB) (p. 11)
Sensitive information (p. 10)

REVIEW PROBLEMS

1. List at least five information elements that should be contained in an informed consent.

2. List four guidelines for conducting ethical research.

3. George, a social work student, is planning to interview social work majors to find out how many of them have cheated on tests while in college. He starts by calling his friends in the same statistics class, and then plans to contact others who have been in his policy and practice classes. George promises all of them anonymity. Is *anonymity* the correct term? If not, what would have been a better term to have used?

4. Could the information that George is planning to collect be considered sensitive information?

5. Pam is a research assistant in a pain management clinic. The physician in charge of running a study testing a new narcotic asks Pam to recruit research subjects while clients are waiting for their appointments. He gives Pam a large loose-leaf notebook so that she can familiarize herself with prior studies conducted with the drug—including those detailing its side effects. He asks Pam to sign up 50 subjects over the next 2 weeks and suggests that he will give her a large raise in pay if she recruits all the patients needed for the study.

   Pam doesn't bother reading all of the material and sets out to get the 50 signatures on the prepared informed consent forms. Although clients ask her some questions that she can't answer, Pam always tells the potential research subjects that they should ask the doctor when they meet with him. After being turned down by the first five people she approached, Pam began suggesting that Dr. Osgood would not be very happy with his patients if they didn't agree to participate. After that, every patient but one signed up to participate in the research.

   Were Pam's actions unethical? Why or why not?

REFERENCES

Centers for Disease Control and Prevention. (1997). *Monthly Vital Statistics Report, 45,* Supp. 2, pp. i, 23.

Congress, E. (1999). *Social work values and ethics: Identifying and resolving ethical dilemmas.* Belmont, CA: Wadsworth.

Epley, N., & Huff, C. (1998). Suspicion, affective response, and educational benefit as a result of deception in psychology research. *Personality and Social Psychology Bulletin, 24,* 759–768.

Esmail, A., Everington, S., & Doyle, H. (1993). Racial discrimination in the allocation of distinction awards? Analysis of list of award holders by type of award, specialty, and region. *British Medical Journal, 316,* 193–194.

Huff, D. (1954). *How to lie with statistics.* New York: Norton.

Linzer, N. (1999). *Ethical dilemmas in social work practice.* Boston: Allyn & Bacon.

Loewenberg, F., & Dolgoff, R. (1996). *Ethical decisions for social work practice.* Itasca, IL: F. E. Peacock.

National Association of Social Workers. (1999). *Code of ethics.* Washington, DC: Author.

Phillips, L., & Cole, W. (1996). *Random House treasury of humorous quotations.* New York: Random House.

Steinman, S. O., Richardson, N. F., & McEnroe, T. (1998). *The ethical decision-making manual for helping professionals.* Belmont, CA: Wadsworth.

CHAPTER THREE

THE NATURE OF DATA

WHAT ARE DATA?

If you've been around children, you've probably been amused when young Tasha points to a dog and says proudly, "cat." Or perhaps you've chuckled when a toddler has gleefully greeted a total stranger as "Daddy." Each of these youngsters is on the right track—learning that objects in his or her world have certain characteristics in common. After all, both cats and dogs have four legs, usually they have tails and are furry. As we get older and learn to discern differences, we recognize that all Toyotas are cars, but that all cars are not Toyotas. If it is important to us, we learn to look at the front grill or the taillights for a certain distinctiveness that would identify one make of car from another. And erroneous or not, what young Tasha has been doing is making observations. To be very simplistic about it, data are nothing more than observations about the world around us.

If we're planning on going outside, we will probably note, for instance, whether it is hot or cold enough to wear a jacket. Sometimes we observe the thermometer to see exactly how hot it is in objective terms. "Ninety-eight degrees!" we might shout to a disbelieving friend. If the plants in the window box are wilted, that's an important piece of data—providing quite different information than if you had opened the door and found 6 inches of snow on the ground.

Besides the weather, we notice how much we're paid, how long we have to wait in a physician's office, what grades we get from our professors, how fast our car is traveling down the highway. In each of these instances, we are measuring something of interest by using standardized categories. **Measurement** involves counting or quantifying our observations using accepted rules or units. Thus, we understand the passing of time by dividing a day into 24 hours, each hour by 60 minutes, and each minute by 60 seconds. Thermometers and speedometers have been scientifically calibrated so that we can have a common understanding of what 98 degrees Fahrenheit or 75 miles per hour means.

In the social sciences, we often design paper-and-pen tests and questionnaires to measure such diverse concepts as intelligence, potentiality for child abuse, attitudes about drinking, or problems like depression. For instance, if you were attempting to assess whether clients entering your residential treatment program were depressed, you might administer a questionnaire that would ask them such questions as these:

Examples of Possible Questionnaire Items for Assessing Depression

	STRONGLY AGREE	AGREE	UNDECIDED	DISAGREE	STRONGLY DISAGREE
1. I feel that life is worthwhile.	☐	☐	☐	☐	☐
2. I enjoy life.	☐	☐	☐	☐	☐
3. I wish that I had never been born.	☐	☐	☐	☐	☐
4. Each day is a burden.	☐	☐	☐	☐	☐
5. I am happy every day.	☐	☐	☐	☐	☐
6. Most days I am lugubrious.	☐	☐	☐	☐	☐
7. Many days I am blue but generally optimistic.	☐	☐	☐	☐	☐
8. I like Drew Carey.	☐	☐	☐	☐	☐
9. The Cleveland Browns are a great team.	☐	☐	☐	☐	☐

An issue of concern for researchers and evaluators is whether the questionnaires and instruments being used to gather data are reliable and valid. **Reliability** refers to a characteristic similar in nature to dependability. That is, a reliable measure tends to consistently provide accurate measurements. Any instrument that assessed a group of individuals as being very depressed at 9:00 a.m. and then four hours later found the same group *not* depressed certainly wouldn't be reliable. How could this happen? Take a close look at the questionnaire items in the preceding table, particularly item 6. Do you know what the term *lugubrious* means? If you are not sure, then it is possible that other people reading the item might guess, too. If the meaning is not perfectly obvious, it is possible to guess one way in the morning and a different way in the afternoon. Unclear and confusing items like items 6 and 7 (how can one be both blue and optimistic?) undermine the reliability of a questionnaire because they create potential scenarios whereby individuals who are depressed might not be able to show or record it and, conversely, those who are *not* depressed might somehow indicate that they *are* depressed because they are puzzled about how to respond to the items. In the process of creating reliable instruments, researchers must weed out troublesome items that don't contribute to a scale's reliability.

Another important consideration when evaluating instruments is **validity.** Validity concerns how well an instrument approximates the concept or construct it was designed to measure. A scale designed to assess depression should provide a reasonable gauge of depression. If it failed to detect depression in a group of individuals who had attempted suicide and consequently been admitted to an inpatient psychiatric unit, then it would not be valid for measuring depression because these individuals represent depression in an extreme form.

Once again, it is possible to wonder how an instrument constructed to measure depression could end up measuring something else. A quick scan of items 8 and 9 above further reveals two more items that do not assist us in assessing an individual's depression and, therefore, undermine the scale's validity. However, these items may not necessarily detract from the instrument's reliability because if someone liked Drew Carey or the Cleveland Browns in the morning, it is very likely that he or she would respond the same way in the afternoon, or whenever asked on a second occasion.

Just as there are various forms of reliability, there are different types of validity and various ways that researchers and evaluators go about demonstrating that newly designed instruments are valid and reliable. However, additional detail about these topics is a subject that lies more in the realm of research methodology than in an introduction to statistics text. Suffice it to say that if no information is available about a questionnaire's or instrument's reliability and validity, then reliability and validity cannot be assumed. The instrument might be completely worthless either because it actually measured a different concept than intended, or because it measured the concept inaccurately. Anytime a new questionnaire or instrument is created for research or evaluation purposes, one should be able to show that it has sufficient reliability and validity. For this reason, many researchers and evaluators look first for instruments that have been published and already have known reliability and validity. Along this line, Joel Fischer and Kevin Corcoran's reference book, *Measures for Clinical Practice* (2000), is a very useful resource. If no good instrument can be found to measure the concept or problem that interests you, then it is logical to construct one of your own.

Whether you are measuring an emotional state, an attitude, or knowledge, the underlying notion is the same—science requires that observations be objective (not influenced by personal bias) and capable of being replicated (verified) by others. The goal is to obtain accurate measurements. The data that are produced are what we interpret with statistical procedures.

LEVELS OF MEASUREMENT

When researchers examine data, they note how precisely the variables have been measured. This is important because determining which procedure to use in an analysis depends, in part, on the level of measurement (type of data) involved. Some statistics work with one kind of data but not with another. To use an example, we understand how data can be categorized by thinking about variables such as cars, breeds of dogs, or restaurants. It is easy to recognize that there are many types of cars and breeds of dogs. Restaurants, too, can be categorized in terms of their specialties, the prices of their entrees, their hours of operation, seating capacity, and so forth. Similarly, data, too, can also be conceptualized as fitting into certain categories. By convention, the categories used to sort data are called **levels of measurement.** Often the lowest levels of variables are considered to be measured (quantified) rather crudely, whereas those at the highest level are judged to be measured very precisely. A couple of categories are in between. We'll start with the lowest level of measurement.

Nominal Measurement

The **nominal level of measurement** is sometimes called the qualitative level because it involves description, the simplest form of measurement. Nominal measurement requires that we assign names or terms to represent the different categories or classifications into which we sort our observations. Clients might be grouped dichotomously, for example, as employed or unemployed, or as child or adult. Such **dichotomous variables** contain only two possible categories. However, sometimes we run into situations where more than two categories apply. In specifying marital status, for instance, a young parent may be married, divorced, separated, widowed, or never married. In some situations, it may be more important to collapse these categories into simply married or not married. As a researcher, that's your call—you get to decide what level of differentiation is important to your project. (If this sounds a little scary, remember you can always consult the professional literature to see how other researchers have approached the same problem.)

When you think about variables that allow the placement of most people into broad, mutually exclusive categories, keep in mind that the nominal level of measurement is very seductive. Sometimes social workers designing questionnaires will create response choices that categorize data in a way that actually loses or masks information. For example, think about a needs assessment where age is recorded this way: young clients, middle-aged clients, elderly clients. Suppose your friend Susie tells you there were 50 young clients, 110 middle-aged ones, and 25 elderly clients. "That's wonderful," you say. "But what I really wanted to know is their average age."

"Ooops," she says. "I guess we should have thought about that earlier."

Nominal data restrict you to sorting the data into defined categories and reporting percentages. With nominal data, you can't compute averages because all you have are tabulations of people, objects, or events by category or classification. When your data are captured at this level, it is not possible to do any sophisticated statistical analyses. Often, it's useful simply to construct bar graphs and pie charts to display nominal data (see Figures 3.1 and 3.2). However, one popular statistical procedure that works well with these types of data is known as chi-square. We'll discuss this procedure in Chapter 11.

Please understand that nominal data categories are fine when they provide the information you need (for example, sociodemographic descriptors). Sometimes it makes perfect sense to use broad, nominal categories. For instance, you might divide your substance abuse clients into those who received inpatient

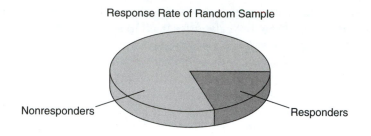

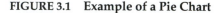

FIGURE 3.1   Example of a Pie Chart

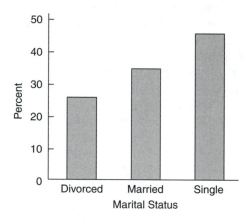

FIGURE 3.2   Example of a Bar Graph

services and those who received outpatient services. However, measuring your dependent variable at the nominal level is sometimes a mistake because it doesn't allow for much precision, and it limits the type of data analysis you can do.

Ordinal Measurement

The **ordinal level of measurement** uses ranking to classify people, objects, and events. Suppose you rank your clients thus: greatly improved, moderately improved, and slightly improved. Ordinal measurement has an order, a clear direction in the gradations of difference—in this case, a hierarchy of improvement. Keep this in mind to help you distinguish between nominal and ordinal levels of measurement.

A scale like the one below would also create ordinal data:

CLIENT IMPROVEMENT SCALE

0	1	2	3
No Improvement	Slight	Moderate	Great Improvement

If you can look at a numerical value such as the 3 above and recognize that it would be a better score than 1, then you have ordinal data, as long as ranking is involved. As the number of categories increases, finer and finer differentiations are possible (resulting in more accurate measurements). At some point, the data no longer would be viewed as ordinal but as interval data, depending on whether there are equal distances between the value positions. On the preceding scale, the distances between values appear equal; however, conceptually there is a great deal of difference between a client who has shown moderate improvement and one with great improvement—but the numerical difference between 2 and 3 is only one unit.

To use a different metaphor, a client who is moderately improved may still be at serious risk for attempting suicide, whereas a client with great improvement may have started a new job, joined a book discussion group, and had only infrequent thoughts of suicide. What is the true distance in the emotional health of these two clients? As with nominal data, it is difficult to know the actual distance between categories that constitute ordinal scales. The numbers we choose to represent positions on these scales are arbitrary. Even though numerical values are assigned to represent moderate improvement, how much improvement is that? How much more is "great" improvement than "moderate" or "slight" improvement? How much does one have to improve to move from slight to moderate improvement? Ordinal data simply recognize a comparison based on ranking. There is no standardized dividing line between ordinal and interval data for you to memorize other than this rule: Ranked data are ordinal data.

However, an ordinal scale does allow you to report that the majority of clients (say, 65%) were moderately improved at discharge, or to compute that the median improvement rating was, say, 2.2 for the 75 clients discharged in the month of July.

Often research instruments will use questions with Likert-type response sets that produce ordinal data. **Likert scales** are standardized categories that are usually in this format: strongly agree, agree, undecided, disagree, strongly disagree; or almost always, frequently, occasionally, rarely, and almost never. Typically, Likert scales are based on an odd number of categories. Five-point scales are often used, but an even number of categories may also be employed. The greater the number of categories, the more differentiations that can be made. Scales containing an odd number of categories usually contain one neutral category. Two examples of Likert scales are as follows:

HOW WOULD YOU RATE OUR SERVICES?
1. Excellent
2. Good
3. Fair
4. Poor

IF I NEEDED HELP AGAIN, I WOULD RETURN HERE.
1. Strongly Agree
2. Agree
3. Undecided
4. Disagree
5. Strongly Disagree

At first glance, you might think that excellent, good, fair, and poor are nominal-level data because they are categories defined by words, but since they are ordered or ranked (excellent is better than good, and good is better than fair), the directionality of this scale produces ordinal data. The same is true for the Strongly Agree–to–Strongly Disagree (Likert) response scale. Because these categories constitute a continuum of agreement, there is a directionality that makes the data created from this scale ordinal data.

Interval Measurement

When data are recorded at the **interval level of measurement,** we can begin to perform more sophisticated statistical procedures. Unlike the problems with nominal and ordinal data, the distances between adjacent positions in an interval scale form standard units with equal intervals. Note in the following example that the Client Improvement Scale has now been modified so that it produces interval-level data.

CLIENT IMPROVEMENT SCALE

(Percent Improved—Subjective Rating)

1 ...... 10 ...... 20 ...... 30 ...... 40 ...... 50 ...... 60 ...... 70 ...... 80 ...... 90 100
No   Great
Improvement   Improvement

This scale employs uniform distances between positions on the continuum. Now anyone can figure out that a client assessed at 90 is 10 points more improved than one assessed at 80. A client with 40 points of improvement would show twice as much improvement as a client registering only 20 points. Such a scale allows us not only to make more accurate (finer) measurements, but also to begin sophisticated data analysis. We could use these interval data to compute a correlation to see if there is a relationship between the level of improvement in our clients and the number of therapy sessions they attended.

Interval data inform us about how much or how much more one score is than others, as illustrated in the second question that follows.

QUESTION	INTERVAL-LEVEL VARIABLE
What was Sally's score on the ACT?	ACT Score
How much higher was Sally's ACT score than Bart's?	ACT Score

Interval-level data allow you to know exactly the distance between a moderate improvement of 65 and a slight improvement of 30. It would also tell you how many points Sally gained on her ACT by taking it a second time or how much better she did than Bart.

Researchers often combine 15 to 20 items measuring the same concept with Likert-type response sets (e.g., strongly agree, agree, undecided, disagree, strongly disagree) to comprise an instrument (see, for example, the McMullin Addiction Thought Scale or the Body Image Avoidance Questionnaire in Fischer & Corcoran, 2000). The scales are summed to produce a total score. Total scores from these and similar instruments produce interval data, even though the individual items constitute ordinal data when examined as single items. Summing all the values from each item produces a theoretical distribution of scores that are generally considered to be interval data. The next time you read the background information on an instrument, look for the **theoretical range of scores.** For instance, a 20-item test with a five-point Likert scale would have a theoretical range of scores of 20 to 100 (where 1 is the lowest possible value times 20 items, and 5 is the highest value times 20 items). This range of possible scores allows enough precision and presumption of equal intervals between scores that most social scientists would consider the data to be interval level.

Ratio Measurement

The **ratio level of measurement** differs from the interval level in only one respect—ratio measurement has a true, or absolute, zero. In other words, a variable reporting zero growth would mean absolutely no growth. Zero weight gain would mean no pounds were added. Zero children in a family would means just exactly that. You'll note in the following examples that questions providing ratio-level data are of the how-many or how-much variety. With ratio data we are able to tell exactly how much or how many and to conclude, for instance, that Rene makes twice as much money as her sister.

QUESTION	RATIO-LEVEL VARIABLE
How much weight did your son gain?	Weight
How much money do you make?	Income
How many clients did you see today?	Productivity
What is your grade-point average?	GPA

If the differences between interval and ratio levels seem like splitting hairs to you, don't be overly concerned. For all practical purposes, the same statistical procedures are used with both interval and ratio data. Both measure **continuous variables** (those like age or income that can fall anywhere along a hypothetical continuum of possible values and can usually be divided into smaller units such as years and months, dollars and cents) as opposed to **discrete variables** (either/or comparisons, such as true/false items). In other words, you really don't have to differentiate between interval and ratio levels of measurement. You will end up treating them both the same. In fact, throughout this text, we refer to interval data as meaning either interval or ratio data.

The reason statisticians make the distinction between the two is that a true zero enables comparisons of magnitude that have precise meaning, such as a salary of $24,000 is twice as large as one of $12,000. In conversation we speak as though our comparisons involving interval-level variables have a zero, when in actuality they don't. We might say, "Luis has no self-esteem at all; the poor kid won't even look at himself in the mirror." With variables like self-esteem or intelligence, it might be possible to score very low, but even the lowest score would not mean that the individual had absolutely no self-esteem or no intelligence.

Because social workers deal with and measure abstract concepts such as self-esteem, life satisfaction, and depression, we develop instruments to aid our assessments. However, even our best instruments are crude and are only approximations of a client's actual self-esteem, life satisfaction, or depression. Who can say that depression lends itself to equal intervals? Though we always strive for greater accuracy, all measurement is somewhat imprecise—that is another reason we are not going to be overly concerned about the distinctions between interval and ratio measurements.

SELECTING A LEVEL OF MEASUREMENT

One thing that is sometimes confusing is that the same variable (age, for example), can be collected at different levels of measurement depending upon the researcher's phrasing of the item. Thus, the question, "How old are you?" produces interval-level data (clients are 17, 23, 44, 58, 73, etc.). However, the researcher could have created ordinal (ranked) data by asking the question this way: "Please indicate your approximate age using this list:"

☐ Under 21
☐ 22 to 29
☐ 30 to 44
☐ Over 45

Similarly, a researcher might gather interval/ratio data but transform it into nominal or ordinal categories for ease of presentation to an audience, as in this example:

NUMBER OF CHILDREN IN CLIENTS' FAMILIES

No children	27%
One or more children	73%

So, when trying to remember the differences between levels of measurement, don't mentally file age as an example of a variable that is always measured at the interval level. Rather than trying to associate specific variables with a level of measurement, a better rule would be to look at the **response set,** or options the responder can choose from. Notice whether the categories have an order or ranking. If so, you have ordinal data. If, knowing one score or value, you can accurately predict the next highest and the next lowest value, and the distances between values are equally spaced, then you have interval/ratio data. If you have discrete categories with no ranking, as in the following example, then you have nominal data:

WHAT KIND OF COMMUNITY DO YOU LIVE IN?
1. Farm/rural area
2. City
3. Suburb/small town

Had these response categories been arranged so a population hierarchy was created (e.g., farms/rural areas at the top, then suburb/small towns, followed by cities), then the same information would be measured at the ordinal level (because of the ranking of population density categories from low to high).

CODING DATA

Notice the numerical value associated with each of the categories identified in the preceding example. A researcher who uses a computer to tabulate questionnaires or survey forms wants to enter large amounts of data the fastest, most accurate way possible and generally wants to tap a single digit on the keyboard to represent a response. An individual living in a suburb or a small town could be coded as a 3, whereas one residing in a city could be assigned a 2. Statistical software programs are quite powerful, and most can incorporate strings of alphabetic characters instead of numbers. However, few researchers would want to type in long phrases such as *farm/rural area.* It is much faster to type a 1, 2, or 3.

It makes no difference whether *city of 50,000 or more* is coded 1, 2, or 3, or even as a 7 or 8, as long as the same rule is applied consistently in working with that variable. However, when there is an absence of something, say, a client has no history of alcoholism, it usually makes sense to code such information with a zero just because it's easier to remember that than some other value.

The total set of responses gathered, whether from a client, a citizen selected randomly from the community, or an employee's evaluation form, is referred to as one **case** in data entry and analysis. Bill Smith's responses constitute a case, and Helen Tomasek's answers form another one. All the cases together form the **data set.**

It's a good practice to make yourself a **codebook,** that is, a reference sheet where you write down your decisions about how you will code the data (e.g., females = 1, males = 2). Although you may have no difficulty remembering the codes you've assigned while you are entering the data, if you get pulled off that assignment for a few days or weeks, you'll be surprised how tough it can be to recall some of the decision rules that you were using earlier.

Sometimes, it is better to be inclusive and create more categories than you might actually end up using. For instance, you might start off with these categories to code the educational attainment of your clients:

CODE	EDUCATION
0	No formal schooling
1	Eighth grade or less
2	Less than high school

3	GED (high school equivalency)
4	High school graduation
5	Some college
6	College graduation

After your data have been collected, you might discover that there were two individuals with no formal schooling and only four with less than an eighth grade education. At that point, you may decide to merge these six clients into the group *less than high school.* Then, you might decide that there's really no need to distinguish between those who have a GED and those with a regular high school diploma, and thus you recode those cases or categories and end up with this new scheme:

CODE	EDUCATION
2	Less than high school
4	High school graduation/GED
5	Some college
6	College graduation

The process known as **recoding** data occurs when the data have already been entered into the computer in defined categories, and you later decide to collapse the categories. Researchers know the importance of keeping track of these data modifications in their codebooks. Here is another caution: In some statistical software programs, once you have recoded the data and saved the file, you have lost the ability to work with the data as they were entered originally (prior to the recoding). So, in addition to keeping notes about what variables you have recoded, you probably want to keep a copy of the data prior to the recoding as a backup.

Depending on the statistical software you use, you may or may not need to keep track of the number of columns each variable requires. Let's think for a moment about variables and the width of a data field or column. Gender requires only one column. Age normally would require two digits (at the ratio level), unless you are collecting data from a sample that includes persons who are older than 99—then you would need three digits for those who are 100 or older. In both of the previous examples about coding educational attainment, one column could record any of the possible categories that we've identified. However, if you used the item, "How many years of education have you completed?" and left a blank for the respondent to write in the actual number of years, then how many columns would be needed?

It is good practice to think about your data and how they should be entered so that you will recognize errors during data entry. In the days when all statistical computing used to be done on large mainframe computers, it was necessary to enter a 9-year-old's age as 09 if the variable of age was defined by two columns. If you had entered 9 when the computer was expecting a two-digit value, a 9 by itself might be transformed to a 90. However, the newer statistical software programs are smart enough to allow you to enter either a 9 or 09. If you would rather use nominal categories such as teen and adult (or simply *t* or *a*) and type in these terms, this will not cause any problem, and SPSS will be able to tally the data just fine as long as you define the data properly.

As we discussed earlier, you can take interval- or ratio-level data and convert them to nominal or ordinal data. That is, you can place specific values (e.g., 45, when a client is 45 years old) into a broad category (e.g., 40 to 49 years of age), but you can't go the other way. You can't identify a person's exact age when the information was obtained by having the respondent check a category such as 40 to 49 years. Often, it is best to enter the exact interval/ratio data values for variables such as age or number of counseling sessions, without trying to force the values into tidy categories. Once you enter all the data and get a printout, then you can decide whether you want to create or collapse categories.

COMPUTER APPLICATION: DEFINING A VARIABLE WITH STATISTICAL SOFTWARE

Before you begin to enter data into a statistical software program for processing, you must first define your variables. Defining a variable in the SPSS follows a series of simple steps. SPSS automatically opens up to the Data Editor Window, which looks like a blank spreadsheet with lots of rows and columns. Each case will constitute its own horizontal row, and each variable will be a vertical column.

Step 1. Click on DATA—a menu will appear. Select DEFINE VARIABLE. A window will open up showing that the first variable has already been designated by SPSS as VAR00001.

Step 2. In that window, click on the LABELS button, and type in the name of the variable (e.g., education or marital status). Click on CONTINUE.

Step 3. Click on the TYPE button. The window will change, and you will have several options. The default (standard) selection is already set for numeric variables. If you will be entering numerical values for this variable, you don't need to change anything and can click on CONTINUE. However, if you decided to type in *male* or *female* instead of using numerical values like 1 and 2, then you'll need to click on the indicator for STRING. String variables are those composed of alphabetic characters, or a combination of alphabetic and numeric characters. When you are ready to move on, click on the CONTINUE button.

Step 4. Set the column width. Although there's no requirement that you inform SPSS that you will have a variable such as age requiring two columns, it is a good idea to indicate this so that if you lose your place and absentmindedly try to enter age into the column designated for gender, SPSS will recognize there is a problem. As a default, SPSS can accommodate variables up to eight columns wide without your giving it any special instructions. Why would you need eight columns? Well, if you were examining something like amount of awards made by philanthropic foundations, an award of $1,000,000 would require seven columns, and an award of $10,000,000 would need eight columns.

Step 5. Designate special values for missing data. If a client refused to tell you his educational level using either of the coding schemes we discussed earlier, then you could click on MISSING VALUES (we're still at the window that lets us define each variable) and indicate a value such as 9 to represent missing values. The importance of this will become more apparent in the next chapter, when we begin to look at our data and the percentages of persons reporting characteristics in each of the categories. Hint: The numeric value you select to stand for missing values should be one easily remembered and not vary a great deal from variable to variable. Otherwise, you'll have too much to remember and mistakes will be made in coding and entering data, unless you are extremely careful.

These simple steps allow you to define your variables in SPSS—a necessary step before any data analysis can be conducted. The process is similar in most other statistical software programs.

TERMS TO KNOW

Case (p. 29)	Measurement (p. 20)
Codebook (p. 29)	Nominal level of measurement (p. 23)
Continuous variable (p. 27)	Ordinal level of measurement (p. 24)
Data set (p. 29)	Ratio level of measurement (p. 27)
Dichotomous variable (p. 23)	Recoding (p. 30)
Discrete variable (p. 27)	Reliability (p. 21)
Interval level of measurement (p. 26)	Response set (p. 28)
Level of measurement (p. 23)	Theoretical range of scores (p. 27)
Likert scales (p. 25)	Validity (p. 21)

REVIEW PROBLEMS

1. For a study she is working on, Jamie categorizes families as either enmeshed or not enmeshed. What level of measurement is she using?

2. Jamie wants to examine how many treatment sessions families have received and will record whatever number they tell her. She's calling this variable *number of treatment sessions.* What is this level of measurement?

3. A fourth-grade teacher ranks students on the basis of their reading level and recommends those at the bottom third for a special remedial program. What level of measurement is she employing?

4. If the variable *students' reading level* is measured in terms of grade level (e.g., second grade, third month; fifth grade, fourth month), would it be considered an interval level of measurement?

5. Ron is conducting a statewide survey of mental health agencies and asks all the directors to respond to his questionnaire on clients who drop out of treatment prematurely and those who do not. Can each agency be considered a case?

6. Give an example of a dichotomous variable.

7. Give an example of a variable not mentioned in the text that is generally measured at the interval or ratio level.

8. Create the categories necessary to code *knowledge of parenting* as an ordinal variable.

REFERENCE

Fischer, J., & Corcoran, K. (2000). *Measures for clinical practice.* New York: The Free Press.

CHAPTER FOUR

CONSTRUCTING AND INTERPRETING FREQUENCY TABLES

Once you've collected information on a question of interest, the first order of business is to organize and present it in some meaningful way. There are at least four ways this can be done: narration, frequency tables, graphs, or cross-tabulation tables. Suppose you opted to describe the people who participated in your agency's parenting classes last month in narrative form. Your report might look something like this:

> Of the 35 people who successfully completed our parenting classes last month, 25 were women and 10 were men. Eleven participants described themselves as single parents, with the other 24 indicating that they had the assistance of a second adult in carrying out their parenting responsibilities. Two individuals reported having 6 children at home, 5 have 4, 4 have 3, 13 have 2, and the remaining 11 have a single child at home. We had 8 African American participants, 2 Asian Americans, 15 Caucasians, and 10 of Hispanic descent.

Although the information presented here is quite thorough, it's easy at times to get lost in the details—especially when lots of categories are needed to describe the answers obtained. When narration is confusing or complex, you can choose one of the other three ways to organize and present your data. Although we'll be illustrating all three of these approaches in this text, this chapter addresses how to construct and interpret a frequency table.

FREQUENCY TABLES

The **simple, or absolute, frequency table** is one of the most straightforward means of demonstrating how often each of the scores or values occurs for selected variables within a data set. A **frequency** is simply a count of the number of cases or characteristics of selected cases—such as the number of treatment sessions attended. Let's return to the data gathered on your parenting class participants. Table 4.1 presents the information, or **raw data,** as it was originally obtained.

TABLE 4.1   Raw Data Collected on Agency's Parenting Class Participants

ID NUMBER	SINGLE PARENT?	NUMBER OF CHILDREN	GENDER	RACE/ETHNICITY
1	No	1	Female	African American
2	Yes	2	Female	Hispanic
3	Yes	3	Female	Caucasian
4	No	2	Male	Caucasian
5	No	2	Male	Asian American
6	No	1	Male	Caucasian
7	Yes	4	Female	African American
8	No	2	Female	Caucasian
9	No	2	Male	Hispanic
10	No	1	Male	Caucasian
11	No	6	Female	African American
12	No	1	Female	African American
13	No	3	Female	Caucasian
14	Yes	2	Female	Asian American
15	No	2	Male	Hispanic
16	No	1	Female	Hispanic
17	No	4	Female	Caucasian
18	No	1	Female	Hispanic
19	Yes	2	Female	Caucasian
20	Yes	1	Female	African American
21	No	4	Female	Hispanic
22	No	2	Female	Caucasian
23	No	1	Male	Caucasian
24	Yes	1	Female	Hispanic
25	No	3	Female	Caucasian
26	Yes	4	Female	Caucasian
27	No	1	Male	African American
28	Yes	2	Female	Hispanic
29	No	1	Female	Caucasian
30	Yes	6	Female	Caucasian
31	No	2	Female	African American
32	No	2	Male	Caucasian
33	Yes	3	Female	Hispanic
34	No	4	Male	Caucasian
35	No	2	Female	Hispanic

As Vogt (1993) notes, it's important to realize that in this case the opposite of raw is *not* cooked. Those accused of having "cooked up" their data find themselves in a very precarious position, indeed.

Let's target the column that contains information about the number of children reported by each of your participants. As you can see, the first participant had one child, the seventh had four, and so on. By putting these data in ascending order—that is, from the smallest value to the largest—we can form an **array,** like the one illustrated in Table 4.2.

Looking at the data in Table 4.2, it's easy to see that most of the people in your parenting classes had one or two youngsters at home, whereas no one reported having five. The largest number of youngsters living in any one home was six. Although we could have discerned these patterns by carefully studying the data presented in Table 4.1, it would have taken us quite a bit longer, and there would have been a high likelihood of our making a calculation error. Transforming these data into a frequency table involves nothing more than consolidating like scores or values.

To construct a simple, or absolute, frequency table for a given variable, identify the different scores or values the variable can meaningfully take on. For example, using the data presented in Table 4.2, we know that the number of children these parents have living with them at home varies from one to six, with 1, 2, 3, 4, and 6 constituting the actual scores or values reported. These values are placed in the first column, labeled number of children. A second column is created that will contain the frequency with which each value occurs. Then, using hash marks or some other symbol, record each time a particular value appears, as shown:

NUMBER OF CHILDREN	FREQUENCY	
1	///// ///// /	= 11
2	///// ///// ///	= 13
3	////	= 4
4	/////	= 5
6	//	= 2

Once you've recorded the scores or values reported by everyone in your data set, you simply tally these responses. Table 4.3 illustrates how the data presented in these two columns are used in constructing a simple frequency table.

Frequency tables help us actually visualize how the information we've gathered is distributed, or spread out. This is why you'll often see frequency tables referred to as **frequency distributions.** In Table 4.3, for example, we can readily see that parents who have two children living at home constitute the largest group ($n = 13$), with parents of single children being the next largest ($n = 11$). Only two families had six children living at home.

Obtaining a frequency distribution with SPSS is very simple: After the data are entered into the spreadsheet, simply click on the ANALYZE button, then select DESCRIPTIVE STATISTICS and FREQUENCIES. A new screen appears, showing all the vari-

TABLE 4.2   An Array: Number of Children Reported by Participants

ID NUMBER	NUMBER OF CHILDREN
1	1
6	1
10	1
12	1
16	1
18	1
20	1
23	1
24	1
27	1
29	1
2	2
4	2
5	2
8	2
9	2
14	2
15	2
19	2
22	2
28	2
31	2
32	2
35	2
3	3
13	3
25	3
33	3
7	4
17	4
21	4
26	4
34	4
11	6
30	6

ables that have been entered into the computer. Now just highlight the variable(s) you want to be portrayed, and voilà! A table containing all the information we present in Table 4.3 is produced.

Frequency distributions can be created with all variables, regardless of the level of measurement involved. Let's consider an example using a nominal-level variable. Returning for a moment to the data in Table 4.1, it appears that more women participated in your agency's parenting classes than men. As Table 4.4 demonstrates,

TABLE 4.3   Frequency Distribution: Number of Children Reported by Parenting Class Participants

NUMBER OF CHILDREN (X)*	FREQUENCY (f)**
1	11
2	13
3	4
4	5
5	0
6	2
N*** =	35

*As a matter of convention, an uppercase X is used when referring to the scores obtained for a variable. In this case, the X refers to the number of children.

**Similarly, a lowercase f often is used to symbolize a frequency, or count.

***An uppercase N is used to designate the total number of scores.

TABLE 4.4   Frequency Distribution: Parenting Class Participants' Gender

GENDER (x)	FREQUENCY (f)
Female (1)*	25
Male (2)*	10
N =	35

*These numbers were arbitrarily assigned to distinguish the two gender categories from one another in preparing the data for entry into a data analysis program, such as SPSS.

another frequency table allows us to see at a glance that women are indeed participating in these parenting classes at a substantially higher rate than men.

CUMULATIVE FREQUENCIES

When data are measured at an ordinal level or higher, it can be helpful to add a third column to the simple frequency table, where a cumulative frequency, or running count, is kept. The **cumulative frequency** associated with a given score tells us how many respondents scored at that value or lower. For instance, in looking at Table 4.5, we can see that 24 (11 + 13) of the 35 parenting class participants had

TABLE 4.5 Cumulative Frequency Distribution: Number of Children Reported by Parenting Class Participants

NUMBER OF CHILDREN (X)	FREQUENCY (f)	CUMULATIVE FREQUENCY (Cf)*
1	11	11
2	13	24
3	4	28
4	5	33
6	2	35
	$N = \overline{35}$	

*Cf is the abbreviation typically used when referring to a cumulative frequency.

two or fewer children at home. Notice, too, how the last value in the cumulative frequency column equals the total number of scores contained in the data set. This tells us that we haven't overlooked any scores in tallying this column.

GROUPED FREQUENCIES

Suppose University Anywhere surveyed its most recent class of MSW graduates. Among other things, the faculty and administration were interested in knowing how many of those graduates found jobs in social work. These fictitious data are presented in Table 4.6.

As evidenced in Table 4.6, the salaries reported by University Anywhere's most recent alums ranged from a low of $22,000 to a high of $51,000. However, given the large number of salary categories listed, as well as the fact that the dollar increments between the categories are not equal, it's a little difficult to determine what to make of these data. In such instances, it is generally helpful to combine adjacent categories in some meaningful way. The question is, how do we decide what's meaningful? The answer is, it depends on what categorical divisions you believe will best help you and your audience understand the data. Generally this means reducing the number of categories, while retaining as much measurement precision as is possible.

As a rule of thumb, Craft (1990) suggests using at least 6 categories or intervals, but not more than 15, in a frequency distribution.

Ideally, in redefining your categories, you'll want to group scores so that the values are as **homogeneous** as possible—that is, the values you've clustered

TABLE 4.6   Cumulative Frequency Distribution: Starting Salaries for First Full-Time Social Work Positions Obtained by MSW Alumni

STARTING SALARY (X)*	FREQUENCY (f)	CUMULATIVE FREQUENCY (Cf)
$22,000	3	3
23,000	2	5
24,000	1	6
25,000	1	7
26,000	2	9
27,000	5	14
28,000	8	22
29,000	2	24
30,000	6	30
31,000	2	32
32,000	4	36
34,000	2	38
35,000	1	39
36,000	3	42
38,000	1	43
39,000	2	45
40,000	3	48
51,000	1	49
	$N = \overline{49}$	

*Annual salary, rounded to nearest $1,000.00

together look more like those in the group to which they're assigned, than like the values outside that group. In terms of measurement precision, if your data originally were gathered at an interval level of measurement, it's often important for later analyses to retain that level of measure. Thus, while you strive to reduce the number of categories involved, you'll want to ensure equality or standardization among the groupings you create.

The **grouped frequency distribution** presented in Table 4.7 illustrates how University Anywhere's salary data could be collapsed into $5,000 intervals, thereby retaining the interval nature of the original data. To clarify, note that, although the intervals between the categories listed in Table 4.6 are *not equal*, the original data were collected in $100.00 increments—making it an interval-level variable.

From the information presented in Table 4.7, it's much easier to detect patterns, or trends, within the data. For example, it becomes abundantly clear that many of these graduates started their social work careers earning between $25,000 and $35,000 a year (i.e., 18 + 14 = 32/49). Similarly, it's easy to see that very few of these new MSWs obtained positions paying less than $25,000 ($n = 6$) or more than $40,000 ($n = 4$).

TABLE 4.7   Grouped Cumulative Frequency Distribution: Starting Salaries for First Full-Time Social Work Positions Obtained by MSW Alumni

STARTING SALARY (X)	FREQUENCY (f)	CUMULATIVE FREQUENCY (Cf)
$20,000 to $24,999	6	6
25,000 to 29,999	18	24
30,000 to 34,999	14	38
35,000 to 39,999	7	45
40,000 to 44,999	3	48
45,000 to 49,999	0	48
50,000 to 54,999	1	49
	$N = \overline{49}$	

At times you may want to divide your scores so that each category contains approximately the same number of cases. For instance, you might divide annual income into the lowest third, middle third, and upper third of the values reported and designate these categories as low, medium, and high incomes, respectively. Alternatively, there may be a theoretical or practice-relevant reason for the categories you stipulate. Suppose, for example, your agency served adults 65 years of age and over. Because of the biopsychosocial differences typically experienced by people in their 60s, 80s, and 100s, you might choose to categorize your agency's clients into mathematically unequal—but functionally similar—age brackets, such as 65 to 84, 85 to 99, and 100 and over.

UNDERSTANDING THE STUFF OF WHICH TABLES ARE MADE

As demonstrated throughout this chapter, tables allow us to convey a lot of data in an efficient way. Although we're given a great deal of latitude in deciding when to use a table, various conventions have been established to promote consistency in the type of information to include and how best to present it. You'll find several of these table-building customs in Figure 4.1. Knowing these rules of thumb will make it easier for you to construct, read, interpret, and compare tabular data.

RELATIVE FREQUENCIES

In addition to absolute frequencies and running counts, it's often useful to convey the relative standing of each category—that is, to show what portion of the responses obtained were associated with each of the different scores or values

FIGURE 4.1   **The Anatomy of a Table**

Tables are typically **numbered** in order of their presentation. Table 4.8 is labeled such because it is the eighth table introduced in the fourth chapter.

Tables are given brief **titles** that usually describe the variable(s), respondents, and type of analysis involved.

TABLE 4.8   **Frequency Table: Starting Salaries for First Full-Time Social Work Positions Obtained by MSW Alumni**

STARTING SALARY (X)	FREQUENCY (f)	CUMULATIVE FREQUENCY (Cf)	PROPORTION	PERCENT (%)	CUMULATIVE PERCENT (%)
$20,000 to $24,999	6	6	.1224	12	12
25,000 to 29,999	18	24	.3673	37	49
30,000 to 34,999	14	38	.2857	29	78
35,000 to 39,999	7	45	.1428	14	92
40,000 to 44,999	3	48	.0612	6	98
45,000 to 49,999	0	48	.0000	0	98
50,000 to 54,999	1	49	.0204	2	100
	$N = 49$		1.0000	100	

Horizontal lines are used to mark the beginning and the end of the data that make up the body of the table.

Headings are used to convey how the data presented in the body of the table are organized. Note: Standard abbreviations and symbols can be used in table headings without elaboration (e.g., f, %).

reported. That's why frequency data are often presented in terms of proportions or percentages—or what some refer to as **relative frequencies** (Frankfort-Nachmias, 1997).

Key to the concept of a **proportion** is the premise that the whole (or all) of something is equal to 1. So, if we're talking about the frequency associated with a score as being a portion of all the responses we obtained, we can refer to that category in terms of a proportion or a percent. Theoretically, a proportion can range from no part of something to all of it, so the values it can meaningfully take on range from 0 to 1. A proportion is obtained by dividing the frequency of a category by the total number of observations. If you've forgotten the specifics of calculating a proportion, consult Formulae Alert 4.1.

Column 4 in Table 4.8 presents the alumni salary data in terms of proportions. In examining these data, we find that the proportion of alumni who reported earning between $35,000 and $39,999 annually is .1428. In contrast, the proportion of

---

FORMULAE ALERT 4.1

To calculate a **proportion (P),** simply divide the number of responses in a category (f) by the total number of observations made (N).

$$P = f/N$$

For example: Seven of University Anywhere's 49 alumni earned between $35,000 and $39,999. To determine what part or proportion of the whole this category represents, we divide 7 by 49 and get .1428.

We can easily convert a proportion into a **percentage** by multiplying it by 100.

$$f/N \times 100 = \%$$

Applying this step to our previous calculation, we get

$$7/49 = .1428 \times 100 = 14.28\%$$

This can be rounded to 14%.

---

alumni earning between $25,000 and $29,999 is much larger ($P = .3673$). Note, too, how this column of proportions tallies to 1 (i.e., a single whole). As our remarks concerning proportions reflect, however, intuitively it's difficult to interpret what to make of a proportion. Fortunately, proportions are easily converted to a medium we're all much more familiar with—percentage. To derive a **percentage,** simply multiply the proportion by 100 (for a more detailed description of this process, refer again to Formulae Alert 4.1).

When we talk in terms of percentages, the underlying logic is that the whole (or all) of something is equal to 100%. If you'll return to Table 4.8 for a moment and look at column 5, you'll find the frequencies for the different alumni salary categories conveyed in percentages. Including these data can further our understanding of the information presented. Specifically, not only do we know how many of these graduates reported earning between $25,000 and $29,999 a year ($n = 18$), we also know that 37% of University Anywhere's MSW alumni make this amount.

Another important reason for including relative frequencies is that they allow us to compare distributions across studies without having to have groups of equal size. If the data are presented in percentages, for instance, we can compare MSW alumni salaries across universities, without being overly concerned about the differences in the number of those graduating.

Caution is called for, however, when comparing percentages among subcategories of very different sizes. A specific example is presented later in the "Cautionary Notes" section of this chapter.

Just as a cumulative frequency tells us where a particular category falls in relationship to the rest of the distribution, the **cumulative percentage** also conveys information about the relative standing of a category. Again, let's look at Table 4.8. The data presented in the last column, labeled "Cumulative Percent," tells us that nearly half (49%) of the alumni surveyed report earning $29,999 annually, or less. Slightly over three-quarters (78%) of this group earned $34,999 a year, or less. What other conclusions can we draw from these data? Among other observations, it seems that only about 12% of the students currently enrolled in University Anywhere's MSW program will earn less than $25,000 a year in their first full-time social work position.

CAUTIONARY NOTES REGARDING DATA MISREPRESENTATION

Because percentages alone can provide insufficient, if not misleading, information, it's usually a good idea to report the associated frequencies as well. For example, suppose your university learns that approximately 22% of its MSW program applicants each year are seeking training in administration—rather than the clinical concentration offered. By itself, this figure doesn't give university officials enough information to determine if the demand is sufficiently large to consider adding an administrative track. After all, how many potential graduate students are we talking about? Twenty-two percent of 50 (11) certainly suggests a much smaller demand than 22% of 300 (66).

Also, we can inadvertently mislead our audience when we draw conclusions on the basis of percentages derived from categories of vastly different sizes. Consider, for example, how proud the administrator of a local mental health clinic felt when he recently told the director of the state's mental health department about the great success the clinic was having with its new group treatment program. Specifically, he claimed that "since starting this approach a year ago, the clinic has achieved a treatment success rate of at least 85% for clients in all but one diagnostic category." As Table 4.9 reflects, the actual data suggest a much less promising assessment (i.e., a 64% overall success rate) for this new treatment approach when the agency's clientele are considered as a whole.

It's rather unlikely that this administrator intentionally sought to deceive the state director. Nevertheless, by focusing solely on the pattern suggested by the percent of successful cases achieved among categories of very different sizes, the true impact of this treatment approach was easy to overlook. To avoid such distortions, it's wise to include the actual subgroup frequencies on which the percentages are based.

TABLE 4.9 Success Rate of Clients in Local Mental Health Clinic's Group Treatment Program by Diagnostic Category

DIAGNOSTIC CATEGORY	NUMBER OF SUCCESSFUL CASES	PERCENT (%)
1	12 of 14	86
2	30 of 90	33
3	85 of 100	85
4	7 of 8	88
5	9 of 10	90
	Totals: 143 of 222	64

It can also be misleading when percentages are used to relay data on small samples. It seems rather meaningless, for instance, for your agency to boast about a 75% success rate for its intensive family preservation program—if that 75% means your agency successfully reunited three of only four families it worked with during the past year. Remember that percentages refer to portions of 100. That's why when data on small samples (e.g., $n \leq 30$) are presented in percentages, they're commonly afforded greater importance than their numbers warrant.

COMPUTER APPLICATION: CREATING A FREQUENCY DISTRIBUTION

The MSW starting salary data presented in Table 4.10 were created by activating SPSS by selecting the ANALYZE button, then highlighting DESCRIPTIVE STATISTICS and from that menu choosing FREQUENCIES. These data also were used to construct Table 4.6 (p. 40), where we manually constructed a cumulative frequency distribution to deposit the starting salaries reported by University Anywhere's alumni. However, there are a few important differences between these two tables. Why don't you take a moment to compare these tables and try to discover them before reading further? First, did you notice that the number of respondents ("Total," or N) referenced in the two tables differ? Table 4.6 involves an N of 49, whereas Table 4.10 lists a total of 60. Why the difference? Well, in Table 4.6 we presented salary data for University Anywhere's *valid* cases which, in this instance, means only those respondents who obtained a position in social work since receiving their MSW and gave complete answers to the question about starting salaries. Therefore, the data presented in Table 4.6 were taken from the sections of columns 1 and 2 in Table 4.10, labeled "Valid" (i.e., approximately the top two-thirds). The data contained in columns 4 and 5 of Table 4.10, labeled "Valid Percent" and "Cumulative Percent," respectively, also could have been used to communicate information about the salaries earned by University Anywhere's recent graduates.

TABLE 4.10 Starting Salary for First Full-Time Post-MSW Social Work Job

	SALARY REPORTED ($)	FREQUENCY (f)	PERCENT (%)	VALID PERCENT (%)	CUMULATIVE PERCENT (%)
Valid	22,000.00	3	5.0	6.1	6.1
	23,000.00	2	3.3	4.1	10.2
	24,000.00	1	1.7	2.0	12.2
	25,000.00	1	1.7	2.0	14.3
	26,000.00	2	3.3	4.1	18.4
	27,000.00	4	6.7	8.2	26.5
	27,300.00	1	1.7	2.0	28.6
	28,000.00	8	13.3	16.3	44.9
	28,800.00	1	1.7	2.0	46.9
	29,000.00	1	1.7	2.0	49.0
	30,000.00	6	10.0	12.2	61.2
	31,000.00	2	3.3	4.1	65.3
	32,000.00	4	6.7	8.2	73.5
	34,000.00	2	3.3	4.1	77.6
	35,000.00	1	1.7	2.0	79.6
	36,000.00	3	5.0	6.1	85.7
	38,000.00	1	1.7	2.0	87.8
	39,000.00	2	3.3	4.1	91.8
	40,000.00	3	5.0	6.1	98.0
	51,000.00	1	1.7	2.0	100.0
	Total	49	81.7	100.0	
Missing	Still Looking for Job	6	10.0		
	Working but No Salary Data Reported	3	5.0		
	Returned to School	2	3.3		
	Total	11	18.3		
Total		60	100.0		

In contrast, Table 4.10 reveals how all 60 of the alumni surveyed answered (or failed to answer) this salary question. Specifically, in addition to telling us about the 49 people who provided salary data, the information presented in columns 1, 2, and 3 in Table 4.10 tells us something about the cases for which we have no salary data, i.e., the cases with missing salary data. In examining these data, we find that six (10%) of University Anywhere's most recent graduates are still looking for a job. Three others said they were working in social work, but chose not to reveal their starting salaries. As for the two who opted to continue their schooling, well, this question doesn't really apply to them. Decisions regarding which information to use depend on the question(s) you want your frequency table to address. The researcher decides which responses constitute missing data in the construction of each tabular display.

DEVELOPING CATEGORIES
FOR QUALITATIVE DATA

Social workers who are engaged in qualitative research probably do not worry quite as much about levels of measurement as their more quantitatively oriented colleagues. In their reports, the more qualitatively focused researchers might not employ even a single table to show a frequency distribution. After their data have been collected, however, there is still the same need to consolidate, summarize, and condense. While the quantitative researcher relies on counting events, characteristics, and so forth, the qualitative researcher has a somewhat analogous, but still different, set of tasks to accomplish. These tasks are explained in the next section.

Organizing Your Data

Whether data are gathered through participant observation, in-depth interviewing, focus groups—or by examining historical documents, client logs, written reports, or verbatim responses to open-ended questions—qualitative research generates mounds of words known as **text data,** which—like the numbers that make up quantitative data—must be organized somehow before meaningful analysis and interpretation can occur. The first step in this process generally involves using a typewriter or word processing program to convert any printed, verbal, or handwritten materials gathered for the study (e.g., researcher notes or participant responses) into a workable format. More formally, this process is known as **data transcription.**

For those reluctant to use computers, typing up the data will render it more readable and, hence, easier to work with once the process of physically cutting the manuscript into meaningful segments and pasting related sections together is done. As Babbie (1999) observes, however, word processing programs represent "a vast improvement over the cut-and-paste technology of the typewriter" (p. 274). After all, once your data are entered into a computer file, you can easily copy, edit, correct, and even rearrange data segments in any number of ways. In addition, the search function available in most word processing programs allows you to quickly cull through the document for words and phrases you ultimately identify as important to your study. What's more, data files created with standard word processing programs can be saved in formats that are compatible with the ever-growing number of computer software packages being developed specifically for analyzing qualitative data. We'll take a look at the strengths and limitations typically associated with computer-aided qualitative data analysis (CAQDAS) programs such as Ethnograph, NUD*IST, and ATLAS/ti in Chapter 6. For now, it's important that you know they exist and that entering your text data into a standard word processing program will save you time later on should you choose to use one.

Even if you're fortunate enough to have access to someone who is willing and able to help you transcribe your materials, you'll want to transcribe the first several items (e.g., interviews, field notes, or participant responses) yourself. Doing so allows you to develop a genuine feel for the nature and structure of the data. This level of familiarity is key to determining the best way of organizing your transcripts. For example, to retain access to the contextual subtleties captured within a taped interview, you'll want to be sure the transcriptions include not only the questions along with the verbatim responses obtained, but also any nonverbal cues (e.g., an angry tone, nervous giggle, or a lengthy pause) that accompany the respondents' words. In Figure 4.2, we illustrate several transcription guidelines that qualitative researchers typically use to help ensure the clarity, completeness, and readability of their data.

FIGURE 4.2   Sample Transcript of a Fictitious Taped Interview

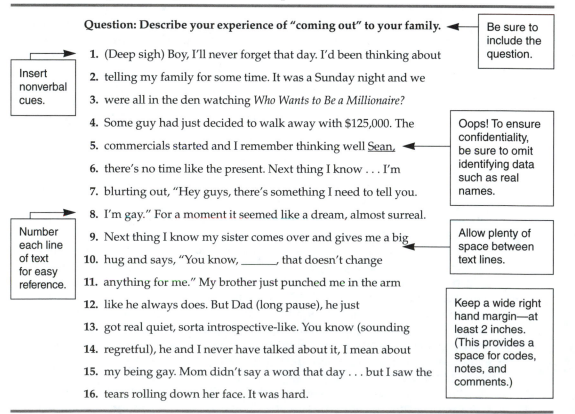

Question: Describe your experience of "coming out" to your family. ◄── Be sure to include the question.

Insert nonverbal cues.

1. (Deep sigh) Boy, I'll never forget that day. I'd been thinking about
2. telling my family for some time. It was a Sunday night and we
3. were all in the den watching *Who Wants to Be a Millionaire?*
4. Some guy had just decided to walk away with $125,000. The
5. commercials started and I remember thinking well Sean, ◄── Oops! To ensure confidentiality, be sure to omit identifying data such as real names.
6. there's no time like the present. Next thing I know . . . I'm
7. blurting out, "Hey guys, there's something I need to tell you.
8. I'm gay." For a moment it seemed like a dream, almost surreal.

Number each line of text for easy reference.

9. Next thing I know my sister comes over and gives me a big ◄── Allow plenty of space between text lines.
10. hug and says, "You know, _____, that doesn't change
11. anything for me." My brother just punched me in the arm
12. like he always does. But Dad (long pause), he just
13. got real quiet, sorta introspective-like. You know (sounding
14. regretful), he and I never have talked about it, I mean about
15. my being gay. Mom didn't say a word that day . . . but I saw the
16. tears rolling down her face. It was hard.

Keep a wide right hand margin—at least 2 inches. (This provides a space for codes, notes, and comments.)

Keeping It on the Record

In a sense, there's a second source of data when you're conducting qualitative analysis. Whether you call it a journal, a process diary, or simply your research notes or memos, you must keep a **written record** of the research process as it unfolds. Actually, this is wise advice to follow whatever type of research you're conducting—but it's crucial for establishing the credibility of a qualitative analysis. Sometimes referred to as an "audit trail" (Tutty, Rothery, & Grinnell, 1996, p. 98), this written record helps the researcher document the various methodological and analytical decisions that were made throughout the investigative process. It also provides a means for others to verify the steps that were taken, and it furnishes the details that would be needed to replicate a study.

Ideally, you'll begin keeping notes during the preparatory phase of your project and continue doing so through completion of the final report. Although there's no one way of structuring this record, Richardson (2000) identifies four valuable categories:

> *Observational notes* contain concrete, detailed descriptions of everything you experienced through your senses. That is, what did you see, touch, hear, feel, and taste?
>
> *Methodological notes* are a record of all the methodological decisions. Included here are decisions about whom to interview (or re-interview), how to dress, what categories to use as you begin coding your data, and how these changed over the course of your analysis.
>
> *Theoretical notes* are where you'll list your initial impressions, tentative explanations, and emerging hypotheses. It's also a place where you can critically assess your thoughts. Be sure to note informative references or sources uncovered, as well.
>
> *Personal notes* are uncensored statements reflecting what you're thinking and feeling about your work and the people you're encountering. Candor is key, so include your frustrations and fears, as well as your triumphs and joys.

Examining the Whole

Alright, you've collected and transcribed your data, and now you're ready to start carefully sifting and sorting through it. There's one more step you need to take, though, before you start formally categorizing, or **coding,** the information you've gathered. To minimize the likelihood of prematurely imposing any conceptual frameworks or definitions on the data, it's important that you read through all the transcripts at least once, without attempting to ascribe meanings or assign codes. The idea here is to become thoroughly familiar with the entire data set. Not only will this help you avoid overlooking important pieces of information, but it will also give you the opportunity to let meanings emerge from the data themselves. At its best, qualitative data analysis is a process of discovery. However, like uncovering the gems amidst a pile of stones, it's not a process that can be hurried.

AN INTRODUCTION TO CODING

In Chapter 2 we showed you how coding—or assigning numbers or other short-hand indicators (e.g., m = male; f = female)—can help us organize quantitative data. Now let's see what the process of coding entails when we're working with qualitative data.

Identifying Meaningful Pieces of Data

In most quantitative studies, each numbered response is seen as constituting a single piece of data (i.e., **datum**). In qualitative studies, however, a datum can consist of a single word, a phrase, or even several pages of text. What determines the length and complexity of each piece of data is the researcher's judgment that the specified segment of text conveys an idea that, in itself, is meaningful to the study. To illustrate this idea, let's look at some examples.

One of the most difficult situations faced by many gays and lesbians is deciding if, when, and how to "come out" to their families. One way of gaining insight into the factors involved in making this decision would be to interview individuals who'd gone through the experience. In Figure 4.2, we presented a segment of a fictitious taped interview that addresses this topic. In Figure 4.3, we've taken a section of that interview and identified six potentially informative pieces of data.

The shaded area in line 1 designates our first unit or piece of data and tells us something about the personal significance of the event. The next chunk contained in the unshaded sections of lines 1 and 2 reveals the process nature of the decision to "come out" to one's family. The shaded area extending from lines 2 through 5 describes the circumstance or setting chosen to share this information. The unshaded area in lines 5 and 6 reflects what might be thought of as the cognitive trig-

---

FIGURE 4.3   Identifying Potentially Meaningful Pieces of Data

---

Question: Describe your experience of "coming out" to your family.

1. (Deep sigh) Boy, I'll never forget that day. I'd been thinking about

2. telling my family for some time. It was a Sunday night and we

3. were all in the den watching *Who Wants to Be a Millionaire?*

4. Some guy had just decided to walk away with $125,000. The

5. commercials started and I remember thinking well _____,

6. there's no time like the present. Next thing I know . . . I'm

7. blurting out, "Hey guys, there's something I need to tell you.

8. I'm gay." For a moment it seemed like a dream, almost surreal.

---

ger, that is, the thoughts that immediately preceded the decision to tell. The shaded sections of lines 7 and 8 reveal the words used to "come out" to one's family. Finally, the unshaded section of line 8 tells us something about the immediate personal reaction (i.e., the mixture of feelings and thoughts) accompanying this disclosure.

As you consider the respondent's statements, you might think of other ways of separating and labeling the relevant pieces of data. Not only is that acceptable, it's expected. What's critical is that you delineate the choices you make, as well as the reasoning behind those choices. Even within the context of a single study, it's more than likely that the initial units of data will be refined and revised as the researcher continues to work with the data. Again, what's important is that the researcher keep track of these analytical decisions. By now the value of maintaining that written record we mentioned earlier should be crystal clear. Let's look at another example of specifying the individual units of data within a study.

The data presented in Table 4.11 were collected as part of a consumer satisfaction/needs assessment survey at the request of a local tribal council. Specifically, tribal leaders were interested in (1) obtaining feedback about the adequacy of services that tribal elders were receiving, and (2) identifying what additional services the elders would like the tribe to provide. Presented in Table 4.11 are the 94 verbatim responses the 60 elders interviewed gave to the question, "What other kinds of services would you like to see offered by tribal agencies?" Given the straightforward nature of the question and the corresponding clarity of the responses, it makes sense in this case to initially treat each verbatim response—whether offered as a paragraph, sentence, phrase, or word—as an independent piece of data. There's really little risk in this decision, as we fully expect that the units of data identified at this stage will undergo a fair amount of refinement and change as the analysis unfolds. What's more, as Williams, Unrau, and Grinnell (1998) observe, it's generally easier to break larger sections up into smaller ones as the analysis proceeds, than to try to reconnect segments that previously were separated. Therefore, when in doubt it's wise to keep connected sections of text intact.

Assigning Initial Codes

A **code** is simply a word, phrase, symbol, or abbreviation used to identify or label a piece of data as fitting into a specified category. To loosely paraphrase Miles and Huberman (1984), codes are categorizing devices derived from our research questions, hypotheses, or conceptual themes that help us retrieve and organize our data.

Take a moment to peruse the list of responses presented in Table 4.11. As you do, we think you'll find it easy to get a sense of the unmet needs identified by this particular group of elders. It would be difficult at this point, though, to establish the importance of any particular need—especially in relationship to the others mentioned. Whether you call it **open coding** (Neuman, 1994), **first-level coding** (Tutty, Rothery, & Grinnell, 1996), or developing an **"ad hoc classificatory" scheme** (Denzin, 1978, p. 48), the first step toward achieving this level of clarification is to categorize your data by putting similar pieces of data together. The classifications presented in Table 4.12 represent our initial attempt to cluster like or similar

TABLE 4.11   Services That Tribal Elders Stated They Would Like to See the Tribe Provide (Raw Data)

Help paying for dental services such as dentures
Short-term loans
Trash pickup services
Don't know
Help with yard work
House repairs
Help with housecleaning
Firewood
Free firewood for wood-burning stoves
Better communication about what services are available
Someone to check on people who are ill more than once a day
Our own nursing home
I'd like to see the police go around more at night
Repair living room window (fogged out; tighten screen)
None
Make seniors the number one priority
Help paying utilities: electric bill, propane, and gas
Road maintenance
Home appliance and plumbing repairs (stove, bathtub)
Emergency monies
Help getting a new heater; heater repair is costly
Good, clean water
Help paying for eyeglasses
Emergency help for elders
Renovate present home. Needs repairs as soon as possible.
Burial money
Gas station
Better health care
We need a store desperately
Emergency funding
Paying heating and electric bills during the winter months
Wood for wood-burning stove
Firewood (delivered)
More money for food
Store to get bread, milk, bacon, etc.
Firewood

Legal help
Clothes (coat and shoes) for winter
Medical assistance at home
Help paying for funeral expenses
Someone to check on elderly—whether they're sick or not
Help with medications
Help with bathing
Legal assistance
Help with heating bills
Help with electric bills
Food baskets
Help with light bill
Burial money
Propane
Short-term loans
Spring water for elders, delivered at times when water is not good for drinking
Someone to come and clean homes for the ones that are unable to do so
Help purchasing firewood
Pay gas and power bills for seniors
Money for a chain-linked fence around our houses
Fence my yard
Don't know
Help paying heating bills
Home repairs
Install sewers
Roof repairs
Home repair and improvement
We would like assistance with improvements on our home, such as roofing and floor repair
Dental assistance
Need more assistance on Christmas holiday
Garbage collection
Emergency assistance for things like replacing the hot water heater, cleaning the stove pipes, repairing floors and roofs, etc.
Checking on homebound people every day to see they are fed, clothed, and bathed
Tribal store on reservation so I would not have to travel so far to buy groceries
Better health services
A senior advocate, that is, a person to look out for seniors' needs

TABLE 4.11   Continued

I see many of the Native American elders placed in homes where they are away from their people and cared for by uncaring people. There must be a way the tribe could plan towards a home on the reservation.	Gas station
	Yard cleanup
	Food baskets on special occasions
	Wood for heat
	Scheduled outings for disabled old, such as dinner, brunch, etc.
Help with electric bill	Paying funeral expenses
More financial assistance for the very old who live on meager incomes	Some of the elders need help in cleaning their homes
Employment	Help getting food
Laundromat to wash clothes	Left blank = 9

objects, activities, and terms together. Despite the crudeness of this coding effort, a number of interesting patterns begin to emerge. For instance, we found that help with home repairs was the most common need mentioned, followed closely by requests for assistance with utility bills.

Reviewing, Refining, and Reorganizing the Categories

Once you've placed your data into conceptually similar clusters (i.e., categories), it's a good time to carefully reexamine the sorting decisions that were made. Specifically, you'll want to pull together all the pieces of data you tagged for inclusion in each category. As you do, review each item to make sure it fits in the category assigned and not somewhere else. This requires a careful look at (and perhaps some refinement of) the criteria established for inclusion and exclusion. For example, you might decide that requests for financial assistance with items like eyeglasses and dentures reflect a call for a more extensive form of health care coverage, rather than independent needs.

Make note of any categories you expected to find, but didn't. You may have incorporated items reflecting the expected categories elsewhere. Suppose, for example, you expected to find a need for additional social services. In looking for items that might fit into such a category you decide that "checking with homebound people everyday to see they are fed, clothed, and bathed" (i.e., a protective service function), and the request for "a senior advocate . . . to look out for seniors . . . ," actually reflect important social service needs. If you believe items associated with an expected category like this remain independently important to the study, you'll want to reassign them to a category of their own.

After completing this review process, it's a good idea to ask a colleague to test your analytic scheme by applying the sorting criteria you've established to a transcript or two. Once these tasks are done, you're ready to pursue the next step in the coding process—examining the relationships that exist among the categories you've identified.

TABLE 4.12   Services That Tribal Elders Stated They Would Like to See the Tribe Provide (Clustered in Terms of Equivalent or Like Responses)

Help paying for dental services such as dentures
Dental assistance

Someone to check on people who are ill more
  than once a day
Someone to check on elderly—whether they're
  sick or not
Checking with homebound people every day
  to see they are fed, clothed, and bathed
Medical **assistance at home**
Help with bathing
Help with medications

Short-term loans
Emergency monies
Emergency funding
Short-term loans
More **financial assistance** for the very old who
  live on meager incomes

House repairs
Repair living room window (fogged out; tighten
  screen)
Home appliance and plumbing repairs (stove,
  bathtub)
Help getting a new heater; heater repair is costly
Renovate present home. Needs repairs as soon
  as possible.
Home repairs
Roof repairs
Home repair and improvement
We would like assistance with improvements on
  our home such as roofing and floor repair
Emergency assistance for things like replacing
  the hot water heater, cleaning the stove pipes,
  repairing floors and roofs, etc.

Help paying utilities: electric bill, propane, and
  gas
Paying heating and electric bills during the
  winter months
Help with heating bills
Help with electric bills
Help with light bill
Propane
Help with electric bill
Pay gas and power bills for seniors
Help paying heating bills

Firewood
Free firewood for wood-burning stoves
Firewood (delivered)
Firewood
Help purchasing firewood
Wood for heat
Wood for wood-burning stove

Employment

I'd like to see the **police** go around more
  at night

Road maintenance

Gas station (2)

Help paying for **eyeglasses**

Emergency help (medical) for elders

Better **health care**
Better health services

Our own **nursing home**
I see many of the Native American elders
  placed in homes where they are away
  from their people and cared for by uncaring
  people. There must be a way the tribe
  could plan towards a home on the
  reservation

Burial money
Help paying **funeral expenses**
Burial money
Paying funeral expenses

Help with **yard work**
Yard cleanup

More money for **food**
Food baskets
Food baskets on special occasions
Help getting food

Clothes (coat and shoes) for winter

Need more **assistance with Christmas** holiday

TABLE 4.12   Continued

Help with **housecleaning**
Someone to come and clean homes for the ones
   who are unable to do so
Some of the elders need help in cleaning their
   homes

Legal help
Legal assistance

Good clean **water**
Spring water for elders, delivered at times when
   water is not good for drinking

Trash pick-up services
Garbage collection

Make **seniors** the **number one** priority
Better communication about what **services** are
   available
A **senior advocate,** that is, a person to look out
   for seniors' needs
Scheduled **outings for disabled old,** such as
   dinner, brunch, etc.

Money for a chain-linked **fence** around our
   houses
Fence my yard

Install **sewers**

We need a **store** desperately
Store to get bread, milk, bacon, etc.
Tribal store on reservation so I would not have
   to travel so far to buy groceries

Laundromat to wash clothes

None

Don't know (2)

Blank (9)

Making Comparisons across Categories

Thus far our focus has been on defining individual pieces of data and making comparisons among them. Now our attention turns to the categories we devised. While this change in focus takes us a step away from the individual responses obtained, it allows us to consider commonalities occurring across cases.

Typically referred to as **axial coding** (Neuman, 1994) or **second-level coding** (Tutty, Rothery, & Grinnell, 1996), this phase involves examining the relationships that occur among our categories. Here, in addition to looking at how categories may be similar or different, we also look for relational connections, such as time order (Does one category always precede another?), co-occurrences (Do two categories just happen to appear together, or does one surface only when the other is present?), and conceptual overlapping (Is one category contained within another, or Does one category actually constitute an alternative form of another?). As you consider these comparisons, you may begin to see relationships emerge that suggest additional, more complex, and perhaps more useful classification schemes. The patterns you find occurring among categories are typically referred to as **themes.** For example, as a social worker familiar with the gerontological literature, you might find it useful to connect various categories in ways that reflect the need for assistance with Activities of Daily Living (ADLs, i.e., bathing, dressing, feeding, transferring) and Instrumental Activities of Daily Living (IADLs, i.e., transportation, administering medication, preparing meals, light housekeeping).

The analytic approach you take will depend on many factors, including the questions, problems, or hypotheses being addressed by your research; the availability of a relevant theoretical framework; or the existence of an empirically derived template (i.e., patterns of relationships that have emerged from the analysis of previous observations), to name a few. The bottom line is that it's a decision that you as the researcher will need to make.

INTERPRETING YOUR FINDINGS

At times, as in the case of our needs assessment example involving the tribal elders, it's sufficient to conclude your analysis by presenting the various themes uncovered. In other instances, it may be appropriate for you to use the concepts, patterns, and themes that emerge to formulate questions and hypotheses for consideration in future studies. At other times, it's possible to link the concepts and categories that emerged in a way that forms a conceptual model or provides a more formal theoretical explanation (e.g., grounded theory).

While an extensive discussion of these interpretive approaches is beyond the scope of an introductory text, we will present select practice-relevant examples for your consideration in future chapters. Those of you seeking more in-depth treatment of the topic are encouraged to see, for example, Lincoln and Guba (1985), Lofland and Lofland (1995), Miles and Huberman (1994), and Strauss and Corbin (1990).

TERMS TO KNOW

Ad hoc classificatory scheme (p. 51)
Array (p. 36)
Axial coding (p. 55)
Code (p. 51)
Coding (p. 49)
Cumulative frequency (p. 38)
Cumulative percentage (p. 44)
Data transcription (p. 47)
Datum (p. 50)
First-level coding (p. 51)
Frequency (p. 35)
Frequency distributions (p. 36)
Grouped frequency distribution (p. 40)

Homogeneous (p. 39)
Open coding (p. 51)
Percentage (p. 43)
Proportion (*P*) (p. 42)
Raw data (p. 35)
Relative frequencies (p. 42)
Second-level coding (p. 55)
Simple (or absolute) frequency table (p. 34)
Text data (p. 47)
Themes (p. 55)
Written record (p. 49)

REVIEW PROBLEMS

The situation: Amber is a social work student who's interning at a local grade school. Recently she and her field instructor began cofacilitating two after-school friendship groups—one for third and fourth grade girls and the other for third and fourth grade boys. Currently they have about 10 participants in each group. In discussing possible topics for future sessions, Amber asked if a session on self-esteem issues might be helpful. Amber's field instructor thought this was a great idea. She suggested that they might be able to clarify specific self-esteem issues of interest by assessing these youngsters' current levels of self-esteem. So Amber located an appropriate 20-item self-esteem scale, and then she and her field instructor administered it at this week's group meetings. The raw scores they obtained are presented as follows:

GIRLS	BOYS
14	14
12	9
10	17
6	11
10	12
16	8
14	11
12	6
9	6
10	14

In reviewing these data, you need to know that the self-esteem scores generated by this measure can range from 0 to 20, with higher scores suggesting higher self-esteem.

1. Below, we've placed the girls' self-esteem scores in an array. We'd like you to do the same with the boys' self-esteem scores.

   Girls' Self-Esteem Scores: 6, 9, 10, 10, 10, 12, 12, 14, 14, 16
   Boys' Self-Esteem Scores: ___, ___, ___, ___, ___, ___, ___, ___, ___, ___

2. Using the data in our array, we prepared the girls' self-esteem scores for entry into a frequency table. Go ahead and do the same with the boys' self-esteem scores.

GIRLS' SCORES	FREQUENCY (f)		BOYS' SCORES	FREQUENCY (f)
6	/	1		
9	/	1		
10	///	3		
12	//	2		
14	//	2		
16	/	1		
Total:		10		

3. We used the data we compiled on the self-esteem scores obtained from the girls' friendship group as the basis for building Table 4.13. Using the data you compiled for the self-esteem scores from the boys' friendship group, construct Table 4.14 by transferring (and, where appropriate, computing) the data called for by each column heading.

4. How many girls obtained a self-esteem score of 10? How many boys?

TABLE 4.13   **Absolute and Cumulative Frequencies and Percentages: Self-Esteem Scores for Participants in Girls' Friendship Group**

SELF-ESTEEM SCORES	FREQUENCY (f)	CUMULATIVE FREQUENCY (Cf)	PERCENT (%)	CUMULATIVE PERCENT (%)
6	1	1	10	10
9	1	2	10	20
10	3	5	30	50
12	2	7	20	70
14	2	9	20	90
16	1	10	10	100
	$N = 10$		100	

TABLE 4.14   **Absolute and Cumulative Frequencies and Percentages: Self-Esteem Scores for Participants in Boys' Friendship Group**

SELF-ESTEEM SCORES	FREQUENCY (f)	CUMULATIVE FREQUENCY (Cf)	PERCENT (%)	CUMULATIVE PERCENT (%)
6				
8				
9				
11				
12				
14				
17				
	$N = 10$		100	

5. What percentage of boys obtained a self-esteem score of 10 or lower?

6. What percentage of girls obtained a self-esteem score of 11 or higher?

7. In this instance, would Amber be wise to report the underlying frequencies when she's presenting percentages? Why or why not?

8. According to this chapter, which are easier to interpret—proportions or percentages? Explain your answer.

9. Describe the categories and themes you would use to present the social services needs suggested by the data contained in Table 4.11 to the tribal leaders.

REFERENCES

Babbie, E. (1999). *The basics of social research.* Belmont, CA: Wadsworth.
Craft, J. L. (1990). *Statistics and data analysis for social workers.* Itasca, IL: F. E. Peacock.

Denzin, N. K. (1978). *The research act: A theoretical introduction to sociological methods.* San Francisco: McGraw-Hill.

Frankfort-Nachmias, C. (1997). *Social statistics for a diverse society.* Thousand Oaks, CA: Pine Forge Press.

Lincoln, Y. S., & Guba, E. G. (1985). *Naturalistic inquiry.* Beverly Hills, CA: Sage.

Lofland, J., & Lofland, L. H. (1995). *Analyzing social settings* (3rd ed.). Belmont, CA: Wadsworth.

Miles, M. B., & Huberman, A. M. (1984). *Qualitative data analysis.* Beverly Hills, CA: Sage.

Miles, M. B., & Huberman, A. M. (1994). *Qualitative data analysis: An expanded sourcebook* (2nd ed.). Thousand Oaks, CA: Sage.

Neuman, W. L. (1994). *Social research methods* (2nd ed.). Boston: Allyn & Bacon.

Richardson, L. (2000). Writing: A method of inquiry. In N. K. Denzin & Y. S. Lincoln (Eds.), *Handbook of qualitative research* (2nd ed., pp. 923–948). Thousand Oaks, CA: Sage.

Strauss, A. L., & Corbin, J. (1990). *Basics of qualitative research: Grounded theory procedures and techniques.* Newbury Park, CA: Sage.

Tutty, L. M., Rothery, M. A., & Grinnell, R. M., Jr. (1996). *Qualitative research for social workers.* Boston: Allyn & Bacon.

Vogt, W. P. (1993). *Dictionary of statistics and methodology.* Newbury Park, CA: Sage.

Williams, M., Unrau, Y. A., & Grinnell, R. M., Jr. (1998). *Introduction to social work research.* Itasca, IL: F. E. Peacock.

CHAPTER FIVE

PREPARING AND INTERPRETING GRAPHICAL REPRESENTATIONS

Graphical displays provide another means of organizing and presenting data. Variably referred to as graphs, charts, or diagrams, these techniques are used to augment or replace information that might otherwise be presented in a table or in narrative form. While some researchers attempt to draw careful distinctions among the terms *chart, graph,* and *diagram,* it's common to refer to any illustration (other than a table) included in a formal report or manuscript as a **figure** (American Psychological Association, 1994).

As we noted earlier, tables typically contain the exact scores or results obtained from a study. In contrast, figures simplify and condense the data to convey only the essential facts. This reduction in the amount and type of data presented tends to make the information easier to read and more readily understood. Also, by streamlining the results in this manner, you allow your viewer to see at a glance the overall pattern of the data. It's akin to taking a panoramic shot versus a close-up, with the trade-off being a loss of detail in exchange for a glimpse of the bigger picture. This broader perspective is particularly helpful in highlighting the distribution of scores obtained for a single variable, or in demonstrating how scores achieved on one variable relate to those obtained on another.

The graphics functions associated with most of today's word processing and statistical software packages provide access to a wide variety of graphical displays. In this chapter, however, we'll focus on the techniques most likely to be used by social workers. In general, decisions about which approach to use will depend on how the variables were measured, as well as how best to keep the presentation clear.

UNDERSTANDING THE STUFF OF WHICH GRAPHS ARE MADE

As with tables, several rules of thumb have emerged with respect to constructing graphs. The most common conventions of graph construction are presented in Figure 5.1. Go ahead and take a few minutes to review these items. We think you'll

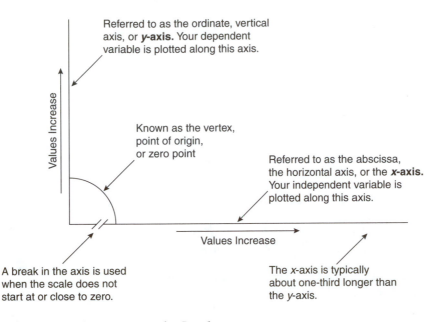

Referred to as the ordinate, vertical axis, or **y-axis.** Your dependent variable is plotted along this axis.

Values Increase

Known as the vertex, point of origin, or zero point

Referred to as the abscissa, the horizontal axis, or the **x-axis.** Your independent variable is plotted along this axis.

Values Increase

A break in the axis is used when the scale does not start at or close to zero.

The x-axis is typically about one-third longer than the y-axis.

FIGURE 5.1   The Anatomy of a Graph

find that becoming familiar with these guidelines will make it easier for you to construct, interpret, and compare data presented through graphical displays.

BAR GRAPHS

Bar graphs are used to depict frequency data associated with a nominal-level variable. In Figure 5.2 we use a bar graph to display the different types of counseling services that were provided by Agency ABC during the past month.

Notice how the bars are of equal width and, rather than touching, they're spaced evenly along the horizontal axis. Maintaining this distance between the bars is important because it reminds the viewer that the categories displayed represent differences in type or kind—as opposed to amount. In Figure 5.2 we used both words and numbers to label each category. The words delineate the type of counseling associated with each bar, whereas the numbers, which hold no numerical value, indicate only how each category was identified for data entry purposes. Given the categorical nature of the data, these labeling decisions were arbitrary. We could have introduced these bars alphabetically, in order of increasing or decreasing frequency, or even randomly and not altered the meaning of the data.

The height of the bar is used to communicate how frequently the category occurred. Looking at Figure 5.2, it's easy to see that Agency ABC delivered more individual counseling last month than any other counseling service. What conclusion can be drawn by comparing the height of the bar representing individual

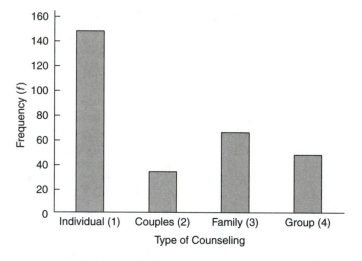

FIGURE 5.2   Bar Graph of Counseling Services Provided by Agency ABC Last Month

counseling with the one for family counseling? (Hint: The bar representing family counseling is half as tall as the one for individual counseling.)

PIE GRAPHS

Another means of displaying data is the **pie, or circle, graph.** It can be used with nominal-, ordinal-, interval-, or ratio-level measures—as long as it makes sense to think about the categories or values that make up the variable as constituting a whole. The pie graph is especially useful when you want to illustrate what percentage or proportion of the data are associated with each of the different values or categories involved. Moreover, as illustrated in Figure 5.3, the close, visual proximity of this information makes it possible to quickly ascertain the relative importance (i.e., prevalence) of each category or value. The steps involved in constructing a pie graph are described in Formulae Alert 5.1.

HISTOGRAMS

Histograms provide a useful way of displaying frequency information gathered on ordinal-, interval-, or ratio-level data. Like the bar graph, the histogram uses bars of different heights to convey how frequently the categories or values associated with a variable occurred. Similarly, the widths of the bars are usually equal. On occasion, however, you'll encounter an interval- or ratio-level measure in which several response categories were collapsed. In such instances, the researcher has the option of proportionately widening the bar used in the histogram to reflect the expanded range of values captured by the category.

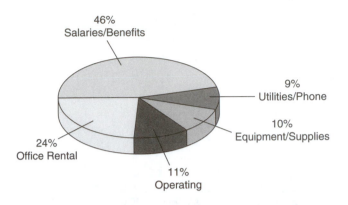

**FIGURE 5.3   Pie Graph of Agency ABC's Expenditures
for Fiscal Year 2000–2001**

FORMULAE ALERT 5.1

In constructing a pie graph, it's helpful to think of it as a circle consisting of 360°. Each category or value is represented by a piece of the pie. You'll be slicing the pie so that the size of each piece corresponds to the percentage or proportion of the data represented by the category or value involved.

For example, suppose Agency ABC's entire budget for fiscal year 2000–2001 was $100,000. Let's say its monthly rent was $2,000. To determine the percentage of the budget expended on rent, you'd multiply the monthly cost by 12, for an annual total of $24,000. Then you'd divide this amount by the total budget (i.e., $24,000/$100,000). The result, of course, is .24, which is converted to a percent by multiplying by 100 (24%).

To determine how large you should cut the slice of pie representing rent, you'd simply multiply the percent of the budget allocated to rent by 360°. The answer is 86.4°, which is nearly a quarter of the pie (or 90°). To complete your pie, simply repeat this procedure for each of the other budget categories. Using a protractor and compass, you could develop a drawing like the one presented in Figure 5.3. Alternatively, with a couple of extra key strokes, you can take advantage of the pie chart option offered by most word processing and statistical software packages.

Unlike the bar graph, the sides of adjacent bars in a histogram touch each other. This is because the categories used at these levels of measurement represent differences in the amount of the variable being depicted—as opposed to differences in type or kind. In addition, the position of the bars along the horizontal axis is determined by the value associated with each category. As Figure 5.4 illustrates, the smallest value category is placed closest to the vertex or zero point, followed by the next largest category, and so on.

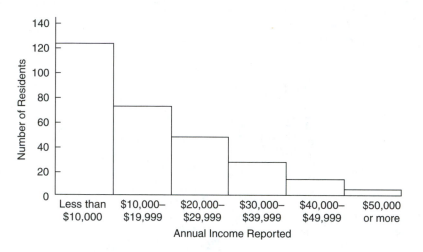

FIGURE 5.4   Histogram of Annual Incomes Reported by Residents of the Eaton County Extended Care Facility

Imagine you are doing your field placement at a county facility that provides long-term care for older adults. As part of your orientation, your field supervisor shares demographic data about the facility's current residents. Figure 5.4 displays the annual income data that's been gathered. Does it surprise you to see how many of the facility's residents maintain incomes near poverty level? Why or why not?

Let's return for a moment to the scenario suggested by Figure 5.2, which depicts the counseling services provided by Agency ABC. Suppose the Agency's Board of Directors is interested in learning more about the 150 people who received individual counseling services from the agency last month. In particular, they want to know if the populations targeted for help as identified in the agency's mission statement are indeed being served. For illustrative purposes, let's assume that Agency ABC seeks to provide individual counseling services for area residents of all ages. The data presented in Figure 5.5 depict the ages of the people who received individual counseling services during the previous month.

As a board member, how would you say the agency is doing in achieving this part of its mission? What additional data might help you in making this assessment? For example, how could you use census data to help make your assessment?

FREQUENCY POLYGONS

As you may recall from an introductory geometry class, a **polygon** is a closed geometric figure that is bounded by three or more lines. The **frequency polygon,** sometimes referred to as a **line graph,** is a special type of polygon that can be used as an alternative to the histogram to portray the overall shape of a distribution of scores. Like the histogram, the scores or values associated with a variable are plot-

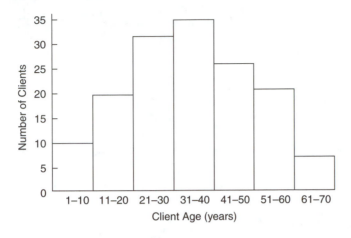

FIGURE 5.5   Histogram Depicting Ages of Clients Receiving Individual Counseling Services from Agency ABC Last Month

ted along the horizontal axis, or *x*-axis, and the frequencies are noted along the vertical axis, or *y*-axis. Instead of bars, however, a single point is plotted for each score which designates how often that score or value was observed. The frequency polygon is completed by connecting adjacent points with straight lines.

The frequency polygon presented in Figure 5.6 depicts the same client age data that are presented as a histogram in Figure 5.5. Take a moment to compare these two figures. Let's focus first on similarities. Both figures show us how individual

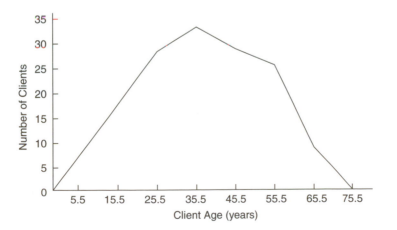

FIGURE 5.6   Frequency Polygon Depicting Ages of Clients Receiving Individual Counseling Services from Agency ABC Last Month

counseling services provided by Agency ABC last month were distributed across age groups. Consequently, both allow us to quickly discern that people in the middle groups received more individual counseling than those in the youngest and oldest categories.

Structurally, however, there are differences between the two figures. First, because the frequency polygon is a closed figure, it is necessary to extend our figure on both sides (i.e., a category beyond the smallest and largest values that we actually observed). Doing so allows us to anchor our endpoints on the *x*-axis, thereby ensuring we'll be able to create a closed geometric figure. Second, the category labels used in the frequency polygon consist of a single number, as opposed to the range of ages used to label the categories included in our histogram. This is because when scores are grouped into intervals, as they are in this example, it is customary to use the midpoint to identify each category contained within the frequency polygon. For additional details on how to compute the **midpoint,** be sure to check out Formulae Alert 5.2.

In general, whether you choose to use a histogram or a frequency polygon to show how the scores you obtained are distributed is really a matter of personal preference. It might be noted, though, that some researchers think it's inappropriate to use a frequency polygon to display ordinal data, because ordinal measures lack a standard unit of measure—a feature believed to be essential for making the cross-category comparisons made possible by these kinds of graphs. Exceptions are allowed, however, when the information obtained by an ordinal measure can be thought of as inherently interval or ratio. Examples of such data include age, number of children, income, height, and so forth.

USING FIGURES TO DISPLAY DIFFERENCES ACROSS GROUPS

Figures also can be useful when you want to compare scores across two or more groups. As you might suspect, level of measurement remains an important factor

FORMULAE ALERT 5.2

The procedure used to find the midpoint of a category or group of scores is really quite simple. First, identify the smallest and largest values making up the category. Then add those values together and divide the sum by 2. For example, in Figure 5.5 our third category consists of clients between the ages of 21 and 30 who received individual counseling from Agency ABC last month. To derive the midpoint for this category, you would add 21 and 30, which gives you a total of 51. Divide this figure by 2, and you've got the midpoint for the category. If you want to see if your answer is correct, compare it with the one presented in Figure 5.6.

in determining which approach to use. If your data are nominal or ordinal, bar graphs and pie charts work well. When the comparisons you're making involve interval- or ratio-level variables, histograms and frequency polygons emerge as the graphical displays of choice. You'll find two literature-based examples of such graphing techniques in Figure 5.7.

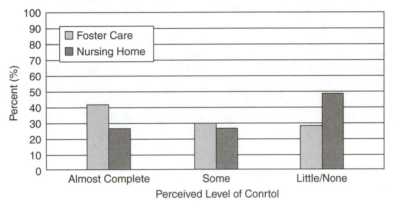

Source: Data used in this example were extrapolated from tabular data presented in "Choosing an Adult Foster Care Home or a Nursing Home: Residents' Perceptions about Decision Making and Control," by J. Reinardy and R. A. Kane, 1999, *Social Work, 44,* p. 578.

Source: These data were adapted from a graph presented in "A Comparison of Two Welfare-to-Work Case Management Models," by T. Brock and K. Harknett, 1998, *Social Service Review, 72* (4), p. 514.

FIGURE 5.7   Using (a) Bar Graphs and (b) Frequency Polygons to Display Data Obtained on More Than One Group

STEM-AND-LEAF DIAGRAMS

The **stem-and-leaf diagram** was developed by Tukey (1977) in the late 1960s. This clever data presentation format actually provides viewers with more information than that found in a histogram or a frequency polygon. That's because, in addition to conveying how the data are distributed, a stem-and-leaf diagram also contains the original scores obtained.

Imagine you're working in a medical center that specializes in treating people diagnosed with chronic pain and depression. You've been asked to develop a biofeedback-relaxation training component for the program. Among the physiological indicators you've selected to help clients monitor the progress they make as they learn how to relax is pulse rate. This week as you worked with your first group of clients, you obtained the following data:

CLIENT	PULSE RATE	CLIENT	PULSE RATE
George	88	Tiffany	65
Valerie	91	David	84
Dean	87	Tameka	82
Mary	76	Tyler	75
Ivan	72	Melody	82
Olena	88	Yolanda	86
Norlene	98	Laura	84
Will	73	Dan	99
Teresa	82	Sam	66
Windy	68	Melisa	95
Maureen	78	Shelley	87
Tom	85	Christine	88
Wendell	74	Chelsie	93

Suppose you wanted to share these data with your colleagues at the next client review meeting. In thinking about how you might do this, you decide that a stem-and-leaf diagram might be just the ticket. First, you need to decide on a stem. To do this, it might help to think back to when you learned about numbers as being made up of ones, tens, hundreds, thousands, and so forth. While thinking in these terms, you want to identify the core numbers on which the actual scores you want to report are based. For example, when dealing with two-digit numbers, such as the pulse-rate data presented here, the values associated with your largest (i.e., the tens) column is typically used to build the stem. Since the pulse rates observed range from a low in the 60s to a high in the 90s, you'd place 6, 7, 8, and 9 in a column, draw lines down the sides of the column and, voilà, you've got a stem:

```
6 | 5
7 |
8 | 8
9 |
```

Now start inserting the second digit of each pulse rate (i.e., the leaf) next to its associated tens unit. For example, since George's pulse rate was 88, place an 8 in the row that signifies values in the 80s. Tiffany's pulse rate of 65 is recorded by placing a 5 in the row set aside for values in the 60s. If you were to continue this procedure until all these pulse rates were entered, your diagram would look like the one in Figure 5.8.

Note how a histogram-like figure appears when you turn the diagram on its side. In Figure 5.9 we've accentuated this feature by placing the numbers contained in each row in ascending order and then shading these data. What impact does ordering the data have? Do you think shading improves the presentation?

Although the stem-and-leaf diagram is rarely used in social work literature, other fields have found this visual display an effective means of conducting preliminary data analysis (Franzosi, 1994; Sklar & Armstrong, 1994). Specifically, by instantly providing information about the high and low values, as well as the spread and clustering of the scores, the stem-and-leaf diagram provides quick insight into the overall structure of a data set. To demonstrate these features, Franzosi (1994) drew on the work of Bollen and Jackman (1985) and prepared a stem-and-leaf diagram much like the one displayed in Figure 5.10. As you view these data, what impressions about the data set do you form? Did you notice how the data points tend to cluster together toward the lower end of the scale, with one notable exception—the single data point located at position |9| 4? The clarity made possible by the level of detail conveyed through tools like the stem-and-leaf diagram have led some to suggest that increasing their use would lead to sounder, more replicable research conclusions (see, for example, Sklar & Armstrong, 1994). What do you think?

FIGURE 5.8   **Stem-and-Leaf Diagram: Clients' Initial Pulse Rates**

6	5 6 8
7	6 5 2 3 8 4
8	8 4 7 2 2 8 6 4 2 7 5 8
9	1 8 9 5 3

FIGURE 5.9   **Ordered and Shaded Stem-and-Leaf Diagram: Clients' Initial Pulse Rates**

6	5 6 8
7	2 3 4 5 6 8
8	2 2 2 4 4 5 6 7 7 8 8 8
9	1 3 5 8 9

FIGURE 5.10   **Stem-and-Leaf Diagram for Income Inequality**

```
1 | 9 9
2 | 2 4 7 8 9 9
3 | 0 1 4 4 5 6 8
4 | 4
5 | 6
6 |
7 |
8 |
9 | 4
```

Note that each stem digit = 1.0, and each leaf digit = 0.1 (i.e., |1| 9 represents 1.9).

GRAPHICAL DISPLAYS WITH SINGLE-SYSTEM DESIGNS

Single-system designs provide social workers with an easy-to-use, affordable means of monitoring client performance. It's important to keep in mind that, as it's used here, the term *client* applies to any system in which a professional social worker may intervene, including individuals, couples, families, groups, organizations, and communities.

As illustrated in Figure 5.11, in its most basic form, a single-system design consists of baseline (A) and intervention time frames (B), during which repeated measures of a targeted client behavior are obtained and recorded. It is the visual presentation or graph of the client's performance throughout these time periods that constitutes "the essence of the single-system design" (Royse, 1999, p. 45). To illustrate how easy it is to interpret the graphing component of the single-system design, let's look at some examples from the professional social work literature.

The healing effect often associated with "the laying on of hands" has long intrigued many in the helping professions. In an effort to examine how touch might augment a more traditional social work approach, Cheung (1999) used an ABAB single-system design ($n = 8$) to evaluate the impact of a social worker–massage therapist team intervention on the physical functioning of nursing home residents. In Figure 5.12, you'll find the average weekly Activities of Daily Living (ADLs) scores obtained for two of the eight residents who participated in Cheung's study. (ADLs include such tasks as, eating, toileting, dressing, personal hygiene, and transferring.) Possible scores on this instrument ranged from 0 to 36, with higher scores reflecting higher levels of functioning. Take a moment, if you will, to review these data.

As you can see from the data presented in Figure 5.12, a notable decrease occurred in Client A's ADL level during the third week of treatment. What's more,

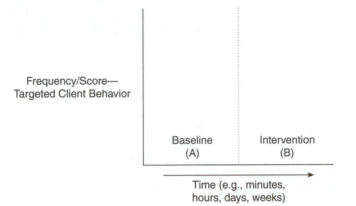

FIGURE 5.11   Basic Elements of a Single-System Design

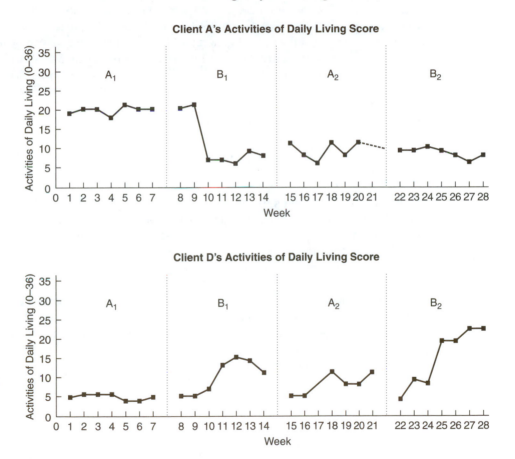

FIGURE 5.12   Sample Graphs from a Single-System Study

Source: From "Effectiveness of Social Work Treatment and Massage Therapy for Nursing Home Clients," by M. Cheung, 1999, *Research on Social Work Practice, 9,* pp. 237–238. Copyright © 1999 by Sage Publications, Inc.

this reduced level of functioning continued throughout the remainder of the study. Given these observations, it seems fair to say that this innovative treatment didn't have the hoped-for effect on Client A's level of functioning. Before you draw any definitive conclusions about the efficacy of this treatment approach overall, however, it's important to note that Client A experienced an exacerbation of symptoms associated with a preexisting medical condition at that exact point in time. In research parlance, then, a historical event emerged that served to seriously threaten the internal validity of this component of the study. In contrast, an increase in Client D's ADL scores was observed during both intervention periods (i.e., B_1 and B_2), with the greatest amount of gain occurring during the second treatment phase.

Despite the varied nature of Cheung's results, practice evaluations like this are important because they provide practitioners with insights into the potential benefits and limitations of a given intervention. In an effort to promote greater use of practice evaluations of this nature among social work practitioners, Auerbach (1996) recently developed a computer program designed specifically to facilitate the entry, analysis, and presentation of data acquired through research carried out with single systems. An example of the output generated through this program can be found in Figure 5.13. Specifically, Figure 5.13 presents data gathered by an MSW student who assisted a classroom teacher in addressing a 9-year-old student's disruptive classroom behavior. The treatment involved giving the youngster the special responsibility of distributing all classroom materials. In looking at these data, the decrease that occurred in this youngster's tendency to get out of his seat is easy to detect.

In Figure 5.13, you'll also find three additional pieces of information displayed that you can use to help to visually assess the nature of the behavioral change observed:

1. A solid line represents the average, or mean, number of times the youngster got out of his seat during the baseline (preintervention) period.
2. A dotted line represents the value two standard deviations above this pretreatment average.
3. A dashed line represents the point two standard deviations below this mean.

The technical importance of these values will become clearer once we've discussed measures of central tendency, dispersion, and confidence intervals. For now, all you need to know is that *desired behavior* is defined as the area outside this 2 standard deviation band (Conboy et al., 2000). In this instance, since a decrease in the incidence of the behavior is being sought, we're looking for behavior below the mean and the 2 standard deviation band (dashed line). Is this what was found?

For many, these visual findings—considered in conjunction with feedback from the student and teacher—would be sufficient to determine whether the intervention had been successful. Others, however, believe additional statistical analyses are needed to determine if the results obtained are "real" or merely the work of chance. As you'll learn in the chapters ahead, determining what role chance played in producing the research findings obtained is the essence of inferential statistics. There are many inferential statistical techniques that can be used to analyze single-system data.

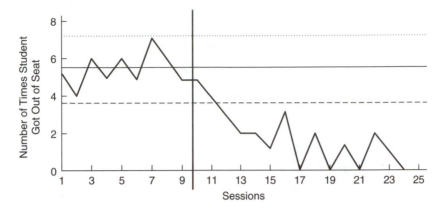

FIGURE 5.13   Computer-Generated Output for Single-System Design

Source: From "MSW Student Satisfaction with Using Single-System-Design Computer Software to Evaluate Social Work Practice," by A. Conboy, C. Auerbach, A. Beckerman, D. Schnall, and H. LaPorte, 2000, *Research on Social Work Practice, 10,* p. 133. Copyright © 2000 by Sage Publications, Inc.

For more detailed explanations of these analytic strategies, see, for example, Bloom, Fischer, and Orme (1995) and Rubin and Babbie (2001). It's our contention, however, that in most cases statistical analysis is not required for single-system data.

GRAPHICALLY DISPLAYING QUALITATIVE DATA

Although most graphical displays are best suited for communicating quantitative data, the bar graph and pie chart provide two ways of presenting qualitative data in graphic form. To illustrate, let's return to the needs assessment data presented in the previous chapter (see Table 4.11, p. 52). Suppose, after carefully considering the 94 responses received from the tribes' elders, you identify seven categories that you believe capture the nature of the needs reported. Specifically, the domains you identify include medical/dental ($n = 19$), financial ($n = 10$), public works/community development ($n = 16$), housekeeping/home maintenance ($n = 15$), utilities/firewood ($n = 17$), advocacy/legal ($n = 5$), and don't know/no answer ($n = 12$). You could narratively describe these data. However, given the number of categories involved, such description could get rather cumbersome. Alternatively, you could develop a pie chart, such as the one presented in Figure 5.14. As a member of the tribal council, would you find this graphical summary helpful? Why or why not?

RECOGNIZING DISTORTED DATA

If misused, graphical displays can distort, rather than communicate, data. For instance, compare the two graphs in Figure 5.15. The first bar graph suggests that

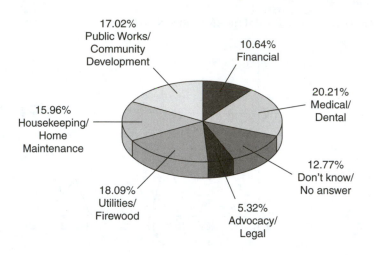

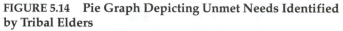

FIGURE 5.14   Pie Graph Depicting Unmet Needs Identified by Tribal Elders

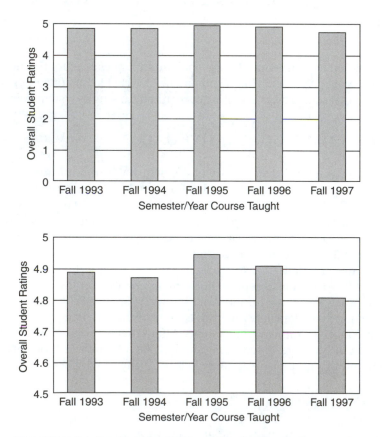

FIGURE 5.15   Bar Graphs: Students' Evaluations of an Instructor's Teaching

student evaluations of the instructor's teaching have remained extremely stable (and positive!) over the five-year period reported. In the second figure, however, the instructor's performance appears to have been rather erratic (and less positive), despite the fact that the same numbers are used in both instances. What do you think accounts for these apparent differences?

If you said the differences are simply due to variations in the values used to define the vertical axis, or *y*-axis, in the two drawings, you're absolutely on target. In the second bar graph, the differences between the evaluations received by this instructor from year to year have been exaggerated by cutting off, or **truncating,** the vertical axis. To avoid such distortions, begin both bar graph axes at zero whenever possible. If you find it necessary to violate this practice—as when you're reporting age data on adults, for example—be sure to signal your decision to do so clearly. As we illustrated in Figure 5.1, this break in scale is typically communicated by inserting two forward slashes (//) on the truncated or shortened axis.

With the graphics available through today's word processing programs, you'll likely find all kinds of ways of using pictures to communicate information. Although we don't want to discourage your creativity, we do feel a word of caution is warranted. Consider this scenario: Imagine you're the director of a small, private, nonprofit agency, and you've just discovered that the county finance committee is planning to cut your agency's block grant funding next year by twice the amount it did this year. In an effort to alert your agency's key community supporters, you prepare the following graphic illustration:

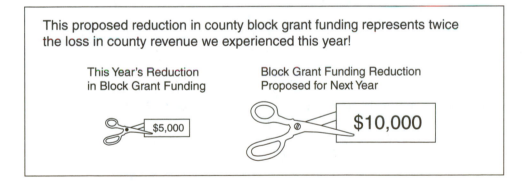

This proposed reduction in county block grant funding represents twice the loss in county revenue we experienced this year!

| This Year's Reduction in Block Grant Funding | Block Grant Funding Reduction Proposed for Next Year |

Since the proposed cuts are twice as large as those the agency absorbed this year, you simply doubled the size of the scissors when you prepared your graphic. So, what's the problem? Well, when you double the size of a figure, you're actually making it twice as tall *and* twice as wide. As a result, your new picture takes up 4 times the space your original did. Essentially, you've exaggerated the difference you want to portray by 100%. It's an honest enough mistake, but it means you need to be on the lookout for such distortions in both your own work and that of others. Remember, the goal of a graphical display is to enhance, not distort, communication.

COMPUTER APPLICATION: CREATING GRAPHICAL DISPLAYS WITH SPSS

Using the client pulse rate data presented earlier, we used the graphing capabilities of SPSS to generate the pie graph depicted in Figure 5.16.

A pie graph generated using SPSS is interpreted in exactly the same way as one that's been developed by hand. In the pie graph presented in Figure 5.16, the labels are outside of the graph and connected to their corresponding pieces by a line. The number inside each piece of pie represents the percentage of the whole that's occupied by that category. The benefit of using computer-generated graphical representations is the ease and precision with which they are created. In addition, such programs generally give you the ability to customize output in ways that allow you to more effectively communicate patterns in the data. For example, SPSS' graphical interface includes features that allow you to change the information contained in the labels of graphs, as well as other features that let you highlight important parts of the data, such as "exploding" a pie graph. Using these features, we modified the pie graph in Figure 5.16 to obtain Figure 5.17. Note that the labels now include not only the percentage of cases, but also the number of cases (count) included in each piece of the graph. Also, the largest piece of the pie was "exploded," or visually separated from the rest of the pie to highlight the fact that nearly half of the clients' initial pulse rates fell within this category.

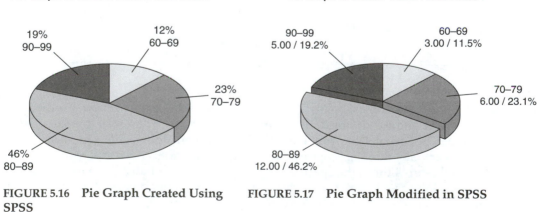

FIGURE 5.16   Pie Graph Created Using SPSS

FIGURE 5.17   Pie Graph Modified in SPSS

TERMS TO KNOW

Bar graph (p. 61)
Circle graph (p. 62)
Figure (p. 60)
Frequency polygon (p. 64)
Histogram (p. 62)
Line graph (p. 64)
Midpoint (p. 66)

Pie graph (p. 62)
Polygon (p. 64)
Single-system design (p. 70)
Stem-and-leaf diagram (p. 68)
Truncating (p. 75)
x-axis (p. 61)
y-axis (p. 61)

REVIEW PROBLEMS

The situation: Your good friend, Chelsie, is a social worker with the New Mexico State Department of Child and Family Services. The adoption unit with which she works is currently undergoing its annual program review. As a part of this process, each worker has been asked to provide select demographic information about his or her current open cases. In response to this request, Chelsie prepared the following table:

AGE AT LAST BIRTHDAY	RACE	GENDER
11	Caucasian	Male
3	Caucasian	Female
4	Hispanic	Male
5	Hispanic	Male
0	African American	Male
1	Caucasian	Female
10	Hispanic	Female
3	Hispanic	Male
6	Caucasian	Male
3	Hispanic	Female
8	African American	Female
0	Hispanic	Female
2	Caucasian	Male
2	African American	Female
7	Hispanic	Female
0	Caucasian	Female
9	Caucasian	Male
1	Caucasian	Male
6	Hispanic	Male
0	Caucasian	Male
5	Caucasian	Female
4	Hispanic	Female
7	African American	Male
1	Caucasian	Male
3	Caucasian	Female

$N = 25$

1. Knowing that you're currently taking an introductory statistics course, Chelsie asks you to help her prepare graphical displays for these data. What kinds of graphs would you suggest she consider for each of these variables? Be sure to tell Chelsie why you're recommending the display(s) you do.

2. Histograms and bar graphs look very much alike, yet they serve different purposes. Under what circumstances would you choose to use a histogram rather than a bar graph?

3. Using the client demographic data your friend Chelsie collected, prepare an appropriate graphical display for the variable age.

4. Figure 5.18 is a histogram of the client pulse data that we presented previously in a stem-and-leaf diagram (see Figure 5.9). Take a moment and carefully compare Figures 5.9 and 5.18. In what ways are they similar? How are they different?

5. Figure 5.6 contains a histogram of the ages of clients receiving individual counseling services from Agency ABC last month. Recall that the mission of the agency is to provide individual counseling services for residents of all ages. Suppose that you were a board member of this agency and received these data as part of a month-end report on service delivery. How would you say the agency is doing in achieving this part of its mission? What additional data might you request to help you in making this assessment? For example, how could you use census data to help make your assessment?

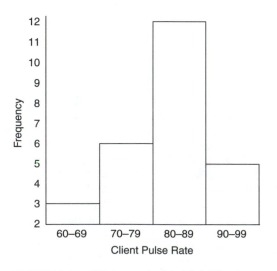

FIGURE 5.18   Histogram of Initial Client Pulse Rates

REFERENCES

American Psychological Association. (1994). *Publication manual of the American Psychological Association* (4th ed.). Washington, DC: Author.

Auerbach, C. (1996). *Statistics for single subject design (Beta version)*. (Available from A. M. Conboy, Social Work Projects Coordinator, The New York Academy of Medicine, 1216 Fifth Avenue, New York, NY 10029; e-mail: aconboy@nyam.org.)

Bloom, M., Fischer, J., & Orme, J. G. (1995). *Evaluating practice: Guidelines for the accountable professional* (2nd ed.). Boston: Allyn & Bacon.

Bollen, K. A., & Jackman, R. W. (1985). Regression diagnostics: An expository treatment of outliers and influential cases. *Sociological Methods and Research, 13*(4), 510–542.

Brock, T., & Harknett, K. (1998, December). A comparison of two welfare-to-work case management models. *Social Service Review, 72*(4), 495–520.

Cheung, M. (1999). Effectiveness of social work treatment and massage therapy for nursing home clients. *Research on Social Work Practice, 9,* 229–247.

Conboy, A., Auerbach, C., Beckerman, A., Schnall, D., & LaPorte, H. (2000). MSW student satisfaction with using single-system-design computer software to evaluate social work practice. *Research on Social Work, 10,* 127–138.

Franzosi, R. (1994). Outside and inside the regression "black box" from exploratory to interior data analysis. *Quality and Quantity, 28,* 21–53.

Reinardy, J., & Kane, R. A. (1999). Choosing an adult foster care home or a nursing home: Residents' perceptions about decision making and control. *Social Work, 44,* 571–585.

Royse, D. (1999). *Research methods in social work* (3rd ed.). Chicago: Nelson-Hall.

Rubin, A., & Babbie, E. (2001). *Research methods for social work* (4th ed.). Belmont, CA: Brooks/Cole.

Sklar, M. G., & Armstrong, R. D. (1994). Robust estimation procedures and visual display techniques for a two-way classification model. *Quality & Quantity, 28,* 284–304.

Tukey, J. W. (1977). *Exploratory data analysis.* Reading, MA: Addison-Wesley.

CHAPTER SIX

COMPUTING AND INTERPRETING MEASURES OF CENTRAL TENDENCY

In Chapters 4 and 5, we showed you how frequency tables and graphical displays can be used to organize and present data. In this and the following chapter, we'll show you several descriptive procedures you can use to summarize data in even more succinct ways. In fact, **descriptive measures** typically allow us to reduce a data set to a single label or value. For example, it's not uncommon for students to use their cumulative grade point average (GPA) as an indicator of their overall academic performance. Likewise, a social work practitioner might report on the progress of her clients in a treatment group by using an average depression score—derived by averaging participants' scores on a measure such as the Beck Depression Inventory. It's this use of a single number to summarize an entire set of scores that explains why these descriptive procedures are also referred to as **data reduction techniques.**

Descriptive analytic techniques are typically classified into two categories. The first type tells us how the values in a given distribution of scores *cluster,* and indicates where the typical or average score is found. These descriptive measures are referred to as **measures of central tendency** and constitute the focus of this chapter. The second type tells us how the scores in a distribution are *spread out*, or dispersed. Therefore, these measures are referred to as **measures of dispersion,** or variability. We'll address these descriptive measures in Chapter 7.

IDENTIFYING THE TYPICAL RESPONSE

As a social work student, it's likely that you often think about what's "typical" or "average." In a human behavior class, for example, you might talk about the developmental tasks of the typical two-year-old. In seminar you might discuss a typical client in some agency, or the average student caseload. What's meant by *typical* or *average* in these instances is not always clear. In the context of social work research, however, such ambiguity is averted by introducing terms that help us distinguish between the three different kinds of averages: the mode, the median, and the mean. Each provides a way of summarizing data with a single label or value, as well as producing a common reference point for making comparisons across groups. Together these measures also provide a foundation for more sophisticated kinds of statistical analyses. Let's start by examining the characteristics associated with the simplest type of average—the mode.

THE MODE

The **mode** is the category or score that occurs the most often in a data set. It also can be thought of as the most common or popular response obtained. Finding the mode is simply a matter of determining which category or value within a set of scores occurs most often. There really is no formula for calculating the mode, but frequency tables and graphical displays of frequency distributions make finding the mode a relatively quick and easy task. To illustrate, let's look at the starting salaries obtained by clients who completed involvement in a job training program during the past 6 months (see Table 6.1). To obtain the mode, simply identify the salary category with the highest frequency (f). If you selected $18,000 as the mode, you're correct. Twenty-one of the 100 clients who completed this program during the past 6 months started at this salary level—that's 7 more than the next largest category.

Using the histogram in Figure 6.1, how would you go about finding the mode? Simply locate the tallest bar. What value on the horizontal axis is associated with

TABLE 6.1   Frequency Distribution: Starting Salaries Obtained by Job Training Program Graduates during the Past 6 Months

STARTING SALARY	FREQUENCY (f)
$16,000	3
17,000	2
18,000	21
19,000	2
20,000	4
21,000	3
24,000	11
25,000	14
26,000	12
27,000	13
28,000	9
30,000	5
32,000	1
	$N = 100$

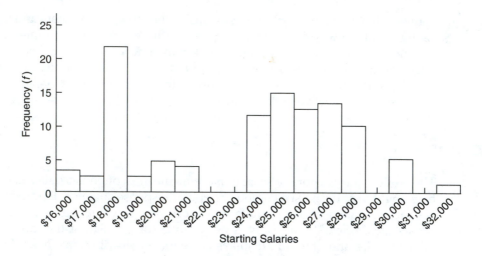

FIGURE 6.1   Histogram: Starting Salaries Obtained by Job Training Program Graduates during the Past 6 Months

this bar? Since the data are identical to that presented in Table 6.1, it's not surprising that $18,000 again emerges as the modal client starting salary. To find the mode of a distribution presented in a bar chart or frequency polygon, simply follow the same steps you took with this histogram—locate the tallest bar or the highest point in the distribution, and then note the score or label on the *x*-axis directly below it.

Distributions such as our client salary data, in which one score or category clearly occurs more frequently than any of the others, are referred to as **unimodal distributions.** These distributions have one major peak. If no score occurs more than once, or if every score occurs the same number of times, the distribution is said to have **no mode.** When there is a tie between the two most frequently occurring categories, the distribution is described as **bimodal.** For example, Tom is a case manager at an outpatient mental health clinic. His caseload consists of 25 clients who have been diagnosed with conditions that place them within the following major diagnostic categories:

DIAGNOSTIC CATEGORY	NUMBER OF CLIENTS
Anxiety disorders	8
Eating disorders	4
Mood disorders	8
Personality disorders	3
Schizophrenia and other psychotic disorders	2

In this example, it's easy to see that the largest number of people in any category is eight. In fact, eight of Tom's clients experience anxiety disorders, while another eight experience some type of mood disorder. Which condition would you say typifies the people with whom Tom currently works? Both do, of course, so

Tom's caseload is considered bimodal with respect to the diagnostic characteristics of his clients. If three or more categories tie for having the largest frequency, the distribution is referred to as **multimodal.**

As Knoke and Bohrnstedt (1994) observe, the term *bimodal* technically applies only to distributions in which the two categories occurring the most often occur exactly the same number of times. In practice, though, researchers often use the term *bimodal* to describe distributions in which the two most frequently occurring categories have *approximately* the same number of cases or observations. This practice, however, is not followed by many statistical packages, such as SPSS, which require an exact match in the number of occurrences to identify a distribution as bimodal or multimodal. It's important, therefore, that you visually inspect your data to rule out the existence of a distribution that would be considered by many researchers to be, in essence, bimodal or multimodal.

Although the mode can be used with variables operationalized at any level of measurement, it is the only measure of central tendency that can be used with nominal level measures. Given this circumstance, why is the mode rarely mentioned in descriptions of nominal level data? That's because it's often more useful to report frequencies or percentages with a nominal-level variable, rather than the modal category alone. For instance, let's return for a moment to the gender data gathered on the people completing a parenting skills class (Table 4.1, page 35). A quick count reveals that there were 25 women and 10 men participating in this training. You could report that women constituted the modal category, but you can just as easily say that 71% (n = 25) of the participants were women and 29% (n = 10) were men. Which of these descriptions do you find most informative?

Craft (1990) has suggested it might be more accurate to think of the mode as an indicator of what's typical rather than a measure of central tendency. After all, as our client salary data revealed (Table 6.1), the mode need not be located anywhere near the center of a distribution, nor does it necessarily signify where the majority of the cases cluster. Its legitimacy as a measure of central tendency also has been questioned on the grounds that, since distributions can be bimodal and even multimodal, the mode doesn't consistently allow us to reduce the information in a data set to a single number.

Modality, however, does provide an important tool for describing distributions that don't possess any clear central tendencies. Suppose, for instance, your supervisor asked you to conduct a client satisfaction survey. Among the questions you asked was an item that addressed client satisfaction with the agency's walk-in clinic hours. Let's assume that walk-in services are available only on weekdays from 10:00 A.M. until 2:00 P.M. The responses obtained from the first 100 clients polled are presented in Figure 6.2.

With distinctive clusters of scores like this, it's likely you're dealing with two separate subgroups of clients. There's a strong possibility that this bimodal distribution was produced because one group of clients (i.e., those who work during the day) found the clinic's walk-in hours inconvenient, while another group (i.e., those who don't work during the day) were quite satisfied. Consequently, there is

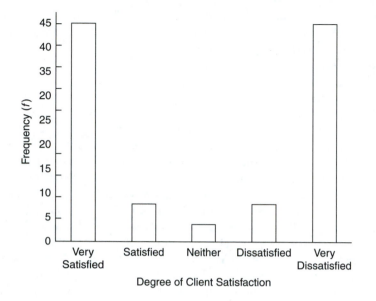

FIGURE 6.2   **Bar Graph: Client Satisfaction with Walk-In Clinic Hours**

no single indicator of central tendency that would accurately characterize your clients' satisfaction with the agency's walk-in clinic hours. In such cases, it's wise to report both modal categories as well as their respective percentages, and then proceed cautiously with any further interpretation until additional data are obtained.

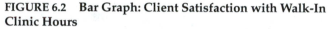

REPORTING THE MODE

In research articles and professional reports, the abbreviation **Mo** is often used to symbolize the mode. It's important to note that measures of central tendency are rarely printed without a reference to an appropriate measure of dispersion (e.g., standard deviation). Consequently, you'll typically find a reference to the range accompanying a report of the mode. In a formal presentation, you may encounter something like this: "while the ages of the clients participating in this study ranged from 16 to 38, there were more 22-year-olds than any other age group (Mo = 22)."

When presenting the mode for grouped frequency data, such as the client age data depicted in Figure 5.5 (p. 65), you can report the *group or category* with the largest frequency (e.g., "the modal category consisted of clients between the ages of 31 and 40"), or you can use the category's *midpoint* (e.g., "a modal age of 35.5 was obtained"). For information on how a midpoint is computed, see Formulae Alert 5.2 (p. 66).

Again, if you find more than one mode, be sure to report them all.

THE MEDIAN

Another indicator of central tendency is the **median.** This measure can be used whenever you're working with data that can be rank ordered, that is, data that have been gathered at an ordinal level of measurement or above. Alternatively referred to as the midpoint, the 2nd quartile, or the 50th percentile, the median is the point that divides the number of observations in an ordered distribution into two equal portions or halves. Like the double yellow line running down the middle of a road, the median can be thought of as dividing a continuum of scores in half.

Finding the median when there are a small number of observations or scores is basically a matter of ordering and counting. Consider the data in Table 6.2, which depicts the number of community-based care management cases opened last quarter by the social workers on staff at an area agency on aging.

To find the median for this data set, first we place the observations made regarding the number of cases each worker opened in ascending order, as shown in Table 6.3: 0, 10, 12, 13, 14, 16, 20. Next, to locate the median value, we count the number of cases or observations that were made, add 1, and divide that sum by 2 [$(N + 1) \div 2$ = the location of the median]. In this example, we have a total of seven observations. By adding 1 to this total and then dividing the sum by 2 [$(7 + 1) \div 2 = 8 \div 2 = 4$], we learn that the median occupies the fourth position within the ordered list of observations. To find the median, we next start with the smallest observation in the array and count until we reach the fourth observation. Doing so, we find that Allen's 13 cases is in the fourth position. It is also the point that divides our array in half, with three observations located above it and three observations below it. We conclude, therefore, that our median is 13.

In cases such as this where there are an odd number of observations, the value of the median is usually a value that someone actually attained. However, when a distribution contains an even number of observations or cases, this isn't necessarily

TABLE 6.2   Area Agency on Aging Community-Based Care Management Cases Opened Last Quarter by Social Worker

SOCIAL WORKER	NUMBER OF CASES OPENED LAST QUARTER
Allen	13
Betty	0
Carol	12
David	10
Ellen	20
Francine	16
Georgina	14

TABLE 6.3   Area Agency on Aging Community-Based Care Management Cases Opened Last Quarter by Social Worker (in Ascending Order by Number of Cases)

SOCIAL WORKER	NUMBER OF CASES OPENED LAST QUARTER
Betty	0
David	10
Carol	12
Allen	13
Georgina	14
Francine	16
Ellen	20

the case. That's because an additional step is involved in ascertaining the median when we have an even number of categories or observations. Suppose in reexamining the data presented in Table 6.2, the agency's director decided that, since Betty started with the agency only a week before the end of last quarter, she really shouldn't be included in the quarterly report. The director's decision to omit Betty is now reflected in Table 6.4. How would you go about helping the director find the median for this new data set? First, you place the scores or observations made in order from smallest to largest: 10, 12, 13, 14, 16, 20 (see Table 6.5). Now count the number of observations, add 1, and divide the sum by 2. Take a moment to do that now.

In computing the location of the median, you should have obtained 3.5 [(6 + 1) ÷ 2 = 3.5], which means that the median lies halfway between the third and fourth observations. To determine the value of the median, start with the smallest observation in your array, and locate both the third and fourth observations. In this case, you'll find that the third score is 13 and the fourth is 14. The value of the median is then derived by adding these two scores together and then dividing that sum by 2, as follows: [(13 + 14) ÷ 2 = 13.5]. Even though no agency worker actually opened 13.5 cases this past quarter, that is the median, since 13.5 is the point that divides this array precisely in half, with three observations located above it and three located below it.

When you work with large data sets, the easiest way to order the scores is to create a cumulative frequency distribution, such as the one presented in Table 6.6. Once this is accomplished, the process of finding the median is basically the same as the one we just described. Table 6.6 shows the length of 907 telephone calls taken by crisis call workers during the month of June. Note that each call made is an observation. If we add 1 to this total and divide the sum by 2 [(907) + 1 ÷ 2 = 454], we discover that the median is represented by the 454th call. Looking down the cumulative frequency column, we find that the 454th call is found in that group of calls lasting 4 minutes. Hence, we say that the median length of calls fielded by workers at the crisis call center in June was 4 minutes.

TABLE 6.4   Area Agency on Aging Community-Based Care Management Cases Opened Last Quarter by Social Worker— Omitting New Workers

SOCIAL WORKER	NUMBER OF CASES OPENED LAST QUARTER
Allen	13
Carol	12
David	10
Ellen	20
Francine	16
Georgina	14

TABLE 6.5   Area Agency on Aging Community-Based Care Management Cases Opened Last Quarter by Social Worker— Omitting New Workers (in Ascending Order by Number of Cases)

SOCIAL WORKER	NUMBER OF CASES OPENED LAST QUARTER
David	10
Carol	12
Allen	13
Georgina	14
Francine	16
Ellen	20

TABLE 6.6 Cumulative Frequency Distribution: Length of Calls Fielded by Crisis Call Center in June

LENGTH OF CALL IN MINUTES (X)	FREQUENCY (f)	CUMULATIVE FREQUENCY (Cf)	PERCENT (%)	CUMULATIVE PERCENT (%)
1	135	135	14.88	14.88
2	82	217	9.04	23.92
3	129	346	14.22	38.14
4	112	458	12.35	50.49
5	65	523	7.17	57.66
7	84	607	9.26	66.92
9	45	652	4.96	71.88
10	56	708	6.17	78.05
12	38	746	4.20	82.25
13	33	779	3.64	85.89
14	23	802	2.54	88.43
15	18	820	1.98	90.41
16	24	844	2.65	93.06
18	16	860	1.76	94.82
20	25	885	2.76	97.58
23	14	899	1.54	99.12
24	5	904	0.55	99.67
28	2	906	0.22	99.89
35	1	907	0.11	100.00
	N = 907		100.00	

Because the median is the value that divides the scores in an ordered distribution precisely in half, it also can be thought of as the score or category that corresponds with the point in a frequency distribution where the cumulative percentage reaches 50%. To illustrate, let's return to the data displayed in Table 6.6. Starting with the smallest value in the array (which in this case is located at the top of the cumulative percentage column), let's scan down until we've captured 50% of the calls involved. It's important to note that we'll need some latitude in searching for this 50% mark because it's unusual for a category to cumulate to exactly 50%. As we proceed down the cumulative percent column, we find at the 3-minute category that we've accounted for 38.14% of the calls. It isn't until we reach the 4-minute category that we capture just over 50% (50.49). Thus, we again conclude that the median length of calls taken by workers at the crisis call center during June was 4 minutes. Fifty percent of the calls were 4 minutes or shorter, and roughly 50% were 4 minutes or longer.

Often the data of interest to social workers—such as statistics on child abuse, teenage pregnancy, new AIDS cases, or suicide rates—are available only in grouped or tabular form. Fortunately, this approach—equating the median with the point in a distribution of ordered scores where the cumulative percentage reaches 50%—can be used when working with grouped data, as well. Consider, for example, the client education data reported in Table 6.7. To find the median level of

TABLE 6.7   Years of Education Completed by Family Assistance Recipients (Head of Household)

YEARS OF EDUCATION	FREQUENCY (f)	PERCENT (%)	CUMULATIVE PERCENT (%)
17 or more	3	4.0	100.0
16	7	9.0	96.0
13–15	15	19.2	97.0
12	31	39.7	67.8
8–11	20	25.6	28.1
Less than 8	2	2.5	2.5
	N = 78		

education achieved by these program participants, start with the smallest value in the array (which in this instance is at the bottom of the cumulative percentage column), and scan upward until you find the category where the cumulative percentage reaches 50%. As you proceed, note how just over a quarter (28.1%) report completing 8 to 11 years of education or less. Continuing on, you'll find 67.8% of the clients completed 12 years of education or less. This large category includes the cumulative percentage of 50%, and thus represents the median level of education attained by participants in this family assistance program.

Many statistics texts conceptualize the median as the 50th percentile and recommend using a rather complex formula for determining its value. For the more adventuresome among you, we present this approach in Formulae Alert 6.1.

Note: Computerized statistical packages such as SPSS and the data analysis component of Microsoft Excel calculate the median by selecting the middle observation for an array containing an odd number of observations, and averaging the two middlemost scores when there are an even number of observations.

REPORTING THE MEDIAN

In research articles and professional reports, the median is often abbreviated as **Mdn** or **Mn.** When reporting the median, it is customary to include a description of the interquartile range. Here's an example of what you might find: "Although the calls fielded by center staff in June ranged in length from 1 to 35 minutes, the average or median length of calls was 4 minutes (Mdn = 4)."

When reporting the median for grouped frequency data, the median is typically described in terms of the category within which it falls, i.e., "a median income of $8,000 to $10,000 was discovered for this group, which is considerably lower than their age counterparts nationally (national Mdn = $24,000 to $26,000)."

FORMULAE ALERT 6.1

The median can be thought of as the 50th percentile, or the point in an ordered distribution below which 50% of the observations fall. The formula for computing percentiles, therefore, provides another way of determining the median. In fact, many statistics texts present this as the preferred way of calculating the median—especially when one is working with continuous scores. The specific procedure for calculating the median as the 50th percentile is as follows:

$$Mdn = LRL_{Mdn} + \left[\frac{.50(N) - Cf_{bMdn}}{f_{wMdn}} \right] \times W_{Mdn}$$

where

Mdn = median

LRL_{Mdn}* = lower real limit of the category containing the 50th percentile (Mdn)

N = total number of scores or observations

Cf_{bMdn} = cumulative frequency for all categories below (i.e., leading up to but not including) the one containing the 50th percentile (Mdn)

f_{wMdn} = number of observations, or frequency, within the interval or category containing the 50th percentile (Mdn)

W_{Mdn} = width of the interval containing the 50th percentile (Mdn), which is derived by subtracting the category's lower real limit from its upper real limit

Let's apply this formula to the client education data presented in Table 6.7. Earlier we used the cumulative percentage column and determined that the median lies somewhere within the 12-year interval. Inserting this, along with the other pertinent information used in the percentile formula, we get

$$Mdn = 11.5 + \left[\frac{.50(78) - 22}{31} \right] \times 1 = 12.05 \text{ years}$$

*Remember that when we're working with continuous numbers (whether grouped or not), the space between integers theoretically contains an infinite number of values. Thus, while we typically talk in terms of whole numbers, we do so implicitly knowing that we're rounding our figures. For example, in summarizing a case, you might report that your client is 38 years of age. The reality is he's likely a tad older or younger than this, depending on the procedure you used to collect/round this information (e.g., age at nearest birthday? age at last birthday?). When we talk about a category's lower and upper real limits, we're explicitly acknowledging the additional values typically included. In "real limit" terms, for instance, 3 is believed to encompass all values extending from 2.5 (its lower real limit, or LRL) to 3.5 (its upper real limit, or URL). Likewise, 4 extends from 3.5 to 4.5. Notice how the upper real limit of 3 becomes the lower real limit of 4. The LRL concept applies similarly to data presented in groups. If you were working with a response category of 10 to 15, for example, the LRL would be 9.5, and the URL would be 15.5.

THE MEAN

The measure of central tendency that social workers tend to know best is the **mean.** Technically referred to as the arithmetic mean, it is defined as the sum of all the scores contained in a data set, divided by the number of scores summed. The formula used to calculate the mean can be found in Formulae Alert 6.2.

Note: Although there are several types of means (e.g., arithmetic, geometric, harmonic), whenever the term is used without a modifier, it's presumed to refer to the arithmetic mean.

To illustrate, let's help Tawny determine how well she's doing in her statistics course by figuring out her average (mean) performance on the five quizzes she's taken thus far. The specific scores she's achieved are 88, 95, 92, 90, and 100.

To compute the mean, we first add all her quiz scores together: $88 + 95 + 92 + 90 + 100 = 465$. Now we divide this sum by the number of quizzes involved: $465 \div 5 = 93$. Tawny's average (mean) quiz score is 93.

One of the defining characteristics of the mean is that it constitutes the numerical center of a distribution. That is, it's the point in a data set around which the values of all the observations balance. Using Tawny's quiz scores, we demonstrate this numerical balancing feature in Table 6.8. The data presented in column 3 tell you precisely how much each individual quiz score differs from the mean. The balance, or equity, that exists among these differences (also known as deviations) becomes apparent when we add them together and discover that they cancel one another out—that is, they sum to zero.

FORMULAE ALERT 6.2

The formula for calculating the mean is as follows:

$$\overline{X} = \frac{\sum X_s}{N}$$

where
$\overline{X}$ (Read X-bar*) = sample mean
Σ (the Greek letter uppercase sigma) = sum, or add up, all the items to the right of this symbol
X_s = all scores contained in the data set
N = total number of scores in the data set

Note: the Greek letter μ (mu) is used in place of X-bar when computing the mean for a population.

TABLE 6.8   Deviation of Tawny's Quiz Scores from the Mean

QUIZ SCORE	MEAN	QUIZ SCORE – MEAN
88	93	–5
90	93	–3
92	93	–1
95	93	2
100	93	7
		Sum = 0

The mean as a center point is also illustrated graphically in Figure 6.3. As you look at these data, picture the number line as an old-fashioned playground teeter-totter and the mean (93) as its fulcrum. In preparing Figure 6.3, we converted Tawny's scores into the number of points each deviated from the mean, and then placed these values on top of our number line. When you disregard the plus and minus signs, the "weight" symbolized by these distances actually balances around the mean (i.e., nine deviation points located both to the right and left of the mean). Note how the positioning of these values along the teeter-totter is no accident—clustered placement of the negative values on the left serves to offset the pull exerted by the 7 on the right (i.e., positive) end.

By incorporating the value of every score in its computation, the mean allows us to make use of all the information available within a data set. Although this gives the mean certain properties that render it desirable for use in more sophisticated analyses, it also makes it vulnerable to the influence of extreme scores. Let's see, for instance, what would have happened to Tawny's average if she had missed the first quiz. In that case, her quiz scores would have been 0, 95, 92, 90, and 100. This set of numbers yields a new mean score of 75.4 (0 + 95 + 92 + 90 + 100 = 377; 377 ÷ 5 = 75.4)—a figure which in no way represents Tawny's typical performance. Clearly her average was pulled down drastically by the one missed quiz. When you have a score that differs so dramatically from the other scores in a data set (like Tawny's zero), it's thought of as an **outlier**. Distributions of scores that contain outliers—whether the deviant scores are markedly higher or lower than the

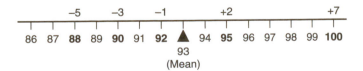

FIGURE 6.3   A Display of Tawny's Individual Quiz Scores Presented in Terms of Their Respective Distances from the Mean

rest—are referred to as **skewed.** (The topic of skewed distributions is addressed more fully in Chapter 8.) What's the moral to this story? Well, there are two. First, be wary of using the mean as an indicator of central tendency when you have unrepresentative, extreme scores that produce skewed distributions. In such situations, the median is the best measure of central tendency. Second, be sure not to miss any quizzes in your statistics class!

Computing the Mean from Grouped Data

When working with large data sets, the task of summing individual scores can get cumbersome. As with the median, the process is rendered more efficient if we construct a frequency distribution first. Let's return to the crisis call center data in Table 6.6. The length of call (X) is presented in the first column. The second column tells us how many times calls of each length occurred. We recognize that we could derive the mean by adding each call's length as many times as it appears in the frequency column. That is, a call length of 1 minute would be entered into our equation 135 times, 2-minute calls would be added in 82 times, and so forth. However, as the data in Table 6.9 suggest, this process can be simplified greatly by creating a new column in which each score (X) is multiplied by its respective frequency (f) of occurrence. Now all we have to do is tally the numbers in column 3 and divide this sum by the total number of observations involved. Applying these steps to the data in Table 6.9, we get an average (mean) call of 6.83 minutes [(135 + 164 + 387 + . . . + 35) = 6,194 ÷ 907 = 6.83].

A unique circumstance arises when we work with frequency distributions involving dichotomous variables. As you may recall, dichotomous variables are those consisting of only two categories, such as, yes/no, or male/female. If we code one category as 0 and the other as 1, the mean will be equivalent to the proportion of cases having a score of 1. Let's use the data in Table 6.10 to illustrate this phenomenon. As above, we calculate the mean for this distribution by tallying the data in column three (0 + 92 = 92) and dividing this sum by the total

---

■ ■ ■ ■ ■

✍ REPORTING THE MEAN

In research articles and professional reports, you'll find the sample mean abbreviated as $\overline{X}$ (X-bar) or as an underlined or italicized em (M, *M*). The Greek letter μ (mu) is used to signify a population mean. Here's an example of what you might encounter: "The mean increase in self-esteem achieved by women completing the 8-week assertiveness training program (*M* = 2.85) was higher than the increase realized by women in the 4-week program (*M* = 1.33)."

In addition, the mean is typically accompanied by its standard deviation (defined in Chapter 7). For example, "The age range of the clients participating in this treatment was 14 to 21 years, with a mean age of 17.9 (*SD* = 1.84)."

TABLE 6.9 Frequency Distribution: Length of Calls Fielded by Crisis Call Center in June

LENGTH OF CALL, IN MINUTES (X)	FREQUENCY (f)	LENGTH OF CALL × FREQUENCY (X × f)
1	135	135
2	82	164
3	129	387
4	112	448
5	65	325
7	84	588
9	45	405
10	56	560
12	38	456
13	33	429
14	23	322
15	18	270
16	24	384
18	16	288
20	25	500
23	14	322
24	5	120
28	2	56
35	1	35
	N = 907	Total = 6,194

number of observations (135). Our outcome (mean) is .6814, which is the proportion of cases with a score or code of 1 (females). Do you have an idea of how you could use this information to determine the proportion of male cases involved? (Hint: Think about what happens if you subtract .6814 from 1). Admittedly, the mean in this instance (i.e., 0.6814) isn't easy to interpret because it lies between 0 and 1. In such instances, the mode usually becomes the central tendency measure of choice.

TABLE 6.10 Gender Data: Clients Served by Project Restart from January through June

GENDER (X)	FREQUENCY (f)	GENDER × FREQUENCY (X × f)
Male (0)	43	0
Female (1)	92	92
	N = 135	

DECIDING WHICH MEASURE TO USE

Deciding which descriptive measure of central tendency to use depends on a number of factors, including (1) your data's level of measurement, (2) the shape of the distribution, and (3) whether you intend to use the data to estimate population parameters in subsequent analyses. We'll discuss these each in turn.

Level of Measurement

If your data are gathered at a nominal level, the mode is the only indicator of central tendency you should use. With ordinal-level measures, you can usually use both the mode and the median. As illustrated by the client satisfaction data in Figure 6.2, though, a notable exception arises when encountering a bimodal distribution in which the values of the modal categories differ substantially. Given the ordinal level of this measure, you might be tempted to report the median response (which in this case would be neither *satisfied* nor *dissatisfied*). Doing so, however, would obscure the **bifurcated,** or split, view clients expressed on this issue. In such cases no single indicator of central tendency will describe the distribution accurately, so you need to report both modes. When working with interval- ratio-level measures, you can use the mode, the median, or the mean to describe your data. The median and mean are the measures most often reported.

Shape of Distribution

The mean, median, and mode will be close in value whenever the scores in a unimodal distribution cluster in a symmetric fashion around the center. In such instances, the mean is the preferred indicator of central tendency when working with interval-, or ratio-level data; the median is recommended when the data are measured at an ordinal level.

In skewed distributions, the values of the mean, median, and mode will differ. The mean, given its susceptibility to the influence of outliers, will be pulled toward the values of the extreme scores. The mode will fall toward the opposite end of the distribution (the end without outliers). The median will be found sitting between the other two, dividing the number of cases precisely in half. Because it's not sensitive to extreme scores, the median is considered more resistant to outliers than the mean and, therefore, is the preferred indicator of central tendency when there is a skewed distribution. It is possible, though, to increase the resistance of the mean by trimming a small percentage (e.g., 5%) of cases off both the low and high ends of a distribution. The remaining values—the middle 90%—are then used to calculate what's referred to as a **trimmed mean.**

Intended Use of Inferential Statistics

If we examined measures of central tendency from repeated samples that have been drawn from a select population, we'd find less variability among the values of the means than that which occurs among the medians or modes. Such consistency or stability is quite desirable when one is using sample statistics to estimate population parameters. Consequently, the mean is the central tendency statistic of choice whenever subsequent analyses of an inferential nature are planned.

We hope you'll find these guidelines helpful. However, you need to know that even the experts don't always agree on when it's best to use each measure. It's important to remember that the mean, median, and mode are merely tools designed to help us summarize and communicate our data clearly. Misusing them may prove to be not only uninformative, but also misleading. Because each measure tells us something unique about a distribution, whenever you're uncertain about which one to use, present all the indicators of central tendency you have available.

COMPUTER APPLICATION: MEASURES OF CENTRAL TENDENCY

Suppose that you worked in an agency that advocates for children in foster care. You have been asked to compile data on the length of time that the clients receiving services from your agency are spending within the foster care system before being either reunified with their families or placed for permanent adoption. Examination of case files for the last 200 cases closed yields the data in Table 6.11 about the length of time (in months) that your clients spent in foster care.

TABLE 6.11   Raw Data: Number of Months Clients Spent in Foster Care

28	7	43	65	64	69	1	29	62	10
18	3	2	12	16	1	21	25	40	26
27	26	66	34	31	22	70	58	71	18
69	4	50	59	70	34	22	54	25	56
5	14	5	26	35	37	27	71	3	17
0	67	7	18	56	49	58	52	6	10
54	45	13	29	40	51	40	13	70	49
38	57	58	19	13	62	8	4	55	53
71	67	65	39	36	49	35	10	3	57
48	53	42	11	64	27	14	15	24	23
22	58	50	20	65	3	51	33	37	18
21	58	57	49	54	68	45	52	70	27
61	40	63	32	16	62	20	51	51	27
24	6	70	21	38	29	72	64	59	65
41	51	29	8	65	28	7	56	56	48
47	19	55	50	62	0	49	67	3	37
66	69	43	40	70	35	18	59	36	61
48	67	33	12	4	0	39	44	35	42
43	67	38	10	6	41	60	5	20	50
30	26	31	24	15	53	38	66	43	38

TABLE 6.12   Central Tendency Output Using SPSS

N = 200	Missing Cases = 0

STATISTICS	MONTHS
Mean	37.635
Median	38
Mode	70

TABLE 6.13   Central Tendency Output Using Excel

STATISTICS	MONTHS
Mean	37.635
Standard error	1.504234851
Median	38
Mode	70
Standard deviation	21.27309328
Sample variance	452.5444975
Kurtosis	−1.201251322
Skewness	−0.115029699
Range	72
Minimum	0
Maximum	72
Sum	7257
Count	200

The following output was generated for the data in Table 6.11 using SPSS (see Table 6.12) and the data analysis functions of Microsoft Excel (see Table 6.13). As you can see, we got a lot more output from Excel than we did from SPSS. This is simply because we had the ability to select only the output we wanted in SPSS, whereas Excel generates a predetermined package of descriptive statistics. The additional information generated by Excel can also be produced by SPSS by asking for it in the STATISTICS dialog box. Notice, however, that the mean, median, and mode calculated by the two programs are the same ($\overline{X}$ = 37.635, Mdn = 38, Mo = 70).

Note: Excel frequently encounters problems in generating the mode for a data set, in which case it will return the error code "#NUM!" In such cases, you need to sort and examine the data directly. We think you'll find the frequency tables or graphical displays useful for this.

DESCRIBING THE TYPICAL QUALITATIVE RESPONSE

Initially, the goal of data reduction may seem at odds with the qualitative research objective of helping us better understand phenomena through the use of narrative description that is rich and detailed. Yet as we saw in Chapter 4, a critical aspect of qualitative analysis is the consolidation of data that occurs as we code and categorize our observations. Although the focus of qualitative research may be as much on describing what's unique as on describing what's typical, our understanding of

■ ■ ■ ■ ■

INTRODUCTION TO COMPUTER-ASSISTED QUALITATIVE DATA ANALYSIS (CAQDA) SOFTWARE

Although **computer-assisted qualitative data analysis (CAQDA)** software is relatively new, at present there are over two dozen different packages available, with new ones entering the market every day. As Dohan and Sanchez-Jankowski (1998) note, "no one package dominates" (p. 478), so the decision regarding which one, if any, to use is one that you, the researcher, must make.

Generally speaking, CAQDA software provides you with a variety of tools to help you organize and manage your data. Typically, these programs include functions that make it easy to do the following:

- Mark or tag meaningful segments of data
- Assign (or reassign) codes
- Quickly search your files for relevant data segments, and assemble all supporting materials
- Link-related data segments, and present these connections as conceptual networks or graphic maps
- Record your own thoughts, ideas, and theories about the analytic process

Some programs also provide tools designed to assist you in carrying out the more complex comparing, contrasting, and linking tasks involved in theory building and hypothesis testing.

It's important to note that, although CAQDA software can help us manage the vast amount of material typically gathered in carrying out a qualitative research effort, it cannot do the hard work for us. That is, it's still up to the researcher to identify meaningful data segments, assign codes, and determine what the data under examination mean (Drisko, 1998; Weitzman, 2000).

CAQDA software packages mentioned most frequently in social work literature include HyperRESEARCH, NUD*IST, ATLAS/ti, and Ethnograph. If you're thinking about using a CAQDA software package to assist you in carrying out a qualitative analysis, Weitzman and Miles (1995) suggest you consider the following: What kind of research are you planning to undertake? What will the data you gather look like? What kinds of conclusions do you plan to draw from your data? Would you be buying the software for use on one project or many? In addition, we agree with Drisko's (1998) suggestion that you should get some hands-on experience with the software package you're considering before you purchase it. Many of the major software vendors allow you to download demonstration versions from the Internet for this purpose.

the phenomenon under study can be enhanced by knowing the frequency with which the various responses, categories, and themes surfaced, as well as which occurred most often. As Huberman and Miles (1996) observe, counting not only provides a way of familiarizing ourselves with what's there, it also helps keep us honest (p. 187). To illustrate the potentially informative nature of this counting approach, we've replicated in Figure 6.4 the results of the needs assessment conducted with tribal elders (presented previously in Figure 5.14, p. 74).

Qualitative researchers also find quantitative indicators of central tendency (i.e., the mode, median, and mean) useful for describing the significant characteristics of their samples. Note, for example, how important the average age of the participants becomes in establishing the focus and context of the following study.

Interested in learning more about the caregiving experiences of grandparents, Poindexter and Linsk (1999) interviewed seven African American women who had assumed primary parenting responsibilities for their minor grandchildren because of the occurrence of HIV/AIDS within their families. In describing their sample, the researchers noted that their participants ranged in age from 46 to 60, with an average age of 55. These numerical data provide unambiguous empirical support for the researchers' subsequent observation that "none of these women would be considered 'elderly' by gerontological standards, but as grandmothers their experiences and concerns were intergenerational" (p. 67). The focus of the investigation is clarified even further when the researchers point out that the defining characteristic of the participants "was their stage rather than their age" (p. 67).

From a "noncounting" perspective, if we view indicators of central tendency as reflecting how our observations tend to cluster, or coalesce, then the conceptual themes, models, prototypes, and theories developed through qualitative research might be thought of in these terms, as well. Let's consider, for example, Reese, Ahern, Nair, O'Faire, and Warren's (1999) investigation of the factors influencing African Americans' underutilization of hospice. Although this participatory action research endeavor encompassed both qualitative and quantitative investigative

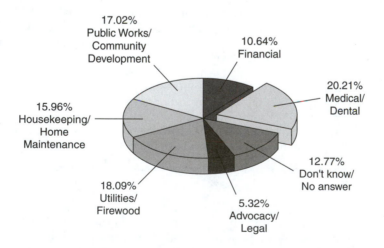

FIGURE 6.4   Highlighting the Typical Qualitative Response:
An Example Using Counts

strategies, given the focus of this discussion, we'll limit our remarks to the qualitative phase of the study.

Citing "the importance of the church in African American communities and the importance of the pastor as a community leader," the researchers asked six pastoral ministers why each thought "there are very few African American patients in hospice" (Reese et al., 1999, p. 553). The senior researcher manually analyzed the transcripts derived from the tape-recorded interviews. Subsequently, the transcripts were independently reviewed by another member of the research team. To further verify the credibility of their conclusions, the researchers then presented their findings to the respondents for review and feedback. This process resulted in the identification of two major types of barriers to hospice care—cultural and institutional.

As Janesick (2000) observes, "validation in qualitative analysis has to do with . . . whether the explanation fits the description" (p. 393). That is, does the explanation offered seem credible? Suggested ways of establishing the credibility of a qualitative analysis include member checks (i.e., allowing participants to review the transcripts and conclusions drawn) and keeping an audit trail (i.e., written record) that others can use to verify or double-check the analytic decisions made.

In providing a conceptual rallying point, if you will, each theme might be thought of as a type of "conceptual average." Two distinct cultural barriers were identified: (1) differences in values surrounding medical care, and (2) differences in religious beliefs. In terms of medical care, the participants suggested there existed a marked resistance to accepting, planning for, or discussing terminality of life, and a concomitant preference for life-sustaining versus palliative care—perspectives that clearly stand in opposition to the philosophy of hospice. In addition, preferences for home remedies over those provided by doctors, and assistance from family members as opposed to assistance from strangers, also were noted (Reese et al., 1999, p. 553). With respect to spiritual differences, the respondents indicated that "many African Americans would rather pray for a miracle, than accept terminality"; to do otherwise, they suggested, would be viewed as "a lack of faith" (p. 554). Participants also suggested a prevailing belief that God—not the availability or lack of medical treatment—determines whether one lives or dies. The institutional barriers mentioned included (1) a lack of familiarity with hospice within the African American community, (2) the belief that services like hospice are unaffordable without insurance, (3) a generalized lack of trust in the health care system, and (4) the dearth of African American staff within local health care agencies.

Based on these findings, Reese et al. (1999) identified several recommendations for social work practice. As you reflect on the preceding observations, what practice implications do you find?

TERMS TO KNOW

Bifurcated data (p. 94)

Bimodal distribution (p. 82)

Computer-assisted qualitative data analysis (CAQDA) (p. 97)

Data reduction techniques (p. 80)

Descriptive measures (p. 80)

Distribution with no mode (p. 82)

Mean ($\overline{X}$) or (M) (p. 90)

Measures of central tendency (p. 80)

Measures of dispersion (p. 80)

Median (Mdn) (p. 85)

Mode (Mo) (p. 81)

Multimodal distribution (p. 83)

Outlier (p. 91)

Skewed distribution (p. 92)

Trimmed mean (p. 94)

Unimodal distribution (p. 82)

REVIEW PROBLEMS

The situation: You're a family preservation worker for Clark County's Department of Child and Family Services. You and several of your colleagues are concerned about the rapidly growing size of your caseloads. When you shared this concern with your boss, she seemed interested and suggested you gather additional data on the topic. Following are the data you've assembled so far regarding the caseloads for each worker for each of the last two years.

SOCIAL WORKER	CASELOAD SIZE (1998)	CASELOAD SIZE (1999)
A	10	5
B	10	5
C	10	5
D	12	5
E	8	10
F	10	20
G	10	30
H	12	40
I	10	30
J	10	20
K	11	10
L	9	5
M	7	5
N	13	5
O	10	5

1. The key question of interest is, has the average caseload increased? As the first step in addressing this matter, compute the mode, median, and mean for each distribution.

2. Compare the measures of central tendency you derived across years. What do you find?

3. Is the mean a good indicator of the typical caseload size for both years? Why or why not?

4. Which of these findings will most accurately summarize what's been happening with regard to the size of these caseloads?

5. If you were in your supervisor's shoes, what would you do with these data?

REFERENCES

Craft, J. L. (1990). *Statistics and data analysis for social workers* (2nd ed.). Itasca, IL: F. E. Peacock.

Dohan, D., & Sanchez-Jankowski, M. (1998). Using computers to analyze ethnographic field data: Theoretical and practical considerations. *Annual Review Sociology, 24,* 477–498.

Drisko, J. W. (1998). Using qualitative data analysis software. *Computers in Human Services, 15,* 1–19.

Huberman, A. M., & Miles, M. B. (1996). Data management and analysis methods. In N. K. Denzin & Y. S. Lincoln (Eds.), *Collecting and interpreting qualitative materials* (pp. 179–210). Thousand Oaks, CA: Sage.

Janesick, V. J. (2000). The choreography of qualitative research design. In N. K. Denzin & Y. S. Lincoln (Eds.), *Handbook of qualitative research* (2nd ed., pp. 379–399). Thousand Oaks, CA: Sage.

Knoke, D., & Bohrnstedt, G. W. (1994). *Statistics for social data analysis* (3rd ed.). Itasca, IL: F. E. Peacock.

Poindexter, C. C., & Linsk, N. L. (1999). "I'm just glad that I'm here": Stories of seven African-American HIV-affected grandmothers. *Journal of Gerontological Social Work, 32,* 63–81.

Reese, D. J., Ahern, R. E., Nair, S., O'Faire, J. D., & Warren, C. (1999). Hospice access and use by African Americans: Addressing cultural and institutional barriers through participatory research. *Social Work, 44,* 549–559.

Weitzman, E. A. (2000). Software and qualitative research. In N. K. Denzin & Y. S. Lincoln (Eds.), *Handbook of qualitative research* (2nd ed., pp. 803–820). Thousand Oaks, CA: Sage.

Weitzman, E. A., & Miles, M. B. (1995). *Computer programs for qualitative data analysis: A software sourcebook.* Thousand Oaks, CA: Sage.

......

CHAPTER SEVEN

COMPUTING AND INTERPRETING MEASURES OF DISPERSION

While it's important for social workers to know what's average or typical, it's also critical for us to understand how clients and their circumstances vary. We know, for example, that some people respond well to AA's 12-step program, whereas others abhor the notion of such an approach. Likewise, some policy change efforts require a direct, hard-sell strategy, whereas others fare better when more subtle techniques are used. Not all clients or policy makers conform to the same profile. From a research perspective, often it is the exceptions to the rule—the *variation* in the data that isn't well represented by a measure of central tendency—that's interesting. Knowing the mean, median, and mode are like having one quadrant of a road map. However, having information about the dispersion of key variables adds another quadrant to our map.

In your field practicum, you might hear comments about the range of differences that exist in caseworkers' salaries or in the varied cultural backgrounds of the clients the agency serves. Like our everyday observations about what's "typical," these verbal referents to variability are open to subjective interpretation. Just as measures of central tendency provide a way of systematically describing how scores cluster, measures of dispersion or variability give us a more precise means of conveying how scores scatter across a distribution. Without information on both centrality and dispersion, our ability to understand a data set remains incomplete.

To illustrate, let's look at the client anxiety data presented in Table 7.1 for inpatient and outpatient clients at a state mental health facility. If we limit our focus to comparisons of the mean, median, and modal scores reported for each group, we're likely to conclude that the anxiety levels experienced by clients receiving inpatient and outpatient services are identical. This impression is readily challenged, however, when the graphical representation of these data presented in Figure 7.1 is considered. Notice how the anxiety scores of clients being served on an outpatient basis are spread out across the continuum of possible values, whereas the scores achieved by those receiving inpatient services cluster between

TABLE 7.1   Frequency Distribution of Anxiety Scores Obtained by Inpatient and Outpatient Clients at a State Mental Health Facility

ANXIETY LEVEL	OUTPATIENT CLIENTS FREQUENCY (f)	INPATIENT CLIENTS FREQUENCY (f)
10	3	0
9	6	0
8	7	5
7	9	12
6	15	16
5	20	34
4	14	15
3	10	14
2	8	4
1	5	0
0	3	0
	$N = 100$	$N = 100$
	$\overline{X} = 5, \text{Mdn} = 5,$	$\overline{X} = 5, \text{Mdn} = 5,$
	$\text{Mo} = 5$	$\text{Mo} = 5$

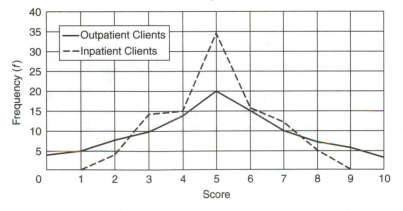

FIGURE 7.1   **Frequency Polygon of Anxiety Scores Obtained from Inpatient and Outpatient Clients at a State Mental Health Facility**

the values of 2 and 8. Without additional information about how the scores within each group are dispersed, there would be no way of detecting these different distribution patterns.

There are several indicators of dispersion. In this chapter we'll examine four of those you're most likely to encounter as a social work practitioner: the range, the interquartile range, the variance, and the standard deviation. Let's start by addressing that old standby—the range.

THE RANGE

The **range** is the easiest measure of dispersion to calculate and the simplest to understand. It is derived by subtracting the lowest value or score in a distribution from the highest. Given the simplicity of this procedure, you can get a general idea of the variability characterizing a data set almost instantaneously.

Imagine you're a hospital social worker who's cofacilitating an educational group for women preparing to give birth to their first child. The ages of the participants in this group are: 18, 21, 23, 25, 26, and 38. To determine the range of ages involved, just subtract 18 from 38 (i.e., 38 − 18 = 20). Almost at a glance, the 20-year span that exists among members of the group becomes apparent. By providing an understanding of how the scores in a data set are spread out, the range also can be useful in determining the number and size of intervals to use in constructing grouped frequencies.

Technical Note: Some statistics texts suggest that in order to accurately capture the distance between the largest and smallest values in a data set, you need to add one to the subtraction step described above (i.e., largest value minus lowest value plus 1). As Jaeger (1983) notes, this adjustment is of limited practical importance. While it does provide a way of accommodating the "real limits" of the upper and lower scores of a distribution, its impact on the value of the range is generally minimal. In the case of the parent support group data, the lower limit of 18 is 17.5, and the upper limit of 38 is 38.5. Substituting these values for those we originally entered, we get: 38.5 − 17.5, which yields a revised range of 21. The term *inclusive range* is sometimes used to distinguish this range from the one defined as the difference between the upper and lower score. Statistical packages like SPSS utilize the simpler approach. We present both approaches so you'll be prepared when you encounter them in the professional literature.

On the down side, because it is dependent on just two scores from the data set, the range (like the mean) is susceptible to the influence of extremely high or low scores (i.e., outliers). Thus, when a distribution of scores contains outliers, the range will yield an exaggerated notion of the variability that exists within a distribution.

This dependence on only two scores also makes the range vulnerable to the addition or removal of high- or low-end scores. For example, suppose the 38-year-old mother-to-be drops out of your educational group. What happens to the age range of the participants who remain? It instantly drops from 20 years to 8, even though no other changes in membership occurred. This instability, coupled with the fact that the range tells us nothing about the positioning or values of the other scores in the distribution, renders it a fairly weak measure of variability.

PERCENTILES AND QUARTILES

Before introducing our next measure of dispersion, there are a couple of terms we need to clarify. In the previous chapter, we characterized the median as the 50th percentile, or the point in an ordered distribution of scores below which 50% of the scores fall. More generally, percentiles can be thought of as an indicator of position; that is, they specify a point below which a designated percentage of cases fall. Thus, a client of an outpatient mental health center who scored at the 70th percentile on a depression scale would be more depressed than the average client (at the 50th percentile). In fact, compared to the population on which the norms were prepared, the client at the 70th percentile would be more depressed than all but 30% of outpatients.

Another commonly used measure of position is the quartile. **Quartiles** are the points in an array that divide the scores into four equally sized clusters or groups. The 1st quartile (25th percentile) is the point in an array below which 25% of the scores fall. As you know, the median (50th percentile) constitutes the 2nd quartile. Any guesses on which percentile doubles as the 3rd quartile? Yep, it's the 75th percentile—the point below which three-fourths, or 75%, of the cases can be found.

THE INTERQUARTILE RANGE

The **interquartile range,** or **hinge spread,** is a variant of the range that manages to avoid the problem caused by outliers by focusing on the middle 50% of scores. It is defined as the range of values, or distance, between the 1st and 3rd quartiles (or 25th and 75th percentiles). There are several ways of determining the interquartile range. We believe the easiest way of accomplishing this when you're working with large data sets is to start by developing a cumulative frequency distribution. To determine the value of the 1st quartile, scan the cumulative percent column until you reach the category or score that encompasses 25% of the observations. Make a note of this value. Now continue scanning the cumulative percent column until you locate the point that accounts for at least 75% of the scores (i.e., the 3rd quartile). Note this value, too. The value of the interquartile range is then calculated by subtracting the 1st quartile from the 3rd quartile.

Let's apply these steps to our inpatient/outpatient anxiety data. In looking at Table 7.2, you'll see that we've added percentage and cumulative percentage columns to the frequency data we presented earlier in Table 7.1. To find the interquartile range for the outpatient group, we start with the smallest value in the array (located at the bottom cumulative percent columns) and scan upward until we've located the spot that accounts for 25% of the cases. Note that the score associated with this point is 3 for the outpatient group. Thus, 3 represents our 1st quartile. We continue scanning upward until we locate the point where we've accounted for 75% of the cases. Note that the value associated with this point for the outpatient group is 6, which represents our 3rd quartile. Subtracting

TABLE 7.2   Frequency Distribution of Anxiety Scores Obtained by Inpatient and Outpatient Clients at a State Mental Health Facility

ANXIETY LEVEL	OUTPATIENT CLIENTS FREQUENCY (f)	PERCENT (%)	CUMULATIVE PERCENT (%)	INPATIENT CLIENTS FREQUENCY (f)	PERCENT (%)	CUMULATIVE PERCENT (%)
10	3	3	100	0	0	
9	6	6	97	0	0	
8	7	7	91	5	5	100
7	9	9	84	12	12	95
6	15	15	75	16	16	83
5	20	20	60	34	34	67
4	14	14	40	15	15	33
3	10	10	26	14	14	18
2	8	8	16	4	4	4
1	5	5	8	0	0	0
0	3	3	3	0	0	0
	$N = 100$	100		$N = 100$	100	
	$\overline{X} = 5,$			$\overline{X} = 5,$		
	Mdn = 5,			Mdn = 5,		
	Mo = 5			Mo = 5		

the 1st quartile from the 3rd quartile (6 − 3 = 3), we find that the interquartile range of the anxiety scores for the outpatient group is 3. Those of you who want a more precise way of identifying the 1st and 3rd quartiles will find the formula presented in Formulae Alert 6.1 (p. 89) helpful, but simply remember to substitute 0.25 and 0.75 for 0.50 when computing the 1st and 3rd quartiles, respectively.

Note: As with the range, some statistics texts suggest adding 1 to the subtraction procedure just described (i.e., 3rd quartile minus 1st quartile plus 1 = interquartile range). The decision regarding which strategy to use is up to you and your instructor. Regardless of the strategy that you decide on, be consistent in the method you use.

The interquartile range is often used along with the median to describe distributions involving ordinal level measures. Although it is considered more resistant to the impact of outliers than the range, the interquartile range is still computed on the basis of only two scores. Consequently, like the range, the interquartile range fails to tell us anything about the positioning or values of the other scores within a data set.

THE SEMI-INTERQUARTILE RANGE

A related index of dispersion you're apt to encounter is the **semi-interquartile range** (often referred to as Q). It is derived by dividing the interquartile range in half. For reasonably symmetric distributions, the semi-interquartile range will provide a general indicator of how scores vary around the median.

Returning to our outpatient/inpatient anxiety data for a moment, recall that we computed an interquartile range of 3 for the outpatient group. To find the semi-interquartile range, we simply divide this value in half (i.e., 3 ÷ 2 = 1.5). Since our outpatient anxiety scores are distributed in a fairly symmetric fashion, we conclude that the middle 50% of scores in this distribution will not extend more than 1.5 points above or below the median. In other words, at least half the outpatient anxiety scores will fall between 3.5 and 6.5 (i.e., 5 ± 1.5).

Since the semi-interquartile range is based on the interquartile range, it shares that measure's strengths and weaknesses. Specifically, the semi-interquartile range is essentially immune from the impact of outliers, yet it fails to convey any information about the positioning or values beyond the scores used for its computation.

THE VARIANCE

As we've repeatedly noted, a major shortfall of the range and interquartile range is their inability to attend to all the scores within a data set. As a result, they don't capitalize on all the information available, nor do they provide a means of describing the typical or average deviation. Two indexes of dispersion that manage to overcome these limitations are the variance and its mathematically related counterpart, the standard deviation. Let's focus first on the variance.

We start this discussion by taking you back for a moment to the information we presented in the previous chapter on Tawny's quiz scores. Recall that the scores she has achieved thus far include 88, 95, 92, 90, and 100, with an average (i.e., mean) quiz score of 93. The data we presented previously in Table 6.8 (p. 91) to illustrate the balancing role of the mean has been expanded in Table 7.3. We draw your attention to the data in column three, which depict how much each score differs, or deviates, from the mean. The distance between a score and its mean is referred to as a **deviation** (which is often abbreviated as d). Because they always sum to zero, these deviations give no indication of how much the scores in a data set vary from the mean. The data contained in column 4 correct this limitation by eliminating the impact of the negative entries through squaring. The sum of these squared deviations (also known as the sum of the squares, or SS) quantitatively describes the total amount of variability found within the data set. The **variance,** or **mean square,** is nothing more than the arithmetic average of these squared deviations. The symbol used to denote a sample variance is s^2.

If we use the data presented in Table 7.3, we find that the variance for this sample of Tawny's quiz scores is 22 [SS ÷ (n − 1)* or 88 ÷ 4 = 22]. (See the following

TABLE 7.3   Deviation and Squared Deviation of Tawny's Quiz Scores from the Mean

QUIZ SCORE (X)	MEAN ($\overline{X}$)	DEVIATION (QUIZ SCORE − MEAN) $(X - \overline{X})$	SQUARED DEVIATION (QUIZ SCORE − MEAN)^2 $(X - \overline{X})^2$
88	93	−5	25
90	93	−3	9
92	93	−1	1
95	93	2	4
100	93	7	49
(N = 5)		Sum = 0	Sum = 88

technical note for an explanation of why we divide by $n - 1$ in this instance.) But what does this mean? Because the variance represents the amount of dispersion that exists among Tawny's quiz scores in units best described as squared quiz score units, it's difficult to interpret the meaning of this variance of 22 directly. There is no standard referent to help interpret variance—this is a major limitation and explains why it's rarely used as a descriptive index of dispersion. Nevertheless, the variance is useful when comparing variability across samples. Its real value, though, is the contribution it makes to a myriad of other statistical analyses, and for this reason it is an indicator of dispersion that we need to learn.

Technical Note: Technically, our definition of the variance as the arithmetic average of the sum of the squared deviations applies to data gathered on a population. The symbol used to denote this population parameter is σ^2 (the lowercase Greek letter sigma). In most circumstances, however, you'll be dealing with data gathered from a sample. The variance that is calculated on sample data still looks at the average or mean of the squared deviations, but it is derived by dividing the sum of the squared deviations by $n - 1$. This adjustment is required to reduce the bias that emerges when one uses a variance based on sample data to estimate the variance of a population. Without it, you're very likely to underestimate the variance of the population. Many of the statistical packages, such as SPSS, use the $n - 1$ formula. You may wish to consult more advanced statistics texts (e.g., Kiess, 1996) for a more detailed discussion of this topic.

THE STANDARD DEVIATION

The **standard deviation** (*SD*; also seen in other statistics literature as *sd, s, S*) is simply the square root of the variance; that is, it's the square root of the average squared deviation from the mean. Basically, it tells us how far the average score in a distribution varies from the mean. By "unsquaring" the variance, the standard deviation represents a conversion back to the unit of measure used with the original scores, making it much more interpretable than the variance. It's this added descriptive value that makes it the most widely used measure of dispersion.

Let's return to Tawny's quiz scores one more time. Taking the square root of the variance we calculated previously (i.e., $\sqrt{22}$), a standard deviation of 4.69 is derived. This finding indicates that Tawny's scores tend to fluctuate about 4.69 points around her mean quiz score of 93.

As an index of variability, we can expect that the more the scores in a distribution are spread out, the larger the standard deviation will be. In turn, when scores are tightly compacted and not widely dispersed, the smaller the standard deviation we'll find. In the rare instance where all the scores in a distribution are equal, both the standard deviation and variance will be 0. In no instance, however, should you derive a standard deviation or variance with a negative value. If this happens, you'll want to rerun your analysis! For those of you who are interested, we present the deviation method of calculating the standard deviation in Formulae Alert 7.1, along with an algebraically simplified version. To determine the variance, simply square the value obtained for the standard deviation.

In addition to giving us a picture of how scores disperse themselves around the mean, the standard deviation allows us to compare the variability that exists among different groups or samples. One of its most useful functions, though, emerges in the context of the normal, or bell-shaped, curve, which we'll discuss in detail in Chapter 8.

Because the standard deviation and variance are computed in reference to the mean, they're best suited for data measured at an interval, or ratio, level. In practice,

FORMULAE ALERT 7.1

There are several formulas for calculating the sample standard deviation, and all of them are algebraic derivatives of the following deviation method:

$$SD = \sqrt{\frac{\sum (x - \overline{X})^2}{n - 1}}$$

where
SD = sample standard deviation
x = score
$\overline{X}$ = sample mean
n = total number of observations in the sample

Here is one alternative formula:

$$s = \sqrt{\frac{\sum x^2 - (\sum x)^2 / n}{n - 1}}$$

though, you'll often find the mean and standard deviation reported for data measured at the ordinal level. This most frequently occurs when ordinal-level measures have been used so often that they come to be viewed as standardized (i.e., approximating interval data). Examples you'll find in social work research include scales developed to measure phenomena such as self-esteem, depression, well-being, life satisfaction, and so forth.

The mathematical dependence on the mean makes the variance and standard deviation sensitive to the influence of outliers. Therefore, when you're working with a distribution that is skewed, your best bet is to describe your data using the median and interquartile range.

COMPUTER APPLICATION: MEASURES OF DISPERSION

Calculating measures of dispersion using SPSS is similar to calculating measures of central tendency—it is simply a matter of asking for different output. Using the data presented in Chapter 6 for length of time in foster care, we generated the data in Table 7.4, using SPSS.

Recall from Chapter 6 that the output from Microsoft Excel we generated for descriptive statistics included several items that we ignored at that time. Many of those items should now be recognizable to you as measures of dispersion. The output obtained from Excel has been reproduced in Table 7.5 for comparison.

TABLE 7.4 Measures of Dispersion Output Generated with SPSS Data for Length of Time in Foster Care

$N = 200$		Missing Cases $= 0$
STATISTICS		**MONTHS**
Standard deviation		21.2731
Variance		452.5445
Range		72.00
Minimum		0.00
Maximum		72.00
Percentiles	25	20.0000
	50	38.0000
	75	56.0000

TABLE 7.5 Measures of Dispersion Output Generated with Excel: Data for Length of Time in Foster Care

MONTHS

Mean	37.635
Standard error	1.504234851
Median	38
Mode	70
Standard deviation	21.27309328
Sample variance	452.5444975
Kurtosis	−1.201251322
Skewness	−0.115029699
Range	72
Minimum	0
Maximum	72
Sum	7257
Count	200

THE BOXPLOT: OBTAINING A FIVE-NUMBER SUMMARY

The **boxplot,** or **box-and-whisker diagram,** developed by John Tukey (1977), provides a graphical means of summarizing how the values in a data set are dispersed. Based on what's known as the **five-number summary,** the boxplot depicts five important indicators of dispersion: the minimum, the 1st quartile, the median, the 3rd quartile, and the maximum.

Depending on the software you use, the information contained within the boxplot may vary. Typically, though, you'll find the following:

1. A center box in which (a) the top and bottom (also referred to as the "hinges") represent the 3rd and 1st quartile, respectively; and (b) the area within the box encompasses all the scores falling between these points (i.e., the interquartile range)
2. A thick line within the box that delineates where the median falls
3. Vertical lines depicting the distance from the center box to the largest and smallest observed scores not perceived as potential outliers
4. Horizontal lines marking where the largest and smallest observed values (not perceived as potential outliers) fall. If there are no outliers in the data set, these lines will represent the values of the minimum and maximum observed scores.
5. Identification of outliers (values that fall a distance that's more than 1.5 times the value of the interquartile range above or below the hinges of the central box) and **extreme scores** (values that fall a distance that's more than 3 times the value of the interquartile range beyond the hinges of the central box)

Figure 7.2 contains boxplot diagrams for the inpatient/outpatient anxiety data presented in Table 7.1. By simultaneously plotting select indicators of dispersion for

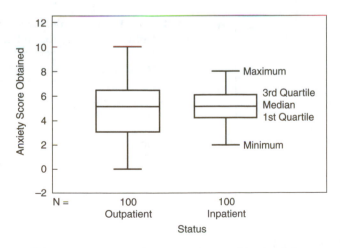

FIGURE 7.2   Boxplot of Anxiety Scores Obtained from Clients Receiving Inpatient and Outpatient Services at a State Mental Health Facility

each group on the same scale, this approach lets us quickly see the similarities and differences that occur between the distributions.

To use a different example, the boxplot presented in Figure 7.3 was generated using data about the ages of participants in a summer day camp program sponsored by the local department of parks and recreation. Different software may use different symbols; in this illustration generated using SPSS, outliers are demarcated by O, and extreme scores are indicated by $*$.

A QUALITATIVE DESCRIPTION
OF THE VARIABILITY IN RESPONSES

The **index of qualitative variation (IQV)** provides a way of describing the variation or heterogeneity that exists within a categorical distribution (i.e., qualitative or nominal-level data). Although its title may sound a bit sophisticated, it's really nothing more than a ratio of the differences you observed to the maximum number of differences that are possible—presented in terms of a percent (i.e., multiplied by 100).

To illustrate, suppose that as part of a needs assessment you gathered the data in Table 7.6 concerning the racial/ethnic characteristics of youngsters age 18 and younger living within your agency's service area. The index of qualitative variation allows you to compare the observed differences in the racial/ethnic makeup of your service area's youth with the maximum possible variation that could occur. The formula for this procedure is presented in Formulae Alert 7.2 (p. 113). Computation of the index for these data yields a result of 0.8296, which means that 83% of the racial/ethnic variation that could exist within this group does. In other words, the youngsters living within your agency's service area appear to be pretty ethnically diverse.

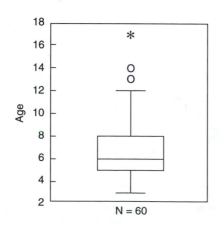

FIGURE 7.3   Boxplot of Ages
of Participants in Summer Day
Camp Program

TABLE 7.6   Ethnic Breakdown of People
Age 18 and Younger Living in Service Area

RACE/ETHNICITY	FREQUENCY (f)
African American	75
Asian/Pacific Islander	50
Caucasian	500
Hispanic	125
Native American	250
	$N = 1,000$

FORMULAE ALERT 7.2

The formula for determining the index of qualitative variation (IQV) is

$$\text{IQV} = \frac{\sum n_i n_j}{[k(k-1)] \div 2 \times [N \div k]^2}$$

where $\sum$ = the sum of . . .

$n_i n_j$ = Product of the number of observations in each category (n_i) and the number of observations in each of the other categories (n_j)

k = Number of categories

N = Total number of observations

n = Number of observations in each category

If we apply this formula to the data presented in Table 7.6, we find

$$\text{IQV} = \frac{\begin{array}{c}(75 \times 50) + (75 \times 500) + (75 \times 125) + (75 \times 250) + (50 \times 500) + (50 \times 125) + (50 \times 250) \\ + (500 \times 125) + (500 \times 250) + (125 \times 250)\end{array}}{[5(4) \div 2] \times [1{,}000 \div 5]^2}$$

$$= \frac{3{,}750 + 37{,}500 + 9{,}375 + 18{,}750 + 25{,}000 + 6{,}250 + 12{,}500 + 62{,}500 + 125{,}000 + 31{,}250}{10(200)^2}$$

$$= 331{,}875 \div 400{,}000 = .8296$$

The formula for the index of dispersion (D) is

$$D = \frac{k(N^2 - \sum f^2)}{N^2(k-1)}$$

where k = Number of categories

N = Total number of observations

f^2 = Frequency, or number, of observations in each category, squared

Applied to the data in Table 7.6, we get:

$$D = \frac{5[1{,}000^2 - (75^2 + 50^2 + 500^2 + 125^2 + 250^2)]}{1{,}000^2 \times (5-1)}$$

$$= \frac{5[1{,}000{,}000 - (5{,}625 + 22{,}500 + 250{,}000 + 15{,}625 + 40{,}000)]}{1{,}000{,}000 \times 4}$$

$$= [5(1{,}000{,}000 - 333{,}750)] \div 4{,}000{,}000 = 3{,}331{,}250 \div 4{,}000{,}000 = .8328$$

Another measure of variability that can be used with categorical data is the **index of dispersion (D).** Technically, this measure provides a ratio of the number of unique pairs that can be created out of the observed scores to the total number of unique pairs possible. The index of dispersion provides essentially the same information as the index of qualitative variation, but it is much easier to compute (see Formulae Alert 7.2).

For example, suppose your classmate is doing a social work field practicum at the U.S. Bureau of Indian Affairs. The ethnic breakdown of youth (age 18 and younger) residing in that agency's service area (which consists of the region's eight different tribal reservations) is portrayed in Table 7.7. What's your guess as to what the index of qualitative variation will be? If you said 0, or none, you're absolutely correct. A look at the IQV calculation quickly verifies this conclusion:

$$IQV = \frac{0(0) + 0(0) + 0(0) + 0(680) + 0(0) + 0(0) + 0(0) + 0(680) + 0(0) + 0(680)}{[5(4) \div 2] \times [680 \div 5]^2}$$

$$= \frac{0}{184,960}$$

TABLE 7.7   Ethnic Breakdown of People Age 18 and Younger Living in Service Area

RACE/ETHNICITY	FREQUENCY (f)
African American	0
Asian/Pacific Islander	0
Caucasian	0
Hispanic	0
Native American	680
	$N = 680$

TERMS TO KNOW

Box-and-whisker diagram (p. 111)
Boxplot (p. 111)
Deviation (d) (p. 107)
Extreme scores (p. 111)
Five-number summary (p. 111)
Hinge spread (p. 105)
Index of dispersion (D) (p. 114)
Index of qualitative variation (IQV)
   (p. 112)

Interquartile range (p. 105)
Mean square (p. 107)
Quartiles (p. 105)
Range (p. 104)
Semi-interquartile range (p. 107)
Standard deviation (SD) (p. 108)
Variance (p. 107)

REVIEW PROBLEMS

1. Referring back to Table 7.1, calculate the ranges of the anxiety scores obtained for both the inpatient and outpatient groups.

2. Returning to the data presented in Table 7.2, identify the anxiety score associated with the 1st quartile for clients receiving inpatient services. Now identify the anxiety score associated with the 3rd quartile for this group. What is the interquartile range of the anxiety scores of the inpatient group?

3. Take a moment to review the boxplots presented in Figure 7.2. What conclusion can you draw about the anxiety levels of the individuals receiving inpatient services versus those being served on an outpatient basis? What do you think accounts for the variability in anxiety patterns these data portray?

4. Suppose that you were a hospital social worker facilitating support groups for children and adults who are undergoing chemotherapy treatment for cancer. You are preparing a report for your supervisor on the group, and one of the things that she is interested in knowing is the average number of sessions members have been attending for the previous 3 months. You have collected the information in Table 7.8 to answer this question.

    So far you've completed the analysis of the information on the children's group and calculated the standard deviation to be 3.197 ($\sqrt{92/n-1} = \sqrt{92/9}$). Complete the analysis for the adult group by filling in the remainder of the table and calculating the standard deviation for this group. Do the groups have different or similar standard deviations?

TABLE 7.8 Attendance of Group Members over the Previous 3 Months, by Age

	Children's Group			Adult Group		
NUMBER OF SESSIONS ATTENDED (X)	DEVIATION (d) $(X - \bar{X}_1)$	SQUARED DEVIATION $(d)^2$ $(X - \bar{X}_1)^2$	NUMBER OF SESSIONS ATTENDED (X)	DEVIATION (d) $(X - \bar{X}_2)$	SQUARED DEVIATION $(d)^2$ $(X - \bar{X}_2)^2$	
6	−4	16	5			
11	1	1	5			
14	4	16	16			
10	0	0	16			
5	−5	25	6			
10	0	0	15			
9	−1	1	13			
15	5	25	4			
12	2	4	6			
8	−2	4	14			
$\bar{X}_1$ = 10	Sum = 0	Sum = 92	$\bar{X}_2$ =	Sum =	Sum =	

R E F E R E N C E S

Kiess, H. O. (1996). *Statistical concepts for the behavioral sciences* (2nd ed.). Boston: Allyn & Bacon.

Jaeger, R. M. (1983). *Statistics: A spectator sport.* Newbury Park, CA: Sage.

Tukey, J. W. (1977). *Exploratory data analysis.* Reading, MA: Addison-Wesley.

CHAPTER EIGHT

THE NORMAL DISTRIBUTION

In Chapter 5 we showed you how frequency polygons and histograms can help us get a sense of how the scores associated with an interval- or ratio-level variable are distributed. In this chapter, we'll explore how we can use information about the shape of such distributions to get a more precise understanding of our data.

WHAT SHAPE ARE YOUR DATA IN?

Suppose you totally bombed the first test in your social work policy course. Devastated, you decide to find out if you are the only one who failed the quiz. As you gather information from your classmates, you get the sense that all but a few suffered the same misfortune. As a student of statistics, you know that plotting the data you gather from the 18 students you spoke with would provide a way of checking out your impression, so you develop the frequency polygon presented in Figure 8.1.

From Figure 8.1, you can see that the bulk of the students received test scores of 50 or less (μ = 42.78). In fact, only three students got a grade higher than 60. Note the **asymmetrical** (unbalanced) pattern that emerges when scores cluster at one end of a distribution like this. We refer to such distributions as **skewed.** The

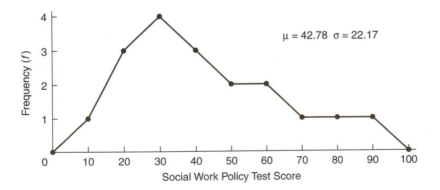

FIGURE 8.1   **Frequency Polygon of Scores on First Social Work Policy Test**

end of the distribution containing the fewest number of scores is commonly referred to as the **tail.** When scores cluster at the left end of the distribution, with the tail located on the right end of the *x*-axis, where the scores are larger in value (as in Figure 8.1), the distribution is said to be **positively skewed.** Of course, as a member of this policy class you'd probably describe this distribution of test scores as anything but positive!

Bravely, you share your findings with your policy instructor. In doing so, you discover that she, too, is concerned about the class's poor performance. In fact, she has conducted an item analysis of the test, which prompted her to rework several questions and, to your relief, she has decided to re-administer the test. The scores you and your classmates (N = 20) achieve on this second, revised test are presented in Figure 8.2.

Notice how the scores continue to cluster in an asymmetrical, or skewed, fashion. This time, though, the infrequently occurring scores that make up the tail are located on the left side of the *x*-axis, which indicates they're lower in value than the majority of scores. These atypical values will tend to pull the distribution's mean (μ = 62.22) toward the negative end of the number line. Even though as a group you and your class scored about 20 points better on the revised policy test, the distribution is actually **negatively skewed.** Note the tail and shape of the distribution.

You shouldn't have any trouble confusing positive and negative skew if you remember that the end of the distribution that contains the fewest number of scores (often outliers) is the tail. Picture an arrow on the end of the tail. If the arrow points toward the right, or the positive end of a number line, the distribution is positively skewed. If the arrow points to the left (i.e., toward zero and any potential negative numbers on the *x*-axis), the distribution is negatively skewed. We display this idea graphically in Figure 8.3.

There are formulas for determining the precise amount of skewness present in a distribution (see, for example, Formulae Alert 8.1). However, you can get a rough idea of the amount of skewness present by comparing the value of a distribution's median with its mean. If you remember our previous conversation about

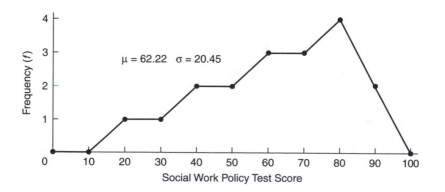

FIGURE 8.2 Frequency Polygon of Scores on the Re-Administered Social Work Policy Test

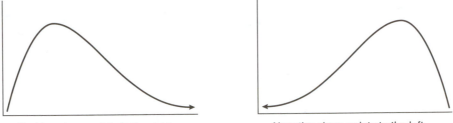

Positive skew, points to the right   Negative skew, points to the left

FIGURE 8.3   Differentiating Positive and Negative Skewness Based on Tail of the Distribution

the mean's susceptibility to outliers, you'll recall that when there are outliers, the value of the mean is easily pulled off center, toward the values of the atypical scores. However, the median is resistant to such influences. As Figure 8.4 illustrates, when the mean is larger in value than the median, there is some positive skewness. When the mean is smaller in value than the median, there is some negative skewness. The larger the difference between the values of the mean and median of a distribution, the greater the degree of skewness present. Of course, when the median and mean are equal, the distribution has no skew.

FORMULAE ALERT 8.1

Skewness provides an indication of how symmetrically (evenly) the scores in a distribution are scattered around the mean. One measure of skewness in a distribution is

$$\frac{n}{(n-1)(n-2)} \sum \left(\frac{X - \overline{X}}{s} \right)^3$$

where n = sample size
X = score
$\overline{X}$ = sample mean
s = sample standard deviation

Given the availability of computer software that can generate this measure of skewness for us, we're not going to hand-calculate an example for you. Instead, we draw your attention to the central tendency output generated on the foster care data in Chapter 6 (see p. 96). In this case, we obtained a skewness measure of −0.115, which suggests the data are slightly negatively skewed. Given this finding, would you expect the mean to be greater or smaller than the median? You can check the accuracy of your response by examining the data in Table 6.13 (p. 96).

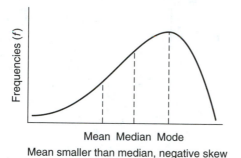
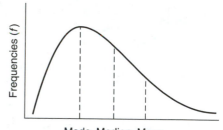

Mean smaller than median, negative skew

Mean larger than median, positive skew

FIGURE 8.4   Effect of Skewness on the Position of the Mean Relative to the Median

Interpreting Skewness

As a rule, the mean and median of a distribution are likely to vary somewhat. So at what point do we become concerned about the impact of skewness? Fortunately, with computer programs such as Excel and SPSS to do the computations for us, it's easy to generate a precise measure of skewness. When interpreting this figure, remember that the closer your skewness measure is to zero (a skewness measure of zero signals perfect symmetry, a rare occurrence), the closer your distribution is to having symmetry. As you might expect, a negative skewness measure indicates your distribution is negatively skewed. Likewise, a positive skewness measure denotes a positive skew.

Knowing whether a distribution is skewed or not, and to what degree, is important in helping you determine which indicator of central tendency (the mean or median) will best represent your data. In addition, as you'll learn in later chapters, there are several inferential statistical procedures that should not be used when the data you're working with are markedly skewed. According to Sprinthall (1994), a distribution is considered "markedly skewed" when a skewness value greater than 1.00 or smaller than −1.00 (e.g., −1.25) is obtained. If the absolute value of the skewness measure is greater than zero, but less than one, the distribution is generally described as "slightly" or "moderately" skewed. In such cases, you shouldn't be concerned about skewness and can feel confident about reporting the mean as a representative indicator of central tendency.

Another way to think about the lack of symmetry that exists in a markedly skewed distribution is in terms of its deviation from normality. We'll be addressing the notion of normality in more detail momentarily. For now, it may be helpful to know that if the ratio you get when you divide your skewness measure by its standard error is greater than 2.00 or smaller than −2.00 (e.g., −2.50), you can reject the idea that your distribution is "normal" (SPSS, 1998). Otherwise, you can assume your distribution is normal and not be concerned about violating the assumptions regarding normality that are important to most inferential statistical tests.

VIEWING SYMMETRY IN THE CONTEXT OF MODALITY

Earlier we showed you how modality can affect the use and interpretation of measures of central tendency. Specifically, when distributions are distinctively split, such as the bimodal case we presented in Chapter 6 of the clusters of very satisfied and very dissatisfied clients (p. 82), no measure of central tendency will accurately summarize the data. Likewise, measures of symmetry are difficult to interpret both when no mode exists and when multiple modes exist. To illustrate, consider the various distributions portrayed in Figure 8.5.

Which of these distributions do you think would be the easiest to interpret? The answer, of course, is the one that's both symmetrical and unimodal. Indicators

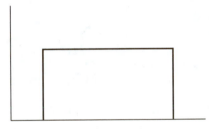

Symmetrical, no mode

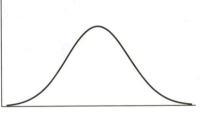

Symmetrical, unimodal

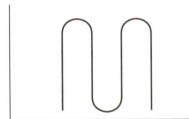

Symmetrical, bimodal

Asymmetrical, bimodal

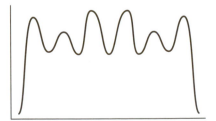

Symmetrical, multi-modal

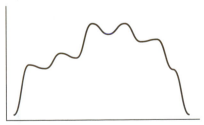

Asymmetrical, multi-modal

FIGURE 8.5   A Sampling of Varied Distributions

of symmetry, whether conveyed through a measure of skewness or a graphical display such as a histogram or frequency polygon, can be important to rendering your description of a data set complete. When you have symmetrical distributions that are not unimodal, however, measures of skewness alone will yield an incomplete, if not misleading, picture of what's happening with the data. So when you're working with uniform (no mode), bimodal, or multimodal distributions, your best bet is to routinely address the issue of skewness through the use of graphical displays.

Measures of skewness are used to determine whether the data we're working with are normally distributed. In the chapters ahead, you'll see how the decision about whether a variable is distributed normally becomes critical to the completion and interpretation of many inferential statistical tests. Now it's time to focus on the distribution that's so important to the field of statistics—the normal curve.

DEFINING PROPERTIES OF NORMAL DISTRIBUTIONS

We suspect that somewhere in your academic career you've come across a discussion or two concerning the **standard normal distribution,** or the **bell-shaped curve** (see Figure 8.6).

Before tackling the specifics of the standard normal curve, let's consider the general properties that set normal curves apart from other types of distributions. Like many of the examples found earlier in this chapter, **normal distributions** are **symmetrical**—that is, if we draw an imaginary line down the exact center, or midpoint, of a normal distribution and fold it in half, the right side of the figure would perfectly mirror the left. You can also think of that imaginary line as signaling the single highest point in the data set, which makes the normal curve unimodal. This point is also where you will find the median and the mean, so for normal distributions, all three measures of central tendency—the mode, the median, and the mean—will be equal. To remind us that theoretical distributions can accommodate

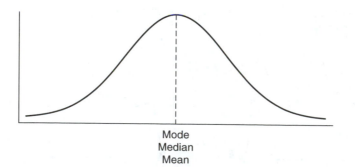

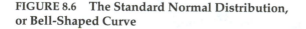
Mode
Median
Mean

FIGURE 8.6   **The Standard Normal Distribution, or Bell-Shaped Curve**

all possible scores—no matter how unlikely a specific value may be—the tails of a normal curve will never touch the *x*-axis. We describe this feature as **asymptotic.**

In Figure 8.7, the *x*-axis below the normal curve is divided into six equal sections, three sections on the right side of the mean, and three on the left. The actual size or length of these sections is determined by the value of the distribution's standard deviation. As we'll see momentarily, nearly all (> 99%) of the scores associated with a normally distributed variable will fall within the area defined by these six sections.

Two values, the mean and standard deviation, determine the actual shape of any given normal distribution. This principle is demonstrated graphically in Figure 8.8. Notice how the distributions in the first graph (a) have different ranges, even though they share the same mean. Also, note that scores in the taller distribution are much more compressed than those in the shorter, flatter one. The two distributions in the second graph (b) have equivalent standard deviations, but different means. In addition, the range of the values contained within each distribution is completely different—the scores in the distribution on the right are larger than those in the distribution on the left. In the third graph (c), each distribution has a different standard deviation and a different mean. Again, scores in the taller distribution are more homogenous, or alike, whereas the scores in the flatter distribution vary more.

Did you notice how some of the normal curves in Figure 8.8 are more peaked, whereas others are flatter and more spread out? This feature, known as **kurtosis,** is a direct function of the size of the standard deviation. Specifically, curves associated with distributions that have large standard deviations are more spread out or flat and are referred to as **platykurtic.** Tall, or peaked, curves occur when distributions have small standard deviations, and these curves are referred to as **leptokurtic.** The term **mesokurtic** is reserved for distributions whose curves are neither peaked nor flat but, as Goldilocks would say, "just right". The shape we all know as the standard normal, or bell-shaped, curve is a mesokurtic curve.

As with symmetry, it's possible to calculate a precise measure of kurtosis (see Formulae Alert 8.2). You also can estimate the kurtosis of a distribution by applying what's called "the 1/6 rule" (Sprinthall, 1994, p. 55). Based on the notion that

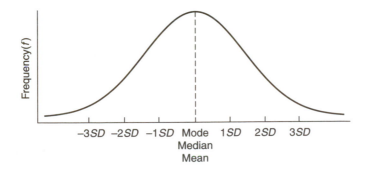

FIGURE 8.7   Key Elements of a Normal Distribution

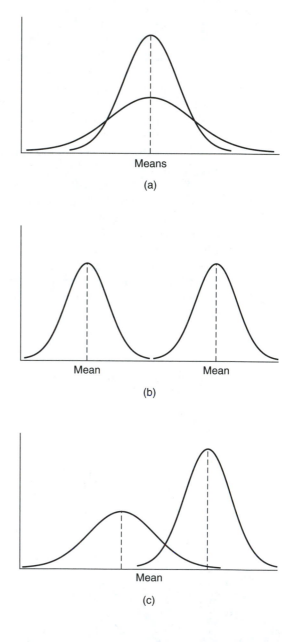

FIGURE 8.8   Influence of Mean and Standard Deviation on the Shape of Normal Distributions. (a) equal means but different standard deviations, (b) different means but equal standard deviations, and (c) different means and different standard deviations.

nearly all the scores of a normally distributed variable will fall within three standard deviations above and below the mean, the standard deviation can be thought of as representing about one-sixth of a distribution's range. Therefore, simply dividing any range by six should give a good idea of what the standard deviation ought to be. If the standard deviation derived for a normally distributed variable is larger than one-sixth of the range, the distribution is somewhat flat (i.e., platykur-

FORMULAE ALERT 8.2

Kurtosis provides an indication of how peaked or flat a distribution is relative to the standard normal curve. One measure of kurtosis in a distribution is as follows:

$$\left[\frac{n(n+1)}{(n-1)(n-2)(n-3)} \sum \left(\frac{X - \overline{X}}{s} \right)^4 \right] - \frac{3(n-1)^2}{(n-2)(n-3)}$$

where n = sample size
         X = score
         $\overline{X}$ = sample mean
         s = sample standard deviation

Don't feel bad—we, too, find this formula to be more than just a little intimidating. Thankfully, computer software can generate this measure of kurtosis for us. Look at the dispersion output generated on the foster care data in Chapter 6 (see Table 6.13, p. 96). In this case, we obtained a kurtosis measure of −1.201, which suggests the data are somewhat platykurtic.

tic). Distributions with standard deviations smaller than one-sixth their respective ranges tend to be peaked (i.e., leptokurtic). Can you guess how you'd characterize a distribution whose standard deviation is approximately 1/6th the value of the range? Yes, it's normally distributed (i.e., mesokurtic)!

Note: Some students find it helpful to pair the terms associated with kurtosis with objects or actions exhibiting similar traits. For example, platykurtic distributions are flatter, like plates, whereas leptokurtic distributions tend to "leap" off the x-axis.

Interpreting Kurtosis

We can use measures of kurtosis to help determine whether or not our data approximate the standard normal curve. As a rule of thumb, a kurtosis near zero suggests a mesokurtic, or bell-shaped, distribution. Kurtosis measures greater than 1.00 (e.g., 1.25) indicate tall, peaked, or leptokurtic, curves. In turn, flatter, or platykurtic, curves are denoted by kurtosis measures with values smaller than −1.00 (e.g., −1.25). As with symmetry, assumptions about a distribution being normal are rejected when the ratio of the kurtosis measure to its standard error (i.e., our kurtosis value divided by its standard error) is greater than positive 2.00 (e.g.,

2.50) or smaller than –2.00 (e.g., –4.00). Should this occur, proceed cautiously in using statistical tests that list "normality" among their assumptions for use.

To summarize our discussion thus far, the mean, median, and mode in a normal distribution are equal. In addition, the shape of a normal curve is symmetrical, unimodal, and asymptotic. Also, by now, you should realize that the entity known as the standard normal curve possesses features in terms of symmetry and kurtosis that set it apart from other distributions. In the next section we'll delve further into these and other distinguishing features of the standard normal curve.

THE AREA UNDER A NORMAL CURVE

In Chapter 4, we discussed the frequency, or count, associated with a given score as constituting a proportion of all the responses obtained, and we referred to this as a relative frequency. As illustrated in Figure 4.1 (p. 42), the proportions associated with all the different scores in a data set combine to form a single entity—that is, they sum to 1. Since a normal curve is nothing more than a graphical presentation of a relative frequency distribution, it makes sense to think of the area under the curve as containing a continuous distribution of scores that, together, constitute a whole entity, or 1. The ability to think about a distribution in this way is critical to understanding what the area under a normal curve represents.

Note: As you might recall from previous math courses, by continuous we mean that between any two scores there theoretically exists an infinite number of values or scores. For instance, between 1 and 2 there is 1.5, 1.9, 1.887.

Several mathematicians, including Jacob Bernoulli (1654–1705) and Karl Friedrich Gauss (1777–1855), are credited with discovering the normal curve (Kiess, 1996). A key tenet derived from their work is that for any normally distributed interval- or ratio-level variable, we will find specific proportions of scores lying within specified intervals about the mean. These relationships are depicted in Figure 8.9.

As you look at Figure 8.9 you may be thinking, "That's nice, but what exactly does this mean?" The standard deviations provide markers we can use to understand how scores in a normal distribution are distributed about the mean. Specifically, when working with a normal distribution, you can expect .3413, or 34.13%, of the scores, cases, or observations to lie between the mean and one standard deviation above (to the right of) the mean. Likewise, because the distribution is symmetrical with the left side mirroring the right, we'll find that .3413, or 34.13%, of the scores fall between the mean and one standard deviation below (to the left of) the mean.

We can add the proportions associated with different segments to draw additional conclusions. Taking the information we just highlighted, we discover that

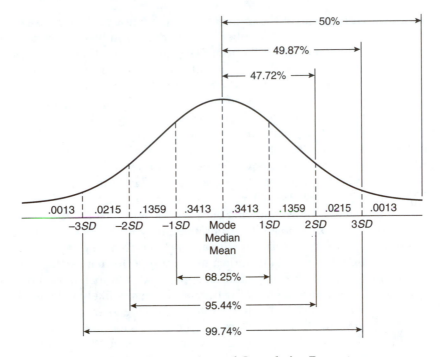

FIGURE 8.9   Relative Frequencies and Cumulative Percentages of Scores within Specified Intervals of a Normal Distribution

.6826, or 68.26% (.3413 + .3413 = .6826), of all scores fall within plus or minus one standard deviation of the mean. Similarly, 49.87% [(.3413 + .1359 + .0215) × 100 = 49.87%] of the scores will fall between the mean and three standard deviations above or below it. If we add in the proportion of scores associated with the extreme portion of the tails (i.e., the segments of the curve that correspond with the areas beyond the three standard deviations above and below the mean), we learn that 50% [(.4987 + .0013) × 100 = 50%] of the scores will be located on each side of the mean. This makes sense because, in the case of a normal curve, the median and mean are essentially interchangeable.

Notice how as we move away from the mean the proportion, or percentage, of scores associated with each segment—also referred to as the area under the curve—becomes smaller, even though the length of each segment is defined in terms of the same standard deviation unit. As you can see in Figure 8.9, this is because the height of the curve, which corresponds to the number of scores involved, becomes progressively shorter as we move further from the mean.

Information about areas under the normal curve can be useful. Consider the following hypothetical example: Suppose your agency provides job training and placement services for men and women seeking reentry into the labor market. As part of its assessment package, the agency incorporates an intelligence test that, when used with the general population, generates scores that are normally distributed with a mean of 100 and a standard deviation of 15. Suppose further that, although your clients face a number of challenges, you have no reason to believe that they will perform differently from the general population on this test, and you have no reason to assume the instrument is biased in terms of cultural, socioeconomic, age, language, gender, or educational factors (this is a lot to assume!).

In the preceding year, the agency administered this intelligence test to the 120 clients it served. The question is, how many of the agency's clients scored between the mean (100) and two standard deviations above the mean? By looking at Figure 8.9, we know we should find .3418 of the 120 client test scores between the mean and one standard deviation above the mean. Another .1359 should lie between one and two standard deviations above the mean. Therefore, we can expect to find 47.72% [(.3413 + .1359) × 100 = 47.72%], or approximately 57 (.4772 × 120 = 57.26) of the agency's clients scoring between 100 and 130 on this test.

To take this example a bit further, imagine your agency is in the process of developing a contract for services with a computer training program. Suppose this program's eligibility criteria include a minimum performance of 110 on the same intelligence test. In order to negotiate an appropriate number of training slots, your supervisor wants an estimate of the number of clients likely to be eligible for the program. She's asked you to pull this information together.

As Figure 8.10 illustrates, the point where 110 is located doesn't coincide with any of the distribution's standard deviations. Consequently, the information presented in Figure 8.9 isn't going to help you address your supervisor's question directly. Does this mean you won't be able to provide an estimate? Not at all. Because normal distributions are defined mathematically, it's possible to determine the exact relative frequency associated with any specified interval of scores within such distributions—as long as the values of the mean and standard deviation are known. There is one little problem, though. The mathematical complexity of the equations involved in this process tend to intimidate even the most mathematically adept among us. Fortunately, we can find the proportions associated with any designated area under a normal curve once we know how to find areas under the standard normal distribution, or **z-curve.**

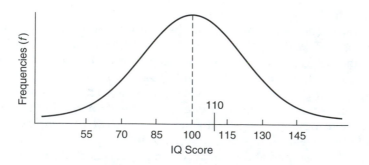

FIGURE 8.10   **Distribution Depicting Intelligence Test Scores**

THE STANDARD NORMAL DISTRIBUTION, OR z-CURVE

As we shall soon see, the versatility and simplicity of the standard normal distribution, or z-curve, renders it nothing less than a mathematic marvel. Among its many contributions, the standard normal distribution permits us to

- Determine the exact proportion or percentage of scores that fall between *any* two scores in a normal distribution (i.e., not just the area(s) between standard deviation scores)
- Assess how a score relates to the other scores in a distribution (i.e., its relative standing)
- Compare scores across normal distributions that have different means and standard deviations
- Estimate the probability of an event's occurrence

Defining Characteristics

In designing the standard normal distribution, mathematicians created a uni-modal, symmetric (i.e., no skewness), asymptotic, bell-shaped (i.e., mesokurtic) curve with a mean (μ) of 0 and a standard deviation (σ) of 1. As with other normal distributions, the total area under the standard normal distribution is equal to 1, with most (99.74%) of its area lying between ±3 standard deviations from the mean (see Figure 8.11).

Note: The terms standard normal distribution and z-curve can be used interchangeably to refer to what's commonly known as the bell-shaped curve.

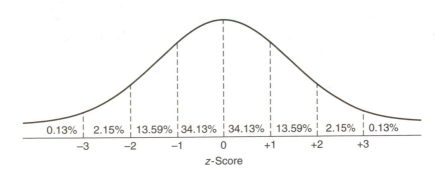

FIGURE 8.11   Standard Normal Distribution, or z-Curve, with a Mean of 0 and a Standard Deviation of 1. The percentage of scores between the specified z-score is shown.

z-Scores

Because the standard normal distribution is so important, tables such as Table 8.1 have been developed that specify the exact percentage of scores that fall between any given z-score and its mean. By now you're probably wondering, "What is this z-score?" Well, a **z-score** is a mathematical way of converting a raw score drawn from a normal distribution to a score in a *standardized* normal distribution. We think you'll find the formula behind this mathematical transformation informative:

$$z\text{-score} = \frac{(\text{Raw Score} - \text{Mean})}{\text{Standard Deviation}} = \frac{\text{Deviation Score}}{\text{Standard Deviation}}$$

Notice how the numerator is equivalent to what we described in Chapter 7 (p. 107) as a deviation (i.e., the distance between a score and its mean). If a score (x) is larger than its mean ($\bar{x}$ or μ), the deviation score will be positive, which in turn will render the derived z-score positive. If a score (x) is smaller than its mean ($\bar{x}$ or μ), the deviation score will be negative, which will make the derived z-score negative.

The denominator in the preceding equation consists of the standard deviation for the distribution. In dividing a deviation score by the standard deviation involved, you're simply converting the difference between a score and its mean to standard deviation units. Thus, the z-score becomes a way of expressing how many standard deviation units a score falls below or above its mean. It's this grounding in standard deviation units that results in statisticians referring to the z-score as a **standard score.** To illustrate the utility of the z-score, we return to our computer training program scenario.

Using z-Scores to Define Specific Areas under the Standard Normal Distribution

Recall that your supervisor asked for an estimate of the number of clients likely to meet the computer training program's required intelligence test score (i.e., IQ ≥ 110). Given the context of this discussion, can you guess the first step to addressing this issue? First, you need to convert the targeted score (x) to a z-score. Using the information already obtained about the population's mean and standard deviation, we get the following:

$$z\text{-score} = \frac{(110 - 100)}{15} = \frac{10}{15} = 0.667$$

Because you want to know what proportion or percentage of the agency's clients can be expected to achieve an IQ score of 110 or higher, you need to determine the area under the standard normal curve associated with a z-score of 0.67 or higher (see shaded area in Figure 8.12).

To find this area of the curve, you'll need to turn to Table 8.1. First, scan down the left-hand column until you've located the row labeled 0.6. Place your left finger there to mark that spot. Now focus on the top row, which is labeled z. Move your right finger across this row until you find the second decimal associated with our z-score, .07. As you move your fingers across the 0.6 row and down the .07 column, the number you should find is 24.86. This is the percentage of scores that fall between our raw score (110) and our mean (100). This is interesting, but it doesn't tell us how many scores fall above a score of 110. Don't worry— because you know that 50% of the scores are contained in the area above the mean, all you have to do is subtract 24.86 from 50.00 to find the percentage of scores that lie above this point. When you do the subtraction, you learn that 25.14% of the scores are apt to fall above 110. Based on the number of clients served this past year (n = 120), therefore, you tell your boss that she can expect about 30 clients a year (120 × 0.2514 = 30) to meet the intelligence criterion for the computer training program.

Note: When you work with z-scores, it's critical to remember that the typical z-score table gives you the percentage of scores falling between a selected z-score and the mean. It does *not* tell you what percentage of scores or observations fall above a given z-score or below it. Nor does it tell you the percentage of cases lying between two specified z-scores. Making these determinations requires a bit of logic and some simple addition or subtraction on your part. As we did in Figure 8.12, it's often helpful to draw the z-curve and highlight the area you're targeting. This is why the rule of thumb, "When in doubt, draw it out," is a good one to follow.

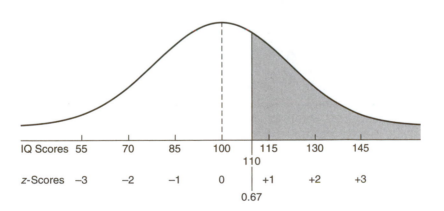

FIGURE 8.12   Area under the Normal Curve Associated with IQ Scores of 110 or Higher

TABLE 8.1   Percent of Area under the Standard Normal Curve between $\overline{X}$ and z

z	.00	.01	.02	.03	.04	.05	.06	.07	.08	.09
0.0	00.00	00.40	00.80	01.20	01.60	01.99	02.39	02.79	03.19	03.59
0.1	03.98	04.38	04.78	05.17	05.57	05.96	06.36	06.75	07.14	07.53
0.2	07.93	08.32	08.71	09.10	09.48	09.87	10.26	10.64	11.03	11.41
0.3	11.79	12.17	12.55	12.93	13.31	13.68	14.06	14.43	14.80	15.17
0.4	15.54	15.91	16.28	16.64	17.00	17.36	17.72	18.08	18.44	18.79
0.5	19.15	19.50	19.85	20.19	20.54	20.88	21.23	21.57	21.90	22.24
0.6	22.57	22.91	23.24	23.57	23.89	24.22	24.54	24.86	25.17	25.49
0.7	25.80	26.11	26.42	26.73	27.04	27.34	27.64	27.94	28.23	28.52
0.8	28.81	29.10	29.39	29.67	29.95	30.23	30.51	30.78	31.06	31.33
0.9	31.59	31.86	32.12	32.38	32.64	32.90	33.15	33.40	33.65	33.89
1.0	34.13	34.38	34.61	34.85	35.08	35.31	35.54	35.77	35.99	36.21
1.1	36.43	36.65	36.86	37.08	37.29	37.49	37.70	37.90	38.10	38.30
1.2	38.49	38.69	38.88	39.07	39.25	39.44	39.62	39.80	39.97	40.15
1.3	40.32	40.49	40.66	40.82	40.99	41.15	41.31	41.47	41.62	41.77
1.4	41.92	42.07	42.22	42.36	42.51	42.65	42.79	42.92	43.06	43.19
1.5	43.32	43.45	43.57	43.70	43.83	43.94	44.06	44.18	44.29	44.41
1.6	44.52	44.63	44.74	44.84	44.95	45.05	45.15	45.25	45.35	45.45
1.7	45.54	45.64	45.73	45.82	45.91	45.99	46.08	46.16	46.25	46.33
1.8	46.41	46.49	46.56	46.64	46.71	46.78	46.86	46.93	46.99	47.06
1.9	47.13	47.19	47.26	47.32	47.38	47.44	47.50	47.56	47.61	47.67
2.0	47.72	47.78	47.83	47.88	47.93	47.98	48.03	48.08	48.12	48.17
2.1	48.21	48.26	48.30	48.34	48.38	48.42	48.46	48.50	48.54	48.57
2.2	48.61	48.64	48.68	48.71	48.75	48.78	48.81	48.84	48.87	48.90
2.3	48.93	48.96	48.98	49.01	49.04	49.06	49.09	49.11	49.13	49.16
2.4	49.18	49.20	49.22	49.25	49.27	49.29	49.31	49.32	49.34	49.36
2.5	49.38	49.40	49.41	49.43	49.45	49.46	49.48	49.49	49.51	49.52
2.6	49.53	49.55	49.56	49.57	49.59	49.60	49.61	49.62	49.63	49.64
2.7	49.65	49.66	49.67	49.68	49.69	49.70	49.71	49.72	49.73	49.74
2.8	49.74	49.75	49.76	49.77	49.77	49.78	49.79	49.79	49.80	49.81
2.9	49.81	49.82	49.82	49.83	49.84	49.84	49.85	49.85	49.86	49.86
3.0	49.87									
.	.									
.	.									
.	.									
4.0	49.997									

Using the Standard Normal Curve to Determine a Score's Relative Standing

z-scores also make it possible for us to take a raw score we've obtained for a normally distributed interval- or ratio-level variable and clarify where that score falls with respect to the other scores in the distribution. Probably the easiest way of accomplishing this is to first convert your raw score to a percentile.

Note: Recall that a percentile ranking designates the percent of cases or scores that fall at or below a selected point or score.

For those of you contemplating graduate school, you've likely heard about a test known as the Graduate Record Exam, or GRE. Suppose your classmate, Darnel, obtains a score of 620 on the quantitative subsection of the GRE. Knowing that you're studying statistics, he asks for your help in determining whether this is a good score. In looking at the material Darnel has received from Educational Testing Service, you see that the mean quantitative score for students planning to enter the social sciences is 528 with a standard deviation of 90.

With this information, you can easily convert Darnel's quantitative score to a standard z-score [(620 − 528) ÷ 90 = 1.02]. By doing so, you learn that Darnel's quantitative performance places him slightly beyond a standard deviation above the mean or average performance of university students planning advanced studies in the social sciences. "That's nice," Darnel declares, "but what does that mean?" You realize that to satisfactorily answer him, you're going to need to go a step further. Using Table 8.1, you find that 34.61% of these GRE quantitative scores will fall between a score of 620 and the mean (528). This finding is displayed graphically in Figure 8.13.

To convert a positive z-score, such as this, to a percentile, you add the area associated with the z-score to 50% (the area of the curve located below the mean). In this case, we find that Darnel did better on the GRE math test than 84.61% (50% + 34.61% = 84.61%) of the other social science–bound university students who took the test. It is customary to round to the nearest whole number when working with percentiles, so you can tell Darnel that he scored at the 85th percentile— which means he did better than 85% of his counterparts. Not bad at all!

Hearing how you'd helped Darnel out, Jerry asks you to help him interpret his GRE quantitative score of 500. Following the same steps just described, you first convert Jerry's raw score to a z-score [(500 − 528) ÷ 90 = −.31]. Looking at

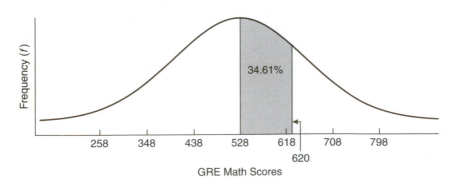

FIGURE 8.13   Distribution of GRE Quantitative Scores for University Students Planning Graduate Studies in the Social Sciences

Table 8.1, you discover that negative scores aren't listed. That's okay—given the symmetry of the standard normal curve, positive and negative z-scores of a given value will deviate the same amount from the mean. Therefore, information about the percentages of half the curve is all you need. Returning to Table 8.1, then, locate the percentage associated with a z-score of .31, which will be equivalent to the percentage associated with −.31. As depicted in Figure 8.14, the value corresponding to a z-score of −.31 is 12.17%.

When you work with z-scores to the left of the mean (i.e., negative scores), the percentile is derived by subtracting the area of the curve you find in Table 8.1 from 50%. Subtracting 12.17 from 50.00, you find that Jerry's GRE quantitative score of 500 places him at the 38th percentile (50% − 12.17% = 37.83%). Though not stellar, Jerry's performance on the math portion of the GRE may be high enough to get him accepted into a masters program.

Using z-Scores to Compare Scores across Distributions

Standard scores, or z-scores, are also useful when we want to compare raw scores that have been drawn from distributions that have different means and standard deviations. To illustrate, let's return to our computer training program example one more time. Suppose your agency decided to contract with the company mentioned earlier for 12 training slots a year. Client demand has been consistent, so the training slots remaining are limited. In fact, you find yourself with three clients vying for the two training slots you have left.

As you review these clients' materials to verify eligibility for the program, you find that your dilemma may be solved. That is, the IQ test scores obtained for these three applicants are Client A = 112, Client B = 122, and Client C = 95. Clearly Client C's score of 95 falls well below the training program's stipulated cutoff of 110. Upon closer inspection of these data, however, you discover that Client C had been referred to your agency by a youth program that employs a different battery of tests.

Specifically, the IQ test Client C completed was based on a mean of 85 and a standard deviation of 10. Digging further, you learn that both tests are considered

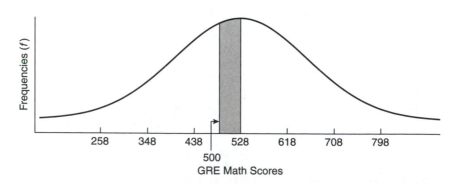

FIGURE 8.14   Distribution of GRE Math Scores for University Students Planning Graduate Studies in the Social Sciences

standardized and possess equivalent indicators of reliability and validity. Knowing a bit about the potential impact of "practice effects" on intelligence tests, you decide not to have Client C take your agency's intelligence test. Instead, you use your knowledge of z-scores, the normal distribution, and percentiles to help you compare these three scores. A summary of your findings is presented in Table 8.2.

Based on your comparative analysis, you decide that although all three candidates meet the training program's IQ entrance criterion, candidates B and C (who ranked at the 93rd and 84th percentiles, respectively) appear stronger than candidate A. There are other factors you'll consider in making your recommendations about this matter, but you no longer believe Client C should be eliminated from consideration for the computer training program solely because of an IQ score that appeared to be lower.

Using the Standard Normal Distribution to Estimate the Probability of an Event

Knowing that a data set is normally distributed—or at least approximately so—allows us to develop a rather complete description of our data. It's not unusual, though, to want to apply findings we derive from a sample to the population from which the sample was drawn. Whenever we undertake such ventures, we enter the realm of inferential statistics. In Chapter 9, you'll see why an understanding of the standard normal curve is critical to the use of inferential statistics.

TABLE 8.2 Comparison of IQ Scores for Clients Applying for an Agency-Sponsored Computer Training Program

z-SCORE	PERCENT OF SCORES BETWEEN RAW SCORE AND MEAN (%)	PERCENTILE RANK
Designated Program Cutoff		
z-score $= \dfrac{(110-100)}{15} = \dfrac{10}{15} = 0.67$	24.86	$+.50 = $ 75th
Client A		
z-score $= \dfrac{(112-100)}{15} = \dfrac{12}{15} = 0.80$	28.81	$+.50 = $ 79th
Client B		
z-score $= \dfrac{(122-100)}{15} = \dfrac{22}{15} = 1.47$	42.92	$+.50 = $ 93rd
Client C		
z-score $= \dfrac{(95-85)}{10} = \dfrac{10}{10} = 1.00$	34.13	$+.50 = $ 84th

■ ■ ■ ■ ■

WHAT TO DO WHEN YOUR DATA ARE NOT NORMALLY DISTRIBUTED

The assumption of normality underlies many inferential statistical procedures. So, what do you do when your data are not normally distributed? The first step in dealing with non-normally distributed data is to review your data. Scatterplots of your data are generally helpful here, as they provide a quick and easy way to identify scores that may be outliers. If you find any, the next step would be to double check your data entry materials to make sure that these data weren't simply misentered.

What do you do when this doesn't solve the problem of nonnormal distribution? We would suggest that you consult a statistician who can direct you to the best option based on the nature of your data. Some possibilities that may be suggested include increasing the size of your sample, trimming your data set to eliminate outliers or extreme scores, or using logarithmic (or other types of data transformations) to bring the data closer to a normal approximation.

COMPUTER APPLICATION: MEASURES OF DISTRIBUTION

Calculating measures of distribution (i.e., skewness and kurtosis) is generally a simple procedure using the computer. Returning to the data for length of time in foster care that we used in Chapters 6 and 7, we produced the following output using SPSS (Table 8.3) and Microsoft Excel (Table 8.4).

TABLE 8.3 Measures of Distribution Output Generated with SPSS: Data for Length of Time in Foster Care

N = 200	Missing Cases = 0
STATISTICS	**MONTHS**
Skewness	−0.115
Standard error of skewness	0.172
Kurtosis	−1.201
Standard error of kurtosis	0.342

TABLE 8.4 Measures of Distribution Output Generated with Excel: Data for Length of Time in Foster Care

MONTHS	
Mean	37.635
Standard error	1.504234851
Median	38
Mode	70
Standard deviation	21.27309328
Sample variance	452.5444975
Kurtosis	−1.201251322
Skewness	−0.115029699
Range	72
Minimum	0
Maximum	72
Sum	7257
Count	200

One thing to note is that, although the measures of skewness and kurtosis are the same, Excel does not generate the standard errors for these statistics. Because one method for determining whether your data are normally distributed is to look at the ratio of kurtosis and skewness measures to their respective standard errors, this omission could be problematic at times. When this is the case, use of a standard statistics package such as SPSS or SAS is advised.

TERMS TO KNOW

Asymmetrical (p. 117)
Asymptotic (p. 123)
Bell-shaped curve (p. 122)
Kurtosis (p. 123)
Leptokurtic (p. 123)
Mesokurtic (p. 123)
Negatively skewed (p. 118)
Normal distribution (p. 122)
Platykurtic (p. 123)

Positively skewed (p. 118)
Skewed (p. 117)
Standard normal distribution (p. 122)
Standard score (p. 130)
Symmetrical (p. 122)
Tail (p. 118)
z-curve (p. 128)
z-score (p. 130)

REVIEW PROBLEMS

1. In most cases the variable *annual income* is positively skewed.
   a. Describe what this means in terms of how income is typically distributed.
   b. In a positively skewed distribution, where will you find the median relative to the mean?
   c. When income is positively skewed, which measure will provide the most accurate indication of "average"—the median or the mean? Explain.

2. In Table 8.3 measures of skewness and kurtosis are presented for the data on length of time in foster care that we introduced in Chapter 6. How would you interpret these findings?

3. In a normal distribution, what percentage of scores would you expect to find within ± 2 standard deviations of the mean?

4. Describe the characteristics of the theoretical standard normal distribution, or bell-shaped curve.

5. Mrs. Townsend, a ninth-grade teacher, is concerned about a student in her homeroom section named Maggie. Recently, she approached your field instructor, a school social worker, with her concerns. Mrs. Townsend mentioned, for example, that over the past several weeks this previously spunky, engaged young woman has become quite withdrawn. She's started skipping lunch and has fallen asleep several times during study hall. In addition, Maggie's grades have begun to tumble. In meeting with Maggie, your field instructor administered a depression scale that has been standardized for use with adolescents. Scores derived from this instrument are distributed normally with a mean of 30 and a standard deviation of 5. Knowing

you're taking a statistics course, your field supervisor asks you to convert Maggie's score of 38 to a standard score (z-score). She'd also like you to interpret Maggie's score in terms of a percentile ranking.

REFERENCES

Kiess, H. O. (1996). *Statistical concepts for the behavioral sciences* (2nd ed.). Boston: Allyn & Bacon.
Sprinthall, R. C. (1994). *Basic statistical analysis* (4th ed.). Boston: Allyn & Bacon.
SPSS. (1998). *SPSS base 8.0: Applications guide.* Chicago: Author.

..... ━━━━━━━━━━━━━━━━━━━━━━━━━

CHAPTER NINE

INFERENTIAL STATISTICS: UNDERSTANDING PROBABILITY AND SAMPLING

Up to this point we've been focusing on different strategies you can use to organize and summarize your data. Collectively, these strategies are referred to as descriptive techniques. Sometimes these descriptive approaches may be all you need to adequately relay your findings. This is most likely to be the case when you've collected data from the entire group of people, events, or objects you've targeted for study (i.e., the population).

Often, however, the populations social workers are interested in studying are too large or dispersed to investigate directly. Suppose, for example, you're interested in assessing how a new treatment approach would work for people who wish to stop drinking. Even if you narrowed that interest to teens in your community who want to stop drinking, the logistical problems associated with identifying all these individuals, let alone involving all of them in your study, are staggering. That's why we typically select samples, or subsets, of cases from the populations we're interested in studying. Our intention, of course, is to use the data we gather from our sample to describe what's happening within the larger population from which the sample is drawn.

Formally, a **population** is any collection of people, events, institutions, or other objects of study that a researcher wishes to investigate. For any given study, therefore, members of the population are distinguished by the characteristics specified by the researcher. In the preceding example, your population of interest could be defined in terms of age (teens), geography (a particular community), a problematic behavior (drinking), or by a specific motivational level (those who've expressed a desire to change).

A **sample** is a subset or part of a population of interest. So technically, a sample can consist of one member of a population, or up to all but one of the people, events, or objects that make up that population. Of course, the number we include in our sample usually lies somewhere between these extremes. We'll discuss the role and function of sample size in more depth later. For now, it's important only that you understand that a sample is a portion of the larger whole that you, as the researcher, identified as the population of interest. Moreover, it's that part of the larger entity that will provide information for your study.

As noted earlier, at times it's sufficient to simply describe the data we've collected, whether it came from a sample or an entire population (e.g., all clients served by an agency to date). Frequently, however, our goal is to extend the observations about the characteristics of a sample (and the ways these characteristics or variables are related to one another) to the population from which the sample was drawn. Whenever we attempt to infer, or generalize, findings we obtain from a sample to the population from which the sample was drawn, we enter the world of **inferential statistics.** Before we delve into this topic, however, there are a couple of key concepts we need to introduce.

PARAMETERS VERSUS STATISTICS

Parameters are numerical descriptors of the features or characteristics of a population. For example, if the population we're interested in is all children involved in our county's foster care system, the average age of these youngsters would constitute one parameter. Others could include the ratio of boys to girls, the variation in their levels of self-esteem, the average length of time in foster care, and so on. In contrast, **statistics** can be thought of as the numerical descriptors of the features or characteristics of a *sample.* For example, if we were to compute the average age for a sample of 100 of the youngsters involved in our county's foster care system, that average would constitute a statistic. Statistics are typically represented in formulae and reports by Roman letters (e.g., sample mean = $\overline{X}$), whereas parameters are represented by Greek letters (e.g., population mean = μ).

As Jaeger (1983) observes, one way to help distinguish between parameters and statistics is to remember that the two terms that start with *p* belong together (population, parameter), as do the two terms that begin with *s* (sample, statistic).

INFERENCE: MOVING FROM THE FEW TO THE MANY

As we'll see momentarily, we use estimation procedures to make informed guesses about the values of population parameters based on the sample statistics we have in hand. Hypothesis tests help us evaluate the likelihood that what we observed in our sample is reflective of what's present in the population from which the sample was drawn. Critical to both forms of inference is the assumption that the sample we're using is representative of the population to which we want to generalize.

A **representative sample** mirrors the population from which it was drawn with respect to variables or characteristics believed to be important to your study. Suppose you're interested in examining the relationship between self-esteem and gender. If your population of interest is split evenly in terms of gender, then your sample should have an equal number of men and women, as well. Samples that match their respective populations in this way can be considered representative. Representativeness may not always be achieved, particularly when samples are small or not randomly selected.

PROBABILITY SAMPLING: OUR GATEWAY TO INFERENCE

The term **probability sample** refers to sampling approaches in which each member of the population has a known, nonzero chance of being selected for inclusion in the sample. The most common sampling strategy of this type, of course, is the simple random sample—where we might draw names from a hat, use a table of random numbers, or a computer-generated list of cases to create our sample. In random samples, each member of the population has an equal probability of being selected; hence, they're also known as **equal probability of selection methods (EPSEM)** samples.

Using a probability sampling procedure helps restrict the role of bias, and thereby increases the likelihood that a sample will be representative of its population. However, it does not *guarantee* that a sample will be representative. By chance, it's possible to draw a sample that differs from its population with regard to the variables or characteristics that are important to a study. That is, by chance we could select a sample that's older, less satisfied, less depressed, or wealthier than the population we've targeted for study. Fortunately, in using a probability sampling approach, we have access to a body of statistical theory called inferential statistics that allows us to estimate the likelihood that our sample data reflect what's happening in the population from which the sample was drawn.

Undergirding this branch of statistics is a collection of mathematical principles commonly referred to as the laws of probability. Before we address these directly, though, it's important to point out that research of interest to social workers is often conducted with nonprobability (e.g., convenience, quota, or judgmental) samples. Technically, it's inappropriate to use inferential statistics to generalize findings derived from nonprobability samples to their respective populations. In practice, however, this principle is frequently violated, with the "robustness" of the statistical procedure cited as justifying the action. Indeed, many statistical procedures are robust enough to tolerate violations of the theoretical assumptions upon which they are based. However, as an informed consumer and producer of research, you need to know that findings derived using inferential statistical techniques with data collected from a nonprobability sample are suspect—to the extent that the sampling procedure used varied from an EPSEM model.

PROBABILITY: THE BASICS

In statistics, the term **probability (P)** refers to the mathematical likelihood that an event will occur. A probability can range from 0 (the event has no chance of occurring) to 1.0 (the event is 100% certain to occur). Let's use the following hypothetical example to illustrate some of the other basic principles, or laws, of probability.

Suppose you've been working as a family services worker with the Bureau of Indian Affairs (BIA) for nearly a month. As your 30-day employment probation period is nearing an end, your supervisor asks you to randomly select a sample case from the six cases you've opened thus far for her to review. The six families you've worked with to date, therefore, constitute the population of interest. Figure 9.1 places these families in the order in which their cases were opened.

If you were to select a single case for your supervisor to review, what is the probability that you'd pick the first case you opened, the Sparks family? Well, according to probability theory, the probability of an event is determined by dividing the number of ways that an event or outcome could occur by the total number of outcomes possible. That is,

$$\text{Probability of an event} = \frac{\text{Number of ways the event can occur}}{\text{Total number of outcomes possible}}$$

Figure 9.2 illustrates what the process would look like for this example. Mathematically, then, the probability of selecting the Sparks family is one out of six (1/6). Probabilities are customarily expressed as proportions, however, not fractions. Therefore, we can say that the probability of selecting the first case you opened (i.e., the Sparks family) for your supervisor's review is 0.1667. It might be even easier to convey this information if we convert this proportion to a percent (by multiplying by 100). Doing so, we can say that the probability of selecting the Sparks family—or any one of the other families for that matter—is almost 17%.

Suppose, though, you're especially pleased with the work you've done with the Moyle and Smith families, and you're curious about the probability of randomly picking either of these two cases. Well, another law of probability tells us that we can determine the likelihood of selecting either of two events (i.e., picking family 3 or family 4) by adding their respective probabilities. Since we know the

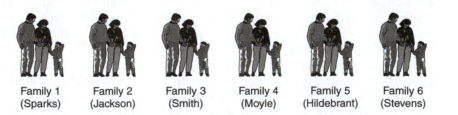

| Family 1 | Family 2 | Family 3 | Family 4 | Family 5 | Family 6 |
| (Sparks) | (Jackson) | (Smith) | (Moyle) | (Hildebrant) | (Stevens) |

FIGURE 9.1   Family Services Cases Opened during First 30 Days of Employment

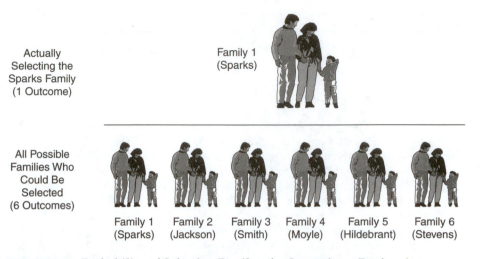

Actually
Selecting the
Sparks Family
(1 Outcome)

Family 1
(Sparks)

All Possible
Families Who
Could Be
Selected
(6 Outcomes)

| Family 1 (Sparks) | Family 2 (Jackson) | Family 3 (Smith) | Family 4 (Moyle) | Family 5 (Hildebrant) | Family 6 (Stevens) |

FIGURE 9.2   Probability of Selecting Family 1 for Supervisory Review

probability of selecting any given family is one in six ($1/6$), the likelihood of selecting either the Moyle family or the Smith family is $1/6 + 1/6 = 2/6 = 1/3$ (0.333). Thus, you've got roughly a 33% chance of picking one of these two cases.

This means you can expect to select either the Moyle family or the Smith family once in every three drawings. Suppose you wanted to practice drawing a random sample using a table of random numbers. You decide to draw single-case samples from this population of six families 12 times (see Formulae Alert 9.1 for details on when and how to use a table of random numbers). How often would you expect to find the Moyle family or the Smith family among those 12 selections? Because we've determined that the probability of selecting one or the other of them in a single drawing is one in three, we can expect that in 12 drawings we would pick one of these two families a third of the time—or four times ($1/3 \times 12 = 4$).

If you were to try this, would you be surprised if you didn't select the Moyle family or the Smith family at all? Would it concern you if you picked one or the other of these families 6 out of 12 times? Actually, neither of these events should be totally unexpected, because our 1-in-3 expectation represents a theoretical probability of what should happen if we were to repeat this selection process an infinite number of times. In other words, it represents what we can expect to happen in the long run. In the short haul, however, deviations from our theoretically predicted pattern can and will occur—if for no other reason than by chance.

Another law governing probability states that the probabilities associated with all the different outcomes that are possible must sum to 1. Consequently, the sum of the probabilities associated with selecting the Sparks family, the Jackson family, the Smith family, the Moyle family, the Hildebrant family, and the Stevens family for your supervisor to review equals $1/6 + 1/6 + 1/6 + 1/6 + 1/6 + 1/6 = 1.0$.

FORMULAE ALERT 9.1: USING A TABLE OF RANDOM NUMBERS

A table of random numbers is simply a list of numbers for which there is no discernible pattern or sequence among the numbers presented. In the long run, each number occurs the same number of times. Tables of random numbers can be found in most research and statistics texts. They're primarily used to randomly select samples or randomly assign subjects to treatment groups in experimental designs (Vogt, 1993). Let's use an example to see how we can use a table of random numbers to draw a random sample.

Suppose your agency is interested in following up with the clients it has served over the past two years. Although it would be desirable to touch base with all 1,250 clients served during this time frame, the agency director decides that, given financial and time constraints, a random sample of 125 clients will be included in the follow-up study. The first step involved in selecting a random sample is to assign each client a number. Because there are 1,250 potential participants, each number will need to encompass four digits. The first client will be labeled 0001, the second 0002, the third 0003, and so forth. Before proceeding, decide what direction you will go once you've established a starting point. For example, you may want to proceed down columns, across rows, or even in an angled fashion. Whatever you choose is ok, as long as the pattern is systematic and specified ahead of time.

Once you've assigned a number to each of the agency's clients served over the past two years, it's time to start selecting those to be included in the sample. Close your eyes and pick a spot on the partial table of random numbers—this spot constitutes your starting point. For the sake of illustration, imagine you picked the first number in column three (the outlined cell).

	1	2	3	4	5	6	7	8	9	10	11
1	18103	57740	84378	25338	12566	58678	44947	05585	15011	35126	60756
	59533	38867	62300	08150	17983	16439	11458	18593	46573	88072	55322
	79936	56865	05859	90109	31595	01547	85590	91610	48360	27354	18549
	69445	18663	72695	52185	20847	12234	90511	33703	93093	48708	83149
5	33488	36320	17617	30017	08272	84115	27156	30613	39975	18317	76988
	52267	67689	93394	01514	26358	85104	20285	29975	72905	86385	90229
	13916	47564	81056	97736	85977	29372	74461	18551	91977	59931	76468
	16308	60756	92144	49444	53900	70960	63990	75601	14342	51038	94342
	19885	55322	44819	01189	65255	64835	44919	05944	36857	82834	45834
10	04146	18594	29852	71582	85030	51132	01915	92747	06907	47358	60952

Because each client has been assigned a four-digit number label, our search for sample participants will start with the first four digits in column 3 or 8437. Since there are only 1,250 people in our population, we'll discard number 8437. We decide to go down

FORMULAE ALERT 9.1: *Continued*

the column and land next on 6230. Since 6230 is also too large, we move on. The first number to fall within our range of 0001 to 1250 is 0585, so the person associated with the file numbered 0585 becomes the first member of our sample. To obtain a random sample of 125—simply continue this search pattern (carving out subsequent blocks of columns of 4 digits) until you've encountered 125 numbers that fall within the designated range. Since none of the remaining numbers included in the shaded area of column 3 fall between 0001 and 1250, you would continue your search for potential participants in the next column which is formed by combining the last (fifth) digit of column 3 with the first three digits of column 4 (i.e., 8253). Can you identify our second sample member? If you said the person associated with file number 0081, you're absolutely correct. In turn, you'll find the third participant is the person with file number 0931, and so on.

What if your supervisor asked you to randomly select two cases for review? What's the probability of you picking the two cases where you were especially proud of your work—the Moyle family *and* the Smith family? According to another law of probability, you can determine the likelihood of two events both occurring by multiplying their respective individual probabilities. Thus, the probability of selecting both the Moyle family and the Smith family for your supervisor to review is $1/6 \times 1/6 = 1/36$ (0.0278 or 2.78%). Notice how the likelihood that you'll pick *both* of these cases in a sample of two becomes rather slight. You'll find that we've summarized relevant laws of probability in Formulae Alert 9.2.

As you think about this scenario, we hope you can see how the application of a random selection approach is likely to result in a different sample of cases than those you would probably have chosen if you were to handpick the files you would like your supervisor to review. Which approach do you think is most likely to yield a representative sample of the work you've done with the agency's clientele thus far?

The preceding examples illustrate how easy it is to calculate probabilities when we're working with small populations consisting of a definable number of discrete outcomes. Many times, however, we're interested in studying variables that are measured continuously, meaning there are no interruptions between the values an outcome theoretically can take on. Consider, for example, characteristics such as height, weight, age, and income. Although you might describe yourself as being 5 feet 10 inches tall, you may actually be 5 feet, 10.25 inches tall, or even a smidgen taller than that. The likelihood of anyone being *exactly* 5 feet 10 inches tall is pretty slim.

As with frequency distributions, the probabilities associated with the scores or values a continuous variable can take on, can be connected by a single, continuous

FORMULAE ALERT 9.2

Probability of an Event (E)

$$P(E) = \frac{\text{Number of ways the event can occur}}{\text{Total number of outcomes possible}}$$

Addition Rule: The Probability of Event A *or* Event B *or* Both

$$P(\text{A or B}) = P(\text{A}) + P(\text{B}) - P(\text{A and B})$$

Note: The addition rule is defined to include the occurrences of both events because if both occur, you have satisfied the condition of one or the other occurring. However, if Event A and Event B are mutually exclusive, meaning that they cannot occur simultaneously, the $P(\text{A and B})$ will be equal to zero, and the following special addition rule may be used.

Special Addition Rule: The Probability of Event A *or* Event B When Event A and Event B Are Mutually Exclusive

$$P(\text{A or B}) = P(\text{A}) + P(\text{B})$$

Multiplication Rule: The Probability of Event A *and* Event B

$$P(\text{A and B}) = P(\text{A}) \times P(\text{B} \mid \text{A})$$

Note: If Event A and Event B are independent events, meaning that the occurrence of one event does not change the probability of the other event occurring, then $P(\text{B} \mid \text{A}) = P(\text{B})$, and the special multiplication rule may be used. The probability of selecting both A *and* B is equal to the probability of selecting A times the probability of selecting B, given that A has already been selected.

Special Multiplication Rule: The Probability of Event A *and* Event B When Event A and Event B Are Independent

$$P(\text{A and B}) = P(\text{A}) \times P(\text{B})$$

Complement Rule: The Probability of Event E *Not* Occurring

$$P(\text{not E}) = 1 - P(\text{E})$$

EXAMPLE

These probability rules can be combined in many different ways to determine the specific probability of any defined event. Returning to our example of randomly selecting two cases for supervisory review, let's consider the probabilities associated with selecting the cases you were especially proud of, the Moyle family and the Smith family, for your supervisor to review. Because the selections of two cases are independent events, the special multiplication rule and the complement rule may be combined to determine the probabilities associated with each of the four possible outcomes related to selecting these two cases. As you can see, the probability of selecting both families is 0.0278, whereas the

FORMULAE ALERT 9.2: *Continued*

probability of selecting neither of these two families is 0.6944. The addition rule can be used to determine that the probability of selecting at least one of the families is 0.3056 [$P(S) + P(M) - P(S \text{ and } M) = 0.1667 + 0.1667 - 0.0278 = 0.3056$], which is equivalent to the addition of the probabilities associated with selecting both cases [$P(M \text{ and } S)$], and the two events of selecting one case and not the other [$P(S \text{ and not } M)$; $P(M \text{ and not } S)$] ($0.0278 + 0.1389 + 0.1389 = 0.3056$). It might be easier to derive the probability of selecting at least one of these cases by viewing this outcome as the complement to selecting neither of the cases [$1 - P(\text{not } S \text{ and not } M) = 1 - 0.6944 = 0.3056$].

	Probability of selecting the Moyle family: $P(M) = 1/6 \ (0.1667)$	Probability of *not* selecting the Moyle family: $P(\text{not } M) = 1 - P(M)$ $= 1 - 1/6$ $= 5/6 \ (0.8333)$
Probability of selecting the Smith family: $P(S) = 1/6 \ (0.1667)$	Probability of selecting *both* the Moyle family and the Smith family (Multiplication Rule): $P(M \text{ and } S) = P(M) \times P(S)$ $= 1/6 \times 1/6$ $= 1/36 \ (0.0278)$	Probability of selecting the Smith family and *not* the Moyle family (Multiplication and Complement Rules): $P(S \text{ and not } M) = P(S) \times P(\text{not } M)$ $= 1/6 \times 5/6$ $= 5/36 \ (0.1389)$
Probability of *not* selecting the Smith family: $P(\text{not } S) = 1 - P(S)$ $= 1 - 1/6$ $= 5/6 \ (0.8333)$	Probability of selecting the Moyle family and *not* the Smith family (Multiplication and Complement Rules): $P(M \text{ and not } S) = P(M) \times P(\text{not } S)$ $= 1/6 \times 5/6$ $= 5/36 \ (0.1389)$	Probability of *not* selecting either family (Multiplication and Complement Rules): $P(\text{not } M \text{ and not } S) =$ $P(\text{not } M) \times P(\text{not } S) =$ $5/6 \times 5/6 = 25/36 \ (0.6944)$

line. You're already somewhat familiar with the most famous probability distribution around—the standard normal curve.

The Standard Normal Curve as a Probability Distribution

Up to now, we've conceptualized the normal curve as a way of describing areas below, above, or between scores in terms of the proportion or percentage of scores involved. We also have seen that by viewing the normal curve as a theoretical frequency distribution, we can convert specified areas under the curve into the number of cases involved. Now let's see how the standard normal curve also serves as a probability distribution for normally distributed, continuous variables.

To illustrate, let's return for a moment to the computer training program scenario we introduced in Chapter 8. Recall that you're working for an agency that offers job training and placement services for men and women seeking reentry into the labor market. Suppose that the agency recently contracted with a local computer training program for 12 training slots this year. To date, the scores your clients have obtained on a standardized intelligence test have coincided with national norms (i.e., $\mu = 100$, $\sigma = 15$). In light of this information, what's the probability that a client selected at random will score at or above the minimum IQ score required for entry into the computer training program (i.e., IQ = 110 or higher)?

Answering this question becomes quite simple once you recognize the relationship that exists among percentages, proportions, and probabilities in regard to the standard normal curve. Previously we described the normal curve as a graphical presentation of a relative frequency distribution, and we suggested you think of the area under the normal curve as encompassing 100% of the scores contained in a data set. We argued further that by accounting for all, or 100%, of the scores associated with a variable, we could think of this area as constituting a whole entity. Whole entities are defined mathematically as unity, or 1.00. Similarly, the concept of probability is based on the fact that the probabilities associated with all, or 100%, of the events or outcomes that could occur will sum to 1.00. Are you beginning to see a pattern?

Whether we're talking in terms of percentages, proportions, or probabilities, the total number of outcomes can be thought of as constituting 100% of the outcomes or scores possible. While percentages vary from 0 to 100%, proportions and probabilities vary from 0 to 1.00. In fact, it may be helpful to think of probabilities as a type of proportion, in which 0 indicates an event has no chance of occurring, and 1.00 suggests its occurrence is a virtual certainty. Conversions among these entities is simply a matter of multiplying or dividing by 100, depending on whether you want to move toward or away from the context of percentages.

Given the close association that exists among percentages, proportions, and probabilities, it shouldn't be surprising to learn that we estimate probabilities the same way we found areas that represent a percentage or proportion of cases under the standard normal curve. As you'll recall from Chapter 8, the first step consists of converting our targeted IQ score of 110 to a z-score: z-score = 110 − 100/15 = 0.667. Next we need to define the area under the standard normal curve that's associated with a z-score of 0.67 or higher. To help conceptualize this process, the data presented previously in Figure 8.12 (p. 131) have been reproduced in Figure 9.3.

As before, finding this area of the curve requires that we scan down the left column of a z-score table (see Table 8.1, page 132) until we locate the row labeled 0.6. Now, focusing on the row labeled z, move across until you find the second decimal associated with our z-score: 0.07. As we bring these points together by moving across the 0.6 row and down the .07 column, we find that 24.86 marks the spot where the row and column converge. This is the percentage of cases that fall between a raw IQ score of 110 and the distribution mean of 100. Subtracting 24.86% from the 50% of scores that make up the right half of the curve, we find that 25.14% of our IQ scores fall at or above the targeted IQ score of 110.

Another way of expressing this is to say that 25.14% of all of the scores will be found at or above 110. The probability of your randomly selecting a client with an

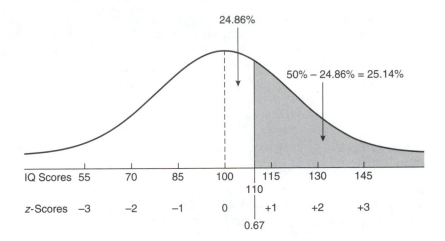

FIGURE 9.3 Area under the Normal Curve Associated with IQ Scores of 110 or Higher

IQ score of 110 or higher is derived by dropping the % signs and dividing 25.14/100. This yields a probability of 0.2514. Therefore, the probability that a client selected at random will score at or above the minimum score required for entry into the computer training program is 0.2514, or approximately one in four.

Contrasting Probability with Odds

Probability statements describe the number of times we anticipate an event will occur in relationship to the total number of outcomes that are possible. In contrast, odds convey the chances *against* an event occurring in relationship to the chances that it will occur. For example, we've determined that the probability of randomly selecting a client whose IQ score is 110 or higher is 0.25, or one in four. This statement emphasizes the likelihood that you will pick a client who meets this criterion. In contrast, the odds of your randomly selecting a client whose IQ score is 110 or higher are 3:1. How did we get that?

We simply converted our probability statement to an odds ratio. That is, we stated the likelihood of *not* randomly selecting a client with an IQ of 110 or greater compared to the likelihood of doing so. We accomplished this by returning our probability statement to a fraction (i.e., 0.25 = 1/4). The numerator tells us how likely it is that an event will occur. Thus, in this instance we have 1 chance (in 4) of randomly selecting a client who scores 110 or higher on the IQ test. By subtracting the numerator contained in a probability statement from its denominator (i.e., 4 − 1 = 3), we can determine how likely it is that the event will *not* occur. Doing so, we find we have three chances in four of *not* selecting a client with an IQ of 110. Thus, we conclude that the odds against randomly selecting a client who meets the IQ eligibility criteria for the computer training program are 3:1 (i.e., three nays to one yea).

In this section we saw how combining an understanding of the laws of probability with knowledge of the standard normal curve allows us to estimate the likelihood of randomly selecting a score that falls within a defined interval of normally distributed scores. Probability theory is also an integral part of the logic that informs statistical inference, that is, the practice of estimating parameters on the basis of statistics (Williams, 1986). To understand this connection, it's helpful to examine the relationships that exist among three distinct and important distributions: the sample distribution, the population distribution, and a new concept that's critical to the process of making inferences—the sampling distribution. So, without further adieu, let's turn our attention to these phenomena.

The Sampling Distribution: Bridging the Gap between a Sample and Its Population

The world of inferential statistics poses an interesting intellectual challenge. Typically, researchers have a great deal of information about a sample of people, objects, or interactions, yet what is of interest is how accurately those sample data reflect the population from which the sample was drawn.

As you've seen in previous chapters, you can describe the sample data you've gathered using measures of central tendency and indicators of dispersion. You can even illustrate these data pictorially with charts and graphs. When you add measures of skewness and kurtosis to this information, a fairly complete picture emerges of how the targeted behavior, trait, or other characteristic is distributed within your sample.

Having been derived from empirical observations, a distribution of sample scores is a known entity. In inferential statistics, the goal is to move from this known sample distribution to a potentially observable—yet unknown—population distribution. After all, if we knew how often our targeted characteristic, behavior, or trait occurred within the population, we wouldn't need to infer this information. To help us move from the known (sample distribution) to the unknown (population distribution), we use a theoretical device known as the sampling distribution (Healey, 1996). As you'll see momentarily, by drawing on the laws of probability, we're able to deduce a great deal about the features of this theoretical distribution.

You may be asking yourselves, Why, if you've already taken the necessary steps to ensure that the sample selected is representative of the population from which it was drawn, would it be necessary to use another device to help you move, or generalize, from your sample to its population. The answer lies in the fact that no matter how careful you are in selecting your sample, you have no way of knowing that it mirrors its population exactly. In fact, probability theory tells us we can expect samples to vary somewhat from their respective populations simply because of chance fluctuations that occur in the short term. This variability among samples is partly due to the fact that the likelihood of drawing two identical samples is very small.

The term used to describe the difference between a sample's statistics and its population's parameters is **sampling error.** The key challenge in making inferences about population parameters on the basis of sample statistics is in estimating how much sampling error exists. How likely is it, for example, that the average, or mean, self-esteem score you obtained from your randomly drawn sample of 50 ninth graders reflects the "true," or actual, average self-esteem score for all ninth graders in the school district (i.e., your targeted population)? Regardless of which inferential statistical test you choose to use, a sampling distribution has been developed to help you determine the probability that chance, or sampling error—not reality—is responsible for your findings.

In contrast to the frequency distributions involving individual, or raw, scores that were presented in previous chapters, a **sampling distribution** is a theoretical frequency distribution of a sample statistic such as a mean, proportion, standard deviation, and so forth. Technically, the data points contained in a sampling distribution represent the values of the statistic that would be generated for an infinite number of samples of the same size taken from a given population. However, given the impossibility of ever obtaining an infinite number of samples, the sampling distribution remains an abstract, theoretical construct—that is, you'll never really touch it or see it. To help you better understand what it is and how it works, though, we will simulate how a sampling distribution of a statistic such as the mean might be constructed.

Simulating a Sampling Distribution

Suppose, in an effort to learn more about the 2,500 seniors who currently use its Meals on Wheels program, an area agency on aging decides to survey a sample of the program's participants. Among the data that the agency intends to collect is information on the program participants' ages. We can simulate the underlying theoretical sampling distribution of the mean for this variable by randomly drawing many samples of the same size from the population of recipients. To accomplish this, we would start by randomly drawing a sample of a given size—for example, five program participants—interview them, compute the average age for the group, and then plot that finding on a graph. After returning the names of these five participants to the pool of 2,500, we would select a second sample of five seniors, interview them, compute their group's average age, and plot that figure on a graph. Figure 9.4 depicts the mean ages ($\overline{X}$) we derived by following these procedures for six separate randomly selected samples.

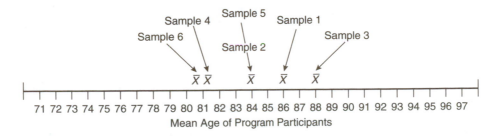

FIGURE 9.4   Mean Age Computed on Six Samples of Meals on Wheels Participants ($n = 5$)

CHARACTERISTICS OF A SAMPLING DISTRIBUTION OF THE MEAN

Now imagine what Figure 9.4 would look like if we plotted the mean age obtained for a thousand samples of $n = 5$ Meals on Wheels recipients. What shape do you think this distribution of means would take on? Do you think they'd cluster in any predictable way? What kind of spread, or variation, would you expect to find among their values? Let's take a moment to address each of these questions individually.

Defining the Sampling Distribution in Terms of Shape

Given what we know about probability theory, it seems reasonable to expect some variation among the values contained in a sampling distribution of means, if for no other reason than there are chance fluctuations in the participants selected for inclusion each time. Also, because these fluctuations are random, we'd expect to get sample means that are larger than the true population mean age, μ, about as often as we'd get sample means that are smaller than μ.

For the sake of discussion, let's assume that the true mean age for this population of service recipients is 84. A sampling distribution of the mean age for 1,000 samples of five Meals on Wheels participants is presented in Figure 9.5. As you look at these data, notice how the values of the sample means vary from one another as probability theory would lead us to expect. Notice, too, how the scores that are greater and less than 84 (μ) are fairly equally distributed. This leads us to another important principle of probability that applies to the shape of the sampling distribution of the mean—the **central limit theorem**. Essentially, this theorem states that as the size of the sample becomes sufficiently large, the sampling distri-

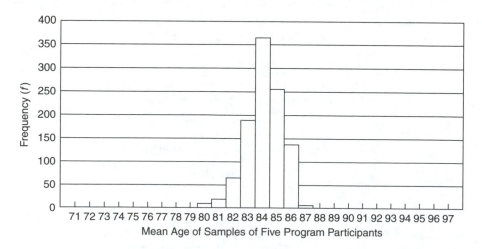

FIGURE 9.5   **Sampling Distribution of the Mean ($n = 5$) for 1,000 Samples Drawn from the Population of Meals on Wheels Participants**

bution of the means will become normal—regardless of how the characteristic is distributed within the population.

An important question, of course, is how large a sample is "sufficiently large?" The answer depends on how the variable is distributed within the population from which the sample is drawn. When a variable is distributed normally within the population, sampling distributions based on sample sizes as small as 5 or 10 will begin to approach normality (Kiess, 1996). If the underlying population distribution is skewed, then larger sample sizes are required for the sampling distribution of the mean to approach normality. However, there seems to be little agreement among statisticians regarding the size of sample needed to reach this outcome when working with non-normal population distributions. Estimates vary from $n = 30$ (Kiess, 1996), to $n = 60$ (Pyrczak, 1995), to $n = 100$ (Kiess, 1996; Healey, 1996). As a rule of thumb, we suggest the larger the sample, the better. In our experience, though, samples of $n = 30$ are generally sufficient for a sampling distribution of the mean to begin taking on the appearance of a normal distribution.

Defining the Sampling Distribution in Terms of Central Tendency

In addition to defining the shape, the mathematical principles undergirding the central limit theorem also tell us that the mean of the sample means in a theoretical sampling distribution (symbolized as $\mu_{\bar{x}}$)[*] will be equal to the population mean (μ). Intuitively, this makes sense, because we know that most of the scores (in this case, sample means) contained in a normal distribution will cluster around the population mean (μ).

Defining the Sampling Distribution in Terms of Dispersion

The amount of variation that exists among the sample means ($\bar{X}$) contained within a sampling distribution of the means is defined in terms of the standard error of the mean. According to the central limit theorem, the **standard error of the mean** (symbolized as $\sigma_{\bar{x}}$) is equal to the standard deviation of the population (σ; see the following Technical Note) divided by the square root of the sample size ($\sqrt{n}$). Keep in mind that the standard error of the mean (or, more simply, the standard error) is really nothing more than the standard deviation of the theoretical sampling distribution. We use a different term to describe it merely as a way of distinguishing the standard deviation of the sampling distribution from the standard deviations we compute using sample or population raw scores. Actually, the use of the term *error* in this instance seems especially fitting because it refers to the random fluctuation that occurs by chance or error when we are computing the same statistic on random samples of the same size drawn from the same population.

---

[*] The $\mu_{\bar{x}}$ refers to the mean of means—the mean of a sampling distribution of the means.

Technical Note: Typically, the standard deviation of the population (σ) is unknown. Nevertheless, we can estimate the standard error of the mean by substituting the estimated population standard deviation (SD) for the population parameter (σ)—that is, the estimated standard error of the sampling distribution ($S_{\bar{x}} = SD \sqrt{n}$), where SD is determined from the sample scores using the formula ($\Sigma[X - \bar{X}]^2)/n - 1$).

The amount of variation found within a sampling distribution is a function of the two elements involved in computing the standard error of the mean—the population standard deviation (whether it's the actual population standard deviation, σ, or its estimated counterpart s) and the sample size. To illustrate, suppose all the members of our population of Meals on Wheels recipients are the same age. In this case, the standard deviation of the population (σ) would be zero. Furthermore, all means derived from the population—regardless of sample size—would be identical. Because there would be no fluctuation among the mean ages derived, the standard error of the mean would also be zero ($\sigma_{\bar{x}} = 0/\sqrt{n} = 0$). However, the likelihood of encountering no variation in a characteristic of interest is extremely small (unless, of course, you were intentionally using it in your research as a constant). Nonetheless, the example helps us see how the amount of variability in the population affects the size of the standard error of the mean. Specifically, less variability in the population yields a smaller standard error of the mean.

As Figure 9.6 illustrates, the size of the sample also influences the standard error. Notice how the width of the distribution of means shrinks as the size of the sample increases from $n = 2$ to $n = 5$ to $n = 10$. Logically, this makes sense, because with very small samples it would be easy to randomly select only extreme (high or low) mean values ($\bar{X}$). As the sample size increases, the chances of including only extreme scores diminishes substantially.

The critical role of the sampling distribution in inferential statistics can't be overemphasized. As you'll soon see, whether you're using estimation procedures or testing hypotheses, the steps you take will involve generalizing from the value of a known sample statistic to an unknown population parameter by means of a theoretical sampling distribution.

ESTIMATION PROCEDURES

One branch of inferential statistics consists of **estimation procedures** that allow us to make educated guesses about the values of population parameters on the basis of sample statistics. For example, the sample mean ($\bar{X}$) is frequently used to estimate the mean of the population (μ). When a sample statistic is used to estimate a population parameter in terms of a single value like this, the process is known as **point estimation.**

Importantly, when it comes to providing point estimates of population parameters, not all sample statistics are equally suited to the task. A good estimator is

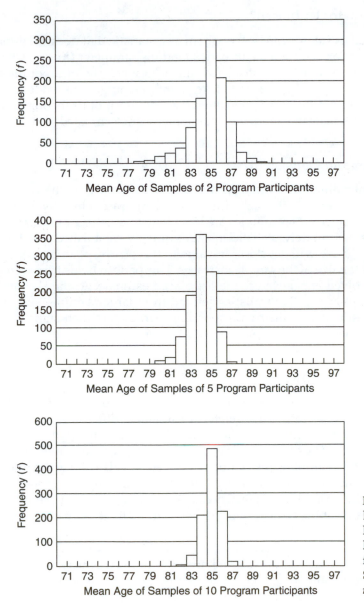

FIGURE 9.6 Sampling Distributions of the Meals on Wheels Participants' Mean Age for Different Size Samples ($n = 2, n = 5, n = 10$)

a statistic that yields an unbiased, consistent, and efficient approximation of the population parameter it estimates. But how do you know if a given statistic possesses these traits? If you're thinking that the sampling distribution probably plays a role here, you're absolutely correct! Let's take a look at how the various features of a given statistic's sampling distribution can be used to help us determine if it's unbiased, consistent, and efficient.

Is the Estimator Unbiased?

An **unbiased estimator** can be thought of as a statistic that doesn't systematically underestimate or overestimate its corresponding parameter (Keiss, 1996). In more specific terms, a statistic is considered unbiased when the mean of the statistical values you'd obtain, if you were to take an infinite number of random samples of the same size from the same population (i.e., the mean of its theoretical sampling distribution), equals the population parameter being estimated.

Is the Estimator Consistent?

A **consistent estimator** is a statistic that tends to get closer to the value of the parameter it estimates as the size of the sample increases. Intuitively, this feature makes sense, since larger samples are less likely to capture only extreme (high or low) scores. Fortunately, statisticians have already established that the statistics we're likely to use will get closer in value to their corresponding population parameters as the size of the sample increases. This pattern holds true even when the statistic involved is believed to yield a biased estimate. At the bottom line, this means we can expect that statistics derived from larger samples will yield more consistent estimates of their corresponding parameters than statistics based on smaller samples.

Is the Estimator Efficient?

The efficiency of a statistic refers to its level of precision, or how closely it corresponds to the value of the parameter it estimates. Efficiency is reflected in the amount of variation observed among the values contained within the statistic's sampling distribution. In fact, efficiency is actually measured in terms of the standard error of the sampling distribution involved. An **efficient estimator** is a statistic with a small standard error, that is, one whose sampling distribution is found to cluster tightly around its mean. Therefore, the more efficient the estimator, the closer the value of the statistic will be to the parameter it estimates.

Note: As noted previously, the standard error is a function of the variability that exists within the population and the sample size. Because we can't alter the variability that exists within a population, increasing the efficiency of an estimator (i.e., reducing the standard error) becomes a matter of increasing the sample size.

It's important to remember, though, that even if you can establish that a given statistic yields an unbiased, consistent, and efficient estimate of its corresponding parameter, you can't rule out the possibility that its value may differ from the "true" value of the parameter—if for no other reason than chance. Although a statistic possessing these characteristics serves as your best guess of the value of the parameter involved, you have no way of knowing how much confidence to put in the accuracy of that guess. There is, however, a type of estimation procedure known as **interval estimation** that allows you to delineate a range of values within which the targeted population parameter is expected to fall; at the same time, the interval estimation enables you to specify how confident you are that the targeted population parameter actually falls within the range. Let's use a field-based example to illustrate how this type of estimation procedure works.

Suppose you're doing your field practicum with the state division of child and family services. Concerned about the increase in turnover that's occurred over the last 12 months among social workers employed within the division's child protective service (CPS) units, the agency's director has asked your practicum supervisor to look into the matter. Seeing this as a great opportunity to address several of the research-related performance objectives you included in your field practicum learning agreement, you enthusiastically offer your assistance.

Given time and budgetary restraints, a decision is made to survey a random sample consisting of 100 of the 1,285 social workers currently working in CPS units statewide. The instrument developed for use in this study includes standardized measures of job satisfaction, locus of control, and burnout, as well as select demographic (e.g., age, gender) and job-related (e.g., years in position, current caseload size) questions. In calculating the results, you find that the average burnout score achieved by the 100 social workers surveyed is 15 with a standard deviation of 2.3.

Although this sample average ($\overline{X}$) provides a good estimate of the average burnout level experienced among CPS social workers statewide (i.e., the population mean, μ), without further information, you can't say how much confidence you'd put in the accuracy of the estimate. In fact, you're aware of the role chance fluctuations can play in these situations, and you'd be justified in wondering whether this particular estimate might just be a fluke. Well, there's no need to panic because this is precisely the kind of circumstance in which an interval estimate is helpful.

CONSTRUCTING AN INTERVAL ESTIMATE (A CONFIDENCE INTERVAL)

As the heading above suggests, another name for an interval estimate is **confidence interval.** Constructing a confidence interval not only generates an interval, or range, of scores around a point estimate, but it also allows you to state how confident you are that the interval likely contains the population parameter being estimated.

In building a confidence interval, the first thing you need to do is decide on the risk you're willing to take that your estimate may be wrong. Your estimate is wrong if the interval you develop doesn't include the true population parameter. The term **alpha (α)** is used to describe this risk factor, or probability of error. In selecting an alpha level, you'll want to think about the consequences associated with making a mistake (i.e., What happens if you're wrong?). Unless it's a life or death circumstance or a decision that would prove very costly in other ways, the alpha level most commonly used is 0.05. That is, most social scientists are willing to risk being wrong 5 times out of 100, or 5% of the time. Since the probabilities associated with all possible outcomes must sum to 1.0, when you set the probability of error, or alpha level (α), at 0.05, you're simultaneously setting the chances of the estimate being correct at 0.95. That is, an alpha level of 0.05 yields a corresponding confidence level of 95%.

Suppose, after weighing the consequences associated with misestimating the level of burnout experienced by the state's CPS social workers, you decide to set your alpha level at 0.05. Let's take a moment to think about the implications of this decision in terms of the underlying, theoretical sampling distribution involved. First, given the random nature of sampling error, you can expect to get a sample mean ($\overline{X}$) that overestimates the average population burnout score (μ), just as often as you get an $\overline{X}$ that underestimates it. It would seem to make sense, therefore, to split the 5% level of risk you're willing to take evenly between the high and low ends (or right and left tails) of the sampling distribution. Figure 9.7 depicts how a hypothetical sampling distribution of mean burnout scores would look once this 5% probability of error is split in half.

Secondly, given the central limit theorem and the relatively large sample involved ($n = 100$), you can expect the mean scores contained within the underlying sampling distribution to be distributed normally. This point is critical because it is this assumption that will allow us to use the standard normal curve in formulating a confidence interval for these data.

To help us navigate the conceptual terrain that exists between the sample data we have on hand (empirical phenomena) and the normal curve (an abstract construct), we'll once again call upon the standard z-curve. We begin our journey, therefore, by locating the z-scores that correspond with the points that separate the

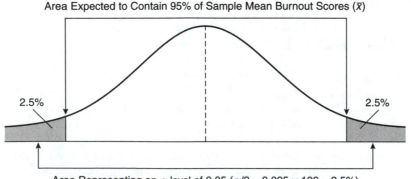

FIGURE 9.7   **Sampling Distribution for Mean Burnout Scores Associated with a 95% Confidence Interval (Alpha Level Set at 0.05)**

area of the curve where 95% of the sample means $(\overline{X})$ are expected to fall, from the areas expected to hold the other 5%. To accomplish this, we'll simply reverse the procedures we followed previously, when we used z-scores to define targeted areas under the normal curve.

Take a moment to examine the right side of the curve depicted in Figure 9.8. Notice how the arrow designating the 95% cutoff point divides this half of the curve into two sections. If we subtract the 2.5% associated with the alpha level selected from this half (50%) of the curve, we're left with an area that encompasses 47.5% of the total curve. To convert this percentage to a z-score, we need to use a table like the one in Chapter 8 (see Table 8.1, p. 132). As you review Table 8.1, recall that the numbers contained in this table tell us the percent of area under the normal curve that falls between a selected score and the mean of the distribution. Recall, too, that each numerical entry corresponds to an actual z-score. Now locate the number that falls closest to the area being targeted (i.e., 47.5%).

As it happens, 47.50 is one of the actual values contained in Table 8.1. (You'll discover later that this is not the case for alpha levels of .10 and .01.) To determine the relevant z-score, follow the row containing 47.50 to the left until you reach the first column (labeled z), and note this value (i.e., 1.9). Next, trace the column containing 47.50 to the top row (which is also labeled z), and note this value (i.e., .06). Now add these values together (1.9 + .06). Doing so, we find that the z-score that corresponds to the 95% cutoff point for the right (or positive) side of the curve is +1.96. Furthermore, given the symmetrical nature of the normal curve, we can deduce that a z-score of –1.96 will coincide with the 95% cutoff point denoted for the left (or negative) side of the curve (see Figure 9.9). Knowing the value of the z-score involved, we're now ready to build a 95% confidence interval for the average burnout level experienced by the social workers currently working in CPS.

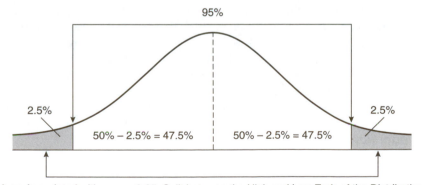

FIGURE 9.8   **Areas under the Normal Curve Defined in Terms of Percent, When α = 0.05**

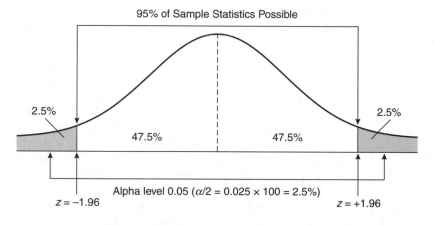

95% of Sample Statistics Possible

2.5%   2.5%

47.5%   47.5%

Alpha level 0.05 ($\alpha/2 = 0.025 \times 100 = 2.5\%$)

$z = -1.96$ $z = +1.96$

FIGURE 9.9   Area under the Normal Curve Defined in Terms of z-Scores Associated with a 95% Confidence Interval

The formula used to construct a confidence interval is presented in Formulae Alert 9.3. If we insert the relevant figures from the burnout data into this formula (i.e., $\overline{X} = 15, z = 1.96, SD = 2.3$, and $n = 100$), we get the following:

$$15 \pm (1.96)\,(2.3/\sqrt{100})$$

$$15 \pm 0.4508$$

To construct a 95% confidence interval for these data, we'll simply add, then subtract, 0.4508 to the sample mean burnout score reported above (i.e., $\overline{X} = 15$). Take a moment to do that now.

In completing these calculations, you'll find the scores that define this particular interval estimate are 14.5492 and 15.4508. Now, when you and your supervisor report your findings to the agency's director, not only can you say that the average burnout score achieved by the 100 CPS social workers sampled was 15 (*SD* = 2.3), but you can also say you're 95% certain that the average burnout level experienced by social workers working within the state's CPS units falls within the range of 14.55 to 15.45. To establish what these data mean, however, you'll need to gather some additional data. For example, to determine whether this level of burnout is considered high, average, or low, it might be helpful to gather information from other studies of social worker burnout, where instruments similar to yours were used.

Parameter Estimates Involving Small Samples

As we've seen, estimation procedures involving large samples—or those completed when the population standard deviation (σ) is actually known—rely heavily on the principles and assumptions of the central limit theorem. But what

FORMULAE ALERT 9.3

The formula used to construct a confidence interval for a sample mean, using a large sample when s serves as an estimate for σ is as follows:

$$\text{confidence interval (ci)} = \overline{X} \pm z(SD / \sqrt{n})$$

where
$\overline{X}$ = sample mean
z = z-score associated with a selected alpha level
SD = estimated population standard deviation, determined using the formula $\Sigma(X - \overline{X})^2 / n - 1$
$SD / \sqrt{n}$ = standard error of the mean

In those rare circumstances in which the standard deviation of the population (σ) is known, the formula is simplified as follows:

$$\text{ci} = \overline{X} \pm z(\sigma / \sqrt{n})$$

where
$\overline{X}$ = sample mean
z = z-score associated with a selected alpha level
$\sigma / \sqrt{n}$ = the standard error of the mean

happens when we're working with smaller samples and the population standard deviation isn't known? Is it possible under such conditions to make meaningful estimates of population parameters based on the sample statistics in hand? Thanks to the work of William Sealy Gossett, the answer is yes!

Specifically, in 1908, writing under the pen name of "Student," Gossett introduced the formula for determining the standard error which, in turn, led to the creation of a new series of distributions, known collectively as the t-ratio, or Student's t (Sprinthall, 1994). Like the z-distribution, t-distributions are bell-shaped and symmetrical with a mean of zero (Knoke & Bohrnstedt, 1994). In contrast to the single curve that makes up the standard normal (z) distribution, though, the t-ratio refers to a family of distributions whose shapes differ from one another on the basis of the sample sizes and standard deviations involved. In particular, t-distributions derived from smaller samples will have larger variances (and consequently, larger standard errors) than the standard normal distribution. As a result, they'll be somewhat flatter and more spread out than the standard normal (z) curve. Note, however, that the t-distribution starts to approximate the standard normal (z) curve as the size of the sample increases (see Figure 9.10).

As you look at the data presented in Figure 9.10, notice the new term *degrees of freedom* (abbreviated *df*). We'll discuss this concept in more detail in the chapters ahead. For now, it's important only to know that in making interval estimates

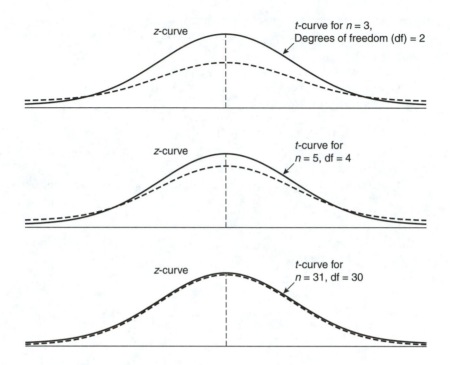

FIGURE 9.10   Comparison of *t*-Distributions to the Standard Normal (*z*) Distributions, Based on Sample Sizes of 3, 5, and 31

using *t*-distributions, degrees of freedom are used to compensate for the bias that occurs when calculating standard deviations on small samples. When working with *t*-distributions, we determine the degrees of freedom involved by subtracting 1 from the original sample size (i.e., $n - 1$). Figure 9.10 depicts *t*-distributions for sample sizes of 3, 5, and 31. Another distinction between the *z*- and *t*-distributions is that the *t*-distribution technically requires that the sample come from a normally distributed population. Because the effect of violating this assumption is minimal, however, it's generally acceptable to use *t*-distributions with nonnormal populations (the exception being the markedly nonnormal population distribution). As you'll soon see, *t*-distributions play an integral part in many tests involving statistical hypotheses. For now, just be aware that a confidence interval based on a *t*-distribution differs from one that uses the standard normal (*z*) curve. To illustrate this difference, let's see what would happen to the 95% confidence interval developed for the burnout data, if the number of CPS social workers interviewed is substantially decreased.

Specifically, suppose our sample consisted of 25 ($n = 25$) CPS social workers instead of 100. With a sample this small, and without knowing the population standard deviation, we can't legitimately use a *z*-distribution to create a confidence interval. As you'll learn momentarily, though, the *t*-distribution associated with 24 ($n - 1$, or $25 - 1$) degrees of freedom provides a valid way (i.e., a valid theoretical sampling distribution) of constructing a confidence interval for a sample of this size.

You'll find the formula for constructing a confidence interval using a t-distribution in Formulae Alert 9.4. It might be helpful to take a moment to compare this formula with the one presented in Formulae Alert 9.3: You'll notice that the only difference between the two is the use of a t-value instead of a z-value in the second formula. Like the process we followed to find a value for z, the first step in locating t is to set our alpha level. Since the outcomes associated with a misestimation haven't changed, let's retain an alpha level of 0.05. Also, because we're as likely to overestimate the average level of burnout as we are to underestimate it, let's again split our probability of risk between the right and left tails (this is also referred to as a two-tailed test).

Unlike before, when we used a single standardized distribution to transform a targeted area under the curve to a z-value, we're now faced with a variety of t-distributions that change in shape according to sample size. This is where knowledge of the degrees of freedom involved comes into play. In this instance, we'll want to target a t-distribution associated with $n - 1$, or 24, degrees of freedom. Combining this information with the alpha level of 0.05, we used a table of critical t-values (see Table 9.1) and found a t-value of 2.064 located at the point where a two-tailed test for an alpha level of 0.05 and 24 degrees of freedom intersect. As illustrated in Formulae Alert 9.4, when we insert this t-value along with the other pertinent information ($\overline{X} = 15$, $SD = 2.3$, $n = 25$) into the formula, we get a 95% confidence interval that ranges from 14.0506 to 15.9494.

FORMULAE ALERT 9.4

To create a confidence interval using the t-ratio rather than z, simply substitute s for σ and insert the t-value adjusted for the size of the sample (df = $n - 1$) and α level involved. For example,

$$ci = \overline{X} \pm (t)(s / \sqrt{n})$$

$$ci = 15 \pm 2.064(0.46)$$

$$ci = 15 \pm 0.9494$$

$$ci = 14.0506, 15.9494$$

The t-value 2.064 was obtained from a table of critical t-values (see Table 9.1). In this case, we located a t-value of 2.064 for $n - 1$ or 24, df for a two-tailed test using an alpha of 0.05.

TABLE 9.1   Critical Values for Selected
***t*-Distributions**

DEGREES OF FREEDOM	LEVEL OF SIGNIFICANCE FOR TWO-TAILED TEST	
	.05	.01
1	12.706	63.657
2	4.303	9.925
3	3.182	5.841
4	2.776	4.604
5	2.571	4.032
6	2.447	3.707
7	2.365	3.499
8	2.306	3.555
9	2.262	3.250
10	2.228	3.169
11	2.201	3.106
12	2.179	3.055
13	2.160	3.012
14	2.145	2.977
15	2.131	2.947
16	2.120	2.921
17	2.110	2.898
18	2.101	2.878
19	2.093	2.861
20	2.086	2.845
21	2.080	2.831
22	2.074	2.819
23	2.069	2.807
24	2.064	2.797
25	2.060	2.787
26	2.056	2.779
27	2.052	2.771
28	2.048	2.763
29	2.045	2.756
30	2.042	2.750
> 30	1.960	2.576

The burnout data collected from these two samples are summarized in Table 9.2. Focus, for a moment, on the size of the confidence intervals involved. Why do you think the interval based on the smaller sample is a full point wider than the interval developed for the larger sample, even though the means and standard deviations are the same? In answering this question, you might find it helpful to think about the impact of dividing 2.3 (s) by 5 (i.e., $\sqrt{25}$) instead of by 10 (i.e., $\sqrt{100}$), and multiplying those quotients by a t of 2.06, or a z of 1.96.

TABLE 9.2   CPS Social Workers' Burnout Data

POPULATION	SAMPLE SIZE	AVERAGE BURNOUT SCORE	STANDARD DEVIATION	95% CONFIDENCE INTERVAL	RANGE
CPS Social Workers $N = 1{,}285$	100	15	2.3	14.55 – 15.45	0.90
CPS Social Workers $N = 1{,}285$	25	15	2.3	14.05 – 15.94	1.89

Interval Estimates Involving Proportions

Though you may not realize it, the interval estimate involving proportions is the one you're probably most familiar with. How many times have you heard, for example, something like, "Candidate A is leading in the polls with 64% of the vote, plus or minus 3%"? Or, "It's been estimated that 48 to 52% of our nation's children live in poverty"? How do researchers and pollsters arrive at these kinds of estimates? And, further, how are they best interpreted?

As you'll see, the procedure for building a confidence interval using a sample proportion is similar in many ways to the approach used to create an interval estimate based on a sample mean. Because it's a different statistic, though, we need to use a different theoretical sampling distribution.

Drawing again on the central limit theorem, we know that the sampling distribution for a proportion, like that for a mean, will be normal in shape, and its mean (known as μ_p) will be equal to the population proportion (symbolized as P_μ). In contrast to the sampling distribution for a mean, however, the standard deviation for this distribution is equal to the square root of the population proportion (P_μ), multiplied by 1 minus this figure ($1 - P_\mu$), divided by the size of the sample. That is, $\sqrt{P_\mu (1 - P_\mu)/n}$.

At first glance this description and its accompanying formula may seem a bit daunting. As we examine the elements individually, though, you'll see that the process is really quite simple. Critical to this formula is the population proportion, or P_μ. Since this is precisely the value we're trying to estimate and, therefore, an unknown value, you'd be wise to ask, "How can we possibly move forward?" The answer is, "Very conservatively." Specifically, the solution statisticians have devised involves setting the value of the population proportion at 0.5 ($P_\mu = 0.5$). As a result, the second term (i.e., $1 - P_\mu$) is automatically set at 0.5 as well (i.e., $1 - 0.5 = 0.5$). Although it may seem that arbitrarily assigning a value for P_μ is a bit presumptuous, if you look a little further you'll see that this actually represents a very conservative solution.

In setting P_μ at 0.5, the product obtained by multiplying $P_\mu (1 - P_\mu)$ will always be 0.25. Believe it or not, this is the largest value this expression will ever attain. That is, if we were to set the population proportion (P_μ) at any other value, the product obtained in multiplying $P_\mu (1 - P_\mu)$ would always be smaller than

0.25. For example, suppose we set the population proportion at 0.75: In carrying out the expression 0.75 × 0.25, we get 0.1875. So in setting the population at 0.5, we're sure to obtain the maximum value for the expression $P_\mu(1 - P_\mu)$. In turn, we're ensuring that the width of the confidence interval we estimate will be as wide as possible. That's why this approach is seen as the most conservative way of resolving the dilemma posed by needing to include an unknown value when building this type of interval estimate.

The formula for creating a confidence interval on the basis of a sample proportion can be found in Formulae Alert 9.5. To better understand how you, as a social worker, might find the procedure useful, consider the following illustration. Suppose you're the student representative on the legislative committee of your state's chapter of the National Association of Social Workers (NASW). Suppose further that your state legislature is considering adopting a welfare reform package that social workers throughout the state oppose because they believe it would unfairly disadvantage single-parent households, most of whom are women.

FORMULAE ALERT 9.5

The formula for constructing a confidence interval based on a sample proportion is

$$ci = P_s \pm z\sqrt{P_\mu(1 - P_\mu)/n}$$

where: P_s = sample proportion
z = relevant z-score, given the alpha level selected
P_μ = population proportion, which is typically assigned a value of 0.5
n = sample size

Suppose a professional polling firm randomly interviewed 500 voters and found that 52% of them were in favor of a pending piece of controversial legislation. To be as accurate as possible, the firm would likely construct a confidence interval for this finding. Inserting the data into the formula presented above, they'd find the following:

$$ci = 0.52 \pm 1.96\sqrt{0.5\,(1 - 0.5)/500}$$

$$ci = 0.52 \pm 1.96\sqrt{0.25/500}$$

$$ci = 0.52 \pm 1.96\,(0.02236)$$

$$ci = 0.52 \pm 0.04$$

Their conclusion might read, "In a recently conducted survey of 500 voters, 52% said they were in favor of the legislation. The estimate is accurate to within ±4%."

Your committee has been actively lobbying for the bill's defeat, and to date your efforts have been successful. Yesterday, however, the results of a public opinion poll suggested "overwhelming public support for the bill." Specifically, the media reported that 52% of the 500 voters randomly polled said they were in favor of the bill. What is more, they cast the finding as constituting, "a public mandate to the legislature to pass the legislation." Finding this development disconcerting, the legislative committee called an emergency planning session. Knowing that you're

REPORTING DATA ASSOCIATED WITH INTERVAL ESTIMATES

There are a number of statistical elements involved in creating interval estimates, and each has its own symbol or abbreviation. Although many of these symbols and abbreviations are already familiar to you, we've summarized here the statistical characters you're likely to see and use in reporting interval estimates.

Mean	μ or $\overline{X}$
Standard deviation	SD, sd, S, or s
Standard error	SE
t-value	t
z-value	z
Confidence interval	ci
Proportion	P
alpha	α

When reporting the standard error of the mean, it is customary to report all the items the reader would need to build a confidence interval, including the sample size (n), the mean (μ or $\overline{X}$), and the standard deviation (SD). Here's an example of what you might find in a research article or professional report: "The 100 CPS social workers randomly surveyed exhibited a rather modest level of perceived locus of control, obtaining a mean score of 14 on a 20-point scale where higher scores reflect a greater sense of personal control ($SD = 5$, $SE = 0.98$)."

Likewise, reports that present confidence intervals are usually accompanied by data regarding the mean, the standard deviation, and the sample size. For example, you might encounter a statement like the following in a research article or professional report: "In an on the job satisfaction inventory, CPS social workers achieved a mean score of 83 ($SD = 16$, $n = 100$, $SE = 3.14$), and a 95% ci equal to 79.86 − 86.14."

Sometimes authors decide to leave the arithmetic to us, as evidenced in the statement below: "Current support for the social work licensing bill introduced in this legislative session is estimated at 38% (±3%)." Given these data, it's up to the reader to construct the ci involved, if desired. Note too, that the confidence level associated with this interval is not explicitly stated. In such cases, a 95% level of confidence is generally assumed.

When we report more than one confidence interval in a single report, we typically summarize these data in tabular format, as illustrated in Table 9.2.

currently enrolled in a statistics class, the other members of the committee asked your opinion of the findings reported. Does 52% of the vote represent an overwhelming majority? Does this figure warrant the label of a "public mandate"? What are the chances of the estimate being wrong?

In response, you decide to develop a 95% confidence interval based on the sample data reported. Doing so, you find that the proportion of voters in favor of the proposed welfare reform legislation is between 0.48 and 0.56. Said differently, between 48% and 56% of the state's voters are in favor of the welfare reform legislation currently being considered. Given this finding, what recommendations would you make to the committee? In particular, how should the committee respond to the recent media assertion of a "public mandate" supporting the bill's passage?

Interpreting Interval Estimates

In comparison to point estimates, interval estimates are a bit more difficult to produce, but safer to use, since they're more likely to capture the population value being estimated (Healey, 1996). As, Knoke and Bohrnstedt (1991, 1994) observe, though, a word of caution is in order when it comes to interpreting confidence intervals. In saying we're 95% **certain** that the population mean falls between two specified scores, we're "guesstimating," or inferring, the value of μ from the sample data, but we'll never know for certain if it falls within a given interval. What we're really saying in stating that we're 95% confident or certain, is that the interval or range of scores presented was determined using a strategy that produces correct estimates 95% of the time (Moore & McCabe, 1999). Another way of thinking about this is to see the interval as the result of using a procedure that guarantees that, in the long run, 95% of the intervals produced will contain μ (Knoke & Bohrnstedt, 1991). Although the distinction suggested here may seem subtle, it's an important one to keep in mind when reading or reporting data about confidence intervals.

TERMS TO KNOW

Alpha (α) (p. 157)
Central limit theorem (p. 152)
Certain (p. 168)
Confidence interval (ci) (p. 157)
Consistent estimator (p. 156)
Efficient estimator (p. 156)
Equal probability of selection methods (EPSEM) (p. 141)
Estimation procedures (p. 154)
Inferential statistics (p. 140)
Interval estimation (p. 157)
Parameters (p. 140)

Point estimation (p. 154)
Population (p. 139)
Probability (P) (p. 142)
Probability sample (p. 141)
Representative sample (p. 141)
Sample (p. 139)
Sampling distribution (μ) (p. 151)
Sampling error (p. 150)
Standard error of the mean ($\sigma_{\bar{x}}$) (p. 153)
Statistics (p. 140)
Unbiased estimator (p. 156)

REVIEW PROBLEMS

1. You are a case manager at a local agency that provides support for people recovering from alcohol addiction. The clients currently on your caseload have attained the following sobriety times (in months):

CLIENT	KRANTZ	HALL	MACK	JOHNS	HOSE	SIMMS	CAGE	JONES	CROSS	QUINN
Length of Time Sober (Months)	6	12	16	4	18	10	13	5	11	7

As part of the annual evaluation of the agency's effectiveness that will be presented in a proposal for continued funding through the community development block grant (CDBG), the director has asked each of the 15 case managers on staff to randomly select one of their current clients for review. You know that one of the characteristics that the funders look at when determining effectiveness of programs such as yours is the length of sobriety time achieved by the individuals receiving services. Determine the probabilities associated with each of the following scenarios:

The client you select will have at least 1 year of sobriety
The client you select will have at least 1½ years of sobriety
The client you select will have less than 1 year of sobriety
The client you select will have less than 6 months of sobriety

Now imagine the director has asked you to choose two clients for inclusion in the agency's review. What's the likelihood of your randomly selecting the two clients on your caseload who have the longest periods of sobriety (i.e., Mack and Hose)?

2. Throughout the chapter, we used several examples involving 95% confidence intervals. We also mentioned that there may be times when other confidence levels are more appropriate for the question you are posing. In Figure 9.11, we illustrate the areas under the normal curve defined in terms of a z-score associated with a 90% confidence interval. Finding the z-score for this illustration was a little trickier than the process we followed when we established z-scores for the 95% confidence interval (see Figure 9.9). Specifically, in looking at Table 8.1 (p. 132), you'll find there is no proportion or percentage that corresponds exactly with half of 90% or 45%. The closest we come to .4500 is .4495 and .4505. In resolving such dilemmas, to be on the safe side, statisticians tend to take the more conservative route. In this instance, this means targeting the larger of the two options, .4505. If you look carefully at Table 8.1, you'll see this point is associated with z-values of 1.6 (row) and .05 (column), yielding an overall z-score of 1.65, and its symmetrically placed counterpart is −1.65. This information is graphically depicted in Figure 9.11.

Following steps similar to those just illustrated, fill out the relevant information associated with a 99% confidence interval, in Figure 9.12.

3. Suppose you sampled 100 clients and found the mean attained sobriety time to be 10.2 months, with a standard deviation of 4.71. Construct a 99% confidence interval for the mean length of sobriety time achieved by these clients.

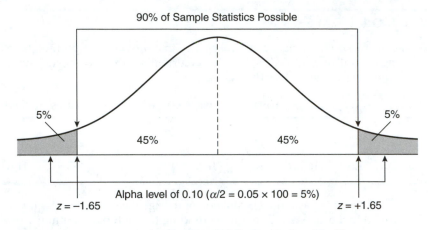

FIGURE 9.11   **Areas under the Normal Curve Defined in Terms of Percent and *z*-scores when Alpha (α) = 0.10**

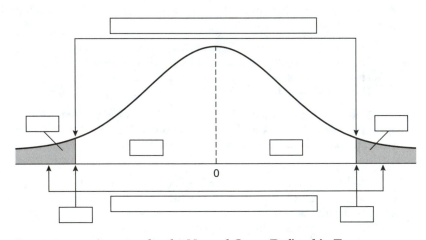
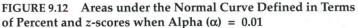

FIGURE 9.12   **Areas under the Normal Curve Defined in Terms of Percent and *z*-scores when Alpha (α) = 0.01**

REFERENCES

Glass, G. V., & Hopkins, K. D. (1984). *Statistical methods in education and psychology* (2nd ed.). Englewood Cliffs, NJ: Prentice-Hall.

Healey, J. F. (1996). *Statistics: A tool for social research* (4th ed.). Belmont, CA: Wadsworth.

Jaeger, R. M. (1983). *Statistics: A spectator sport.* Newbury Park, CA: Sage.

Kiess, H. O. (1996). *Statistical concepts for the behavioral sciences* (2nd ed.). Boston: Allyn & Bacon.

Knoke, D., & Bohrnstedt, G. (1991). *Basic social statistics.* Itasca, IL: F. E. Peacock.

Knoke, D., & Bohrnstedt, G. (1994). *Statistics for social data analysis* (3rd ed.). Itasca, IL: F. E. Peacock.

Moore, D., & McCabe, G. (1999). *Introduction to the practice of statistics* (3rd ed.). New York: W. H. Freeman.

Pyrczak, F. (1995). *Making sense of statistics: A conceptual overview.* Los Angeles: Pyrczak.

Sprinthall, R. C. (1994). *Basic statistical analysis* (4th ed.). Boston: Allyn & Bacon.

Vogt, W. P. (1993). *Dictionary of statistics and methodology: A nontechnical guide for the social sciences.* Newbury Park, CA: Sage.

Williams, F. (1986). *Reasoning with statistics: How to read quantitative research* (3rd ed.). New York: Holt, Rinehart and Winston.

CHAPTER TEN

HYPOTHESIS TESTING

The other main branch of inferential statistics consists of **hypothesis testing,** or what some refer to as **significance testing.** As with estimation procedures, hypothesis testing uses known sample statistics to make statements about unknown population parameters by way of a theoretical sampling distribution. Although estimation procedures allow us to make educated guesses about the values of selected population parameters, hypothesis testing provides a decision-making framework for determining whether an estimated value for a given population parameter is reasonable. Crucial to this decision-making process are two complementary, yet mutually exclusive statements about the predicted value of the targeted population parameter. These statements—more commonly known as hypotheses—are the focus of this chapter.

DEFINING THE RESEARCH AND STATISTICAL HYPOTHESES

At the foundation of most social work research endeavors is the desire to answer questions that are important to professionals in the field and the people we serve. For example, a social worker at a community mental health agency might be interested in knowing if an insight-oriented approach to treating depression in teenagers might produce more long-term positive effects than the cognitive-behavioral approach currently being used. Another may want to know if age negatively affects adult clients' receptivity to becoming involved in mental health treatment. The administrator of a child welfare unit may want to see if experience, as reflected by a specified minimum time in position, positively influences the rate of success achieved with respect to permanency plans.

The actual research question selected might be derived from the research findings reported by others in the literature or from those presented at professional conferences. Alternatively, the research question might be sparked by an interest in testing the assumptions or explanations associated with a given theory. Or the question may emanate from one's own practice observations and experiences. Regardless of the source of the query, once the research question is stated in terms of a tentative direction or solution, it becomes what's known as a research hypothesis.

Note: Alternative terms used to describe the research hypothesis within the literature include *experimental hypothesis, alternative hypothesis,* or *substantive hypothesis* (Weinbach & Grinnell, 1998).

In more specific terms, a **research hypothesis** (usually abbreviated as H_1) is a declarative sentence that states how two or more variables are believed to relate to, or differ from, one another. To illustrate, let's take the example questions just mentioned and reframe them into statements that describe the specific relationships we'd expect to find if we were to actually conduct a relevant study. In other words, let's convert these questions into research hypotheses.

- The proposed insight-oriented approach to treating teenagers diagnosed with depression will have longer-lasting positive effects than those achieved through the cognitive-behavioral approach currently being used.
- Older people will exhibit less receptiveness toward involvement in mental health services than those who are younger.
- Social workers with 2 or more years experience will exhibit higher success rates in permanency planning than social workers with less experience.

By clearly stipulating the specific relationships expected, the research hypothesis not only helps focus a study, but also helps identify which research design and measures to use. When we carry out a study, we use statistical analysis to see if the relationship(s) predicted by the research hypothesis occurred. For example, suppose we believe that males currently participating in an agency's adolescent substance abuse treatment program have greater difficulties with anger management than females in the program. To test this idea, we can randomly select a group consisting of male and female program participants and administer a standardized measure of anger control. If, in analyzing the data we find males and females both have a mean anger control score of 45 (on a 60-point scale), we could conclude that, at least for our sample, anger management scores do not appear to vary by gender.

Suppose, however, that the mean anger control score achieved by the young women sampled was 20, whereas the mean score obtained by the young men was 55. In contrast to our first example, these findings would clearly suggest there's a relationship between gender and anger management. However, rarely are patterns in sample data so definitive. Even when they are, though, we don't know what role, if any, sampling error or chance fluctuations may have played in producing the results observed. In fact, without additional information, we can't say anything about the likelihood of a similar pattern occurring within the population from which the sample was drawn. As with estimation, if we want to go beyond describing the sample data in hand and enter into the realm of statistical inference (i.e., generalize to the population from which the sample came), we need to gain access to the relevant theoretical sampling distribution involved. Our efforts to bridge the gap between these empirical and theoretical domains begin by calling on the logical opposite of the research hypothesis—an entity known as the statistical hypothesis, or null hypothesis.

Derived from the research hypothesis, the **null hypothesis** (abbreviated H_0 and pronounced "H-aught") states that, despite what the sample data suggest, *no real relationship or difference exists* among these variables in the population from which the sample is drawn. Return, for a moment, to the research hypothesis that asserts that experienced social workers will exhibit a higher rate of success with respect to their permanency planning endeavors than their less experienced counterparts. If we were to take the opposite stance, we'd maintain that experience, at least as it's operationalized here, is *not* related to the success rate achieved. That's precisely what the null hypothesis argues. More formally, the null hypothesis would state,

> There is no relationship between worker experience and permanency planning success rates.

This statement is expressed mathematically as follows:

$$H_0: \text{Parameter} = 0$$

Technically, the symbol associated with the population parameter you're inferring (e.g., χ^2 or ρ) would be inserted in place of the word *Parameter*.

As you consider this expression, notice how the null hypothesis not only *posits a relationship* that directly opposes the research hypothesis, but also introduces the population parameter into the equation. In doing these two things, null hypothesis transforms the context of our statement from what we expect to find within the sample data collected for a specific research effort, to the relationship expected to occur within the population from which the sample came. It is the null hypothesis, therefore, that opens the door to the theoretical sampling distributions that underlie the statistical findings we want to test and which constitute the heart of the probability theory. Before we get into the specifics of how this process works, though, let's look at some of the other important features of research and statistical hypotheses, and the relationship between them.

DIRECTIONALITY: WHICH WAY WILL THE DATA FLOW?

Given our person-in-environment focus, social workers are generally interested in doing research that helps us understand or explain the similarities and differences that occur among people as they interact with their social, psychological, and physical environments. What is it about some youngsters, for example, that makes them more resilient than others to the threat that an academic failure poses for their self-esteem? Does the "12-step" approach to treating addictions work equally well for men and women? Given such interests, you'll find that social work research generally uses two kinds of research hypotheses. One type, called a **nondirectional,** or **two-tailed, research hypothesis,** states that two variables are expected to relate to, or differ from, one another, but this hypothesis doesn't predict the direction this relationship will take.

For example, suppose a medical social worker believes that age and knowledge of HIV/AIDS risk factors are related, but doesn't have enough information to hypothesize which ages will score higher. Because she is unable to predict which scores on the age variable will be associated with which scores on the HIV/AIDS knowledge test, the direction of the relationship must remain unspecified. This is when a nondirectional, or two-tailed, hypothesis of association, such as the following, would be appropriate:

Age is related to knowledge of HIV/AIDS risk factors.

Similarly, another social worker may believe that clients participating in group treatment will express different levels of service satisfaction than those receiving individual treatment. Yet, he doesn't have sufficient information to say which approach is likely to yield higher (or lower) levels of satisfaction. Again, a nondirectional, or two-tailed, hypothesis of difference, such as the following, would work best:

Client satisfaction levels will differ according to the type of counseling received (group versus individual).

The second type of research hypothesis that is commonly used in social work research is the **directional,** or **one-tailed, hypothesis,** which states not only that two variables will relate to, or differ from, one another, but it also indicates the direction that this relationship is expected to take. For example, suppose after years of study and practice, you developed a new group approach for treating individuals with anorexia. To date, you've informally piloted the approach and obtained good short- and long-term results in the areas of weight gain and self-esteem. Now you'd like to formally test your approach by randomly assigning participants to two different treatment options: the new group treatment, and the treatment approach traditionally used within the agency.

After you obtain approval from the agency and from the human subjects committee, and, of course, the informed consent from a pool of potential participants, your study is ready to go. Take a moment to think about what you expect the study to reveal. Specifically, do you believe participants receiving your new treatment approach will do better, worse, or about the same as those who receive the agency's existing treatment? Given your preliminary findings, chances are you believe the two treatment groups will not only experience different outcomes, but you expect those who receive your new treatment approach will actually do better.

If this is so, then the following directional, or one-tailed, hypothesis of difference would be warranted:

> Clients participating in the new group treatment approach will exhibit higher weight gain and self-esteem scores at 3- and 6-month follow-up than those who receive the agency's existing intervention.

Shifting gears for a moment, imagine you're a social worker at a local rehabilitation hospital. Recently you've noticed that patients who are visited regularly by family and friends seem to have shorter hospital stays than those visited infrequently or not at all. Since data pertaining to visitors and length of stay are kept on all patients, you decide to examine this relationship more systematically. Given the pattern you've been observing, a directional, or one-tailed, hypothesis of association such as the following appears to be in order. Do you agree?

> The more frequently a patient receives visits from family and friends, the shorter the amount of time spent in the hospital.

Since applying the notion of directionality to the "tails" encompassed within a theoretical sampling distribution can get a bit tricky, we decided to illustrate this for you pictorially (see Figure 10.1).

THE NULL AS A RESEARCH HYPOTHESIS

While it may seem to contradict all that's been said on the topic thus far, it's important to point out that on rare occasions the question of interest to the researcher—and hence the foundation of the research hypothesis—is one that challenges the existence of any real relationship or difference between the variables under study. In these cases, the research and null hypotheses are one and the same. In social work research, such hypotheses generally are used to challenge false assumptions about the relationship that exists between two variables. Examples would include any research effort that seeks to dispel ageist, sexist, classist, racist, or heterosexist assumptions and beliefs. Can you think of a null research hypothesis you'd like to see tested?

As you process the idea of a null research hypothesis, don't let this exception cloud your thinking about statistical hypothesis testing. The hypothesis that's tested in statistical analysis is the null hypothesis. In positing no relationship or difference between the variables under study, the null hypothesis generally expresses the logical opposite of what the researcher believes is true at the onset of an investigation (i.e., the research hypothesis). As you'll see momentarily, the dichotomy established by keeping the null and research hypotheses distinct, yet complementary, in a logical sense, is important to the interpretive part of the hypothesis-testing process.

The terms *two-tailed,* or *nondirectional*, apply to hypotheses that state that there is a relationship or difference between the variables under study, and we're not certain what direction that relationship will take.

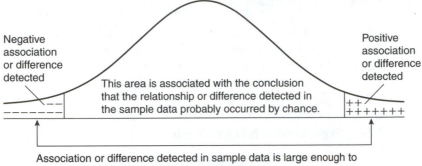

Negative association or difference detected

This area is associated with the conclusion that the relationship or difference detected in the sample data probably occurred by chance.

Positive association or difference detected

Association or difference detected in sample data is large enough to conclude it isn't likely to have occurred by chance.

The terms *one-tailed,* or *directional*, apply to hypotheses that state that there is a relationship or difference between two variables under study, and we're predicting the direction that relationship is expected to take. As indicated below, the predicted relationship can occur in two directions: a positive association or difference, or a negative association or difference.

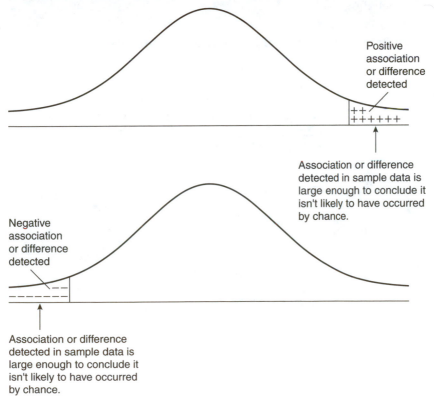

Positive association or difference detected

Association or difference detected in sample data is large enough to conclude it isn't likely to have occurred by chance.

Negative association or difference detected

Association or difference detected in sample data is large enough to conclude it isn't likely to have occurred by chance.

FIGURE 10.1   Directionality Applied to the Tails of a Theoretical Sampling Distribution

THE HYPOTHESIS-TESTING PROCESS

Although the specific procedures used to test a statistical hypothesis vary according to the question being addressed, the overall format tends to remain rather consistent. Figure 10.2 introduces a five-step model that can be helpful in organizing the generic aspects of the hypothesis-testing process. Let's take a moment to look at each step individually.

Step 1: State the Research Hypothesis

Recall that the research hypothesis is an unambiguous description of the association or difference the researcher expects to find between the variables under study. In a sense, it summarizes the researcher's perception of what is currently known about the phenomenon under investigation. The clarity and specificity used to describe the variables and relationships addressed within the research hypothesis should be such that these descriptions help guide us in the process of conceptualizing and operationalizing the variables as well as in selecting an appropriate research design.

Step 2: State the Null, or Statistical, Hypothesis

Although the exact form of the null hypothesis will vary according to the test we're conducting, it is always a statement of no real difference or relationship. When the focus is one of difference, the null hypothesis is actually arguing that any differences noted within the sample data are not prominent enough to support the conclusion that the scores being compared came from populations that truly differ from one another. That is, the differences observed in the sample statistics are likely to have occurred by chance.

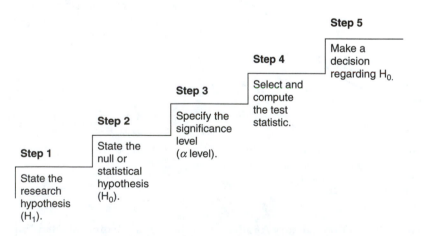

Step 5
Make a decision regarding H_0.

Step 4
Select and compute the test statistic.

Step 3
Specify the significance level (α level).

Step 2
State the null or statistical hypothesis (H_0).

Step 1
State the research hypothesis (H_1).

FIGURE 10.2 **Hypothesis Testing Conceptualized as a Five-Step Process**

In contrast, when the question is one of relationship, the null hypothesis asserts that any associations or correlations observed among the variables under study are not prominent enough to support the conclusion that they actually exist within the population from which the sample was drawn. In other words, the associations detected in the sample data may well have occurred by chance.

Remember, in statistical hypothesis testing it is the null hypothesis, not the research hypothesis, that is tested. In fact, the logic informing the process calls for us to assume the null hypothesis is true until the evidence gathered suggests otherwise. That is, we start out assuming that any difference or relationship detected within our sample data is not real, but merely a result of chance fluctuations. Given the focus on the null hypothesis, the conclusions drawn as a result of statistical hypothesis testing are always in reference to the null hypothesis (e.g., "Reject the null," or "Do not reject the null"). Decisions regarding the research hypothesis are made by default. That is, we substantiate the research hypothesis when we reject the null hypothesis, and, conversely, we reject the reasonableness of the research hypothesis when we retain the null hypothesis. In a convoluted way, this approach makes sense: In forcing us to look for the opposite of what we really expect or believe we'll find, the hypothesis-testing process helps diminish the human tendency of seeing only what we want to see (i.e., it provides some protection against the proverbial self-fulfilling prophecy).

Step 3: Specify the Significance Level

As with estimation procedures, hypothesis testing requires researchers to specify the risk they're willing to take of being wrong. Since the decision in hypothesis testing centers on the null hypothesis, the **significance level** (or **alpha level,** abbreviated as α level) selected actually indicates how big a risk the researcher is willing to take in *rejecting* the null hypothesis (the assertion there really is no relationship) when in fact the null hypothesis is true. In determining the value of the significance level, you'll want to think about the consequences of concluding that an association or difference exists, when in fact it doesn't. For example, if you were comparing the effectiveness of two different treatments, you'd need to ask yourself, What happens if I conclude that treatment A is better than treatment B, when the difference was really just a fluke caused by sampling error?

By convention, the significance level typically selected is 0.05. In choosing this level, the researcher is saying he or she is willing to erroneously reject a null hypothesis 5% of the time. Or, put another way, the researcher is willing to appropriately retain the null hypothesis 95% of the time. Of course when the stakes are high, more conservative significance levels are preferred (e.g., 0.025, 0.01, 0.001).

Frequently, the significance level, or α-level, selected is reported in terms of a lowercase *p*. It's likely you've encountered statements in the literature such as "This difference was significant at the $p < 0.05$ level." The *p* in this instance stands for probability, and the expression itself is really just a shorthand way of saying that the findings reported would be expected to occur by chance less than 5% of the time.

When we select a given significance level, we simultaneously establish the guidelines we'll follow when we make a decision to reject or retain the null hypothesis. Some refer to this process as developing the decision rule. Technically, a **decision rule** is a statement that specifies what values of a sample statistic will prompt you to retain or keep H_0, and what values will lead you to reject H_0. To understand how this works, it may be helpful to recall our previous discussion involving confidence intervals. In particular, remember how we used the α level we selected to find the z- or t-scores that corresponded with the level of confidence being sought? The essential elements of this process are summarized in Figure 10.3.

In hypothesis testing, we use the theoretical sampling distribution in a very similar way. As Figure 10.4 illustrates, though, it is the question we ask of the sampling distribution that's different. Specifically, rather than asking how closely the statistic (e.g., $\overline{X}$) approximates the value of the targeted population parameter (e.g., μ), we're asking how likely it is that we'd observe a difference or association greater than zero in our sample, if these relationships don't really occur within the population from which the sample data came. More simply, we're asking how likely is it that we would obtain sample evidence of a difference or association between the variables under study simply because of sampling error or chance.

In Figure 10.4, we use a z-curve and an α level of 0.05 to illustrate how select scores or critical values within the theoretical sampling distribution are used to separate areas of rejection (the 5% represented by the two shaded areas of the curve) from areas of acceptance (the remaining 95% region making up the center of the curve). Based on this representation, the specific decision rule would state that we'll reject the null hypothesis if we obtain a z-score that equals or falls beyond ±1.96, and that we'll continue to hold the null hypothesis as true (i.e., we won't reject the null) if the z-score obtained lies between the critical values of –1.96 and +1.96. The important point to remember here is that when you're conducting hypothesis testing—whether it involves a question of difference or association—the computation will yield a statistic that's translatable to a position on the relevant

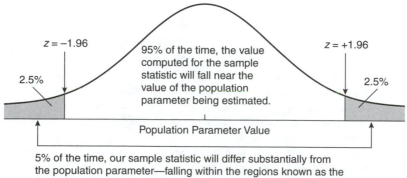

$z = -1.96$

95% of the time, the value computed for the sample statistic will fall near the value of the population parameter being estimated.

$z = +1.96$

2.5%

2.5%

Population Parameter Value

5% of the time, our sample statistic will differ substantially from the population parameter—falling within the regions known as the tails of the distribution (α level 0.05; $\alpha/2 = 0.025 \times 100 = 2.5\%$).

FIGURE 10.3   Areas under the Standard Normal Curve Associated with a 95% Confidence Interval

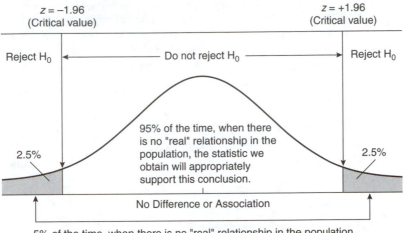

FIGURE 10.4   **Sampling Distribution of the z-Statistic Illustrating the Rejection Regions Established for a Two-Tailed Hypothesis Test with an α of 0.05**

sampling distribution and will convey the probability of the relationship being real, or simply due to chance (DiLeonardi & Curtis, 1988).

Step 4: Select and Compute the Test Statistic

As noted before, decisions about which statistical tests to use are determined in large part by the study questions that have been posed. Additional factors that need to be considered include the type of sampling procedure used and the assumptions being held about the data collected. In terms of sampling, for example, you'll need to specify the size of the sample as well as whether the data were gathered randomly. With respect to the data itself, you'll need to clarify the levels of measurement involved as well as any assumptions you're making about how the variables are distributed (e.g., normality). We address these and other topics to be considered in selecting the most appropriate statistical test in Chapter 15.

Given the availability of statistical software, it's unlikely you'll be computing statistical tests by hand. If you choose to do so, however, calculating the statistic is generally a matter of following the steps that comprise a given analytic procedure. The formulas associated with the inferential statistical procedures you'll most likely need as a professional social worker can be found in the Formulae Alert sections presented in this text. More often than not, though, you'll enter your sample data into a computer program such as SPSS or Excel, and ask the program to conduct the statistical analysis for you. What you'll obtain is the value of the statistic derived from your sample data along with the actual probability of obtaining this value by chance (e.g., $p = 0.0285$).

Note: It's not unusual for a statistical program to present a probability, or *p*-value, of 0.000. If interpreted literally, a probability of 0 would mean there's no way the statistical value reported occurred by chance. Although such definitiveness might be desirable, it's highly unlikely. In fact, the finding is likely an artifact of the program's reporting protocol. Specifically, most statistics programs are capable of calculating statistical values to a very precise level. SPSS, for instance, can display calculations up to 17 decimal places, whereas Excel can display up to 30 decimal places. This level of precision is lost, though, when the program's reporting protocol calls for the calculated value to be truncated (cut) to three or four decimal places. Therefore, if you obtain a *p*-value of 0.000, it's safe to assume that truncation has occurred. The convention is to replace the last zero reported by the computer with a 1 and conclude that the *p*-value was less than 0.001 (i.e., $p < 0.001$).

Step 5: Make a Decision Regarding H_0

The final step involves making a decision regarding H_0 and then, based on this decision, drawing conclusions for the study. In cases in which you've carried out the statistical test by hand, your decision regarding H_0 is made by comparing the calculated value of the statistic obtained with the critical value established for the type of test (i.e., one-tailed or two-tailed) and the α level selected (i.e., 0.05, 0.01, 0.025, or 0.10).

If your observed value falls within the acceptance region of the sampling distribution for the statistical test (e.g., t, z, r, or χ^2) and α level selected, then you would conclude that the sample association or difference observed is too likely to be a chance finding for you to be able to claim it's not due to sampling error or chance. In other words, you'd decide to continue to perceive H_0 as true (i.e., do not reject H_0). If however, the calculated value of the statistic falls within the rejection region(s) of the sampling distribution for the statistical test and α level chosen, you'd conclude that the sample association or difference observed is *not* likely to have occurred simply by chance. Consequently, you would reject H_0 and assert that a significant difference or association was found at the α level selected (e.g., $p \leq 0.05$).

When the statistical test is completed with the assistance of a computer, the decision regarding H_0 is made on the basis of the actual probability, or *p*-value calculated. Specifically, if the *p*-value obtained for the sample statistic is greater than the α level (i.e., significance level) selected, it's appropriate to conclude that the sample association or difference observed is not statistically significant, but likely to have occurred by chance. For example, suppose you obtained a *p*-value of 0.15 with a correlation between two variables. What this says is that you could, in 15 out of every 100 samples selected, obtain evidence of an association of this size by chance. Clearly this exceeds the conventional level of error ($\alpha = 0.05$, or 5%) typically set as acceptable for social work research. Consequently, you'd keep the null hypothesis and continue to believe that no real association exists between the variables examined in the population from which the sample was drawn.

To take another example, suppose you obtained a *p*-value of .03 with a *t*-test. This says that you could expect to get such a difference by chance in only 3 out of every 100 samples drawn. As a result, your decision would be to reject H_0 and assert that the differences observed support the belief that the sample statistics you're comparing represent different populations; that is, the difference is statistically significant.

SEPARATING STATISTICAL FROM SUBSTANTIVE SIGNIFICANCE

In day-to-day conversations, the term *significant* typically is viewed as synonymous with important or profound. In statistical parlance, however, the term *significant* is used to describe statistical test results that accompany a decision to reject H_0. More specifically, when we claim a finding is **statistically significant,** we're saying that the mathematical probability of the event occurring by chance (as indicated by the *p*-value obtained) is less than the rejection level we selected. Does this mean that a statistically significant finding is also substantively important? Not necessarily. The value or meaning of the association or difference observed is a matter the researcher must determine given its potential implications for social work practice.

As Weinbach and Grinnell (1998) note, all statistically significant relationships must be evaluated in light of the question, "So what?" (p. 88). For instance, suppose you found a statistically significant association between birth order and self-esteem. On closer inspection, though, you discover the relationship is so small or weak that the finding holds little meaning for social work practice. In such cases, although the relationship is indeed significant in a statistical sense, its practical value or worth remains questionable (i.e., so what?).

We also need to be cautious about the language we use to describe findings associated with statistical tests that result in our keeping H_0. Although the words *nonsignificant* or *not significant* may appropriately describe such findings, the term *insignificant* suggests something entirely different, doesn't it? Suppose, for example, you help introduce a program designed to strengthen problem-solving skills into a local school latchkey program. What if, after 2 months, you compare youngsters who were randomly assigned to the new program with those who received regular services, and you found no difference in the level of problem-solving skills exhibited? In other words, the new program exerted no statistically significant effect. Is this finding insignificant or inconsequential? Quite the contrary. Such a finding suggests that both programs function similarly when it comes to promoting problem-solving skills. Consequently, unless there are other appealing features associated with your new program (e.g., reduced costs, more updated content), it's unlikely the agency will continue it.

WHY DO WE FAIL TO REJECT, RATHER THAN ACCEPT, H_0?

You may be wondering why, if we reject H_0 when the test statistic falls into the specified rejection region, we don't simply accept H_0 when the test statistic falls within the acceptance region? In part, the answer lies in the logic that informs hypothesis testing. Specifically, the process involves testing an alternative hypothesis of difference or association against an assumption of no relationship. When we fail to reject the null, we also fail to find support for the research or alternative hypothesis being tested. Such a finding, however, does not rule out the possibility that other reasonable alternative hypotheses to the null exist. Nor does the finding rule out the possibility that we arrived at our decision to retain H_0 in error (i.e., by chance). Given these factors, it would seem that to use the lack of current evidence for an alternative explanation as proof that no relationship exists is premature, at best. A much more tentative solution is preferred. In other words, when we decide not to reject H_0, we continue to treat the null hypothesis as true until the evidence gathered suggests otherwise.

TYPE I AND TYPE II ERRORS

In essence, hypothesis testing provides a structure for making decisions regarding the null hypothesis (H_0). Based in probability theory, the process remains vulnerable to the influences of chance or sampling error. Consequently, a degree of uncertainty always characterizes the decisions we make about H_0. As the data presented in Table 10.1 illustrate, there are two kinds of errors one can make when testing H_0 for Type I errors and Type II errors. A **Type I error** occurs when a researcher rejects the null hypothesis and concludes that the association or difference observed within the sample data also exists in the population from which the sample was drawn, when in reality it does *not* exist in the population. Sometimes referred to as a false positive, a Type I error can be thought of as seeing too much in the data (Sprinthall, 1994).

The risk of making a Type I error is actually defined in terms of the alpha level selected. Consequently, a researcher can easily increase or decrease the risk of making this kind of error by appropriately adjusting the α level involved. As noted earlier, the conventional α level set for most social work research is 0.05. When the

TABLE 10.1   Hypothesis-Testing Decision Table

Given the sample data, the researcher decides to . . .

In the population, H_0 actually is . . .	NOT REJECT H_0	REJECT H_0
True	Correct decision made	Type *I*, or α, error Seeing too much in the data
False	Type II or β error Not seeing enough in the data	Correct decision made

stakes are high, though, it's both ethical and wise to reduce the probability of a Type I error by selecting a smaller α level. For example, suppose your agency is planning to use the outcome of a study comparing two treatment strategies to determine which service approach it will continue to offer clients. Given the implications of such a decision for clients and workers alike, the agency wants to be especially cautious to avoid concluding there is a significant difference between the two treatment approaches, when a significant difference doesn't really exist. One way of limiting the likelihood of obtaining such a chance finding is to choose an α level that's more conservative than the conventional 0.05. By setting the α level at 0.01, for example, the agency could reduce the risk of erroneously rejecting the null hypothesis from 5 times out of 100 to 1 in 100. This phenomenon is illustrated in Figure 10.5. As you examine the distributions presented in Figure 10.5, notice how the shaded rejection regions shrink, while the area of acceptance expands, when the α level is changed from 0.05 to 0.01.

In contrast, suppose you are piloting a new treatment to see if the outcomes are promising enough to warrant more rigorous study. The consequences of finding a significant effect at this stage, if there really isn't one, are not truly worrisome, so an α level of 0.10 will probably suffice.

A **Type II error** occurs when there *is* a real association or difference between variables in the population from which the sample is drawn, but given the results of your statistical analysis, you decide to stick with the null. You might want to think of a Type II error as not seeing enough in the data (Sprinthall, 1994). It's important because, whenever a Type II error occurs, we're essentially tossing aside a perfectly sound idea about how select variables are related.

The risk or probability of making a Type II error is known as beta (β). Whereas the probability of making a Type I error is quickly ascertained and easily adjusted through the α level selected, determining and altering the probability of a Type II error is a tad more complicated (Craft, 1990). First of all, we find that the actual value of β is difficult to obtain because it requires a reasonable awareness, or guesstimate, of the very population characteristic we're trying to estimate. Consequently, we find ourselves turning to the logical and probabilistic complement of β, which is referred to as statistical power $(1 - \beta)$. Specifically, **statistical power** refers to the probability of the test rejecting H_0, when H_0 should be rejected—that is, when a real difference or association between the variables under study exists. Because the value for power is derived from β, this value too is difficult to calculate precisely. Fortunately, though, there are several ways we can work toward increasing the power of a statistic. Before addressing these strategies, let's take a moment to consider power as an inherent characteristic of any statistical test.

Recall from our earlier discussions that not all statistics are created equal. The mean, you'll remember, is considered a better measure of central tendency than the mode or the median. In part, this assessment is based on the fact that the mean uses all of the values contained within the data set. As a result, it is suggested that when the level of measurement and the characteristics of the distribution involved warrant it, the mean is the preferred indicator of central tendency because it constitutes the more informative, precise measure.

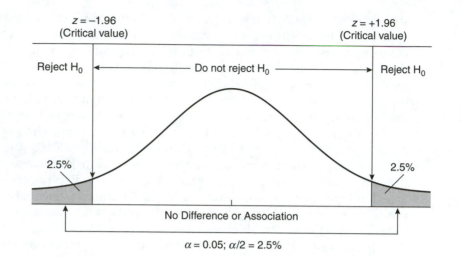

$z = -1.96$
(Critical value)

$z = +1.96$
(Critical value)

Reject H_0 ← ────────── Do not reject H_0 ────────── → Reject H_0

2.5%

2.5%

No Difference or Association

$\alpha = 0.05;\ \alpha/2 = 2.5\%$

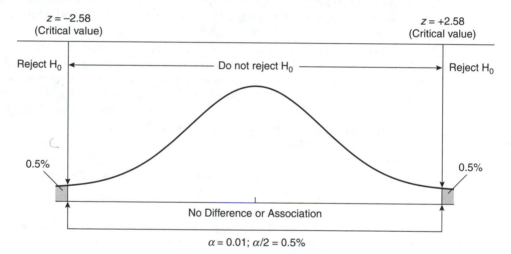

$z = -2.58$
(Critical value)

$z = +2.58$
(Critical value)

Reject H_0 ← ────────── Do not reject H_0 ────────── → Reject H_0

0.5%

0.5%

No Difference or Association

$\alpha = 0.01;\ \alpha/2 = 0.5\%$

FIGURE 10.5   Rejection and Acceptance Regions for α-Levels of 0.05 and 0.01

This same logic applies to the idea of statistical power. Tests that use all the data available (i.e., all the scores) tend to yield more precise results than those relying on group frequencies, or the rank values assigned to cases (Weinbach & Grinnell, 1998). Consequently, all other things being equal, you'll find that some statistical tests are inherently more powerful than others. As discussed later (in Chapter 15) when you go about the task of selecting the statistical tests for your study, you'll want to choose the most powerful tests available, given the study questions and type of data involved.

Beyond the statistical test itself, there are several factors that can influence a test's ability or power to detect significant differences or associations within a data set, including:

1. **Effect size**—defined as the strength of the association or magnitude of the difference that actually exists among variables in the population
2. Degree of variability exhibited by the targeted variables in the population
3. Size of the sample
4. α level
5. Directionality of the test—use of either a one-tailed test or a two-tailed test

Let's take a closer look at how each of these items is related to the potential power of a statistical test. The first item, effect size, refers to the strength or magnitude of the relationship involved. Effect size emphasizes that larger differences and stronger associations are easier to detect. Consequently, strong relationships are more apt to be detected, even when less powerful statistical tests are used. The second factor, the degree of variability existing within targeted variables, is important because the more variation there is among scores, the greater the likelihood of drawing samples that capture a preponderance of high or low values—that is, the greater the probability of sampling error. Both the size of the relationship and the variability of scores observed are characteristics of the population we're seeking to learn more about. Thus, although it's important to understand how these two factors relate to this notion of power, these are not factors that a researcher can or wants to influence, or change.

The third factor, sample size, also impacts statistical power through its effect on sampling error. Specifically, larger samples are less susceptible to the influence of sampling error. Along with independent replication of a study, increasing the size of the sample is one of the most common strategies researchers use to increase the power of an analytic procedure and, thereby, minimize the probability of Type II error. Although the topic is beyond the scope of this text, you should know that many advanced statistics texts go so far as to specify the actual sample size needed for specific tests to achieve their optimal levels of power.

From a probability standpoint, the relationship between Type I and Type II error is not mathematically straightforward. The probability of Type I error is α, whereas the probability of Type II error is β power ($1 - \beta$ not $1 - \alpha$). Nevertheless, the two are inversely affected by our fourth factor, the α level selected. To see this more clearly, it might be helpful to return for a moment to Figure 10.5. Notice how reducing the α level from 0.05 to 0.01 not only decreases the likelihood of committing a Type I error by increasing the acceptance region, but it also increases the chances of committing a Type II error by simultaneously reducing the size of the rejection region. Given this relationship, another way of increasing the power of a statistic (i.e., reducing the probability of a Type II error) is to increase the value of the α level you select (e.g., to move from an α level of 0.01 to one of 0.05).

The last factor in our list, the directionality of the test, affects power in a very practical way, as well. As Figure 10.6 depicts, a one-tailed test with an α level of

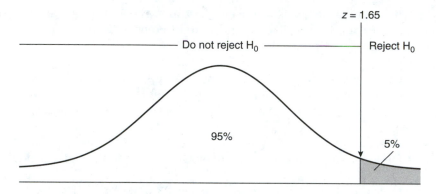

FIGURE 10.6   Rejection and Acceptance Regions for a One-Tailed Hypothesis with α = 0.05

0.05 possesses a larger rejection region to the right of the mean, compared to the rejection regions specified by the two-tailed tests in Figure 10.5, where α levels of both 0.05 and 0.01 are used. When it's appropriate, therefore, to specify the direction of the relationship you're predicting in your research hypothesis, then do so—this will help increase the power of the statistical test you use.

Note that neither Type I nor Type II error is inherently more desirable than the other. The process of selecting an α level represents one area where the researcher attempts to balance the influence of these two types of error. As noted earlier, whether you decide to risk missing a relationship or to risk substantiating one that doesn't exist is based on your professional judgment regarding the value and importance you place on the anticipated consequences associated with each error.

To summarize, all inferential tests—whether they involve estimating the value of a parameter or testing a hypothesis—are based in probability theory. As a result, there's always a chance our findings will be wrong. This fact may seem frustrating at first, but don't get discouraged. Although we may be wrong in our assessments, probability theory allows us to actually convey to our readers the chances that we're wrong. More importantly, in underscoring the probabilistic nature of research findings, inferential statistics serve to reinforce the scientific perspective, which asserts that all knowledge is tentative, and, therefore, to some degree, inquiry must always remain open. In other words, our social work knowledge base represents the best we know—for now.

T E R M S   T O   K N O W

Alpha level (p. 179)
Decision rule (p. 180)
Directional hypothesis (p. 175)
Effect size (p. 187)

Hypothesis testing (p. 172)
Non-directional hypothesis (p. 175)
Null hypothesis (p. 174)
One-tailed hypothesis (p. 175)

Research hypothesis (p. 173)
Significance level (p. 179)
Significance testing (p. 172)
Statistically significant (p. 183)

Statistical power (p. 185)
Two-tailed hypothesis (p. 175)
Type I error (p. 184)
Type II error (p. 185)

REVIEW PROBLEMS

1. Suppose you're evaluating the relationship between a recently initiated employee policy involving flexible hours, and a marked decline in the number of successful case outcomes reported for the last quarter. State your null and research hypotheses. Discuss the factors you'd consider in choosing an appropriate α level.

2. Suppose you are testing two treatment strategies in an effort to determine which is more effective in reducing anxiety. State your statistical (null) and research hypotheses. Assuming the difference observed is large enough to warrant your rejecting H_0 at an α level of 0.05, what's the probability of your committing a Type II error? (Hint: Can you commit a Type II error when you reject the null?)

3. In its mathematical form, the statistical hypothesis specifies a numerical value for a parameter. Therefore, which of the following constitute statistical hypotheses?

   a. $r = 0$
   b. $s = 15$
   c. $\mu = 8$
   d. $\overline{X} = 95$
   e. $\sigma = 4.3$

REFERENCES

Craft, J. L. (1990). *Statistics and data analysis for social workers.* Itasca, IL: Peacock.
DiLeonardi, J., & Curtis, P. (1988). *What to do when the numbers are in: A user's guide to statistical data analysis in the human services.* Chicago: Nelson-Hall.
Sprinthall, R. C. (1994). *Basic statistical analysis* (4th ed.). Boston: Allyn & Bacon.
Weinbach, R. W., & Grinnell, R. M. (1998). *Statistics for social workers* (4th ed.). New York: Longman.

CHAPTER ELEVEN

BIVARIATE ANALYSIS

THE DIFFERENCE BETWEEN UNIVARIATE
AND BIVARIATE ANALYSES

The frequency distributions discussed in Chapter 4 allow the social work researcher to examine one variable at a time—that's why it is also known as **univariate analysis.** Why look at only one variable at a time? Doing so allows us to

- Get a quick count of the number of research subjects
- Assist in cleaning or editing the data
- Understand who has been included or excluded
- Examine the range of values or scores
- Determine the mean, median, and standard deviation

If we reexamine some of the data from Table 4.8, shown here in Table 11.1, we can tell right away that very few of those reporting their starting salaries were making more than $40,000, and most were making between $25,000 and $35,000. No one was making more than $55,000. Perhaps if we had found a salary of $250,000, we might have recognized it as a data entry error when $25,000 should have been recorded. By looking at the high and low values (the range), sometimes errors can be detected. We may even go to greater lengths to verify each entry—for example, by confirming that there are 18 salaries in the $25,000 to $29,999 range.

Once the researcher is satisfied that the data appear to be reasonably accurate, then she or he typically examines the descriptive statistics—the mean, the median, the standard deviation, and so forth. This is the most elementary level of analysis. Unfortunately, this is also where many social workers stop. The analogy here would be like going to a nice restaurant, spreading a fine linen napkin across your lap, taking a sip of the sparkling water with a slice of lemon in it, a taste of the hot bread the waiter brings to the table, and then announcing you are full and ready to go home. The descriptive statistics discussed in the previous chapters merely offer a quick summary of the data, just as you might say about another restaurant, "The Bikers' Den? Oh yes, I've eaten there—worst meal I've ever had." As a rule of thumb, when more information can be had, researchers want it. Regarding lunch at the Bikers' Den, we don't know whether the meal was deliber-

TABLE 11.1   Grouped, Cumulative Frequency Distribution: Starting Salaries for First, Full-Time Social Work Positions Obtained by MSW Alumni

STARTING SALARY (X)	FREQUENCY (f)	CUMULATIVE PERCENT (%)
$20,000 to $24,999	6	12
25,000 to 29,999	18	49
30,000 to 34,999	14	78
35,000 to 39,999	7	92
40,000 to 44,999	3	98
45,000 to 49,999	0	48
50,000 to 54,999	1	100
	N = 49	

ately prepared to be bad, if it was ruined accidentally, whether good meals are normally expected, if the chef was incompetent, or had just smoked too much of an illegal plant. If it were important to us to explore this matter further, we would want to create and test hypotheses.

Although some research questions, such as "What is the average age of our clients?" can be answered with univariate analysis, descriptive statistics are severely limited in the explanations they can provide. Often our questions involve more than just one variable. For example, we may want to know if African American males are underrepresented in the younger client groups—answering this query requires us to have data on both age and race. **Bivariate analysis,** which involves examining a dependent variable using an independent variable, such as race or gender, allows researchers to go beyond mere description of the variables. Bivariate analysis can be used to test for differences between groups and to check for relationships between two variables. This chapter presents information on one particular type of bivariate analysis, the chi-square (χ^2). Bivariate analysis with *t*-tests and ANOVA will be discussed in Chapter 13.

STARTING A BIVARIATE ANALYSIS

Assuming the data in Table 11.1 came from a real sample of MSW social workers starting their first professional positions, what hypothesis involving an additional variable might interest you?

Here are two that we thought of:

Are the starting salaries for males significantly higher than those for females?

Are the starting salaries for whites significantly higher than those for persons of color?

The first hypothesis requires that we employ gender as an independent variable, whereas the second uses race to understand our data. For reasons that we'll explain later, let's first simplify our table so that we have three salary categories.

Collapsing categories is the term used when a researcher reduces the number of categories (e.g., seven income groupings in Table 6.1). In Table 11.2, we expand the $4,999 income brackets we used in Table 11.1 to increments of $9,999. Thus, the two categories $20,000 to $24,999, and $25,000 to $29,999 become the single category $20,000 to $29,999. Most statistical software programs allow for easy conversion or recoding of data in this way.

Table 11.3 shows the same data when we examine them by the independent variable of gender. If you look carefully at these data, you can immediately detect some differences in salaries by gender. Note that the females are bunched in the lowest category, whereas the men are clustered in the middle category. This pattern is more conspicuous when the percentages are viewed (see Table 11.4). We observe that 70% of the women but only 23% of the men are in the $20,000 to $29,999 range, whereas 64% of the men but only 26% of the women are in the second-highest salary category. Men appear to be earning higher salaries. The issue we want to consider, however, is whether this is a statistically significant difference. Would another sample from the same population produce the same results? Is it likely these findings occurred by chance?

When we analyze data, our major concern is whether a particular pattern could have been produced by chance (as in a card game when you are dealt a terrible hand) or whether the pattern is real—meaning that it is likely to be found again in a second or third sample because that's the way the data exist in reality. In other words, statistical significance means that the results or the findings were not likely to have been a fluke, but represent real differences in, for instance, the salaries between men and women.

When the dependent variable exists as categorical data (as in Tables 11.3 and 11.4), and the researcher wants to analyze it with a nominal (or categorical) independent variable (e.g., gender), the appropriate statistic to use is **chi-square.** Chi-square is a statistical procedure that provides a statistical test of association between categorical variables. That is, chi-square is used to determine whether the

TABLE 11.2   Grouped Starting Salaries for First, Full-Time Social Work Jobs Obtained by MSW Alumni (Categories Collapsed)

STARTING SALARY (X)	FREQUENCY (f)
$20,000 to 29,999	24
30,000 to 39,999	21
40,000 to 54,999	4
	N = 49

TABLE 11.3   Grouped Starting Salaries for First
Full-Time Social Work Jobs Obtained by MSW
Alumni, by Gender

	FREQUENCY	FREQUENCY
STARTING SALARY (X)	*Female*	*Male*
$20,000 to 29,999	19	5
30,000 to 39,999	7	14
40,000 to 54,999	1	3
	N = 27	N = 22

TABLE 11.4   Grouped Starting Salaries for First Full-Time
Social Work Jobs Obtained by MSW Alumni, by Gender

	FEMALE		MALE	
STARTING SALARY (X)	N	%	N	%
$20,000 to 29,999	19	70	5	23
30,000 to 39,999	7	26	14	64
40,000 to 54,999	1	4	3	13
	N = 27		N = 22	

proportion of persons with some characteristic or trait is the same for one group (e.g., men) as for another group (e.g., women). If the proportions are quite similar, chi-square will be small and insignificant. When there is an association between variables (suppose e.g., females are more likely to have a certain attitude than males), then chi-square will be larger and significant.

Not only is chi-square used to test for association or independence when one variable is independent of another, but chi-square is also sometimes also used to test for what is known as a **goodness of fit**. In this case, the chi-square procedure is used to determine how well the proportions obtained from a sample compare with the known characteristics found in the population. For instance, assume females comprise 62% of all the clients in a certain outpatient clinic. A recent client satisfaction survey found that 48% of the sample was female. A chi-square in this case would help the researcher determine whether to reject or retain the null hypothesis by indicating whether the sample is significantly different from the larger population.

Chi-square is an extremely popular procedure because it requires measurement of variables at only the nominal level. Also, it is appropriate to use chi-square with ordinal data groupings (e.g., highly motivated, moderately motivated, and low motivated clients). However, chi-square cannot be used with interval-level data unless categories are created.

RECODING WITH SPSS

To recode means to give a different value. Assume the data are already in the computer and the salary categories were originally coded this way:

$20,000 to $24,999 = 1
$25,000 to $29,999 = 2
$30,000 to $34,999 = 3
$35,000 to $39,999 = 4
$40,000 to $44,999 = 5
$50,000 to $54,999 = 6

The researcher could merge categories together by following these steps:

Step 1: Select TRANSFORM from the toolbar. This creates a pop-up menu.

Step 2: Select RECODE from the menu.

Step 3: Choose whether you want to change the original data into new values (by selecting INTO SAME VARIABLES, or preserve the old data while creating a new variable (INTO DIFFERENT VARIABLES). Often it is better to simply create a new variable. However, we are going to select INTO THE SAME VARIABLES for this demonstration.

Step 4: From the list of all variables in your study, indicate which variable you want to recode. Highlight it, and move it to the small window labeled "numeric variables."

Step 5: Indicate the old values you want to rename. Since we want to merge categories, we're going to indicate that we want 2 to become 1. This combines the data from the old categories 1 and 2 into the single category of $20,000 to $29,999. Similarly, we indicate that the value of 4 is to become the value of 3 and that the value of 6 becomes the value of 5.

Step 6: After recording both of these old and new values, select the ADD button.

Step 7: When finished indicating all of the old and new values, press the CONTINUE and then the OK buttons. The statistical program automatically transforms the data producing only the three values of 1, 3, and 5, which correspond to the salary categories shown in Table 11.4.

COMPUTER APPLICATION: COMPUTING CHI-SQUARE

To use SPSS to determine if there are statistically significant differences in salaries (the dependent variable) by gender (the independent variable), first enter the data into the computer. Then choose STATISTICS from the menu, then SUMMARIZE, and then CROSSTABS. In the CROSSTABS dialog box, select from the list of variables two that are of immediate interest. Assign one to be the row variable and one to be the column variable. It doesn't really matter which one goes where, although if you are going to be calculating a lot of chi-squares, it is a good practice to get in the habit of making a rule for yourself, such as always placing the independent variable in the row position and the dependent variable in the column position. That's really all you need to do, although there are other software options you can choose.

In Figure 11.1, you can see that the SPSS CROSSTABS procedure creates boxes, called cells. For reasons that will be explained later, we want to simplify our earlier example by using only two salary categories. Because we have categorical data, not actual salaries, an individual with a salary of $23,000 and one with a salary of $28,560 would both be placed in the same grouping. Those with salaries of $33,000 or $40,000 are assigned to the second category. What's important in chi-square is that there are clear and discrete categories.

In Figure 11.1, you can see that the SPSS software calculated the percentages of males and females across the rows. There are other options, such as computing percentages down the columns. (For example, the 19 females in the first salary category represent 79% of all those persons in the lowest salary category. To simplify our presentation of this material, we're not showing those percentages.)

The results of the chi-square cross-tabulation are displayed in Figure 11.2. The SPSS program uses a formula that we'll demonstrate later in this chapter to estimate how many persons could be expected in each cell. In this example, the probability statement is located in the column labeled "Asymp. Sig. (Two-Sided)". The information presented in Figure 11.2 indicates that the probability that women fell in the lowest salary category by chance alone was approximately 1 time in 1,000 (.001)—which indicates that there are significant differences between males and females in their first-year salaries. Another way of saying this is that we would identify this pattern by *accident* only once in 1,000 samples. The vast majority of the time (999 out of 1,000 times), we would expect to find this pattern in which male social workers starting their first jobs *do* make more money than women MSWs entering their first jobs. The salaries paid do not seem to be independent of gender, but rather dependent on gender.

FIGURE 11.1   Cross-Tabulation of Salary by Gender

GENDER		STARTING MSW SALARIES		
		$20,000 to $29,999	*$30,000 or more*	TOTAL
Female	Count	19	8	27
	Expected count	13.2	13.8	27.0
	% within gender	70.4%	29.6%	100.0%
Male	Count	5	17	22
	Expected count	10.8	11.2	22.0
	% within gender	22.7%	77.3%	100.0%
Total	Count	24	25	49
	Expected count	24.0	25.0	49.0
	% within gender	49.0%	51.0%	100.0%

FIGURE 11.2   Chi-Square Results

	VALUE	df	ASYMP. SIG. (TWO-SIDED)
Pearson chi-square	11.011[a]	1	.001
Number of valid cases (N)	49		

[a]0 cells (.0%) have an expected count of less than 5. The minimum expected count is 10.78.

Note: The abbreviation *Asymp. Sig.* stands for asymptotic significance, and simply means that the significance is based on the assumption of a normal curve, where the ends, or tails, extend toward infinity in both directions and never touch the horizontal axis. The critical region is thus found on both ends of the sampling distribution.

As noted previously, by generally accepted convention, statistical significance is usually set at $p < .05$. This notation means that the researcher has accepted the possibility of chance explaining the obtained results 5 or fewer times per 100 repetitions of the study. Findings that could occur more often would not be called significant. For instance, if a probability of .17 had been produced, this would mean that chance alone could have produced the differences between the groups 17 out of 100 times.

Researchers want to minimize the role of chance in explaining their results. When it is especially important that results be trustworthy, investigators might want a $p < .01$ or even $p < .001$. The more stringent criterion might be adopted if there is a risk that the intervention has some unwanted side effects. The standard of $p < .05$ might also be lowered to $p < .10$ on occasion when the investigator has a small sample in an exploratory study.

The simplest **cross-tabulation,** or chi-square, table—also known as a **contingency table**—is a 2 by 2 (2 × 2) table, which means there are two variables, each having two response options, or subcategories. A 2 × 2 cross-tabulation will always produce four cells. In contrast, Table 11.3 with its three salary categories produces a 2 × 3 cross-tabulation with six cells. Gender is one variable with two attributes (male and female), and the variable of starting salary has three **attributes,** or subcategories.

With chi-square, the researcher has enormous flexibility, and there is no limit on the number of categories in a given contingency table. It is possible to have a 4 × 4, 2 × 8, 3 × 6, or even a 7 × 10 cross-tabulation. However, there are some practical constraints. For one, too many cells can make it difficult to identify patterns and to summarize the data beyond a dismissive pronouncement of not significant or significant differences.

A second problem associated with having too many cells is that the chi-square statistic isn't accurate when more than 20% of the cells have an **expected frequency** of 5 or less. This is something you have to keep in mind if you are calculating chi-square manually (see Formulae Alert 11.1). However, if you use a software program such as SPSS, the computer will inform you of the number of cells with an expected count of less than 5. When this problem arises and you have a variable with many categories, one option is to collapse cells so that there are fewer categories. Recall that Table 11.1 initially had seven categories of income, but these were collapsed into three—now you know why.

When the 49 MSW starting salaries are spread across three salary categories, as in Figure 11.3, two of the six cells have expected frequencies of less than 5— that's because there are only one female and three males in the highest salary category. To calculate the expected frequencies, the software has distributed the four persons in the high-salary group based on the column totals. So the four individuals are proportionately distributed between the males and females. Had there been 15 or 20 persons in that $40,000-and-higher income category, then we would not have the problem with low expected frequencies. But since the computer informs us that 33.3% of the cells have expected counts of 5 or less, we know that the significance level of .004 is not meaningful and should not be taken as an accurate reading. (Note that the underlying assumption of chi-square is that there is no difference in the proportionate distribution of the variables.)

What do we do now? One option would be to increase the size of our sample. However, because the proportion of very high income earners is so low (8.2%), even doubling the number of respondents to 98 would not resolve the problem.

FIGURE 11.3   Cross-Tabulation of Salary by Gender When More Than 20% of Cells Have an Expected Frequency of Less Than 5

GENDER		STARTING MSW SALARIES			
		$20,000 to $29,999	$30,000 or more	$40,000 or more	TOTAL
Female	Count	19	7	1	27
	Expected count	13.2	11.6	2.2	27.0
	% within gender	70.4%	25.9%	3.7%	100.0%
Male	Count	5	14	3	22
	Expected count	10.8	9.4	1.8	22.0
	% within gender	22.7%	63.6%	13.6%	100.0%
Total	Count	24	21	4	49
	Expected count	24.0	21.0	4.0	49.0
	% within gender	49.0%	42.9%	8.2%	100.0%

	VALUE	df	ASYMP. SIG. (TWO-SIDED)
Pearson chi-square	11.105[a]	2	.004
Number of valid cases	49		

[a] Two cells (33.3%) have expected count less than 5. The minimum expected count is 1.80.

FORMULAE ALERT 11.1: CALCULATING CHI-SQUARE MANUALLY

Chi-square is one of the few statistical procedures that can be easily computed by hand. It's a very logical process that will help you to understand how expected frequencies are computed. Let's start with the conceptual model of a 2 × 2 table.

a	b	r_1
c	d	r_2
c_1	c_2	N

In this model, a, b, c, and d represent the observed data in a 2 × 2 table; c_1 and c_2 are the two column totals, and r_1 and r_2 are the two row totals. The row and column totals are sometimes referred to as the **marginals.** As a first step, the expected frequencies for each of the four cells must be computed. We do this by multiplying the column totals by the row totals, and then dividing by the grand total (N).

Using the data from Figure 11.1, we calculate the expected frequency for cell a by multiplying 27 (c_1) by 24 (r_1) and dividing that product, 648, by 49 (N). This produces a quotient of 13.2. The rest of the expected frequencies are calculated in a similar manner:

Expected frequency for b = 22 times 24 divided by 49 = 10.8
Expected frequency for c = 27 times 25 divided by 49 = 13.8
Expected frequency for d = 22 times 25 divided by 49 = 11.2

a	b	r_1
19 (o)	5 (o)	24
13.2 (e)	10.8 (e)	
c	d	r_2
8 (o)	17 (o)	25
13.8 (e)	11.2 (e)	
c_1	c_2	N
27	22	49

The second step is to subtract the expected frequencies from the observed frequencies:

Cell a: 19 (observed) minus 13.2 (expected) = 5.8
Cell b: 5 (observed) minus 10.8 (expected) = −5.8
Cell c: 8 (observed) minus 13.8 (expected) = −5.8
Cell d: 17 (observed) minus 11.2 (expected) = 5.8

FORMULAE ALERT 11.1: *Continued*

The third step is to square the values obtained in the second step, and then divide those products by their corresponding expected frequency. Thus, $(5.8)^2 = 33.64$, and

Cell a: 33.64 divided by 13.2 = 2.55
Cell b: 33.64 divided by 10.8 = 3.11
Cell c: 33.64 divided by 13.8 = 2.43
Cell d: 33.64 divided by 11.2 = 3.00

The fourth step is to sum these four values:

2.55 (cell a) + 3.11 (cell b) + 2.43 (cell c) + 3.00 (cell d) = 11.09

The sum 11.09 is the actual chi-square value. This number doesn't have a lot of meaning unless you have access to a table of chi-square values called critical values. When the chi-square is larger than the critical value, then the findings are statistically significant.

For a 2 × 2 table, the critical value is 3.84 for an alpha level (significance level) of .05, 6.64 for an alpha level of .01, and 10.83 for an alpha level of .001. Because the chi-square we obtained exceeded all of these critical values, we can say that our findings are statistically significant at .001. Had we obtained a small chi-square of, say, 2.25, then our findings would not have been significant even at .05. Had our value been 4.77, then it would have been significant at .05 but not at the more stringent .01.

The formula for computing chi-square manually is as follows:

$$X^2 = \sum \frac{(F_o - F_e)^2}{F_e}$$

where X^2 = chi-square value
F_o = observed frequencies
F_e = expected frequencies
$\sum$ = sum of

Chi-square can also be computed on a pocket calculator using the following formula:

$$X^2 = \frac{N(bc - ad)^2}{(a + b)(r + c)(b + d)(c + d)}$$

where $a, b, c,$ and d = observed frequencies in the four cells
r = row total
c = column total
N = total observed frequencies

(continued)

FORMULAE ALERT 11.1: *Continued*

Another thing you need to know if you are going to calculate these values by hand is the degrees of freedom. Compute the degrees of freedom by multiplying the number of rows of data (don't include the marginals) minus 1, by the number of columns of data (don't include the marginals) minus 1. Thus, for a 2 × 2 table, (2 rows − 1) = 1 times (2 columns − 1) = 1; 1 × 1 = 1. The degrees of freedom for a 2 × 2 table is always 1. The formula for calculating degrees of freedom is

$$df = (r - 1)(c - 1)$$

Once the chi-square value is computed, the researcher consults a specially prepared reference table to determine if that value is significant for a cross-tabulation given the degrees of freedom associated with it. A small portion of such a table has been reproduced here. For a chi-square to be statistically significant at $p < .05$ with 1 degree of freedom (i.e., a 2 × 2 table), the chi-square value has to be larger than the critical value of 3.84. A chi-square of 3.33 would not be significant. Similarly, a chi-square value of 6.99 would not be significant if the researcher had 3 degrees of freedom (i.e., a 2 × 4 table) and was using the significance level of .05.

Critical Values to Use When Manually Calculating Chi-Square

	ALPHA LEVELS		
	.05	*.01*	*.001*
2 × 2 table (df = 1)	3.84	6.64	10.83
2 × 3 table (df = 2)	5.99	6.64	13.82
2 × 4 table (df = 3)	7.81	9.21	16.27
3 × 3 table (df = 4)	9.49	11.34	18.47
4 × 4 table (df = 9)	16.92	21.67	27.88

Doubling what we have would lead us to estimate that in the new sample there would be two females and six males in the $40,000-or-more category. With a total of eight individuals distributed over the two gender classifications (e.g., four in each cell), we'd still have two cells with expected frequencies of less than 5 in the high-income category. (We'll show you how chi-square computes this in the next section.) So our options are to triple the sample size, or reduce the number of salary categories—combine categories as we did earlier. This latter option is often the best course of action.

When chi-square statistics are reported in a professional journal article, the degrees of freedom is always shown so that the reader will know how many cells were involved. This is important because chi-square values tend to increase as cross-tabulation tables become larger (more rows and columns of data). It is possible to obtain a large chi-square value that is not significant simply because there were numerous rows and cells in the comparison. Therefore, chi-square values are always interpreted in terms of the associated degrees of freedom. In the days before personal computers, you would determine whether a given chi-square value was significant by looking at a specially prepared reference table listing significant values by degrees of freedom. Today, the statistical software references these values and calculates the actual probability of obtaining the reported χ^2.

This is the proper way of showing the results of a chi-square test where 1,000 clients were assigned to either one of three intervention groups or a control group (four possible groups total), and these data were then examined by gender: χ^2 (3, $N = 1,000) = 1.33, p = .72$. Note that there are three degrees of freedom, the chi-square is 1.33, and this is not statistically significant ($p > .05$).

■ ■ ■ ■ ■

EXAMPLES OF CHI-SQUARE IN THE PRACTICE LITERATURE

EVALUATION OF HIV PREVENTION

Roffman et al. (1997) designed a study to assess the effectiveness of a 17-session HIV prevention group. The researchers used chi-square to determine if there were significant differences between the control and experiment groups in such variables as education (not a college graduate vs. college graduate or more education), ethnicity (persons of color vs. caucasian), serostatus (negative, positive, or unknown), early sexual abuse (yes vs. no), and size of social support network (less than eight people vs. eight or more people). Table 1 in their article shows the results of 19 different comparisons made using χ^2.

PUBLIC EDUCATION ABOUT ELDER ABUSE

Although social workers might assume that most of the general public knows about and can recognize abuse, a study in Indiana (Blakely & Morris, 1992) found that only 1 in every 43 respondents knew that instances of suspected elder mistreatment are to be reported to an adult protective services investigator. In a study that presented college students with vignettes about elder abuse, Blakely and Dolon (1998) found that students who were studying to become social workers, nurses, or other helping professions were more likely to support an investigation by authorities ($\chi^2 = 16.3$, df $= 4$, $p < .003$). Similarly, students who were preparing to enter the helping professions were not as likely as others to become embarrassed if their concerns were later discovered to be unfounded ($\chi^2 = 24.9$, df $= 4, p = .000$) (1998).

MEASURES OF ASSOCIATION

The chi-square statistic has helped us to discover differences between males and females in their starting salaries, but sometimes researchers have questions they want to approach from another perspective. Instead of looking to see if groups are different, there may be times when you simply want to know if there is a relationship between two variables, and if there is, the strength of that association. The chi-square itself is not a good measure of association (Norusis, 1997), but it does serve as the basis for several other statistics that measure strength of relationship. Three of these statistics are briefly discussed here.

When you have a 2 × 2 chi-square table, **phi** is a statistic unaffected by sample size that measures the strength of association between two nominal- or ordinal-scaled variables. Phi varies from 1 (perfect association) to 0 (absolutely no association—also known as statistical independence).

Once your data have been entered into a computer that has a statistical software program such as SPSS, you follow the same steps to obtain phi that you would use in arriving at a chi-square: Select STATISTICS from the menu, then SUMMARIZE, then STATISTICS from the CROSSTABS dialog menu, and then PHI. Manually, phi is obtained by dividing the obtained chi-square by N, and then taking the square root of that value.

The salary and gender data presented earlier in this chapter in Figure 11.1 yielded a phi statistic of .47, which was significant at .001. In other words, there was a moderately strong relationship between salary and gender. (More about how to gauge this a little later.)

When your chi-square table is larger than a 2 × 2 and you want to measure the strength of association between variables, the **contingency coefficient** is the appropriate statistic. A limitation of the contingency coefficient is that it should be used only with tables that have the same number of rows and columns (e.g., 3 × 3, 4 × 4, 5 × 5).

If you have tables that are larger than a 2 × 2 and do not have the same number of rows and columns, then a third statistic, **Cramer's V,** is the appropriate statistic to select. For 2 × 2 tables, Cramer's V will always equal phi. These two statistics—phi and Cramer's V—will begin to depart from each other as the number of rows and columns increases; however, they should be of the same approximate magnitude. That is, if phi identifies a moderately strong association, so should Cramer's V. When Cramer's V is calculated for the data in Figure 11.3, the product is .48 and thus is identical to the .48 produced by the phi statistic.

When you have a table larger than a 2 × 2 and are confused about which of the various measures of association to use, Cramer's V is recommended. This statistic is known for being robust. That is, it is not influenced by the number of categories or by the distribution of cases across the various rows and columns.

Why, you are probably asking, did we just learn about three different statistical procedures when one, Cramer's V, seems to be the best all-round choice? This question is one of those best left for when you have a couple of hours to spend with your favorite statistician—few of us would probably be interested in the subtle distinctions. Briefly, however, each statistic performs better than one of the others under certain conditions. Also, because statistical software quickly and easily provides these statistics, there may well be occasions when you will want to know how to interpret them.

To assess the strength of association measured by Cramer's V or phi, Craft (1990) suggested the guidelines in Table 11.5.

Note that Cramer's V cannot be interpreted as a proportion or percent of variation explained. The Cramer's V of .47 obtained earlier does not mean that 47% of the salary variance can be accounted for by gender. All that the statistic can do for you in this instance is to show that there is a moderately strong association between the two categorical variables of gender and salary. Tabular presentation of data (e.g., Table 11.4) usually helps the reader to interpret the association.

An association that you discover between two variables does not indicate a causal relationship. Obviously, salaries do not cause or affect one's gender. Admittedly, you could accrue evidence that salary is affected by gender, but we have no basis for stating that amount of salary is caused by one's sex. The problem is much more complex. For instance, we would want to know if males and females applying for the same positions make different wages, or if they typically apply for jobs with different responsibilities. Could age, geographical location, or prior job experience make a difference?

Chi-square is an interesting statistic that, by itself, can be hard to interpret without looking at the cells. Indeed, the direction of the relationship cannot be determined without looking at cell data. Chi-square also has a strange quirk in that statistical significance is often found when large samples are employed. If you had a small sample that did not produce a significant chi-square but you were able to increase all the cells by a given factor (e.g., double the number of respondents in each cell), then the chi-square statistic will be increased by the same factor. In other words, it is possible to manipulate findings that were not originally significant by simply increasing the sample size. This is not to say that every nonsignificant chi-square can be made significant, but many of them can. However, deliberately adding to a sample simply to obtain significant findings would be frowned on by most ethical researchers. Note, though, that the strength of the relationship obtained from Cramer's V or phi would not be affected by increasing the sample size.

TABLE 11.5   Guide for Interpreting Chi-Square Measures of Association

MAGNITUDE OF CRAMER'S V OR PHI	STRENGTH OF ASSOCIATION
less than .10	weak
.11–.25	weak to moderate
.26–.40	moderate
.41–.50	moderate to strong
over .50	strong

CHI-SQUARE WITH A CONTROL VARIABLE

One of the differences between experimentalists in the laboratory and social work researchers is that we social workers do not manipulate our subjects in the same way that animal psychologists do. We can't deprive our clients of food or water to motivate them, nor can we punish those consumers of our services who don't learn the right behaviors. Still, there are aspects of the experimental approach that can be used by social work researchers. Random assignment of subjects to an intervention or control group, for example, helps to eliminate alternative explanations.

Researchers can exert control in other ways, too. On occasion, we might screen our clients before inviting them to participate in some research project. For instance, from all the clients eligible for an intervention, we might eliminate from consideration those with specific traits that might make it more difficult for treatment to be successful. There could be sound reasons for excluding, at least initially, clients with a prior history of substance abuse or with personality disorders. This ability to determine research subjects is an example of one way in which researchers impose control in their studies. Sometimes homogeneous client samples are needed, and other times heterogeneous client samples are needed, depending on the topic being investigated.

Researchers also have the ability to exercise statistical control with selected **control variables.** For example, one explanation we posed earlier about our findings on gender and first-year starting salaries was that geographical location may have played a role. Assuming that we can obtain place of residence information from our subjects, then a three-way chi-square can be calculated. By introducing a third variable such as geographical setting, it is possible to investigate the association between gender and salary holding constant (i.e., controlling) the variable of location—whether the new jobs are in a rural or an urban setting. (The assumption here, of course, is that urban settings would pay better than rural settings.)

COMPUTER APPLICATION: COMPUTING A THREE-WAY CROSS-TABULATION

Looking at data one variable at a time, introducing an independent variable (bivariate analysis), and then examining that relationship via a third variable (control variable) is known as the **elaboration model.** The beauty of this process is that involving a control variable can often help to confirm the existence of a relationship under different conditions.

Figure 11.4 displays the results of a three-way cross-tabulation of our salary data in which gender is the column variable, salaries classified by category are the row variable, and geographic location of the new position is the control variable. You'll note that Figure 11.4 consists of two separate cross-tabulations, one for those 23 students taking jobs in urban areas and one for the 26 students working in rural areas. Accordingly, a chi-square is then computed for each geographic division, although the data are presented as one table.

FIGURE 11.4 **Results of a Three-Way Cross-Tabulation**

| | | | GENDER | | |
LOCALITY	STARTING MSW SALARIES		Female	Male	TOTAL
Urban	$20,000 to 29,999	Count	9	2	11
		Expected count	5.7	5.3	11.0
		% within gender	75.0%	18.2%	47.8%
	$30,00 or more	Count	3	9	12
		Expected count	6.3	5.7	12.0
		% within gender	25.0%	81.8%	52.2%
	Total	Count	12	11	23
		Expected count	12.0	11.0	23.0
		% within gender	100.0%	100.0%	100.0%
Rural	$20,000 to 29,999	Count	10	3	13
		Expected count	7.5	5.5	13.0
		% within gender	66.7%	27.3%	50.0%
	$30,000 or more	Count	5	8	13
		Expected count	7.5	5.5	13.0
		% within gender	33.3%	72.7%	50.0%
	Total	Count	15	11	26
		Expected count	15.0	11.0	26.0
		% within gender	100.0%	100.0%	100.0%

LOCALITY		VALUE	df	ASYMP. SIG. (TWO-SIDED)
Urban	Pearson chi-square	7.425[a]	1	.006
	Number of valid cases (N)	23		
Rural	Pearson chi-square	3.939[b]	1	.047
	Number of valid cases (N)	26		

[a] 0 cells (.0%) have expected count less than 5. The minimum expected count is 5.26.
[b] 0 cells (.0%) have expected count less than 5. The minimum expected count is 5.50.

You can see that the pattern we discovered previously of women being clustered in the lower salary category holds true in both the urban and rural areas. Similarly, the vast majority of men are found in the higher salary category—82% of them in the urban market, and 73% in the rural area. And, as we would expect, the chi-squares obtained when the data are cut into urban and rural segments are both statistically significant (p = .006 and p < .047, respectively). In other words, men made

■ ■ ■ ■ ■ ▬▬▬▬▬▬▬▬▬▬▬▬▬▬▬▬▬▬▬▬▬▬▬▬▬

COMPUTING A THREE-WAY CROSS-TABULATION IN SPSS

Step 1: Enter the data into the computer.

Step 2: Select STATISTICS from the toolbar. This creates a drop-down menu.

Step 3: From the drop-down menu, select CROSSTABS. This creates the CROSSTABS dialog box.

Step 4: In the CROSSTABS dialog box, select from your list of variables the row variable, the column variable, and the control variable. Move the control variable to the window labeled Layer 1 of 1.

Step 5: Click on the STATISTICS button in the dialog box, and check CHI-SQUARE.

higher salaries than women both in the urban and in the rural settings. This particular analysis reveals that the problem of salary inequity is not just a concern in rural areas. It is the control variable locality that allows us to make that determination.

Figure 11.5 shows that moderately strong association between gender and salary still holds for rural data (Cramer's $V = .389$), but that the relationship within the urban segment is stronger (Cramer's $V = .568$).

FIGURE 11.5   Measures of Association for the Three-Way Cross-Tabulation

LOCALITY			VALUE	APPROX. SIG.
Urban		Phi	.568	.006
		Cramer's V	.568	.006
	Number of valid cases (N)		23	
Rural		Phi	.389	.047
		Cramer's V	.389	.047
	Number of valid cases (N)		26	

TERMS TO KNOW

Attribute (p. 196)
Bivariate analysis (p. 191)
Chi-square (p. 192)
Contingency coefficient (p. 202)
Contingency table (p. 196)
Control variable (p. 204)
Cramer's V (p. 202)
Cross-tabulation (p. 196)

Elaboration model (p. 204)
Expected frequencies (p. 196)
Goodness of fit (p. 193)
Marginals (p. 198)
Measures of association (p. 202)
Phi (p. 202)
Univariate analysis (p. 190)

REVIEW PROBLEMS

The situation: Juanita has been hired for a special project to examine the self-esteem of persons with disabilities. She is particularly interested in the "invisibly disabled"—those with hearing impairments, severe learning disorders, heart problems, and so forth. Juanita hypothesizes that students with obvious handicaps will have higher self-esteem than students with hidden impairments. She has collected a sample of 75 students from her university's handicapped student services office. Thirty-six students meet her criterion for being "invisibly disabled," and 39 have a visible disability, such as paraplegia. Juanita administers a self-esteem test to all 120 students and then categorizes the students into three groups: those with low, moderate, and high self-esteem scores:

SELF-ESTEEM	INVISIBLY DISABLED	VISIBLY DISABLED
Low	15	11
Moderate	12	15
High	9	13

1. Calculate the percentages associated with each column. Do the data seem to support Juanita's hypothesis?

2. Calculate chi-square either manually or using statistical software. What is the chi-square? Are the differences between the two groups statistically significant?

3. What logical control variables could help explain these findings? If you want to use these data and make up a third variable for a three-way chi-square, which control variables might be important? List three.

4. When Juanita conducts a three-way chi-square, she obtains a Cramer's V of .144. What should she conclude?

    a. the association between variables is strong
    b. the association between variables is moderate
    c. the association between variables is weak
    d. the square root of phi is the suppressor variable

REFERENCES

Blakely, B. E. & Dolon, R. (1998). A test of public reactions to alleged elder abuse. *Journal of Elder Abuse & Neglect, 9* (4), 43–65.

Blakely, B. E., & Morris, D. C. (1992). Public perceptions of and responses to elder abuse in Middletown. *Journal of Elder Abuse and Neglect, 4* (3), 19–37.

Craft, J. L. (1990). *Statistics and data analysis for social workers.* Itasca, IL: Peacock.

Norusis, M. J. (1997). *SPSS 7.5: Guide to data analysis.* Upper Saddle River, NJ: Prentice-Hall.

Roffman, R. A., Downey, L., Beadnell, B., Gordon, J. R., Craver, J. N. and Stephens, R. S. (1997). Cognitive-behavioral group counseling to prevent HIV transmission in gay and bisexual men: Factors contributing to successful risk reduction. *Research on Social Work Practice, 7* (2), 165–186.

UNDERSTANDING AND INTERPRETING CORRELATION

What is a *correlation?* Sometimes we hear the term used improperly in conversation. Tom may say to his friends, "It doesn't correlate. They promoted Raymond instead of me, but I taught him everything he knows." Although Raymond's promotion may not make any sense to Tom, it is doubtful that his employer actually computed a correlation coefficient using real numerical data. Researchers know that a **correlation** is a numerical statement about the strength of a relationship between two interval-level variables. Variables that have a **positive correlation** move in the same direction together, both variables either increasing or decreasing in value. When variables are positively correlated, an increase in the value of one variable means there is a corresponding increase in the other variable, too. It can also mean that a decrease in one variable will result in a decrease in the other. For instance, if a library has a 15% cut in its funding, it is reasonable to expect that it would be able to purchase fewer books. (Both variables would be decreasing—the library's overall budget and the amount set aside for book purchases.) The opposite would also make sense; if the budget were increased, more books could be bought. A **negative,** or **inverse, correlation** means that as one variable increases, the other decreases. In short, they go in opposite directions.

It should come as no surprise that variables often vary together in predictable ways. Level of education and income often are positively correlated. Generally speaking, individuals with higher levels of education tend to earn more money than those with lower levels of education. Variables that are highly correlated allow us to make predictions using samples of data. Unlike Tom, researchers use the term *correlation* only when they are analyzing actual data. Correlation is an essential component underlying many types of sophisticated statistical procedures, and it has a precise meaning.

As noted earlier, a correlation is a numerical statement about the strength of relationship between two variables. The correlation coefficient is a small value that ranges from –1 to +1 (perfect negative or perfect positive correlations). Often the correlation coefficients we obtain in the social sciences are less than .40. Absolutely no correlation between variables is represented by the value .00. Later in this chapter, we will see how these values are produced. Unless you are informed otherwise, correlations are usually Pearson product–moment correlations (named after the statistician Karl Pearson), and interval-level data are required to calculate them. Correlation is often abbreviated as *r*, and it is sometimes referred to as **Pearson's *r*.**

THE USE OF CORRELATION BY SOCIAL WORKERS

Correlations are frequently used by social workers and social work researchers. Suppose, for instance, that you are an advocate for improving the educational opportunities available in our nation's prisons. Even citizens and policymakers who are most punitive in their thinking have to admit that there is a problem with recidivism—that prison is not a strong deterrent to further crimes, and it does not rehabilitate felons. But what if you could show that there is a strong correlation between additional education acquired in prison and reduced recidivism? Might it be cheaper to provide education for prisoners than building new prisons? (For a study on this topic employing correlation, see Tracy, Smith, & Steurer, 1998.)

Or suppose you are a social worker at a university health clinic, and you begin to notice an apparent relationship between the amount of alcohol college students consume and risky sexual behavior. A correlational study examining such data might provide sufficient information to interest university officials in funding educational efforts to target this problem on campus. See, for instance, Poulson et al. (1998) for a study on this topic.

■ ■ ■ ■ ■ ▬▬

EXAMPLES OF CORRELATION IN THE PRACTICE LITERATURE

Before social workers can be effective in helping to change erroneous notions about welfare recipients, they must first learn what attitudes the public holds. Kaufman, Stuart, and MacNeil (1999) collected statewide data and asked respondents 15 questions about the eligibility requirements pertaining to AFDC and food stamps. Other questions asked about the availability of jobs and child-care options. These researchers then used Pearson correlation coefficients to examine for potential relationships between age, education, income, and the respondents' attitudes toward welfare recipients. They found inverse relationships between attitude toward welfare recipients and education and income. In other words, those with lower education and income levels were more negative in their attitudes toward welfare recipients.

Jackson (1999) investigated the well-being of employed and unemployed single mothers and the influence of nonresident fathers. In reporting the findings, Jackson created a correlation matrix as she examined the relationships among variables. She found that parental stress was related to lower education attainment, male children, and higher scores for depression. The more satisfied the mothers were with the amount of time fathers spent with their children, the fewer problems they reported.

Social workers often need to create scales to measure concepts such as emotional abuse, anxiety, depression, marital satisfaction, and children's adjustment to school. Correlation allows researchers to check for agreement, for instance, between parents' behavioral ratings of children with ADHD with those of the children's elementary teachers. Researchers can also compute correlations to examine the psychometric characteristics of their instruments and scales. Internal consistency (Cronbach's alpha), test-retest reliability, as well as concurrent validity (when you administer your new scale along with one already known to be valid) are all based on correlations. In sum, correlation is a very practical statistical concept that can be used in a variety of applications in the social sciences.

SCATTERGRAMS

Scattergrams help us to understand the concept of correlation. So even though this may seem like something of a detour, you'll soon see how it relates to our topic. A **scattergram** (sometimes also known as a scatterplot) is a graphical representation of cases (individuals) showing simultaneously their values (or scores) on two different variables. Unlike graphs used in single-system research designs (SSRDs), in which frequencies of behavior are reported (typically for one individual) on the vertical axis, and the passage of time is reported on the horizontal axis, scattergrams display values for *many* different individuals, and the independent variable is not limited to a measurement of time, but could be a variable such as yearly income, age, number of children, years of education, and so on. As in SSRDs, however, in scattergrams the independent variable is usually placed on the **abscissa** (the horizontal axis, or *x*-axis), and the dependent variable is shown on the **ordinate** (the vertical axis, or *y*-axis). Scattergrams allow us to see any relationships in the distribution of data. Correlations simply summarize those relationships in numerical terms.

In the scattergram in Figure 12.1, we have plotted the number of episodes of physical abuse reported by four clients on a chart that allows us to see the relationship between abuse incidents and length of time the couples were together. In this example, the dependent variable (sometimes known as the **criterion variable**) is the number of times clients in a shelter for battered spouses say they were physically beaten. You can see that Sally reported being victimized on 12 separate occasions, and Judy reported 2 episodes.

The horizontal axis is used to show data on the second variable, which corresponds to an independent variable known as the **predictor variable.** (The different names for these variables reflect the emphasis away from thinking in terms of causality. In correlation, either variable can be used to predict the other.) Note that the values in a scattergram start at the point where the two axes intersect and grow larger as one moves either vertically or horizontally away from the intersection. Because different variables are involved, the scales for the x and y axes generally do not use the same intervals.

In Figure 12.1 the relationship between episodes of abuse and time spent in an intimate relationship are clear—the longer these clients remain in a relationship

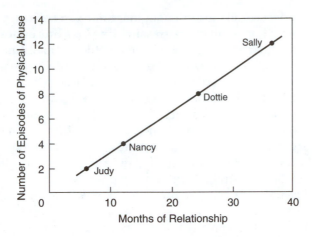

FIGURE 12.1   Scattergram Showing Perfect Correlation

with the violent partner, the more times they can expect to be battered. Look at the following data, which the scattergram is based on. Do you see a pattern? Can you tell whether one variable is increasing at a constant rate? Can you guess what the numerical value of the correlation might be?

CLIENT	VIOLENT EPISODES (Criterion variable)	MONTHS IN RELATIONSHIP (Predictor variable)
Judy	2	6
Nancy	4	12
Dottie	8	24
Sally	12	36

PERFECT CORRELATIONS

Figure 12.1 is an example of a **perfect correlation.** That is to say, these data have a correlation of 1.00. What this means in this particular situation is that as the predictor variable increases by three units on the horizontal axis, the criterion variable (on the vertical axis) increases by one unit. In other words, one could predict that for this sample of victims of domestic violence, there would likely be an abusive episode for every three months that they lived with their partners. A correlation of 1.00 allows for total and complete prediction—there is no unexplained variation between the variables. With a large sample of clients (instead of this small fictitious sample) and a correlation of 1.00, we could accurately predict the number of abusive episodes new clients had experienced if they told us how many months they had been living with their partners.

When there is a perfect correlation, an imaginary line can be drawn through all of the data points. Such a line is called a **regression line** (or a **line of best fit**). So, knowing one variable, say, that the couple had been together about 21 months, we can predict the other variable—there would have been seven abusive episodes. Although this level of precision in prediction is the goal of all science, finding perfect correlations is extremely rare. Seldom can a straight line be drawn through all or even most of the data points when two variables are plotted. Usually, there's just too much individual variation, and the more variation there is, the lower the correlation and the less accurate we would be in making a prediction about one variable from knowing the other. And we don't really "fit" any points to the line when there is a perfect correlation—a straight line simply goes through all the points. However, as you will see a little later, the term *line of best fit* is an apt description when correlations are less than 1.0.

Perfect correlations don't occur often, but they can be produced when two variables are mirror images of each other. Ideally, one ought to come close to a perfect correlation with these two questionnaire items:

On how many occasions has your partner hurt you?
How many times has your partner physically abused you?

If, however, the correlation obtained from these two items was not very high, then it suggests that the respondents probably did not share the same definition of what constituted physical abuse. Or possibly, they were less than honest in reporting these incidents. Many factors can affect the magnitude of correlations. Researchers can determine how well different items on an instrument or scale measure the same concept (e.g., physical abuse) by using computer software to compute a statistical indicator of **inter-item reliability,** which is based on correlations between items. (The internal consistency of a scale has the same meaning as inter-item reliability.)

What does it mean to come close to a perfect correlation? We can use our small sample of data to see how the correlation coefficient is affected by changes in the observed data. If Sally had been in her dangerous relationship 48 months instead of 36 and still experienced 12 separate abusive incidents, the correlation would have been .98, not 1.00. (Remember, though, that this correlation is based on only this sample of four clients.) The correlation would have been a little less than perfect because, although the data fit the general pattern of more abuse within a longer relationship, Sally with 12 episodes in 48 months would have had fewer of these events than a perfect model would have predicted (one incident of abuse for every three months living together should have produced 16 episodes).

A NOTE ABOUT CAUSALITY

Sometimes when there is a high correlation, it is tempting to think that one variable caused the other variable to respond accordingly. However, the fallacy of that assumption can be seen when we think through the possible relationship: Abuse doesn't cause time to pass and there is nothing about the passage of time that by itself causes abuse. These two variables, time and abuse, simply vary together.

Correlation is never proof of causality. For instance, juvenile delinquents tend to have poor grades in school. Often they have attendance problems and have multiple suspensions from school. It is likely that a strong correlation would be found with this group if we were to correlate the number of their arrests with the number of their high school suspensions. Once again, though, the suspensions don't cause the arrests. There are many other variables that contribute to children being arrested and failing in school. Some of these are father's presence or absence in the home, parents' educational achievement, father's arrest record, substance abuse by parents or guardians, domestic violence within the home, and the amount and quality of supervision provided by parents.

Note: Correlation is never proof of causality.

When only two variables are being examined at a time, it is highly likely that other variables are having an effect, too. When you suspect that one or more intervening variables are preventing you from understanding the "true" relationship between two variables, you can statistically control for the extraneous ones by a correlational procedure known as **partial correlation** or partial r. This procedure produces a correlation coefficient, like that obtained between two variables, that allows you to gauge the strength of relationship when other variables may be exerting an influence. (Of course, you have to have data from these other variables.)

OUTLIERS

As data points fan out and away from the regression line, the correlation drops closer to zero. The more the points are scattered, the farther they are from the hypothetical line that tries to run through all of them, the lower the correlation. Outliers are points that stray from the general direction found in the rest of the data.

Let's increase our sample of clients and add in three new ones to demonstrate this idea:

CLIENT	VIOLENT EPISODES (*Criterion variable*)	MONTHS IN RELATIONSHIP (*Predictor variable*)
Judy	2	6
Nancy	4	12
Dottie	8	24
Sally	12	36
Norma	5	10
Adela	12	8
Maria	3	15

Do you still see a pattern of episodes of violence increasing with months in a relationship? It's there, but not quite as obvious because it is less than a perfect correlation. There's more variance in the data, and this can be seen in Figure 12.2. Adela is an outlier—her values represent extreme and atypical points that don't conform to the general pattern indicated by the dotted lines. Adela is in a particularly abusive relationship, and she has experienced more incidents of violence than would be expected. Maria, on the other hand, is in a somewhat less violent relationship than the other clients in her support group. Had she experienced only one abusive incident in 15 months of a relationship, she could be an outlier on the low end.

Sometimes researchers have to decide whether to include or exclude outliers in their statistical computations, because outliers make it difficult for the researcher to determine the actual strength of a relationship between two variables. For instance, without Adela's data in the sample, a strong correlation of .95 is obtained. When Adela is included in the sample, the correlation between the same two variables is reduced to .55. For this reason, researchers ought to produce and examine scattergrams in order to make sure that outliers haven't understated or exaggerated the relationship.

When should outliers be excluded from data analysis? One guideline is to eliminate outliers from analysis whenever the outliers are clearly "oddball" cases that seem to be anomalies, or exceptions to the rule. An easy case for exclusion could be made in a situation like this: Bill has been assigned to work with male batterers who've been referred for counseling. After a screening interview with each prospective member of the group, Bill learns that eight potential group members have been arrested for domestic violence on only one occasion. Tony, however, has been

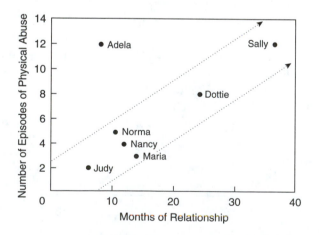

The dotted lines around all of the data points except Adela were added to emphasize how data that are correlated show a direction. Adela is an outlier—her data point lies outside the envelope that can be drawn around the other points.

FIGURE 12.2   Scattergram Showing an Outlier

arrested 10 times. Bill decides Tony's chronic offending requires a more intensive intervention and recommends another group for him. Tony's record of arrests is an outlier that didn't conform to the pattern of the other first-time offenders. When there are flagrant departures from the rest of the data, researchers may decide to exclude individual cases. However, these decisions are never taken lightly. When outliers are excluded routinely, it is usually when there is a good basis for believing certain respondents are unable to provide reliable data or are deliberately lying (e.g., the crack addict who says she's been arrested 900 times). These decisions about omitting cases should be reported for those who read or use your study.

INTERPRETING THE STRENGTH (MAGNITUDE) OF A CORRELATION

Let's first enter the data from the seven clients into the computer. Our SPSS statistical software requires only that from STATISTICS we choose CORRELATE and then BIVARIATE. From that dialog box, we indicate which two variables we wish to correlate. Pearson's r correlation is set as a default. However, you can also choose to compute Spearman's rank-order coefficient or Kendall's tau-b. (More about these types of correlation later in the chapter.) As simple as that, we obtain the output that shows the correlation of abusive episodes and length of relationship is .55, which is not a perfect correlation, but still a fairly strong relationship. But how do you know when to call a relationship a strong one?

By multiplying the correlation coefficient by itself (squaring it), the resulting product indicates the proportion of variation in one variable that is explained by the other. Thus, a correlation of .55 multiplied by itself produces a **coefficient of determination** indicating how much variation within the two variables can be explained. The .30 coefficient of determination (.55 × .55 = .30) means that from the sample of data obtained, we can explain 30% of the variation between episodes of abuse and length of time in an intimate relationship. For a correlation of .35, the coefficient of determination would be .12 (.35 × .35 = .12)—meaning that we could explain only 12% of the variation shared by the two variables. A correlation of .50 accounts for 25% of the variation between two variables. In other words, with a correlation of .50, the researcher is unable to explain 75% of the fluctuation in the two variables. By convention, the guide presented in Table 12.1 is generally accepted for converting the correlation coefficient into descriptive or narrative terms:

TABLE 12.1   Guide for Interpreting the Magnitude of Correlation Coefficients

CORRELATION COEFFICIENT	INTERPRETATION
Less than .20	Slight; inconsequential
.20 to .40	Small; low correlation
.40 to .70	Moderately correlated
.70 to .90	Strong correlation
.90 to 1.00	Very strong correlation

By computing the coefficient of determination (represented by r^2), we realize that a correlation of .90 is not three times better than a correlation of .30, but nine times better (.30 × .30 = 9% of variation explained versus .90 × .90 = 81%). Although the magnitude of the correlation is important, it's not everything, as we'll see in the next section.

STATISTICAL SIGNIFICANCE

The output when our statistical software produces a correlation of .55 for episodes of abuse with length of relationship (for the seven clients in Figure 12.2) also informs us that this finding is not statistically significant (p = .20) (see Table 12.2). This means that we can't place a lot of confidence in this correlation—the coefficient we obtained could have been produced by chance. To say it another way, the relationship might not hold up if we were to add additional clients or to select another sample of clients from the population. An insignificant correlation is one that is not very reliable.

The significance level depends not only on the sample size, but also on whether the data fit a general linear pattern. When a new client, Devonia, is added to the group with her 15 episodes of abuse and 39 months in a relationship with a batterer, the resulting correlation becomes a strong .72. And even though the sample consists of only 8 women, the correlation now is statistically significant (p < .05). From this small sample of data, we would expect other clients' histories would conform to this general pattern. The significant probability was obtained because the addition of Devonia's information helped to confirm the pattern already present in the data and added enough "critical mass" to push it into significance. Correlations tend to be high when a linear direction can be discerned from the scattergram, as in Figure 12.3. When your sample is small, high correlations may be obtained, but it is important to note whether they are significant. It is easier to obtain significance with large samples than with small ones; at the same time, it is also more difficult for lower-magnitude coefficients to be significant when samples are small.

Data don't always fit a linear line. Sometimes the data don't make a pattern. Do you see one in Figure 12.4? In this new group of clients, one experienced a great deal of abuse in the first 6 months of her relationship, yet others had much less abuse over longer relationships. If you don't see a pattern in Figure 12.4, that's because there isn't one. It would be impossible to draw a single line connecting all

TABLE 12.2   Correlation Output

	EPISODES OF ABUSE	MONTHS	SIGNIFICANCE
Pearson's r correlation	1.00	.548	.203
N	7	7	

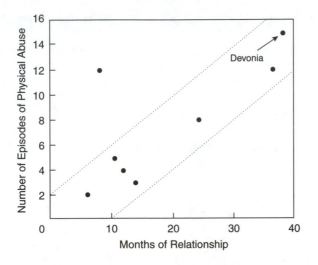

FIGURE 12.3   Scattergram with a Strong Correlation and Outlier

of the data points. The correlation of our two variables with these eight clients is .005, indicating virtually no relationship. Predicting the value of one variable by knowing the other is not possible with these data. This example makes the important point that the correlation always depends on the sample from which the data are derived. Indeed, the worth of any statistical procedure always depends on the quality and size of the sample. It is always risky to generalize from small samples.

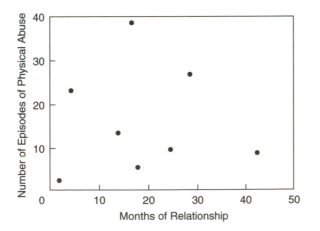

FIGURE 12.4   Scattergram Showing Virtually No Correlation

Furthermore, one should not place confidence in any correlation that is not statistically significant.

Another important point to remember is that, although researchers usually are excited to find statistical significance, significance must be understood within the context of the actual statistical values obtained. For instance, although it is possible to obtain a statistically significant correlation of .04, the low magnitude of this correlation wouldn't allow the researcher to explain even 1% of the variation between the two variables. Thus, the finding may be statistically significant, but it certainly won't be very meaningful. On the other hand, finding a correlation close to 0 between two variables could be very important, depending on the hypothesis and the variables being explored.

NEGATIVE CORRELATIONS

Negative correlations are also known as inverse correlations. In these relationships, as one variable increases, the other variable decreases. For example, suppose Bill had obtained the following data from a group of men who had been arrested for battering:

	SELF-REPORTED NUMBER OF TIMES STRUCK A WOMAN	SCORE ON EMPATHY FOR OTHERS SCALE
Client A	1	70
Client B	3	50
Client C	2	60
Client D	8	30
Client E	22	18
Client F	30	10
Client G	15	26
Client H	6	35
Client I	40	5
Client J	4	48

These data produce a statistically significant ($p < .001$) negative correlation of −.90. The minus sign in front of the correlation indicates that as the number of admitted number of physical assaults increases, the fictitious clients' scores on the Empathy for Others Scale decreases. (A lower score means lower levels of empathy.) Thus, we would be safe in assuming that clients with lower empathy scores would be likely to report a higher number of domestic violence episodes.

Sometimes negative correlations can be recognized in the data even before any calculations are made. This is what you would look for—relatively large values for one variable that correspond to small values for the other variable. (See Formulae Alert 12.1.)

Here's another tip: A negative correlation of −.90 is just as strong as a positive correlation of .90—the only difference is that the negative sign means the values

FORMULAE ALERT 12.1: CALCULATING PEARSON'S r

Although it is a little tedious, Pearson's r can be computed manually. Using the raw scores from the ten clients (A through J) who were arrested for battering (these data are graphed in Figure 12.5), we can calculate the correlation coefficient using the following formula:

$$r = \frac{N\sum XY - \sum X \sum Y}{\sqrt{[N\sum X^2 - (\sum X)^2][N\sum Y^2 - (\sum Y)^2]}}$$

where $\sum X$ = sum of the X scores (number of assaults)
$\sum Y$ = sum of the Y scores (empathy scores)
$\sum XY$ = sum of the product of X and Y scores
$\sum X^2$ = sum of the squared X scores
$\sum Y^2$ = sum of the squared Y scores

Let's start this example by setting up a table:

	X	Y	X²	Y²	XY
Client A	1	70	1	4,900	70
Client B	3	50	9	2,500	150
Client C	2	60	4	3,600	120
Client D	8	30	64	900	240
Client E	22	18	484	324	396
Client F	30	10	900	100	300
Client G	15	26	225	676	390
Client H	6	35	36	1,225	210
Client I	40	5	1,600	25	200
Client J	4	48	16	2,304	192
Totals	131	352	3,339	16,554	2,268

Substituting the relevant values from our table for the elements in the preceding formula, we get

$$r = \frac{(10)(2,268) - (131)(352)}{\sqrt{[(10)(3,339) - (131)^2][(10)(16,554 - (352)^2]}}$$

$$= \frac{22,680 - 46,112}{\sqrt{[33,390 - 17,161][165,540 - 123,904]}}$$

$$= \frac{-23,432}{\sqrt{(16,229)(41,636)}}$$

(continued)

FORMULAE ALERT 12.1: *Continued*

$$= \frac{-23{,}432}{\sqrt{(127.39309)(204.04901)}}$$

$$= \frac{-23{,}432}{25{,}994.433} = -.901$$

Thus, there is a strong negative association ($r = -.90$) between the variables of empathy and the number of assaults. Men who admit to a high frequency of battering tend to have the lowest empathy scores.

associated with the variables being studied move in opposite directions to one another. However, a minus on a correlation coefficient is not like a minus when taking readings from a thermometer. Although minus 30 degrees below zero is certainly a lot colder than 30 degrees above zero, a negative correlation of −.30 does not indicate less of a relationship than a positive correlation of .30. Both the positive and minus correlations indicate an equal level of relationship.

Figure 12.5 is a scattergram of the data clearly showing the inverse relationship of our two variables. Note that, unlike the positive correlations shown in the

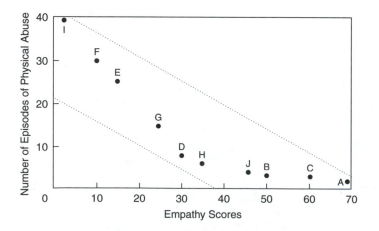

FIGURE 12.5   **Scattergram Showing an Inverse Relationship**

previous scattergrams, the line of data points falls from the highest value for abusive episodes on the left, to the lowest number of abusive episodes on the right.

CONDITIONS NEEDED FOR CORRELATION

There are three basic assumptions, or conditions, that should be examined before the correlation coefficient is computed. First, the data should be measured at the interval level. Second, the data should be reasonably linear, that is, able to conform to a single direction or to a pattern often described as cigar shaped. Lastly, the variances in the x and y variables should be approximately the same. If the variance of one variable is much greater or much less than the variance of the other variable, the data are *not* **homoscedastic.** When the data *are* homoscedastic, the scattergram of that data will look like Figure 12.6, where a band of points can be encompassed easily. Figures 12.3 and 12.5 are also examples of homoscedastic data. On the other hand, when you find O-shaped, U-shaped, J-shaped, or S-shaped patterns in your scattergrams, then your data are said to be **curvilinear,** and they are not homoscedastic, but **heteroscedastic.** (*Homo* derives from a Greek term meaning the same, or equal; *hetero* means other, or different.) Even though it is possible to calculate a correlation with curvilinear data, the correlation coefficient that is produced will not accurately reflect the magnitude of the relationship. It's a good practice to look at scattergrams of your variables, especially if you suspect the presence of curvilinear data. Figure 12.7, like Figure 12.4, is an example of such heteroscedastic data. Generally, you'll know you have heteroscedastic data when you can't easily detect a single direction. As a rule, the narrower the band of data, the higher the correlation; the wider the band of data, the lower the correlation.

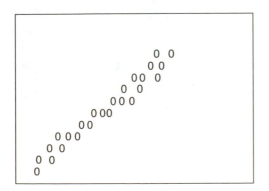

FIGURE 12.6   Scattergram of Homoscedastic Data (A Narrow Band of Data with a High Correlation)

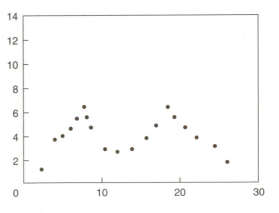

FIGURE 12.7   Scattergram Showing Curvilinear Data

RANK-ORDER CORRELATION

Social workers sometimes create and encounter, ranked data, which require a different type of correlation than Pearson's *r*. Imagine this situation: You and another case manager have been asked to rank which of your severely mentally ill clients will make the best candidates to move into a new supervised living facility. There are only 14 single-bedroom units, and the two case managers must rate all of the clients in their caseloads. The 14 clients who have the lowest rankings (between 1 and 14) will be the ones chosen. Over 50 clients are eligible, but only a few can be selected. Here is a partial list of the ratings assigned:

CLIENT	MY RATING OF CLIENT	DENISE'S RATING	DIFFERENCES IN RANKS
Bob	1	1	0
Sue	2	2	0
Edna	3	10	7
Willy	4	11	7
Polly	5	12	7
Jim	6	13	7
Mary	7	8	1
Pat	8	9	1
Edgar	9	3	6
Eve	10	4	6
Martha	11	5	6
Ronald	12	6	6
Samantha	13	7	6
Russell	14	14	0

We can see that the two case managers don't agree all that often. In fact, they agreed only three times: Bob and Sue were their first and second choices, and Russell was their last pick. The rest of the time there was considerable deviation in the rankings that ranged from one to seven positions apart. The third column shows the differences in the two sets of ratings. These differences are the values that Spearman's rank-order correlation coefficient (also referred to as **Spearman's rho**) uses to quantify the agreement between the two raters. Just by eyeballing the data, you can estimate that there could not be a high correlation. The correlation turns out to be .17, and it is not statistically significant (p = .56). (See Formulae Alert 12.2 to calculate Spearman's rho by hand.) Spearman's rho is interpreted just like Pearson's *r*, in that rho can range from +1 to −1. What Spearman's rho confirms for us is that the two case managers did not agree very often about which clients would make the best candidates for the new facility.

This lack of agreement might be due to different assumptions: One case manager might be thinking about the clients who most urgently needed housing, whereas the other social worker might be weighing personalities more heavily, favoring those with the personal traits of neatness and tidiness. If the criteria on

FORMULAE ALERT 12.2: SPEARMAN'S RANK-ORDER CORRELATION COEFFICIENT

Should you want to compute rho manually, simply follow this formula:

$$r_s = 1 - \frac{6(\sum D^2)}{N(N^2 - 1)}$$

where
r_s = Spearman's rank-order correlation coefficient
$\sum D^2$ = sum of the squared differences between paired ranks
N = number of observations

DIFFERENCES BETWEEN RANKINGS	SQUARED DIFFERENCES
0	0
0	0
7	49
7	49
7	49
7	49
1	1
1	1
6	36
6	36
6	36
6	36
6	36
0	0

Sum of squared differences = 378

$$1 - \frac{6(378)}{14(196 - 1)} = 1 - \frac{2,268}{2,738} = 1 - .83 = .17 \text{ (Spearman's rho)}$$

which the case managers were to make their decisions were not clear and uniform, then it should come as no surprise when a low correlation is obtained. This finding would suggest that the two case managers ought to agree on the criteria for selecting good candidates for the supervised apartments first, possibly write them down, and then begin the rating process all over again.

When you are computing ranks, if there are multiple ties (e.g., where the two case managers give the same ranking to a client), then Kendall's tau-b is the preferred statistic to use instead of Spearman's rho, although both of these bivariate statistical procedures are otherwise very similar. Both of these procedures are commonly found in statistical software packages.

THE CORRELATION MATRIX

Researchers often need to compute more than one correlation coefficient, and the table in which they report these coefficients is known as a **correlation matrix.** As you can see in Figure 12.8, these tables have a distinctive characteristic that makes them easy to spot. Hudson and McMurtry's (1997) article reporting on the reliability and validity of the Multi-Problem Screening Inventory (MPSI) displays two correlation matrixes that we will draw upon in the following example. The MPSI is a relatively new paper-and-pencil multidimensional assessment tool that gathers information on 27 different areas of clients' personal and social functioning. With so many subscales, the authors wanted to know to what extent the subscales are correlated with each other. Figure 12.8 is an excerpt of their findings based on 311 students from schools of social work.

The correlation matrix has the same subscale names in both columns and rows. To read the correlation values in the matrix, choose a row and a column, and find the value at the point where they intersect. We can see from the matrix in Figure 12.8 that any variable correlated with itself is a perfect correlation (1.00) and that a clear diagonal line is apparent. Actually, Figure 12.8 is the lower portion of the correlation matrix; sometimes authors choose to fill in the values for the whole matrix. However, this is unnecessary as the correlation between, say, Depression and Guilt is the same as that for Guilt and Depression. A complete matrix will provide the same data twice.

In this matrix we can also see that the highest correlation (.59) was obtained between the guilt and personal stress subscale scores. The next highest correlation (.58) was obtained between Depression and Personal Stress. The lowest correlation was between Family Problems and Sexual Discord (.11). That particular

FIGURE 12.8   Correlation Matrix of Selected MPSI Subscales

ITEM		DEP	PAR	SEX	STR	FAM	GUI
Depression	(Dep)	1.00					
Partner Problems	(Par)	.45	1.00				
Sexual Discord	(Sex)	.21	.52	1.00			
Personal Stress	(Str)	.58	.23	.21	1.00		
Family Problems	(Fam)	.31	.16	.11	.25	1.00	
Guilt	(Gui)	.54	.30	.32	.59	.30	1.00

From "Comprehensive Assessment in Social Work Practice: The Multi-Problem Screening Inventory," by W. W. Hudson and S. L. McMurtry, 1997, *Research on Social Work Practice, 7*, pp. 96–97.

correlation does not seem to make as much sense (we might expect family problems and sexual problems to correlate more highly) until we remember that many of the subjects in this sample are undergraduate students. Probably most of the subjects are not married, so problems with their families are likely to refer to their biological parents and siblings, not to their own husbands, wives, or partners (if any) with whom they may be having intimate relations.

Correlations are handy tools for summarizing the relationship between two variables, but they won't answer every question. In fact, they may leave you asking a lot more, but they are very useful nonetheless. The biggest caution is to avoid reading too much into them.

MORE ON THE REGRESSION LINE

When there is a correlation between two variables, regression analysis allows researchers to predict the value of one variable when the other is known. Of course, the stronger the correlation coefficient, the more accurate the prediction. The homoscedastic scattergram in Figure 12.6 provides a hint at how it might be possible to predict Y values from known X values. The clue is in the general direction that the data points form. Over the years, mathematicians have worked out the following formula for expressing a linear relationship. This formula, the regression equation, makes prediction possible:

REGRESSION EQUATION

$$Y' = a + bX$$

where Y' = Y value predicted from a specific X value
          a = point where the line intersects the y-axis (the **y-intercept**)
          b = **slope** of the line (the amount Y increases for each unit of increase in X)
          X = X value used to predict Y'

As you can see from Figure 12.9, a regression line plotted using the regression equation attempts to average the distances between the various points using what is called the least squares method. Notice that the line does not pass through many of the data points, and yet it is the line that best approximates the data. Of all the possible lines that can be drawn, the least squares method selects the one with the smallest sum of squared distances from each data point to a hypothetical line. This is where the name line of best fit comes from. The regression line is actually a line of predicted scores, one that's been called a "floating average" (Leonard, 1994). The higher the correlation, the more accurate the predictions can be using the regression equation.

Figure 12.9 uses the data from the 10 clients (A through J) in Bill's therapy group for men who have been arrested for battering. Let's employ the regression

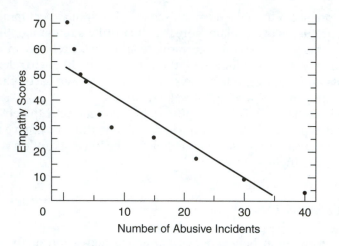

FIGURE 12.9   Regression Line for Empathy Scores and Abusive Episodes

equation to see how well we can predict for hypothetical clients. First, let's plug in the relevant data for the 10 clients. (Formulae Alert 12.3 shows how to calculate the slope and the y-intercept.)

a (y-intercept) = 54.1

b (slope)   = −1.44

Further, let's assume that we want to predict the empathy score for a new client, Mr. Wayclunk. What we know is that he admits to 20 abusive incidents. Plugging the known values into the formula, we obtain

$Y' = a + bX$

$Y' = 54.1 + -1.44\ (20)$

$\quad\ = 54.1 - 28.8 = 25.3$

Thus, we would expect Mr. Wayclunk to have an empathy score of about 25. And we can confirm our calculations by consulting the regression line in Figure 12.9. Draw an imaginary line up from 20 on the x-axis to where it intersects the regression line. Now draw an imaginary line across to the y-axis; the value on the y-axis should be 25. How's that for prediction? This is made possible by the high correlation between the two variables. This ability of the regression equation to allow researchers to estimate possible values of one variable by knowing the other is the basis for multiple regression—a topic that is covered in Chapter 14.

FORMULAE ALERT 12.3: CALCULATING THE SLOPE AND y-INTERCEPT

	ABUSIVE INCIDENTS (X)	X^2	EMPATHY SCORES (Y)	Y^2	XY
Client A	1	1	70	4,900	70
Client B	3	9	50	2,500	150
Client C	2	4	60	3,600	120
Client D	8	64	30	900	240
Client E	22	484	18	324	396
Client F	30	900	10	100	300
Client G	15	225	26	676	390
Client H	6	36	35	1,225	210
Client I	40	1,600	5	25	200
Client J	4	16	48	2,304	192
Totals	131	3,339	352		2,268

How is the slope calculated?

The formula for the slope is

$$b = \frac{N\sum XY - (\sum X)(\sum Y)}{N\sum X^2 - (\sum X)^2}$$

Plugging values into the formula,

$$\frac{(10)(2,268) - (131)(352)}{(10)(3,339) - (131)^2} = \frac{22,680 - 46,112}{33,390 - 17,161} = \frac{-23,432}{16,229} = -1.44 \text{ (slope)}$$

How is the y-intercept calculated?

The formula for the y-intercept is

$$a = \overline{Y} - b\overline{X}$$

where
a = y-intercept (where the regression line intersects the y-axis)
$\overline{Y}$ = mean of Y values
$b\overline{X}$ = slope times the mean of the X values

To calculate the means, $\overline{Y} = 352 \div 10$, or 35.2, and $\overline{X} = 131 \div 10$ or 13.1. Plugging the values into the formula,

$$a = \overline{Y} - b\overline{X} = 35.2 - (-1.44)(13.1) = 35.2 + 18.864 = 54.06 \text{ (y-intercept)}$$

Note: Interactive statistical software allows you to easily calculate the slope and y-intercept of any set of paired data (where you have X and Y values). See, for instance, the web page http://bardeen.physics.csbsju.edu/stats/QFnP_NROW_form.html. A nice feature of this site is that it not only computes the slope, y-intercept, and correlation coefficient, but it also prepares a tidy graph and regression line.

TERMS TO KNOW

Abscissa (p. 210)
Coefficient of determination (p. 215)
Correlation (*r*) (p. 208)
Correlation matrix (p. 224)
Criterion variable (p. 210)
Curvilinear data (p. 221)
Heteroscedastic data (p. 221)
Homoscedastic data (p. 221)
Inter-item reliability (p. 212)
Inverse correlation (p. 208)
Line of best fit (p. 212)
Negative correlation (p. 208)

Ordinate (p. 210)
Partial correlation (p. 213)
Pearson's *r* (p. 209)
Perfect correlation (p. 211)
Positive correlation (p. 208)
Predictor variable (p. 210)
Regression line (p. 212)
Scattergram (p. 210)
Slope (p. 225)
Spearman's rho (p. 222)
y-intercept (p. 225)

REVIEW PROBLEMS

1. True or false—outliers are extreme values that can be either higher or lower than expected.

2. Ginny has some data in which she notices this pattern: When the *y*-axis variable increases two units, the *x*-axis variable increases one unit. Is this a positive correlation?

3. Paige has obtained the following data on a sample of incarcerated crack cocaine users:

NUMBER OF PRISONERS	SELF-REPORTED NUMBER OF TIMES IN DRUG TREATMENT
15	1
20	2
13	3
15	4
25	5
12	6
14	7
10	8
7	9
5	10
1	676

Are there any outliers in this data set? If so, would you exclude them from a correlation analysis? Why?

4. Two social work students correlated the age at which a sample of drug addicts started drinking and started smoking marijuana. They found a correlation of .44. How much variation in the two variables are they able to explain?

5. What are the two ways to identify curvilinear data?

6. True or false—the *x*- and *y*-axes on scattergrams must use the same intervals (e.g., 5- or 10-point intervals).

7. True or false—a strong correlation of .87 is proof of causality.

8. The two case managers have now decided on a clear set of criteria for admission to the new supervised living apartments discussed earlier. Using the following data, compute the new rank-order correlation.

CLIENT	MY RATING OF CLIENT	DENISE'S RATING	DIFFERENCES IN RANKS
Bob	1	1	0
Sue	2	2	0
Edna	3	4	1
Willy	4	3	1
Polly	5	6	1
Jim	6	5	1
Mary	7	12	0
Pat	8	10	2
Edgar	9	13	0
Eve	10	8	2
Martha	11	11	0
Ronald	12	7	0
Samantha	13	9	0
Russell	14	14	0

9. Are there any inverse correlations displayed in the correlation matrix in Figure 12.8?

10. Identify the data pattern in this scattergram without looking back for the proper term. (*Hint:* A broad band of data with low correlation.)

REFERENCES

Hudson, W. W., & McMurtry, S. L. (1997). Comprehensive assessment in social work practice: The multi-problem screening inventory. *Research on Social Work Practice, 7*, pp. 79–98.

Jackson, A. (1999). The effects of nonresident father involvement on single black mothers and their young children. *Social Work, 44* (2), 156–166.

Kaufman, A. V., Stuart, P. H., & MacNeil, G. (1999). Public opinion about welfare in a southeastern state. *Aretê, 24* (3), 54–67.

Leonard, W. M. (1994). *Basic social statistics.* Champaign, IL: Stipes Publishing.

Poulson, R. L., Eppler, M. A., Satterwhite, T. N., Wuensch, K. L., & Bass, L. A. (1998). Alcohol consumption, strength of religious beliefs, and risky sexual behavior in college students. *Journal of American College Health, 46*, pp. 227–233.

Tracy, A., Smith, L. G., & Steurer, S. (1998). Standing up for education: New CEA study seeks to definitively show correlation between education and reduced recidivism. *Corrections Today, 60*, pp. 144–145, 156.

CHAPTER THIRTEEN

t-TESTS AND ANOVA: TESTING HYPOTHESES ABOUT MEANS

Social work researchers often find it to their advantage to avoid creating **categorical data** when the information already occurs naturally as interval level data. Suppose Jereeshe has clients in two different groups and wants to summarize the groups for you. She might do so by discussing how they differ in terms of their age. Her data are arranged as follows:

GROUP 1		GROUP 2	
Client	*Age*	*Client*	*Age*
Bob	34	Tina	18
Ed	34	Ben	18
Grace	35	Vernon	18
Burton	35	Carol	18
Brooke	36	Kathy	19
Moonbeam	37	Jude	19
Phyllis	39	Demarcus	19
Jack	44	Raymond	20
Heshimu	47	C. B.	20
Valerie	49	Sally	21
Average age = 39		Average age = 19	

In these data, the average client in Group 1 is 20 years older than the average client in Group 2. We intuitively understand the average ages of 39 and 19, and we know that, although each group may have many of the same problems, they will have different developmental issues. Although we could force these data into categories such as Young Adults, and Middle-Aged Adults, these groupings would be somewhat subjective and arbitrary. (When does one become middle-aged? And what do you call those who are neither young adults nor middle-aged?) Categories don't always bring the clarity we need to understand the composition of a group. Which of the following examples do you find easier to mentally digest?

1. 40% of the clients were between 34 and 35 years of age.
   30% of the clients were between 36 and 39 years of age.
   30% of the clients were 44 years of age or older.

2. The average age was 39.

Example 1 has more detailed information, but most people find it easier to comprehend example 2. Of course, sometimes we design questionnaires that use categories because category questions intrude less on people's privacy than questions that require people to report specific sensitive information, such as exact annual salary, current age, and how many times a week they drink. From a researcher's perspective, though, categorical data tend to be less satisfying; interval data allow for greater precision and accuracy. When constructing a questionnaire, you should consider in advance how you want to analyze your data. If you think you are interested in averages (as in clients' average age, average number of sessions attended, average pretest and posttest scores), then you will want to avoid collecting categorized data.

As a general rule, it is better to categorize the data *after* you have collected and examined them, than to create broad nominal or ordinal variables ahead of time. Variables that allow your research subjects to cluster their responses into a few responses should be the exception. Here are some realistic, open-ended items that can create useful interval-level data for researchers:

EXAMPLES OF OPEN-ENDED ITEMS PRODUCING INTERVAL DATA
How many visits have you made to our agency?

About how many minutes do you have to wait each time before seeing your counselor?

How many times have you been arrested?

How many days a week do you drink?

How many children do you have?

How much is your rent or house payment each month?

About how much do you spend for groceries each week?

Here are a few questions with predetermined response categories:

EXAMPLES OF ITEMS PRODUCING CATEGORICAL DATA
How many visits have you made to our agency?
□ 1–5 visits
□ 6–10 visits
□ 11 or more visits

How many days a week do you drink?
☐ None
☐ 1 or 2 days a week
☐ 3 or more days a week

How much is your rent or house payment each month?
☐ $100 or less
☐ $101 to 350
☐ $351 to 500
☐ $501 to 1,000
☐ More than $1,000 per month

When you have a dependent variable measured at the interval-level (and you'll know you have interval-level data because you will be able to compute an average that has meaning for that variable), the **t-test** is the statistical procedure to use to test for differences in the means of two groups. Differences between groups can be subtle or starkly apparent. When you can eyeball the groups and see the differences, you may not need a statistical procedure. For those occasions when you want to have the confidence provided by a statistical test, the t-test is a strong, robust procedure based on the means of two (and only two) groups at a time. (A useful mnemonic for remembering that the t-test can be used only when there are two groups is the expression "t for two.")

THE t-TEST

Like the chi-square, the t-test is a tool for bivariate analysis. Specifically, when you have an interval-, or ratio-level dependent variable and a nominal variable that forms only two groups, then the t-test is the appropriate statistical technique. The t-test was invented by W. S. Gosset, a scientist employed by the Guinness brewery around the turn of the century. Guinness would not allow its employees to publish under their own names, so Gosset published his papers under the pseudonym of "Student." At that time, means were investigated using normal probability tables. However, as you know from our discussion in Chapters 9 and 10, the normal curve is "trustworthy" only when the sample is large, and alternative tables did not yet exist for small samples. In 1908, after a year's leave in which he studied intensively with Karl Pearson (noted for his work with correlation coefficients), Gosset wrote a paper titled "The Probable Error of a Mean," which distinguished population parameters from sample estimates. The rest, as they say, is history. Gosset began using the t-statistic with brewery experiments involving samples of various grains and water temperatures, but the statistical procedure did not become popular until much later. Gosset checked his theoretical distributions for t on a data set composed of the body height and middle-finger lengths of 3,000 criminals (Boland, 1984).

The t-test examines the differences between two groups by looking at their means while weighing sampling error. Conceptually, the means from any two groups must be thought of as drawn from the distribution of all possible samples.

The *t*-test, then, is the difference between the group means divided by the standard error of the difference (which is related to sample size and standard deviation). (See Formulae Alert 13.1 for the derivation of the *t*-test.)

Let's go back to Jereeshe's clients. Both of her groups of clients are receiving the same intervention, although on different days of the week. However, she notices after about the third week that the younger group tends to have more absenteeism than the older group. Is this just a coincidence, or is it likely that the groups are really dissimilar in their attendance? To answer this question Jereeshe entered the attendance data from both groups into a statistical software program such as SPSS, and proceeded with her analysis as follows:

■ ■ ■ ■ ■

COMPUTING A *t*-TEST IN SPSS

Step 1: From the menu, select ANALYZE.

Step 2: Choose COMPARE MEANS.

Step 3: Click on INDEPENDENT-SAMPLES *t*-TEST.

Step 4: From there, indicate which variable is the test, or dependent, variable and which variable contains the two groups to be compared (the grouping variable).

Step 5: Define groups by indicating a 1 for those in Group 1 and a 2 for those in Group 2. Then click on CONTINUE and finally, on OK.

These are the data Jereeshe entered into the computer:

Number of Sessions Missed

GROUP 1		GROUP 2	
Bob	4	Tina	5
Ed	3	Ben	5
Grace	2	Vernon	4
Burton	2	Carol	4
Brooke	1	Kathy	3
Moonbeam	1	Jude	3
Phyllis	1	Demarcus	2
Jack	1	Raymond	2
Heshimu	0	C. B.	1
Valerie	0	Sally	1

The first table to be produced by SPSS, Table 13.1, shows that the mean number of absences for Group 1 is 1.5, whereas Group 2 has twice as many (mean = 3)

FORMULAE ALERT: 13.1 DERIVATION OF THE *t*-TEST

With large samples, the *t*-distribution is analogous to a z-distribution. However, you'll recall that the *t*-test was designed for comparisons in which there are a small number of cases (usually 30 or less). What the formula does is estimate the true population parameters (values) using sample statistics as a way of determining how closely the samples conform to the population. The values represented in each of Jereeshe's groups vary freely because she didn't restrict them in any way (e.g., she didn't throw anyone out if they had too many absences). This ability of the variable to vary freely is directly related to the concept of **degrees of freedom** that we first mentioned in connection with chi-square. Degrees of freedom is a numerical way of expressing how much capacity the data have to vary, and conceptually it consists of the sample size minus the number of restrictions on the data. In the *t*-distribution, the population variance is estimated by using $n - 1$. This is a restriction that results in the loss of one degree of freedom for each sample because there are only $n - 1$ quantities left to vary. The total degrees of freedom is found by summing the degrees of freedom for both of the two samples $(n_1 - 1) + (n_2 - 1) = n_1 + n_2 - 2$.

   In the days before statistical software programs, you would have computed the *t*-value of 2.423 associated with our example by using a formula like the one shown here, calculated the df, and then consulted a table containing the critical values of *t* (like Table 9.1). Looking at a specially prepared table of *t*-values found in all the older statistical texts, you would have noticed various columns associated with the different probability levels (e.g., .001, .01, .05) and rows that differentiated degrees of freedom. Finding the row for 18 degrees of freedom $(10 - 1 + 10 - 1 = 18)$, you would then have read over to the column for .05 and found the critical value of 2.101. Since the computed value of 2.423 was greater than that critical value, you would have concluded that this was a significant finding, and that the two groups were, in fact, significantly different.

   Here's what the formula for computing a *t*-value actually looks like when the two groups have approximately equal variances:

$$t = \frac{\overline{X}_1 - \overline{X}_2}{\sqrt{(s^2)\dfrac{N_1 + N_2}{N_1 N_2}}}$$

where
s_1^2 = variance of the first sample
s_2^2 = variance of the second sample
N_1 = size of first sample
N_2 = size of second sample

$$s^2 = \frac{(N_1 - 1)s_1^2 + (N_2 - 1)s_2^2}{N_1 + N_2 - 2}$$

TABLE 13.1   Group Statistics

ABSENCES		N	MEAN	STANDARD DEVIATION	STANDARD ERROR MEAN
Group	1.00	10	1.5000	1.2693	.4014
	2.00	10	3.0000	1.4907	.4714

absences. Is this a statistically significant difference? Table 13.2, the second table prepared by SPSS, presents the results of Levene's test, which helps us decide which of two *t*-test formulas ought to be used. This table shows that the variances in the two groups were not significantly different (e.g., $p > .05$; that is, the groups have similar variances). In other words, there is not a lot of distortion in the data caused by strange outliers and, therefore, the *t*-test formula for assuming equal variances can be used.

Table 13.3 reports the corresponding data from the use of the equal variance *t*-test formula. In Table 13.3, we find the *t*-value, the degrees of freedom, and a *p* value of .026. The latter is evidence that the absentee rates for the two groups are really different because the probability of their occurring at that level by chance

TABLE 13.2   Levene's Test for Equality of Variances

	F	SIGNIFICANCE
Equal variances assumed	.356	.558
Equal variances not assumed		

TABLE 13.3   Independent-Samples *t*-Test

ABSENCES	t	df	SIGNIFICANCE (TWO-TAILED)	MEAN DIFFERENCE	STD. ERROR DIFFERENCE	95% CONFIDENCE INTERVAL OF THE MEAN	
						Lower	*Upper*
Equal variances assumed	−2.423	18	.026	−1.5000	.6191	−2.8008	−.1992

was less than .05. In other words, the absentee rates in these two groups of Jereeshe's clients are statistically significant; the odds of their happening the way they did by chance alone would have been about 3 times in 100 samples of clients. Group 2 really does have greater absenteeism than Group 1.

INDEPENDENT-SAMPLES *t*-TEST

In the previous example, Jereeshe conducted an **independent-samples *t*-test.** It gets its name from the fact that the two groups are not connected or related to each other in a direct way. Although both groups are receiving the same intervention from the same agency, that doesn't affect the statistical view of these two samples as being independent of each other. Similarly, if Jereeshe wants to combine the data from the two different groups and then compare the men with the women, or employed clients with the unemployed clients, she would also be drawing independent samples. Now let's look at what constitutes samples that are not independent.

PAIRED-SAMPLES *t*-TEST

Sometimes the researcher is not as interested in differences between diverse groups as much as in determining if changes occur within a group. The investigator may want to know, for instance, whether his intervention made a difference for those clients who received it. Did clients get better or improve? The **paired-samples *t*-test,** also called the **correlated-samples *t*-test,** doesn't compare the mean of a sample against a population mean—rather, it compares measurements taken at two different points in time from a single group of clients to determine if there is a real difference between the measurements. This is the type of *t*-test one would use any time the same group of subjects is measured twice (e.g., with pretests and posttests) or when the samples are known or logically thought to be correlated. (For instance, there should be a stronger correlation between husbands' and wives' attitudes about child-rearing and marriage than between unrelated men's and women's attitudes.)

The paired-samples *t*-test is also employed when matching is used to construct a second group that closely resembles the first, and when the differences between biological twins are studied. The most frequent use, however, is with pretest-posttest comparisons for one group of subjects. To take a practical example, let's assume that Jereeshe, being a conscientious social worker, is measuring her clients' progress using several standardized instruments. Her prime interest at the moment is in learning if, after a 12-week intervention, her 20 clients in Group 1 and Group 2 have shown any increase in their self-esteem. If not, she wants to make some modifications to the intervention for subsequent groups.

Using a 25-item self-esteem scale that has a theoretical range of scores from 25 to 175 (anything below 100 indicates need of intervention), Jereeshe reasoned that since clients in both groups received the same intervention, she can think about them comprising a single large group and conceptualize the data analysis as fitting a pretest-posttest group research design (O X O). (In this notation the first O represents the pretest, the X represents the intervention, and the second O stands for the posttest.) Jereeshe then went on to obtain the following data from her clients:

Self-Esteem Scores

	PRETEST	POSTTEST		PRETEST	POSTTEST
Bob	74	79	Tina	55	64
Ed	89	94	Ben	68	77
Grace	94	96	Vernon	40	52
Burton	82	88	Carol	74	78
Brooke	67	77	Kathy	93	95
Moonbeam	91	94	Jude	83	90
Phyllis	82	82	Demarcus	81	88
Jack	75	71	Raymond	77	86
Heshimu	85	86	C. B.	89	99
Valerie	67	66	Sally	29	55

Jereeshe can't help but notice that some clients (Jack and Valerie) did worse on the posttest than on the pretest, and Phyllis showed no improvement. Despite some great jumps in scores by Sally, Vernon, C. B., and Brooke, was there enough improvement overall for there to be a statistically significant gain?

Using the SPSS statistical software and following the same basic steps to perform any *t*-test (Step 1: enter the data; Step 2: select STATISTICS and then COMPARE MEANS from the menu), Jereeshe at step 3 selected PAIRED-SAMPLES *t*-TEST. Once the computer output was displayed (see Table 13.4), Jereeshe discovered that the mean of the treatment group increased from 74.75 at pretest to 80.85 at posttest. Further, the computer calculated the odds of these means occurring by chance to have been less than 1 time in 1,000 ($p < .001$) (see Table 13.5). Even though this was not a tightly controlled experiment in which all of the extraneous variables had been eliminated, this statistically significant increase in self-esteem helped Jereeshe feel

TABLE 13.4   Paired-Samples Statistics on Self-Esteem Scores

	MEAN	N	STD. DEVIATION	STD. ERROR MEAN
Pretest	74.7500	20	17.0969	3.8230
Posttest	80.8500	20	13.5502	3.0299

TABLE 13.5   Paired-Samples *t*-Test Results

				95% CONFIDENCE INTERVAL OF THE DIFFERENCE				
	MEAN	STD. DEVIATION	STD. ERROR MEAN	*Lower*	*Upper*	*t*	df	SIGNIFICANCE (TWO-TAILED)
Pair 1	−6.1000	6.2987	1.4084	−9.0479	−3.1521	−4.331	19	.000

good about her intervention and skills as a social worker. It at least suggests that the intervention has potential and deserves further study.

Note: The samples or groups have to be of equal size when performing a paired-samples *t*-test, but they do not have to be of equal size for independent-samples *t*-tests. If you are examining pretests and posttests and have an unequal number (e.g., 40 clients took the pretest but only 35 completed the posttest), the paired samples *t*-test will be based on the 35 pairs, where there is both pretest and posttest data.

ONE-SAMPLE *t*-TESTS

t-tests are wonderfully useful statistical procedures. Besides the uses we have already identified, there is another application that merits discussion. When pop-

■ ■ ■ ■ ■

EXAMPLE OF THE USE OF *t*-TESTS IN THE PRACTICE LITERATURE

Would a 12-week family-based intervention for troubled children actually make a difference? Harrison, Boyle, and Farley (1999) designed a study to look at pretest-posttest differences on the dependent variables of family cohesion, family conflict, parent-child agreement, family time spent together, time spent in the community, mental health of the parents, and parenting styles. The *t*-tests revealed significant improvement at posttest on all of these variables except for parent-child agreement.

Paired *t*-tests were also computed for the pretest and posttest scores on the scales of the Child Behavior Check List. Male children improved on every CBCL scale but one (Schizoid). Female children showed fewer statistically significant reductions in problem behaviors.

ulation parameters are already known, researchers can use the **one-sample *t*-test** to determine if a randomly drawn sample is representative of the population.

Here's a brief example: A recent national survey of men and women on probation revealed that 46.8% had used either alcohol, drugs, or both at the time of their offense. Suppose you are working as a probation officer and want to know how the clients you are supervising compare with the national data. Let's say you randomly select the names of 10 clients and then check their records. These are the data you obtain:

	DRUG/ALCOHOL USE PRIOR TO OFFENSE	CONVERSION CODE*
Robb	Yes	1
Shenelle	No	0
Darryl	Yes	1
Lonnie	Yes	1
Dwana	No	0
Steele	Yes	1
Jim Bob	Yes	1
Reza	No	0
Christy	Yes	1
Ron	No	0

*Although this example uses categorical data by coding a "yes" response as 1 and a "no" response as 0, the statistical software allows us to compare the percentages of those with a drug/alcohol history in the sample against the national benchmark comparison.

In this sample of ten probationers, you count six (60%) whose judgment had been impaired because of drugs or alcohol. This is more than the proportion expected, but is it a statistically significant difference? Is this sample showing a greater problem with chemical dependency than in the population? Might your probationers have more of a problem with substance abuse than one might expect?

Conducting a one-sample *t*-test with the SPSS software follows the same basic steps we've already discussed (select ANALYZE, COMPARE MEANS, then ONE-SAMPLE *t*-TEST). When the ONE-SAMPLE *t*-TEST dialog box appears, you then indicate which variables are to be tested (the test variable) and then put the value against which the sample is to be tested in the TEST VALUE box. (Continuing with this example, we use .4860, the decimal equivalent of 46.8%, for the test value.)

The output reveals that even though 60% of this sample were involved with drugs or alcohol (a mean of .60), the mean difference of .1320 was not statistically significant ($p = .44$). In other words, this small sample of probationers did not

TABLE 13.6   One-Sample *t*-Test, Where 18 of 30 Have Alcohol or Drug History

	N	MEAN	STD. DEVIATION	STD. ERROR MEAN
VAR00001	30	.6000	.4983	9.097E-02

Test Value = .48600

	t	df	SIGNIFICANCE (TWO-TAILED)	MEAN DIFFERENCE	95% CONFIDENCE INTERVAL OF THE DIFFERENCE	
					Lower	Upper
VAR00001	1.253	29	.220	.1140	−7.21E-02	.3001

significantly deviate from the national sample, they were not any more involved with drugs or alcohol than would be expected.

Because of the small sample size, appearances can be a little deceiving. Had 18 of 30 of the probationers been involved with drugs or alcohol, there also would not have been statistical significance ($p = .22$) (see Table 13.6). However, the involvement of 20 out of 30 from your caseload would be significant ($p < .05$) (see Table 13.7).

Let's try a one-sample *t*-test with interval-level data that need no conversion. Jose found that a sample of the children in his caseload had been in foster care an average of 19 months. The statewide average is 17.4 months. Jose wants to know if

TABLE 13.7   One-Sample *t*-test, Where 20 of 30 Have Alcohol or Drug History

	N	MEAN	STD. DEVIATION	STD. ERROR MEAN
VAR00001	30	.6667	.4795	8.754E-02

Test Value = .48600

	t	df	SIGNIFICANCE (TWO-TAILED)	MEAN DIFFERENCE	95% CONFIDENCE INTERVAL OF THE DIFFERENCE	
					Lower	Upper
VAR00001	2.064	29	.048	.1807	1.632E-03	.3597

this average is a significantly longer length of time than is being experienced by other children in foster care?

LENGTH OF TIME IN FOSTER CARE

Hanna	24 months
Abbie	5 months
Syed	17 months
Jhoni	12 months
Nader	15 months
Lee	18 months
Tony	22 months
Yvette	40 months

Table 13.8 shows us that, although 19 months seems like it is significantly longer than the benchmark comparison of 17.4, actually the difference is not significant. Jose does not need to worry that this sample of the children in his caseload are spending more time, on average, than is standard.

ANALYSIS OF VARIANCE (ANOVA)

Analysis of variance, also known as **ANOVA,** or **one-way analysis of variance,** is a helpful statistical procedure when you have an interval-level dependent variable and more than two groups, and you want to know if the means for the groups are similar or different. ANOVA is based on the variance within groups and between groups, and it allows the researcher to understand if the groups significantly vary

TABLE 13.8 One-Sample *t*-Test for Length of Time in Foster Care

	N	MEAN	STD. DEVIATION	STD. ERROR MEAN
VAR00001	8	19.1250	10.2878	3.673

Test Value = 17.40

					95% CONFIDENCE INTERVAL OF THE DIFFERENCE	
	t	df	SIG (2-TAILED)	MEAN DIFFERENCE	*Lower*	*Upper*
VAR00001	.474	7	.650	1.7250	−6.8758	10.3258

from each other. With this procedure, one dependent variable and one independent variable form the groups. The null hypothesis of a one-way ANOVA is that the mean score on the dependent variable is the same in each of the underlying populations represented by the sample groups being compared.

To understand ANOVA, let's start with the following scenario:

■ ■ ■ ■ ■ ■

SCENARIO: PROGRAM EVALUATION

Tiffinea has just been hired as the program evaluator for a large drug-treatment agency that is known for offering a wide array of programs for those with substance-abuse problems. The agency runs three programs: an outpatient drug treatment program, a methadone maintenance program, and a drug-free residential treatment program.

The agency's executive director, Ms. Collins, with a worried look on her face, says, "Tiffinea, our largest funding source is threatening to make a major cut in our funding next year unless we can supply them with data that our programs actually work. I need your help."

Tiffinea asks, "What kind of information are they looking for?"

"We have to follow up on previous clients from all three programs and interview either the clients or their significant others to find out if they are abstinent or still using."

"Okay, I know where to find some questionnaires developed for NIDA (the National Institute on Drug Abuse)—that won't be a problem. Let's see, . . . how many staff can you make available for interviewing?"

"None, I'm afraid. In fact, I'm probably going to have to cut 1½ clinical positions in the next couple of months. Think you can do it with just the help of our social work students?"

"Then we're not talking about interviewing several hundred clients?"

"I was thinking this effort would be on a small scale—maybe 25 former clients from each of the programs, plus a control group. Completing 100 interviews would be good, I think. We'll get the bugs out of the procedure this year, and then begin planning to get better data next year."

The outcome assessment instrument that Tiffinea decides on is very comprehensive; it examines self-reported use of injected drugs as well as drugs that are swallowed, snorted, or smoked. Altogether, more than 75 questions are asked of each respondent, but for the purposes of learning about ANOVA we are chiefly interested in one particular question. This item asks, "How many days have you used alcohol, marijuana, or crack in the last 30 days?"

Twenty-five respondents who had been enrolled for at least 90 days were randomly selected from each program (outpatient, methadone maintenance, and residential). An additional 25 who had begun any of the three programs and then dropped out in the first month of treatment were randomly selected to serve as the control group. A portion of the data that Tiffinea and her two social work interns collect looks like this:

RESPONDENT NUMBER	TREATMENT GROUP	DAYS OF USE REPORTED
31	Outpatient	0
32	Outpatient	0
33	Outpatient	26
34	Outpatient	24
35	Outpatient	24
36	Outpatient	22
37	Outpatient	20
38	Outpatient	18
39	Outpatient	16
40	Outpatient	14
41	Outpatient	12
42	Outpatient	10
43	Outpatient	8
44	Outpatient	6
45	Outpatient	4
46	Methadone	6
47	Methadone	13
48	Methadone	10
49	Methadone	14
50	Methadone	28

To obtain the means from the four groups of respondents, Tiffinea enters all her data into SPSS. She then selects COMPARE MEANS and then MEANS from the SPSS menu. When the dialog box appears, she indicates that Days of Use Reported is the dependent variable, and Treatment Group is the independent variable. The output she receives is as follows:

Number of Days Drugs Used by Treatment Group

TREATMENT GROUP	MEAN	*N*	STD. DEVIATION
Outpatient	8.16	25	9.54
Methadone	14.50	25	9.32
Dropouts (Control)	16.00	25	7.35
Residential	3.08	25	4.99

Looking at the means, we immediately see that the residential and outpatient groups used drugs on fewer occasions than did the control and methadone maintenance groups. For example, residential clients used drugs on average 13 days less than those in the control group and 11 days less than those on methadone. But do these large differences in means represent real differences among the groups? Or do they merely reflect sampling error? Not only is the variance between groups a consideration, there's also variance within groups. Fortunately, ANOVA allows Tiffinea to test the assumption that the group means represent four different population means. A null hypothesis would state that there is no actual difference in the mean scores, and that they deviate from one another largely because of sampling error. A finding of significance would mean that the null hypothesis is rejected.

Analysis of Variance Assumptions

Before conducting an analysis of variance, the researcher should consider four questions. If any of these assumptions cannot be made, then the probability findings produced by the ANOVA procedure may be invalid:

1. Are the data measured at the interval level, and are they a random sample of the larger population?
2. Are the groups independent of each other? (They should consist of different individuals with no overlapping membership. For example, John, Sal, and Fay should not be found in both the Outpatient and Residential Groups. Also, one individual's score should not depend on someone else's score.)
3. Are the data normally distributed?
4. Is there rough equivalence in variance, or approximately the same number of cases in each group?

ANOVA is known for being a powerful (robust) statistical procedure that still performs well even if one or more of the assumptions are violated. In this example, Tiffinea felt that her data met all of the assumptions, so she proceeded to analyze the data.

Computer Application: Conducting an ANOVA

There's absolutely nothing tricky about conducting a one-way analysis of variance using a statistical software program such as SPSS, or the analytic features of a program such as Excel. Tiffinea simply followed these steps: First, she chose ANALYZE from the menu, then ONE-WAY ANALYSIS. When the dialog box opened, she indicated which variable was the dependent variable and which was the factor (independent variable). In this case, the dependent variable is the number of days in the last 30 that former clients have used alcohol, crack, or pot. The independent variable is the treatment group, which allows the means to be computed on the basis of type of intervention clients received.

ANOVA Output

	SUM OF SQUARES	df	MEAN SQUARE	F	SIGNIFICANCE
Between groups	2,673.200	3	891.067	13.88	.001
Within groups					
Total					

From this output, Tiffinea immediately notes that $p < .001$, which confirms that the large differences in means (displayed in the previous table) are not due to sampling error, but indicate that these groups of clients have very different patterns of drug use. Since the residential clients report using drugs less often than the other groups, this finding could likely be interpreted as indicating that the residential program is more effective than the other approaches. However, statistically speaking, the only thing the ANOVA does is to establish that there were differences among the four groups being compared.

Tiffinea doesn't have to interpret, like reading tea leaves, the *F*-statistic produced by the analysis of variance formula. Although she knows that, in general, larger *F*-values are associated with statistically significant findings, her main focus is on whether the group means were truly different, and this is revealed by the probability that these same means would have occurred by chance less than 1 time in 1,000.

When Tiffinea shares her findings with the executive director, Ms. Collins now is intrigued by several new questions:

- Are the residential program clients more successful than clients in the outpatient program?
- Are those clients in the methadone maintenance program really using fewer drugs than clients who have dropped out of treatment and are trying to quit on their own?
- Are clients in the outpatient program actually using fewer drugs than the methadone maintenance clients?

The ANOVA can't answer these questions—the finding of significance simply means only that there were differences among the four groups being compared. In other words, the ANOVA finding can't be used to answer Ms. Collins' questions. However, the ANOVA procedure in SPSS does allow for the computation of optional statistics that will answer her questions. These statistics are discussed in the post hoc comparison subsection presented below.

Degrees of Freedom

The degrees of freedom in an ANOVA is a little easier to understand than those associated with a *t*-test. You'll note in the previous table that degrees of freedom (df) were reported for both the "between groups" category and the "within groups" category. The df for the between groups comparison will always be one less than the number of groups, whereas the df for the within groups category is computed by subtracting one from each of the sample sizes, and then summing the results (e.g., 24 + 24 + 24 + 24 = 96). The total df will always be one less than the total number of subjects. When reporting the results of a one-way analysis of variance in the text of a paper, typically only the degrees of freedom for between groups and within groups are shown, as in this example from the previous table: F (3, 96) = 13.88, p < .001. Thus, a reader of your findings would know by adding 1 to the first df that there were four groups in the study. Similarly, adding the two dfs together and adding 1 to that number would tell the reader there were 100 subjects in the study.

Post Hoc Comparisons

Once an ANOVA has been computed, sometimes the researcher wants to go a step further and test for significant differences between specific pairings of groups (e.g., to compare the outpatient clients to the residential program clients) in order to identify which pairings of means are significantly different from each other. The analysis of variance procedure does not provide this information when there are three or more groups; it tells us only that the means were not similar. When multiple groups are being compared and F is significant, then the researcher has several options for investigating what contributed to the finding of significance. These procedures are called **post hoc tests,** or post hoc multiple comparisons.

The problem is that the more comparisons that are made, the greater the chance of making a Type I error (often called an inflated Type I error risk). With a significance level of .05, the researcher accepts that 5 out of every 100 statistically significant relationships may be produced by chance, and the opposite is true as well—5 out of 100 relationships judged not significant really are. Let's bring this down on a smaller scale. For every 20 significance tests you run, the results of one procedure will be determined more by chance than by real differences. That's what you accept with a p = .05 significance level.

To reduce the problem of finding significance that's actually produced by chance when multiple comparisons will be made with t-tests, the **Bonferroni procedure** calls for the researcher to divide the .05 probability level by the number of statistical tests to be conducted. The resulting value is the new probability level. Thus, if you were planning on conducting five t-tests, then you would require the new significance level of .01 (.05 divided by 5 = .01). Conducting 10 bivariate tests would result in a significance level of .005 (.05 divided by 10 = .005).

Another option is to use SPSS (or similar statistical software) and, for instance, to go to the ANOVA dialog box and select POST HOC. This will allow the researcher to choose from a list of post hoc procedures. An advantage of the SPSS Bonferroni procedure is that it is conservative and produces output that is easy to comprehend. As Table 13.9 shows, it computes the mean differences between each

TABLE 13.9   Bonferroni Post Hoc Output

(I) TREATMENT SETTING	(J) TREATMENT SETTING	MEAN DIFFERENCE (I–J)	STD. ERROR	SIGNIFICANCE	95% CONFIDENCE INTERVAL	
					Lower Bound	Upper Bound
1.00	2.00	–6.3600*	2.266	.036	–12.4655	–.2545
	3.00	–7.8400*	2.266	.005	–13.9455	–1.7345
	4.00	5.0800	2.266	.164	–1.0255	11.1855
2.00	1.00	6.3600*	2.266	.036	.2545	12.4655
	3.00	–1.4800	2.266	1.000	–7.5855	4.6255
	4.00	11.4400*	2.266	.000	5.3345	17.5455
3.00	1.00	7.8400*	2.266	.005	1.7345	13.9455
	2.00	1.4800	2.266	1.000	–4.6255	7.5855
	4.00	12.9200*	2.266	.000	6.8145	19.0255
4.00	1.00	–5.0800	2.266	.164	–11.1855	1.0255
	2.00	–11.4400*	2.266	.000	–17.5455	–5.3345
	3.00	–12.9200*	2.266	.000	–19.0255	–6.8145

*The mean difference is significant at the .05 level.

Key to Treatment Setting Codes: Outpatient Treatment = 1, Methadone Maintenance = 2, Dropouts (Control) = 3, and Residential Program = 4

of all possible pairings of groups, and it indicates with asterisks those that are statistically significant. The printed significance values are the *p*-values of the *t*-test multiplied by the number of comparisons. Thus the Bonferroni procedure corrects for the problem of multiple comparisons.

Note that although eight asterisks are shown in the Bonferroni output, only four pairings of groups are unique and statistically significant. For example, the comparison of group 1, outpatient, with group 3, the control, is the same as comparing group 3 with group 1.

The output shows that the residential treatment group did not obtain significantly better results than the outpatient groups (Ms. Collins' first question). Further, this output reveals that there are significant differences between the outpatient and methadone treatment groups (Ms. Collins' second question), as well as between the methadone maintenance and control groups (Ms. Collins' third question). As one might expect, there were also significant differences between the outpatient and control groups, and between the residential treatment and the control groups. Because the lower means are better (indicating fewer days of drug use), the post hoc testing allows us to conclude that the methadone maintenance was better than doing nothing, that outpatient treatment was more effective than the methadone program, and that although the residential clients reported fewer days of drug use than those in the outpatient group, these differences were not statistically significant.

Besides the Bonferroni procedure, SPSS allows researchers other ways of making post hoc comparisons. The Duncan and Scheffe procedures are also popular. Another possibility would be for the investigator to conduct a series of independent samples *t*-tests. Although it is perfectly acceptable to make a post hoc comparison by using a *t*-test, you should avoid making *many* *t*-test comparisons. Multiple comparisons (for example, when you are calculating 10, 12, or 20 separate *t*-tests) increase the probability that you'll find something significant even when the means really aren't that different. The post hoc procedures such as the Bonferroni procedure have been designed to minimize Type I error and take into consideration that multiple comparisons are being made.

Note: When an ANOVA indicates no significant differences among groups, it is unlikely that significant differences do exist between selected pairs of groups. However, to look at every possible pairing of groups simply to be able to report some finding of significance would be considered by many statisticians to be bad form—a violation of the concept of post hoc testing.

REPORTING *t*-TESTS AND ANOVAS IN MANUSCRIPTS

Most professional journals expect you to report *t*-values and *F*-values, degrees of freedom, and the associated probabilities each time in the manuscript that you indicate use of a statistical procedure. However, some journals will let you get away with not reporting all of that when your findings are not significant. To be on the safe side, follow this format for reporting each computation of a *t*-test or ANOVA: For ANOVAs,

$$F(3, 96) = 13.88, \quad p = .001$$

where 3 = degrees of freedom between groups
    96 = within groups degrees of freedom
  13.88 = *F*-value

For *t*-tests,

$$t(18) = 2.423, \quad p = .03$$

where 18 = degrees of freedom
    2.423 is the computed *t*-value

For further reference, see the *Publication Manual of the American Psychological Association* (APA, 1994).

TERMS TO KNOW

ANOVA (p. 241)

Bonferroni procedure (p. 246)

Categorical data (p. 230)

Correlated-samples *t*-test (p. 236)

Degrees of freedom (p. 234)

Independent-samples *t*-test (p. 236)

One-sample *t*-test (p. 239)

One-way analysis of variance (p. 241)

Paired-samples *t*-test (p. 236)

Post hoc tests (p. 246)

t-test (p. 232)

REVIEW PROBLEMS

The scenario: Robin has been running a shoplifting diversion program for the local municipal court. At the end of 1 year, she examines the re-arrests of the 20 clients she has counseled and the 26 who have dropped out or refused counseling. Those in the psycho-education intervention met every Saturday morning for 10 weeks. Some clients in the control group chose to go to jail rather than get counseling; others dropped out or moved out of the community. These are Robin's data:

Client Re-Arrest Data

CLIENT NUMBER	NUMBER OF RE-ARRESTS	TREATMENT CONDITION
1	1	psycho-education group
2	1	psycho-education group
3	1	psycho-education group
4	1	psycho-education group
5	0	psycho-education group
6	0	psycho-education group
7	0	psycho-education group
8	0	psycho-education group
9	0	psycho-education group
10	0	psycho-education group
11	0	psycho-education group
12	0	psycho-education group
13	0	psycho-education group
14	0	psycho-education group
15	0	psycho-education group
16	0	psycho-education group
17	0	psycho-education group
18	0	psycho-education group
19	0	psycho-education group
20	0	psycho-education group
21	3	no group treatment
22	1	no group treatment
23	1	no group treatment
24	2	no group treatment
25	1	no group treatment

26	1	no group treatment
27	4	no group treatment
28	1	no group treatment
29	0	no group treatment
30	2	no group treatment
31	0	no group treatment
32	3	no group treatment
33	0	no group treatment
34	0	no group treatment
35	0	no group treatment
36	0	no group treatment
37	0	no group treatment
38	0	no group treatment
39	0	no group treatment
40	0	no group treatment
41	0	no group treatment
42	0	no group treatment
43	0	no group treatment
44	0	no group treatment
45	0	no group treatment
46	0	no group treatment

1. Robin's dependent variable is measured at what level?

   (A) NOMINAL   (B) ORDINAL   (C) INTERVAL

2. Compute the mean re-arrest rates for each group. What are they?

3. Robin wants to know if psycho-education intervention is successful. She will know that if the treatment group's re-arrest rate is significantly lower than the control group's rate. To determine statistical significance, which of the following should Robin use:

   (A) ANOVA   (B) PAIRED-SAMPLES *t*-TEST   (C) INDEPENDENT-SAMPLES *t*-TEST

4. If you have access to statistical software, compute a *t*-test using Robin's data. What are the results?

5. Write the results in approved APA style as you would if including them in a manuscript for publication.

   New Scenario: Judge Warner asks Robin to extend her study by including data from 25 individuals who chose jail rather than participating in the diversion program. These are the new data:

Additional Re-Arrest Data

CLIENT NUMBER	NUMBER OF RE-ARRESTS	TREATMENT CONDITION
47	1	Jail
48	1	Jail
49	1	Jail

50	1	Jail
51	0	Jail
52	0	Jail
53	0	Jail
54	0	Jail
55	0	Jail
56	0	Jail
57	2	Jail
58	1	Jail
59	2	Jail
60	3	Jail
61	4	Jail
62	0	Jail
63	1	Jail
64	2	Jail
65	0	Jail
66	0	Jail
67	0	Jail
68	0	Jail
69	0	Jail
70	0	Jail
71	4	Jail

6. What statistical procedure should Robin now use to determine if there are significant differences between the treatment group, the control, and those who went to jail?

   (A) ANOVA   (B) PAIRED-SAMPLES *t*-TEST   (C) INDEPENDENT-SAMPLES *t*-TEST

7. Which group had the highest mean re-arrest rate?

8. If you have access to statistical software, compute a one-way analysis of variance using all of the data. Are the differences among the three groups statistically significant? What is the probability?

9. Write the results in approved APA style as you would if you were including them in a manuscript for publication.

10. True or false—if Robin had pretest and posttest measurements on her treatment group of clients using an impulsiveness scale, it would be appropriate to use the paired-samples *t*-test to examine for any improvement as a result of the intervention.

11. Here is a problem to solve using SPSS or other statistical software: Jose has expanded his sample and now wants to recompute another one-sample *t*-test with the following new data:

Length of Time in Foster Care

Hanna	24 months
Abbie	5 months
Syed	17 months
Jhoni	12 months

Nader	15 months
Lee	18 months
Tony	22 months
Yvette	40 months
Micki	9 months
Jesse	8 months
Marlanda	18 months
Mika	8 months
Ladonna	19 months

Is the new average length of stay in foster care now significantly different from the benchmark comparison of 17.4 months?

REFERENCES

American Psychological Association (APA). (1994). *Publication manual* (4th ed.). Washington, DC: Author.

Boland, P. J. (1984). A biographical glimpse of William Sealy Gosset. *The American Statistician 38,* pp. 179–182.

Harrison, R. S., Boyle, S. W. & Farley, O. W. (1999). Evaluating the outcomes of family-based intervention for troubled children: A pretest-posttest study. *Research on Social Work Practice, 9* (6), 640–655.

CHAPTER FOURTEEN

A GLIMPSE INTO
MULTIVARIATE ANALYSES

The cross-tabulation procedures introduced in Chapter 11 and the correlation techniques presented in Chapter 12 allow the social work researcher to examine how the values or scores associated with one variable (e.g., income) change in relationship to the scores obtained for another variable (e.g., gender). Indeed, by going beyond mere description and allowing us to examine the strength and direction of the relationships that exist between pairs of variables, these analytic procedures permit us to address more complex research questions. Returning to our restaurant comparison for a moment, although the addition of bivariate strategies may enrich one's dining experience, the pièce de résistance (main dish) emerges when the social work researcher enters the world of multivariate analysis.

Specifically, given our profession's person-in-environment focus, most issues and behaviors of concern to social workers involve the interplay of multiple factors or variables. Consider, for example, topics such as poverty, teen suicide, elder abuse, or alcoholism. None of these phenomena is viewed by social work as the result of one variable's influence alone. Rather, they're typically seen as the outcome of various factors coming together in particular ways. Understanding how individual factors influence a problem requires social work researchers and practitioners to disentangle the multiple relationships that exist among the variables. By allowing us to simultaneously examine the interrelationships occurring among three or more variables, multivariate analytic approaches provide one means of facilitating social work's search for a more adequate understanding of the complex phenomena the profession confronts.

Examples of multivariate techniques include multiple correlation, multiple regression, two-way analysis of variance, discriminant analysis, factor analysis, analysis of covariance (ANCOVA), path analysis, logistic regression, and linear structural equation modeling (LISREL). Although in-depth coverage of these techniques is beyond the scope of this text, in this chapter we'll introduce you to three of the most common multivariate strategies you're likely to encounter within the social work literature: multiple correlation, multiple regression, and two-way analysis of variance. We emphasize the introductory nature of this discussion—

whole texts have been written on each of these topics (see, for example, Pedhazur, 1982; Hosmer & Lemeshow, 1989; Hayduk, 1987). Our goal is simply to familiarize you with the analytic purposes served by the three highlighted techniques and to provide guidelines for interpreting their associated findings.

MULTIPLE CORRELATION

In Chapter 12, we learned that the term *correlation* is used by researchers to quantitatively describe the strength and direction of a relationship between two interval-, or ratio-level variables. The **multiple correlation** approach—or more simply, **multiple R**—extends the bivariate Pearson correlation (r) to analytic circumstances involving three or more interval-, or ratio-level variables. Specifically, the approach yields a correlation coefficient (denoted as R to distinguish it from the bivariate correlation coefficient, r), which tells us how much of the variation observed within a selected criterion (i.e., dependent) variable is associated with the variation in scores noted within a given set of two or more predictor (i.e., independent) variables.

Technically speaking, the procedure uses z-scores, calculus, and matrix algebra to simultaneously examine the bivariate correlations occurring between each predictor variable in the set and the criterion variable, as well as the bivariate correlations occurring among the predictor variables themselves. In turn, these data are used to weight the independent contribution made by each predictor variable and to identify which combination of weighted predictor variables correlates most highly with the criterion variable. The set of predictor variables derived through this process should explain more of the variation observed in the criterion variable than any single predictor—or any other grouping of the predictor variables—included in the analysis.

Given its capacity to help select the "best" set of predictors available, multiple correlation emerges as a particularly useful tool within the social worker's analytic arsenal. Among other things, the procedure can be used to help social workers target resources and services toward those most at risk, by allowing them to identify the community, family, and individual characteristics most likely to accompany the occurrence of such varied problems as child abuse, substance abuse, unemployment, and AIDS.

Outcomes Associated with Multiple Correlation

Like the simple bivariate correlation coefficient, r (often referred to as the zero-order correlation), the **coefficient of multiple correlation, R**, is a measure of correlation between variables. In the case of multiple R, however, the predictor variable is actually a composite of two or more predictor variables that have been optimally weighted to yield the highest possible correlation. Also like the correlation coefficient r, the value of multiple R is interpreted as an indication of the strength, or magnitude, of the relationship. Values closer to 0 reflect smaller, less consequential correlations, whereas values closer to +1 or –1 signify stronger, more influential relationships (Williams, 1986).

Note for the advanced student: Theoretically, if all the predictor variables were negatively related to the criterion variable, multiple R could take on a negative value. In actuality, though, most sets of predictor variables contain some items that relate positively with the criterion variable, as well as some that relate negatively. Consequently, for reasons beyond the scope of this text, multiple R will always take on a positive value (Craft, 1990).

The statistical significance of the value obtained for R can be tested against the null hypothesis H_0: $R = 0$. We won't venture into the specific calculations, but the test involved yields a value referred to as an F-statistic, which allows us to evaluate the likelihood that the value obtained for R occurred as the result of sampling error or chance. As described in previous chapters, if the probability associated with the statistic (in this case, F) falls below the rejection level set by the researcher (e.g., $p < .05$), the relationship conveyed by R is considered significant.

Like the coefficient of determination (r^2) generated by the bivariate correlation procedure, the **coefficient of multiple determination R^2** provides a measure of explained variance. That is, **multiple R^2** tells us the proportion of variance in the criterion variable, expressed as a percentage, that can be predicted, accounted for, or explained by the variation occurring within the derived (i.e., composite) predictor variable. An example illustrating how multiple correlation could be used might prove helpful here.

Multiple Correlation in Action

Imagine you're doing your social work internship at an outpatient substance abuse treatment program for adolescents. Teens enrolled in this program participate in both individual and group counseling activities. Although the ultimate treatment outcome sought for each participant is total abstinence, staff use other factors, called intermediate indicators, to measure the progress participants are making toward reaching this goal. In addition to substance-use reports, standardized measures of self-esteem, self-efficacy regarding substance use, and social functioning are routinely administered to program participants. Suppose the most recent data gathered suggest that the program seems to be having a positive effect, as measured by these intermediate outcomes. Interested in knowing specifically how participation in the individual and group counseling activities relate to participants' performance in these areas, your supervisor calculates the bivariate correlations involved. Her findings are presented in Table 14.1.

In looking at these data, it appears that both the number of individual and group counseling sessions attended are positively (and significantly) correlated with all the intermediate outcome indicators. Particularly striking, though, is the strength of the relationships observed between the number of individual and

TABLE 14.1   Zero-Order (Bivariate) Correlations Using Simulated Data for the Adolescent Substance-Abuse Treatment Program (N = 30)

VARIABLE	SOCIAL FUNCTIONING	SELF-ESTEEM	SELF-EFFICACY	NUMBER OF INDIVIDUAL SESSIONS	NUMBER OF GROUP SESSIONS
Social functioning	1.00	.35	.32	.61**	.80**
Self-esteem		1.00	.38*	.46*	.41*
Self-efficacy			1.00	.43*	.44*
Number of individual sessions				1.00	.48*
Number of group sessions					1.00

*p < .01 (two-tailed).

**p < .001 (two-tailed).

group counseling sessions attended and the level of social functioning achieved (r = .61 and .80, respectively). Because each of these treatment approaches correlates so strongly with social functioning, we wonder what their combined effect is. Fortunately, we can use a multivariate correlation analysis to help us clarify the nature of this joint impact. Intuitively, it might seem sensible to determine the combined effect of two predictor variables on a single criterion variable by simply summing the bivariate correlations involved. Unfortunately, that's not how it's done. To understand why, let's see what would happen if we took that approach.

A bivariate correlation (r) of .80 was obtained between group counseling and social functioning. The zero-order correlation (r) found between individual counseling and social functioning was .61. If we simply add these items together, we get a combined correlation—R, of 1.41 (.80 + 61 = 1.41). Because the value of R can never exceed 1.00, a perfect correlation, such an answer is meaningless. What this overrepresentation of the relationship suggests is that some of the variation occurring within the criterion variable is covered, or accounted for, by both predictors. In other words, these predictors have elements in common that contribute to their explaining the same variation in the data.

Don't be discouraged by this apparent conundrum, though; there are various statistical approaches we can use to resolve this problem. One option consists of using a formula such as the one presented in Formulae Alert 14.1. to calculate by hand the multiple correlation coefficient (Multiple R) desired. A much more appealing (and expedient) alternative, however, is to use the linear regression function available through most statistical software packages. Despite the fact that computerized regression procedures yield a great deal of information beyond multiple R and multiple R^2, the pertinent data can be easily extrapolated from the output generated. To illustrate, we ran a linear regression model on the adolescent

---

FORMULAE ALERT 14.1

To calculate a coefficient of multiple correlation, R, for a circumstance involving two predictor variables, simply add the following formula:

$$R_{zxy} = \frac{r^2xz + r^2yz - 2rxzryzrzy}{1 - r^2xy}$$

where x = first predictor variable
         y = second predictor variable
         z = criterion variable
         r = bivariate correlation for the variables that follow (e.g., "r^2xz" is telling us to square the value obtained for the bivariate relationship, r, between the first predictor, x, and the criterion variable, z.

---

substance-abuse treatment center data using the regression feature available in SPSS. The information we gleaned pertaining to multiple R and multiple R^2 are summarized in Table 14.2.

What do the data in Table 14.2 tell us? Since the first row of data focuses only on the relationship between group counseling and social functioning scores, it shouldn't surprise you to learn that the value of multiple R obtained (.80) is identical to the bivariate correlation (r) reported for these two variables in Table 14.1. As the "Guide for Interpreting the Magnitude of Correlation Coefficients" presented in Chapter 12 (see p. 215) suggests, a multiple R of .80 indicates there is a strong correlation between the number of group sessions attended and the level of social functioning achieved. In fact, the corresponding multiple R^2 of .64 suggests that participation in group sessions accounts for about 64% of the variation in social functioning observed among these teens. The F-score and its accompanying significance level ($p < .001$) tell us that the relationship depicted isn't likely to have occurred by chance. The only new concept presented in Table 14.2 is the Adjusted R^2, and its inclusion here warrants a brief explanation.

TABLE 14.2 Multiple Correlation between Social Functioning and Two Predictor Variables: Group Treatment and Individual Treatment

PREDICTORS	MULTIPLE R	MULTIPLE R^2	ADJUSTED R^2	F	SIGNIFICANCE OF F
Group	.80	.64	.63	49.78	.001
Group, Individual	.84	.71	.68	32.34	.001

Why Adjust R^2?

As noted in Chapter 9, not all sample statistics function equally well when it comes to accurately estimating their corresponding population parameters. In the case of multiple R (and by extension, multiple R^2), statisticians have shown that multiple correlation coefficients derived from sample data consistently overestimate the strength of the relationships portrayed, when compared with multiple correlations derived from population data. In statistical parlance, therefore, multiple R and multiple R^2 are believed to be biased estimators of their respective population parameters.

Two factors that influence the level of bias found within this multivariate correlation procedure are the number of cases and the number of variables involved in the analysis. Given this, there are a couple of things researchers can do to offset this tendency toward bias. First, the number of predictor variables should be kept small in relation to the number of cases. As a rule of thumb, there should be at least ten participants (or cases) for each predictor variable included in the analysis. Second, the R^2 reported should be adjusted downward to reflect the actual number of cases and predictor variables included in the analysis; hence, the resulting statistic is called **adjusted R^2**. Application of the equation used to produce this adjustment is reflected in the adjusted R^2 score that is automatically produced by the linear regression feature available in most statistical software packages. If this feature isn't available in the statistical package you use, you can easily calculate an adjusted R^2 by applying the formula presented in Formulae Alert 14.2.

Returning to the data presented in Table 14.2, we find an adjusted R^2 of .63. Given what we now know about the tendency of R^2 to be somewhat inflated, we'd be more accurate in saying that participation in group sessions was found to account for approximately 63% (rather than 64%) of the variation in social functioning observed.

It's not until we focus on the second row of data presented in Table 14.2 that we begin to see how involvement in both group and individual counseling ses-

---

FORMULAE ALERT 14.2

An adjusted R^2 can be easily calculated using the following formula:

$$\text{Adjusted } R^2 = 1 - \left| \left(\frac{N-1}{N-k} \right)(1 - R^2) \right|$$

where N = the number of cases
    k = number of predictor variables
    R^2 = coefficient of multiple determination ($R \times R$)

sions jointly influence these teens' level of social functioning. Specifically, when individual counseling is brought into the analysis, the value of multiple R increases from .80 to .84, suggesting a strong relationship between the number of individual and group sessions attended and the level of social functioning achieved. In light of its tendency to overestimate, let's skip the data pertaining to multiple R^2 and focus directly on the column labeled "Adjusted R^2." Doing so, we find that about 68% of the variation in social functioning observed can be accounted for by the number of individual and group sessions attended. Together, then, individual and group counseling correlate more strongly with social functioning than either variable alone. But is the 4% increase in the amount of variation explained once we add individual counseling to the equation significant? From a statistical standpoint, yes—the F-score ($F = 32.34$) and corresponding significance level ($p < .001$) reported suggest that the odds of finding such a strong relationship by chance are less than 1 in 1,000. The substantive significance, or importance, of this finding, however, is something you and your field supervisor will need to decide. In this example, the data suggest that the group experience has much more influence on social functioning than individual counseling.

Conditions Needed for Multiple Correlation

There are four basic assumptions, or conditions, that should be met before a multiple correlation analysis is undertaken. First, interval-level data (or data that can be treated as interval- or ratio-level, are required for multiple correlation. Does this mean that data measured at the nominal- or ordinal-level can never be used in this type of analysis? No. There is a way to change the appearance of nominal and ordinal data so they look like ratio data. The process involves the creation of dummy variables, a topic we'll reserve for later in our discussion of multiple regression.

Second, the relationships between the criterion variable and the predictors should be reasonably linear. This means the shape of these relationships, as portrayed in scattergrams depicting the relationship between the criterion variable and the predictors in the set, should be cigarlike in appearance.

Third, the data must be homoscedastic. By way of review, it may be helpful to remember that *homo* means equal or same, and *scedasticity* means a tendency to scatter (Vogt, 1993). Literally, therefore, the term means equal scatter, or consistent variance. In practice, this means we expect the scores of the criterion variable to be equally varied, or spread out, as we move across the different values of a given predictor variable. As with linearity, this feature can be assessed by inspecting scattergrams depicting the bivariate relationships that exist between the criterion variable and each predictor. If you uncover a cigarlike shape, you have **homoscedasticity.** In contrast, if your distribution looks like an ice cream cone or set of barbells tilted to the side, or a U, J, or S, you've encountered a condition known as **heteroscedasticity,** and you would be wise to consult a statistician about your options for working with the data.

Finally, the predictor variables should not correlate highly with one another. If they do, you have a condition commonly referred to as either **collinearity** or

multicollinearity. When this occurs, you essentially have two or more predictors taking up a good deal of the same explanatory space. As a result, your findings will be distorted. One way to check for multicollinearity is to carefully examine the bivariate correlations among the predictor variables in the set. If you find two variables with a zero-order correlation of .60 or higher, beware. One solution is to eliminate one of the offending predictors from the analysis. Another is to combine meaningfully related predictors into a single variable. This may be another one of those circumstances in which you'll want to consult an expert.

MULTIPLE REGRESSION

Just as multiple correlation (R) represents an extension of the bivariate correlation (r) approach into the realm of multivariate analysis, **multiple regression** is the multivariate counterpart of the regression procedure involving a single predictor. In Chapter 12, we saw how we could use the simple regression equation ($Y = a + bX$) to estimate the value of one variable, such as Mr. Wayclunk's empathy score, by knowing the value of another variable, such as the number of abusive incidents he reported. Multiple regression extends this process by enabling us to predict the value of a criterion or dependent variable when we know the values of two or more predictor variables. As the following formula illustrates, the multiple regression equation is essentially a longer version of the one used to carry out simple regression.

■ ■ ■ ■ ■ ▬▬▬▬▬▬▬▬▬▬▬▬▬▬▬▬▬▬▬▬▬▬▬▬▬▬

MULTIPLE REGRESSION EQUATION

$$Y' = a + b_1X_1 + b_2X_2 + \ldots b_kX_k$$

where
- Y' = predicted value of the criterion, or dependent, variable
- a = y-intercept (referred to as the constant), which is derived from the means of the observed criterion and predictor variables
- X_1 = first variable entered into the equation
- b_1 = slope associated with the first variable entered into the equation (i.e., the amount of change in Y for each unit increase in X_1^*)
- X_2 = second variable entered into the equation
- b_2 = slope associated with the second variable entered into the equation (i.e., the amount of change in Y for each unit increase in X_2^*)
- X_k = last variable entered into the equation
- b_1 = slope associated with the last variable entered into the equation (i.e., the amount of change in Y for each unit increase in X_k^*)

*The effects of the other predictors are held aside, or held constant.

In contrast to the straight line represented by the simple regression equation, however, the multiple regression equation can be thought of as mathematically defining planes in multidimensional space.

Least Squares Method

As with simple regression, multiple regression employs what's called a least squares method to determine the constant (a) and slope values (b_s) that yield the "best" estimates of the criterion variable possible. Best, in this case, means the regression coefficients (i.e., a and b_s) that will generate predicted values of the criterion variable (Y') that come closer to the actual outcome values observed (Y) than any other combination of coefficients.

Multiple R and Multiple R^2, Revisited

As we learned in the previous section, the overall strength of the relationship between the set of predictor variables included in the analysis and the targeted criterion variable is reflected in the coefficient of multiple correlation R. As you've probably surmised by now, the higher this correlation, the better your predictions will be. When we square R, we derive the coefficient of multiple determination R^2, which tells us how much of the variation observed within the criterion variable can be accounted for, or explained by, the predictor variables included in the set. Thus, the coefficient of multiple determination R^2 is interpreted in the same way in both multiple correlation and multiple regression procedures. Note that the term *model* is often used to refer to the set of predictor variables included within a given regression analysis.

The b Coefficient and the Standardized Beta

Multiple regression also provides a means of assessing the relative contributions made by each predictor variable included in the model. As a measure of association, the slope, or b **coefficient,** computed for each predictor in the regression equation tells us how much of the criterion variable's variation is accounted for by that predictor, alone—while holding aside, or holding constant, the impact exerted by the other predictor variables in the set.

It might be helpful to think of each b coefficient included in a regression equation as a member of a team, whose value depicts only a portion of the prediction made possible by the group. Just like the partial correlation coefficient, the value of the b coefficient reflects its relationship to the criterion variable—after the effects of the other predictor variables have been extracted. Perhaps this explains why it's often referred to as a **partial slope.** More specifically, the value of b (or the partial slope) tells us the amount of change (increase or decrease) that is expected to occur in the criterion variable for every unit change in its corresponding predictor variable (X), while holding constant, or controlling for, the impact of the other predictor variables in the model. However, because differences in scale generally exist among predictor variables, the partial slope (b) isn't especially useful in assessing the relative contribution made by each predictor.

Consider, for example, a study using multiple regression to assess the impact of various factors on perceived health status. Suppose age and income are among the predictor variables included in the study. Although b_{age} would tell us how one's perceived health status would be expected to change for every year added to a respondent's life, and b_{income} would tell us the expected impact of every additional dollar earned, the difference in scale between years and dollars would make direct comparisons of their respective partial slopes difficult. The solution to this quagmire lies with our old friend, the z-score.

As you may recall, converting scores to their respective z-scores places them into a common, standardized distribution that has a mean of 0 and a standard deviation of 1. The values for the partial slopes that emerge as a result of this standardizing process are called **beta weights,** or **beta coefficients.** Like the partial slopes, beta weights (abbreviated β and sometimes characterized as **partial regression coefficients**) describe the amount of variation in the criterion variable that's associated with each predictor variable—independent of the amount of variation accounted for by the other predictor variables in the set. Notably, it is their commonality of scale that renders the beta weights helpful in determining the relative contributions made by the different predictor variables in the model.

Multiple Regression in Action

To get a better understanding of how multiple regression works, let's return to our adolescent substance-abuse treatment center example for a moment, and examine the rest of the output generated by the multiple regression procedure we ran earlier using SPSS. As you look at the data in Table 14.3, one of the first things you'll want to do is determine how well the regression model worked overall. Any ideas on how you'd begin to address this? If you say you'd focus on the data pertaining to the multiple correlation coefficient, R, you're right on the money. Specifically, the F-score (32.34) and its corresponding significance level ($p < .001$) suggest that, as a group, the set of two predictor variables (individual and group counseling) included in the model are significantly correlated with social functioning. An R of .84 indicates that this relationship is rather strong. Furthermore, the adjusted R^2 obtained (.68) tells us that involvement in group and individual counseling

TABLE 14.3   **Multiple Regression of Social Functioning with Group and Individual Counseling**

VARIABLES	b COEFFICIENT	BETA (β)	t	SIGNIFICANCE
Constant (a)	5.16	—	3.24	.003
Group	1.01	.66	5.56	.001
Individual	.23	.29	2.45	.02

$F = 32.34, p < .001;$ df $= 2,27; R = .84; R^2 = .71;$ adjusted $R^2 = .68$

together accounts for just over two-thirds of the variation observed in these teens' levels of social functioning. Overall, therefore, it appears that the regression model involving these two predictors works quite well.

Now let's look at how each predictor variable contributes independently to the predictive capacity of the model. The constant (or y-intercept, a) represents the predicted value of the criterion variable (Y'), when the predictor variables (X_s) are zero. Thus, with no involvement in group or individual counseling, we'd expect these youngsters to obtain a social functioning score of about 5.16. The partial slope (b) associated with group counseling indicates we can expect an increase of approximately 1 point (1.01) in social functioning, for every group session attended. Roughly a quarter of a point (.23) increase is expected to accompany every individual session attended. The t-scores (5.56, 2.45), as well as the corresponding significance levels reported (.001, .02 respectively) indicate that both group and individual counseling make independent contributions to the overall predictive capacity of the model and, further, suggest that these relationships aren't likely to have occurred by chance. Comparing the standardized beta weights (β), we find that the impact made by group counseling is more than twice that accounted for by individual counseling. Both of these sets of statistics once again give us confidence that we can predict social functioning as it is influenced by group and individual counseling within this sample of clients.

Note: The findings presented in Table 14.3 were obtained through SPSS, using the following steps:

Analyze
   Regression
      Linear . . . (opens REGRESSION dialog box)
         Dependent variable selected: Social Functioning
            Independent variables selected: Group Counseling
                                                   Individual Counseling

---

Selecting Variables for Inclusion

There are two critical decisions you need to make when conducting a multiple regression analysis: (1) determining which predictor variables to include in the analysis, and (2) specifying the order in which these items will be entered. There are many different ways of handling these questions, but the two most common approaches are the hierarchical and the stepwise methods of inclusion (DiLeonardi & Curtis, 1988).

In the **hierarchical inclusion** method, researchers draw on their knowledge of the problem—derived from previous observations, empirical studies, or a selected theoretical stance—to tell the computer which predictor variables to enter, as well as the order in which these variables are to be introduced. For instance, Siebert, Mutran, and Reitzes (1999) used hierarchical regression to explore the relative contribution of various factors in predicting life satisfaction among a sample of 800 aging adults. In describing their method of inclusion, the researchers indicated that the batch of predictors entered first consisted of demographic and other background variables that had been found to correlate highly with life satisfaction—either in their study or in studies reported previously by others. Items contained in the next set of predictors were determined by role theory and previous studies. In their words, "Theory guided our decision to look at roles, and previous findings focused our attention on friendship" (p. 527). In particular, they wanted to see how one's identity as a friend and commitment to the role of friendship might clarify the understanding of factors affecting life satisfaction. You'll find an excerpt from their findings in Table 14.4.

From the data in Table 14.4, we can see that there is a moderate correlation ($R = .44$) between the predictors included in the analysis and life satisfaction. In comparing the values reported for the standardized betas (β), we can also see that identity as a friend seems to exert a greater impact in predicting life satisfaction than the demographic and background variables traditionally thought important. In assessing the meaning of this finding, keep in mind that correlation is not causation! Nevertheless, it's an important observation in that it lays the groundwork for potentially fruitful future research as well as practice considerations.

In the **stepwise inclusion** method, the order in which the predictor variables are entered into the analysis is determined on statistical grounds. With this approach, the variable found to correlate most strongly with the criterion variable is entered into the equation first. The remaining variables are then examined in terms of their ability to contribute to the overall predictive capacity of the model. The predictor variable that contributes the most in explaining the variance in the

TABLE 14.4   Hierarchical Regression Analysis for Variables Predicting Life Satisfaction

VARIABLES	b COEFFICIENT	BETA (β)
Items Entered First:		
Married	.153	.180**
Income	.031	.146*
Education	−.001	−.008
Gender (female)	−.047	−.061
Occupational prestige	.001	.031
Density of social support network	.051	.108*
Items Entered Second:		
Commitment to friendship role	.014	.119*
Identity as a friend	.015	.237**

Notes: $R = .44$; $R^2 = .19$

*p < .005;

**p < .0001.

From "Friendship and Social Support: The Importance of Role Identity to Aging Adults," by D. C. Siebert, E. J. Mutran, and D. C. Reitzes, 1999, *Social Work, 44*, p. 529.

criterion variable that, as yet remains unaccounted for, is then introduced. This process—examining the potential contribution of the remaining variables in explaining the variance in the criterion variable not accounted for by the predictor variables already in the model—continues until the potential contribution of the remaining variables is so small, that adding them to the equation would not significantly improve the equation's predictive capacity. It is important to note that as variables are added to the equation, the relative contributions made by items already in the equation can change. When adding a predictor will compromise the contribution made by a variable that was entered previously (statistically the portion of the variance that it explains becomes no longer significant), that predictor is eliminated from the equation. Fortunately, it is unlikely you will ever need to manually calculate a stepwise inclusion procedure, because this task is easily handled by most basic statistics programs.

The work of Cnaan and Cascio (1999) provides a good example of how social workers might use the stepwise inclusion approach. Recognizing the critical role volunteers play in operating human services organizations, these researchers sought to examine the impact of various factors in determining volunteer satisfaction, commitment, and performance. Specifically, responding to criticisms that had been made about previous studies regarding the limited number of variables typically used, Cnaan and Cascio elected to test a large array of independent variables, including 16 demographic characteristics, 9 personality traits, 29 managerial practices, and 17 different symbolic rewards. Table 14.5 shows an excerpt of the findings generated through the stepwise regression portion of their study.

TABLE 14.5   Stepwise Regression Analysis for Variables Predicting Volunteer Satisfaction*

VARIABLES	*b* COEFFICIENT	BETA (β)
Constant	4.27	
Age	−.01	−.24
Liking people	−.023	−.20
Motivation to volunteer	−.19	−.19
In-house lectures	−.20	−.17
Living arrangements	−.27	−.19
Thank-you letters	−.21	−.18
Race (minority)	.16	.13
Involvement in advocacy	−.06	−.12

Notes: *Lower scores denote higher levels of volunteer satisfaction.

$F = 19.24, p < .001, R = .60, R^2 = .36,$ adjusted $R^2 = .34, N = 489$ human service organization volunteers; only variables entering at a statistically significant level were included in this analysis.

From "Performance and Commitment: Issues in the Management of Volunteers in Human Services Organizations," by R. A. Cnaan and T. A. Cascio, 1999, *Journal of Social Service Research, 24,* (3/4), p. 27.

As you can see from the data presented in Table 14.5, although these researchers started with 71 independent variables of interest, the stepwise inclusion procedure was helpful in winnowing this pool down to 8 statistically significant predictors. Clearly, with nearly two thirds of the variance in volunteer satisfaction left unexplained by this group of predictor variables ($1 - R^2 = 1 - .34 = .66$), more work in this area needs to be done. Still, we think it is worth your while to take a moment to think about the implications these findings hold for those working with volunteers in your agency.

Notice the negative signs preceding many of the beta scores (β_s) presented in Table 14.5. Just as the sign preceding a correlation coefficient (r) tells us the direction of the relationship that exists between the two variables involved, the sign that precedes a beta (β) tells us whether a given predictor variable is positively or negatively related to the criterion, or dependent, variable contained in the model. For example, the beta score (β) associated with thank-you letters is $-.18$. What this value indicates is that higher use of thank-you letters was found to be associated with lower volunteer satisfaction scores. Does this mean that those volunteering at agencies who send thank-you letters tend to find their experience less satisfying? Quite the contrary! If you look carefully at the data presented in Table 14.5, you'll see that in this study, lower scores reflect higher levels of volunteer satisfaction. In other words, the practice of sending thank-you letters was associated with an increased sense of satisfaction among volunteers.

Conditions Needed for Multiple Regression

The assumptions or conditions for using multiple regression are identical to those required for multiple correlation. First, the data must be interval or interval-like. Second, the relationships between the criterion variable and the predictors must be reasonably linear. Third, the data must be homoscedastic. Finally, there must be an absence of multicollinearity. (For a more detailed description of these items, please return to the discussion presented earlier in this chapter regarding the conditions needed for multiple correlation.)

Dummy Variables

Earlier we suggested that there is a procedure you can use to change the appearance of a nominal or ordinal variable so it looks like one that's interval, or ratio. Okay, you say, What's the gimmick? Well, it's really a simple matter of distilling the response categories involved down to a binary, dichotomous variable. You may recall from previous discussions that a **dichotomous variable** is one that offers only two response options. Examples include items such as gender (male, female) election results (won, lost) or field placement assessments (satisfactory, unsatisfactory). A **binary variable** is a special kind of dichotomous variable in which 0 is used to signify none of something, and 1 is used to signal the presence of something. If you look at Table 14.4, you'll see that this is precisely what Siebert, Mutran, and Reitzes (1999) did with the variable gender. Essentially, they transformed the variable gender into a measure of what might be termed "femaleness" by assigning a value of 0 to men (i.e., not female) and a score of 1 to women (i.e., female). Coding in this way is believed to render variables such as gender more quantitative, thereby allowing their inclusion in analyses that require higher levels of measurement. But does this new stand-in variable, or **dummy variable** (femaleness) meet the criteria that's been established for interval level measures? Many believe it does, for several reasons: the categories involved (0,1) are mutually exclusive and exhaustive; as you move from one value to the other, you get a sense of more or less of something (i.e., the data have order); there is a standardized unit, or interval (1); and 0 is meaningful in that it represents none of something.

This procedure can also be used with nominal and ordinal variables containing more than two response categories. For example, suppose you were studying depression among older women and believed important information would be lost if you reduced marital status to the dichotomous, binary (dummy) variable, not married = 0 and married = 1. You collected your raw data on marital status in terms of the following categories: Married, Widowed, Separated/Divorced, and Single/Never Married. To make this nominal-level variable more quantitative (and thus more appropriate for inclusion in an analysis such as regression) you might convert it into three different dichotomous, binary predictor variables: (a) Not Married = 0, Married = 1; (b) Not Widowed = 0, Widowed = 1; and (c) Not Separated/Divorced = 0, Separated/Divorced = 1. At this juncture, you're probably wondering why three variables not four? Aren't we overlooking those women who say they're single/never married? In part, the answer is a matter of deductive logic. Think about the woman who is single/never married—how will you code her responses for the three dummy variables you developed for your analysis? You'll assign her zeros for all three of these items, right? Given that constellation of scores, it's easy to deduce that this respondent must be single/never married. To add a fourth category, therefore, would tell us nothing new. Furthermore, the redundancy this fourth item would introduce would inevitably lead to that dreaded condition mentioned earlier—multicollinearity. So when you're creating dummy variables for nominal and ordinal measures containing multiple categories, always introduce at least one less variable than the number of response categories involved. (*Hint:* if you collapse substantively similar categories, you may be able to reduce even further the number of added predictor variables needed.)

TWO-WAY (TWO-FACTOR) ANALYSIS OF VARIANCE

In Chapter 13, we saw how analysis of variance (ANOVA) could be used to test the significance of the differences observed in substance-use patterns reported by four groups of clients: (1) those receiving outpatient services, (2) those participating in a methadone maintenance program, (3) those who dropped out of the program within the first 30 days of treatment (i.e., the controls), and (4) those in residential care. In other words, the procedure allowed us to compare the average number of times clients used drugs during the past 30 days on the basis of a single independent variable—the type of treatment they received. Given the literature's recent focus on the potential need for different substance-abuse treatment approaches for men and women, suppose Ms. Collins asks Tiffinea to determine whether the agency's treatment programs work equally well in decreasing reported instances of substance use for both groups. What Ms. Collins is asking for is a multivariate analysis involving one interval-level dependent variable (number of times selected substances were used), and two categorical independent variables (treatment type and gender). Although this is beyond what a simple ANOVA can handle, you may be wondering if there's a multivariate counterpart to ANOVA like those we found for correlation and regression. You bet there is, but before we address any specifics, we need to introduce a few new terms.

The Language of ANOVA

In ANOVA, the independent, or predictor, variable is referred to as a **factor.** In the drug treatment example described in Chapter 13, therefore, the independent variable, or factor, used was type of treatment. In the new study described above, Ms. Collins is asking Tiffinea to add a second factor (gender) to the analysis. Once ANOVA gets beyond a single predictor, or factor, it's customary to refer to the procedure in terms of the number of factors involved. If Tiffinea conducts the new study, incorporating gender into the analysis, she would be conducting a two-way, or two-factor, analysis of variance, that is, a **two-way ANOVA**. Can you guess what an ANOVA incorporating three factors, or independent variables, would be called? A three-way, or three-factor ANOVA.

Another way of describing an ANOVA using two or more factors is in terms of the number of response options, or value categories, associated with each factor. For instance, in the proposed study involving the substance-abuse treatment agency, there are four different treatment levels, or types of treatment, and two gender categories. Rather than saying Ms. Collins is proposing a two-way ANOVA, you could say she's interested in Tiffinea carrying out a 4 × 2 **factorial design.** Let's illustrate this idea with another example.

Suppose you were studying married couples with children and were interested in knowing how differences in gender (male, female), age (45 to 64, 65 to 84) and number of children (1 to 2, 3 to 4, 5 or more) influence the incidence of marital problems reported. You could analyze these data utilizing a three-way, or three-factor, ANOVA. How would you describe this analysis in terms of a factorial design? That's correct—you would call it a 2 × 2 × 3 factorial design.

The Logic of Two-Way ANOVA

As with simple ANOVA, the purpose of two-way ANOVA is to test the significance of differences occurring among group means. Underlying this test is the assumption that if two (or more) populations have identical means, then we can expect that the means obtained for groups randomly selected from those populations will be similar as well. As you know, probability theory tells us that sample means obtained randomly are likely to vary somewhat, if for no other reason than sampling error. However, probability theory also suggests that if the populations from which the group means were selected are identical, the differences in the mean scores observed should be small (i.e., statistically insignificant).

Admittedly, the name analysis of variance may seem a bit peculiar at first for a collection of statistical strategies designed to test whether the mean scores obtained for a variable differ significantly from one group to another. As Iversen and Norpoth (1984) suggest, perhaps "analysis of means" would be a better title. Once we realize, though, that all of the ANOVA techniques use the ratio of the variance occurring within groups to the variance occurring between the groups, to determine if the groups come from the same or different populations, then the term *analysis of variance* actually seems quite fitting.

Two-Way ANOVA in Action

Let's use a practice-based example to discuss the form and substance of the output generated by the two-way ANOVA procedure. To keep the waters from becoming too muddied, we'll intentionally limit the number of groups involved to four (i.e., a 2×2 factorial design).

Looking at the means presented in Table 14.6, we can see that those who received counseling (mean$_{\text{counseling total}}$ = 3.50) exhibit less depression at 8 weeks than participants placed on the waiting list (mean$_{\text{control-total}}$ = 6.60). Likewise, those who received the new psychotropic medication (mean$_{\text{total-new med}}$ = 4.05) scored lower than participants receiving the placebo (mean$_{\text{total-placebo}}$ = 6.05). What's more, clients who received both counseling and the new medication obtained a lower average depression score than any other group (mean$_{\text{counseling-new med}}$ = 2.50). As with simple ANOVA, however, the question before us is, Do these means represent actual differences among the groups, or do they merely reflect variations resulting from sampling error or chance? As you'll see momentarily, two-way ANOVA allows us to answer this question by simultaneously testing the following three null hypotheses:

Null Hypothesis 1 (H_{01}):   No actual difference in the mean depression scores between those who received counseling and those placed on the waiting list (control)

Null Hypothesis 2 (H_{02}):   No actual difference in the mean depression scores between those who took the new psychotropic medication and those who took the placebo

Null Hypothesis 3 (H_{03}):   No actual difference in the mean depression scores between those receiving counseling alone, and those receiving both counseling and the new psychotropic medication.

■ ■ ■ ■ ■ ▬

SCENARIO: EFFECTIVENESS OF MEDICATION VS. COUNSELING

Imagine you're working for a community mental health center that serves a large metropolitan area. As people come into your agency for assistance, an intake is done which entails a thorough biopsychosocial history and a standardized mental health screening. In recent years, agency funding has failed to keep up with the growing demand for services. Thus, it has become customary to place applicants who are not in need of emergency services on a waiting list. Currently, it is not unusual for applicants to wait between 4 to 6 weeks to receive services.

Concerned about this circumstance, the agency's director, Mr. Chambers, recently asked staff for ideas. Dr. Winters, the agency's consulting psychiatrist, indicated that the agency might be able to acquire additional money for service provision, if it were willing to become part of a mental health research initiative the local university is about to undertake, under the sponsorship of the state department of mental health. Intrigued by the idea, Mr. Chambers asks Dr. Winters for more details.

"Basically," Dr. Winters says, "the university has received a 2-year grant to test the impact of a new antidepressant medication against the effects of cognitive-behavioral therapy in reducing depression. Since many of our agency's clients present with depression, and because cognitive-behavioral counseling is the approach preferred by most of the social workers at this agency, it seems natural for us to get involved." On further exploration, Mr. Chambers verifies that the fit between the objectives of this research project and the agency's and its clients' needs was a good one. Among other things, involvement in the project would allow the agency to hire an additional full-time social worker for the next 2 years—an action that would go a long way in reducing the amount of time applicants currently wait for services.

After working out the logistics with all the relevant university and agency groups and units (i.e., staff, client advisory committee, budget committee, legal committee, institutional review board, and so forth) a system is established whereby people who present to the agency with a depressive condition are given the opportunity to participate in the research. Those who express interest are randomly assigned to one of four treatment conditions:

1. Counseling with Antidepressant
2. Counseling with Placebo
3. No Counseling with Antidepressant
4. No Counseling with Placebo

Following the research protocols established by the university, a measure of each participant's level of depression is obtained after 8 weeks of participation in the study. The mean scores gathered on the first wave of agency participants ($N = 40$) are presented in Table 14.6.

TABLE 14.6   Mean Depression Scores by Counseling and Medication Conditions (N = 40)

COUNSELING CONDITION	MEDICATION CONDITION	MEAN	STD. DEVIATION	N
Control (waiting list)	Placebo	7.60	1.50	10
	New psychotropic	5.60	1.35	10
	Total	6.60	1.73	20
Counseling	Placebo	4.50	.97	10
	New psychotropic	2.50	1.58	10
	Total	3.50	1.64	20
Total	Placebo	6.05	2.01	20
	New psychotropic	4.05	2.14	20
	Total	5.05	2.28	40

When we use two-way ANOVA, we are essentially categorizing participants along two continua. In this instance, clients are being sorted according to whether they received treatment, as well as whether they received the new psychotropic medication or a placebo. Let's reconfigure the data presented in Table 14.6 in a way that renders these comparisons more apparent.

	MEDICATION CONDITION		
COUNSELING CONDITION	*Psychotropic*	*Placebo*	ROW MEANS
Waiting list	M = 5.60	M = 7.60	M = 6.60
Counseling	M = 2.50	M = 4.50	M = 3.50
COLUMN MEANS	M = 4.05	M = 6.05	

The first hypothesis (H_{01}) focuses our attention on the row means. In particular, H_{01} asks, apart from the different medication conditions, do those participating in counseling represent the same population in terms of their mean depression scores as those on the waiting list? In other words, is the roughly three-point (3.10) difference noted between these two mean scores statistically significant? Whenever we focus on the impact of only one factor (or independent variable), while temporarily ignoring the influence of the other, we're targeting what's called a **main effect** (Pyrczak, 1995). Thus, the first hypothesis could be cast more simply as follows: Does counseling exhibit a main effect?

Our second hypothesis (H_{02}) draws our attention to the column means. In particular, it asks, apart from the different counseling conditions, do those who receive the new psychotropic medication represent the same population in terms of their mean depression scores as those receiving the placebo? In other words, is the two-point difference noted between these groups statistically significant? Or, more simply, does medication exhibit a main effect?

In contrast, the third hypothesis (H_{03}) addresses whether the effect of counseling is different when provided in conjunction with the new psychotropic medication as opposed to the placebo. Because it focuses on the combined, or synergistic, effect of the two independent variables (counseling and medication), it is referred to as an **interaction effect.** Pyrczak (1995) describes a fairly simple method you can use to spot an interaction whenever you have at least one factor with only two categories (i.e., rows) involved. First, arrange your group means in rows and columns as we just did in the preceding table. Then subtract the means in the second row from the means in the first row. If the differences obtained are the same, there is no interaction. When we apply this approach to the means involved in this example, we get the following:

	MEDICATION CONDITION	
COUNSELING CONDITION	*Psychotropic*	*Placebo*
Waiting list	$M = 5.60$	$M = 7.60$
Counseling	$M = 2.50$	$M = 4.50$
DIFFERENCE:	3.10	3.10

Because the differences we obtained in carrying out this preliminary procedure are the same, it appears that we'll find no counseling times medication interaction. Let's go ahead and run a two-way ANOVA so we can formally test these three hypotheses.

The Output of Two-Way ANOVA

Table 14.7 contains the output generated by a two-way ANOVA conducted on the first wave of data obtained by the community mental health agency depicted in our preceding scenario. As with a one-way ANOVA, these results are easily obtained through the use of a computerized statistical package such as SPSS.

What can we tell from the output presented in Table 14.7? The first column simply identifies the **source of variance** that is presented in each of the different rows. The data in the second column, labeled **sum of squares,** tell us how much variation was observed in the depression scores obtained overall, as well as how this variation was distributed among the main effects, interaction, and residual or error effect.

TABLE 14.7 Summary of 2 × 2, Counseling-Medication, Two-Way ANOVA for Depression

SOURCE OF VARIANCE	SUM OF SQUARES	df	MEAN SQUARE	F	SIGNIFICANCE
Counseling	96.100	1	96.100	51.027	.001
Medication	40.000	1	40.000	21.240	.001
Counseling and Medication	.000	1	.000	.000	1.00
Error	67.800	36	1.883		
Total	203.900	39			

Note: The findings presented in Table 14.7 were obtained through SPSS using the following steps:

Analyze
General Linear Model (GLM)
Univariate opens the dialog box needed for multifactor ANOVA
Dependent variable selected: Depression Score
Independent variables selected: Counseling
Medication

Note: SPSS uses the univariate option for ANOVA procedures using two more factors. It reserves the GLM multivariate option for ANOVA procedures incorporating two or more dependent variables (i.e., multiple analysis of variance procedures, or MANOVA).

As with simple ANOVA, the total sum of squares is derived by subtracting the overall group mean (or **grand mean**) from each case, and then squaring and summing those differences. Conceptually, the sum of squares for the counseling and medication conditions (i.e., the main effects) are similar to the between-group comparisons calculated in the one-way ANOVA procedure. Specifically, the sum of squares for counseling was derived by subtracting the grand mean from the group means obtained for each category contained within the factor (i.e., those who received counseling and those placed on the waiting list), while temporarily ignoring the influence of the other main effect. The same procedure is carried out on the group means obtained for the medication factor. In turn, the variance associated with individual differences occurring among subjects *within* the four groups defined by these independent variables (i.e., counseling/waiting list and medication/placebo) is referred to as **error**. Finally, the counseling times medication sum of squares (interaction) is determined on the basis of what's left unexplained, once the variation associated with the main effects and error has been extracted. In other words, interaction can be thought of as the special additional effects that occur as the result of combining the independent variables involved (Williams, 1986).

The degrees of freedom for the main and interaction effects is equal to the number of categories involved, minus 1 ($n - 1$). In this case, each condition contains two distinct categories (i.e., counseling or waiting list, medication or placebo, medication/counseling or medication/waiting list), so the degrees of freedom in each instance is 1. The degrees of freedom for error is equal to the number of cases involved minus the number of groups associated with the independent variables, or factors. Thus, the degrees of freedom for error for a 2 × 2 design with 40 cases is 36 ($40 - 4 = 36$). The total degrees of freedom is the number of cases ($N = 40$) minus 1, which in this case is 39.

The values listed in the **mean square** column are derived by dividing the sum of squares associated with each source, by its corresponding degrees of freedom. In a way, the mean square provides a way of factoring in, or adjusting for, the number of cases and categories involved (DiLeonardi & Curtis, 1988).

The F-statistic (also referred to as the F-ratio, or F-score) is found by dividing the mean square derived for each main and interaction effect, by the mean square associated with the error term. Logically, the more variance accounted for by the main effects or their interactions, the less there is available to attribute to error. By extension, the smaller the mean square associated with error (the divisor), the larger the F-ratio score is apt to be. The final column in Table 14.7 conveys the actual significance level computed for each F-statistic reported.

Now that you know the origin and meaning associated with the data presented in Table 14.7, what conclusions would you draw? If you were to say that significant main effects were found for both counseling and medication, although no interaction occurred, you'd be right on target. More specifically, it appears that both counseling and medication significantly reduced the level of depression achieved by clients after 8 weeks of treatment. The effects of counseling remained the same, however, whether or not the new psychotropic medication was administered. Likewise, the effects of the new psychotropic medication—though somewhat smaller than the effects of counseling—remained the same, whether or not counseling was provided. In a journal, these findings might be described as follows:

> A 2 × 2 analysis of variance (ANOVA) factorial design was used to examine the effects of cognitive behavioral counseling and a new psychotropic medication on depression. Both counseling and medication exhibited significant main effects [$F(1,36) = 51.03, p < .001$; $F(1,36) = 21.24, p < .001$; respectively] for decreasing depression. However, no interaction occurred between the two treatment strategies $F(1,36) = .00$, ns.

Conditions Needed for Two-Way ANOVA

The conditions needed for two-way ANOVA are essentially the same as those required for simple ANOVA. First, it is assumed that the data being analyzed are derived from a random sample. Second, it is expected that the dependent variable is measured at an interval level (or higher), and that it is normally distributed within the population from which the sample was drawn. Third, the value categories associated with each of the predictive factors should be independent of one another. In addition, the variance or spread in scores that occurs within each group that's affiliated with a predictor factor should be roughly the same. Finally, the predictive factors should not be highly related (multicollinear) or dependent on one another.

Like ANOVA, the two-way ANOVA procedure is known for being a powerful (i.e., robust) statistical procedure that tends to perform well, even if one or more of these assumptions is violated. Nevertheless, caution is warranted when interpreting the significance of findings derived from a circumstance in which any of these assumptions is not met.

TERMS TO KNOW

Adjusted R^2 (p. 258)	Heteroscedasticity (p. 259)
b coefficient (p. 261)	Hierarchical inclusion (p. 263)
Beta coefficient (p. 262)	Homoscedasticity (p. 259)
Beta weights (p. 262)	Interaction effect (p. 272)
Binary variable (p. 266)	Main effect (p. 271)
Coefficient of multiple correlation (R) (p. 254)	Mean square (p. 274)
	Multicollinearity (p. 260)
Coefficient of multiple determination R^2 (p. 255)	Multiple correlation (p. 254)
	Multiple R (p. 254)
Collinearity (p. 259)	Multiple R^2 (p. 255)
Dichotomous variable (p. 266)	Multiple regression (p. 260)
Dummy variable (p. 267)	Partial regression coefficient (p. 262)
Error (p. 273)	Partial slope (p. 261)
Factor (p. 268)	Source of variance (p. 272)
Factorial design (p. 268)	Stepwise inclusion (p. 264)
F-statistic (score or ratio) (p. 255)	Sum of squares (p. 272)
Grand mean (p. 273)	Two-way ANOVA (p. 268)

REVIEW PROBLEMS

1. Suppose you are investigating how age and income influence the level of burden experienced by adults providing in-home care for frail, elderly, family members. You administer a standardized Caregiver Burden Inventory to a random sample of 80 caregivers selected from area support groups. The bivariate (zero-order) correlations you obtain are presented in Table 14.8. Intrigued by these findings, you decide to conduct a multivariate correlation analysis, with burden as the dependent variable and age and income as the predictors. In doing so, you obtain the following: $R = .51, R^2 = .26$, adjusted $R^2 = .25$ ($F = 10.36, p < .001$). How would you interpret these results?

2. In Table 14.9 you'll find the results of a stepwise regression analysis completed on the fictitious caregiver burden data described in question one.

TABLE 14.8 Zero-Order (Bivariate) Correlations Using Simulated Data for Caregiver Burden Study (N = 80)

VARIABLE	CAREGIVER AGE	CAREGIVER INCOME	CAREGIVER BURDEN
Caregiver Age	1.0	.27*	−.37**
Caregiver Income	0.0	1.00	.42**
Caregiver Burden			1.00

Notes: Higher burden scores signify greater burden.

 *$p < .05$.

** $p < .01$.

TABLE 14.9 Hierarchical Regression Analysis for Variables Predicting Caregiver Burden

VARIABLES	b COEFFICIENT	BETA (β)
Age	−.31	−.28**
Income	.43	.37**

Note: $R = .51$; adjusted $R^2 = .25$; $F = 10.36, p < .001$;
**$p < .003$.

Given the standardized betas (βs) obtained, what can you say about the relationship between age and burden? How does income relate to burden? Are you surprised by either of these findings? Why? Why not?

3. In response to Ms. Collins' questions concerning the possible differential effect the drug treatment approaches may have on men and women, Tiffinea decided to run a two-way ANOVA. In Table 14.10, you'll find the mean number of days respondents reported using drugs according to gender and treatment.

   3.a. Using the data presented in Table 14.10, complete the following chart. Once you've done so, describe what patterns, if any, you see.

	TREATMENT				
GENDER	*Outpatient*	*Methadone*	*Residential*	*Dropouts*	ROW MEANS
Male	$M =$	$M =$	$M =$	$M =$	$M =$
Female	$M =$	$M =$	$M =$	$M =$	$M =$
COLUMN MEANS:	$M =$	$M =$	$M =$	$M =$	

TABLE 14.10   Mean Number of Days Drugs Used by Gender and Treatment

TREATMENT	GENDER	MEAN	STANDARD DEVIATION	N
Outpatient	Male	4.15	5.26	13
	Female	12.50	11.35	12
	Total	8.38	9.54	25
Methadone	Male	12.47	9.31	15
	Female	17.60	8.91	10
	Total	15.03	9.32	25
Residential	Male	1.71	3.50	14
	Female	4.81	6.16	11
	Total	3.27	4.99	25
Dropouts (Controls)	Male	16.77	7.49	13
	Female	15.33	7.23	12
	Total	16.05	7.25	25
Total	Male	8.78	9.01	55
	Female	12.56	9.64	45
	Total	10.46	9.44	100

3.b. After you've reconfigured the data from Table 14.10, apply the approach developed by Pyrczak (1995) for detecting possible interaction effects. (*Hint:* For each treatment condition, subtract the mean score obtained for females from the one reported for the males.) What did you find?

3.c. The results of Tiffinea's two-way ANOVA procedure are presented in Table 14.11. List the three different statistical or null hypotheses Tiffinea is testing in this analysis.

3.d. Given these results, how should Tiffinea answer Ms. Collins' questions?

TABLE 14.11   Summary of 2 × 4, Gender-by-Treatment, Two-Way ANOVA for the Number of Days Drugs Were Used During the Past 30 Days

SOURCE (OF VARIANCE)	SUM OF SQUARES	df	MEAN SQUARE	F	SIGNIFICANCE
Treatment	2667.380	3	889.127	14.975	.001
Gender	353.257	1	353.257	5.950	.017
Treatment × Gender	313.670	3	104.557	1.761	.160
Error	5462.294	92	59.373		
Total	8822.400	99			

REFERENCES

Cnaan, R. A., & Cascio, T. A. (1999). Performance and commitment: Issues in the management of volunteers in human services organizations. *Journal of Social Service Research, 24* (3/4), 1–37.

Craft, J. L. (1990). *Statistics and data analysis for social workers.* Itasca, IL: F. E. Peacock.

DiLeonardi, J. W., & Curtis, P. A. (1988). *What to do when the numbers are in: A user's guide to statistical data analysis in the human services.* Chicago: Nelson-Hall.

Hayduk, K. (1987). *Structural equation modeling with LISREL: Essentials and advances.* Baltimore: The Johns Hopkins University Press.

Hosmer, D. W., & Lemeshow, S. (1989). *Applied logistic regression.* New York: John Wiley & Sons.

Iversen, G. R., & Norpoth, H. (1984). Analysis of variance. *Series: Quantitative Applications in the Social Sciences, 1* (07-001). Beverly Hills, CA: Sage.

Pedhazur, E. J. (1982). *Multiple regression in behavioral research* (2nd ed.). Fort Worth, TX: Holt, Rinehart & Winston.

Pyrczak, F. (1995). *Making sense of statistics.* Los Angeles: Pyrczak.

Siebert, D. C., Mutran, E. J., & Reitzes, D. C. (1999). Friendship and social support: The importance of role identity to aging adults. *Social Work, 44,* 522–532.

Vogt, W. P. (1993). *Dictionary of statistics and methodology: A nontechnical guide for the social services.* Newbury Park, CA: Sage.

Williams, F. (1986). *Reasoning with statistics: How to read quantitative research* (3rd ed.). New York: Holt, Rinehart, & Winston.

■ ■ ■ ■ ■

CHAPTER FIFTEEN

SELECTING THE APPROPRIATE STATISTICAL TEST

CONSTRUCTING CONVINCING AND CREDIBLE RESEARCH

Designing research that will ultimately provide useful information about social problems and guide the interventions of social workers is a lot like trying to find your way around a strange city. Even though you may purchase a map or get directions from "locals," it is still easy to go astray and end up somewhere other than you intended. As a researcher you could be led to the wrong conclusion because of the way you selected your respondents (a selection bias). For instance, imagine you are interested in gathering client satisfaction data from the consumers of a particular program, and you choose to interview a sample of clients who have all had the same social worker. What would that tell you about the clients who received services from other social workers or who were dissatisfied with the agency and dropped out in the first month or two? It is absolutely essential that your research methodology be well planned and balanced (e.g., drawing on a representative sample of the target population) if you want your research to be viewed by others as convincing and credible.

Similarly, you could mislead the readers of your research report if your literature review ignores studies whose findings you don't agree with or if you fail to inform readers about studies that produced results dramatically at odds with yours. And what about your written communication skills? Would a paper full of misspellings and poor grammar give readers any confidence in your competence as a researcher? As you ponder your answer to that question, think about a scenario in which a researcher might use the wrong statistical procedure. What impression would form in your mind about such a researcher? Would you consider this work to reflect competence or incompetence?

Although it is not uncommon for some researchers to prepare instruments and design methodologies while hardly giving a thought to how they might analyze the data to be produced, that is not the recommended course of action. Even knowledgeable researchers with many years of experience sometimes discover that they aren't able to conclude as much from their data as they had intended because, for instance, they failed to consider the level of measurement and the response choices allowed for each of their variables. Particularly when committees are designing questionnaires and revising the wording and phrasing of troublesome items, important but less controversial items may not be scrutinized as closely and, as a result, the response choices may not be mutually exclusive, or they could have other problems. Occasionally data analysis is also frustrated when researchers obtain low response rates or experience severe client attrition, producing smaller samples than planned. Even if researchers have gone to great lengths to ensure that all of these variables are measured at the interval, or ratio level, sophisticated multivariate analyses cannot be conducted if the sample is too small. Just as the researcher must be aware of various problems in the construction or choice of an instrument used for collection of the needed information, the investigator must also be concerned about sample size.

There are enough ways to go astray in the research process without forgetting to plan for statistical analysis or choosing an inappropriate statistical procedure. So if you are a novice researcher, spare yourself a lot of potential problems by thoughtfully considering not only how your data should be analyzed, but also how you want your report to be viewed in the continuum of credible to unconvincing research. Although it might be easy to compartmentalize statistical analysis and think of it as a process entirely separate and removed from your data-collection methodology, you'll have many fewer problems later on if, after you decide on your instrument and methodology, you make it a practice to

1. Examine each of your variables in turn, checking to make sure that each one is appropriately operationalized and will provide data at the level of measurement you need
2. Prepare dummy tables of the analysis you're planning, using the variables you want to collect

Ideally, you will have the opportunity to conduct a pilot study, and from that endeavor you'll have data to use to test whether the variables you are collecting fit the method of analysis you are planning. If you aren't planning a pilot study, it is even more important to create some fictitious data and then go through the exercise of thinking about how you will analyze it, possibly even drafting several tables to highlight findings you think your study is likely to produce.

CONSIDERATIONS IN SELECTING A STATISTICAL TEST

There are many different statistical procedures you can perform—many more than we can discuss in this introductory text; however, there are logical reasons why some statistical tests are employed in one situation and not another. Researchers don't make a wild guess about the best procedure to use, and they don't draw them out of a hat. Instead, they consider the features and properties of their information because the data may not meet certain conditions needed by particular statistical tests. These conditions, also known as assumptions, are usually not empirically verified but are presumed to have been met unless the researcher has reason to suspect a problem. In the following sections of the text, we'll examine some of the necessary and assumed conditions.

Independence of Observations

Suppose for a class project you and each of your classmates in the statistics course are asked to interview 30 social work students about their opinions on whether letter grades or pass/fail grades should be assigned for their practicum courses. Even in a large university, it is unlikely that 20 students enrolled in the statistics course could each find 30 different social work students to interview. More than likely, within a sample of 600 students from the same school, there will be some proportion who have been interviewed more than once. Think about a social work program having 400 social work majors or grad students, and you'll soon realize that the data would be severely biased if a sample of 600 were mandated, because a large proportion of the respondents would be duplicated. Those who allowed themselves to be interviewed on multiple occasions might have similar personalities; maybe they are all easygoing, compliant individuals who have the same thoughts about the grading dilemma, or perhaps they are content with things just the way they are. To the extent that these individuals are interviewed more than once, they are able to register more votes for their position on the practicum grading issue. In such instances, the data are said to be related, not independent, whenever there is a sizeable duplication of respondents in the sample. This is often a problem for researchers.

The independence of observations is the first assumption that needs to be met before a statistical test can be applied. Computers won't know if your observations are independent. Statistical software is not so smart that sirens and red lights will be triggered if you are careless and attempt to interpret data when the observations are not independent. The computer will produce a statistic and a level of significance if you request it, whether or not the data are independent. So you can't pass the buck and think that this is an issue for the computer or someone else to worry about.

What happens if a sloppy researcher ignores this assumption and calculates a chi-square to see, for instance, if there was a difference in grading preference by gender in the sample of 600 students, where about half of them had been interviewed more than once? The simple answer is that it wouldn't be possible to place any confidence in the findings. Why? Because it is very likely that different results would be obtained if all the duplicated interviews were removed. Any findings in which you have no confidence means that they are worthless—the results cannot be considered helpful for deciding the issue one way or the other.

In collecting a convenience sample or even a random sample of data, there's always the possibility that a handful of individuals might be surveyed more than once. Ordinarily, however, this is rarely a problem. Nonetheless, it is the researcher's responsibility always to plan ahead, to anticipate how the data could be compromised, and to prepare a methodology that guarantees the independence of observations as much as possible.

Level of Measurement

As we have previously discussed in this book, the manner in which you have defined and operationalized your variables directly affects the statistical procedures available to you. For instance, you cannot conduct t-tests if you have a nominal-level dependent variable. Although many variables (e.g., gender, marital status) naturally occur at the nominal level of measurement, it is critical that you weigh your variables carefully and consider what information you will be able to derive from them. Sometimes ordinal response categories need to be converted into open-ended items so that variables such as years of education completed can be reported as interval, or ratio variables.

Normally, most studies will have more than one variable of interest. A good rule to observe is that, although your independent (predictor) variables can be nominal or ordinal, it's best to have your dependent variables measured at the interval (ratio) level. If you want to later convert data from your dependent variable into nominal-level categories, that poses no problem. However, it is usually impossible to convert nominal data into interval (ratio) data.

Although it is somewhat controversial, ordinal data can sometimes be treated as interval data. Certainly not all ordinal data can be considered interval data for the purpose of statistical analysis, but data that meets the following criteria may be considered interval: The data must

Be ranked on five or more levels
Come from a normal distribution
Result from a large sample

Good planning beforehand helps the researcher avoid the situation in which ordinal data might have to be treated as interval data. But if this is necessary, the researcher should be a little more cautious than usual in interpreting the results because an ordinal variable with a few gradations (e.g., 5, 6, or 7) compresses potential variation much more than an interval variable does, where there are, for instance, 50 or 100 presumably equal intervals between the lowest and highest possible scores.

Although educators and textbooks usually present the research process as a linear one moving logically from one consideration to another, in reality, researchers have to juggle numerous details in their heads simultaneously. However, deciding on the key variables and how they will be measured must always be in the forefront of planning for any research project. Level of measurement is an early decision the researcher has to make. The next decision is whether the analysis should concern only two variables (bivariate analysis), a series of variables taken two at a time, or whether the analysis will use three or more independent variables to explain variation in the dependent variable (multivariate analysis). If means are going to be compared or many variables will be examined for their effect on a dependent variable, then interval-, or ratio-level measurement is needed.

Normal Distribution

Besides level of measurement, there are several other considerations that influence choice of statistical procedure. For example, most of the statistics discussed in this book require that the dependent variable be normally distributed. Even though a sample of data may not resemble a perfect bell-shaped curve, most large collections of data generally are normally distributed. If you think of the concept of height, for instance, and you gather 100 college students more or less at random and arrange them from the shortest to the tallest, lining up all of the students of the same height behind each other, you might find a pattern something like this:

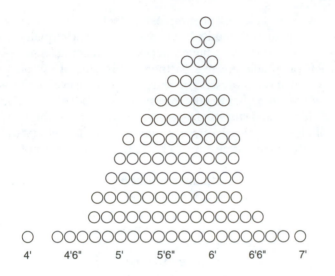

In this example, you find that there are a few vertically challenged students, and a few very tall ones.

If you were to draw several different samples of students, seldom would you find the distribution to be an exact replica of the bell-shaped curve, that is, having absolutely no skewness at either end. Because any sample is one of many possible samples that could be drawn from those enrolled in the university, each sample of students can be expected to be somewhat different from the others. However, most statistical techniques are based on the assumption that the population from which the samples were drawn was approximately normally distributed. This assumption is usually not tested and not one that the researcher worries about if his or her sample is reasonably large (e.g., about 100 cases).

Sample Size

As a rule of thumb, multiple regression and other parametric multivariate techniques require that the sample of data to be analyzed contain ten times more cases (subjects) than variables. If you have, say, 50 variables and 50 cases, then you should not consider using multiple regression, factor analysis, or other procedures that require large numbers of cases—otherwise, the findings won't be meaningful.

Too few subjects can present problems for less powerful statistical procedures, too. Remember that in Chapter 11 it was pointed out that even the simple chi-square procedure can be affected when 20% or more of the cells have an expected frequency of 5 or fewer. When small sample sizes create this problem, the researcher may want to conduct a variation of chi-square called Fisher's exact test, or some other nonparametric test (special statistical tests designed for small samples).

Types of Samples

The first distinction we can make about samples is whether the sample is drawn from a quantitative or a qualitative study. If you are conducting a qualitative study and have four or six subjects who you have interviewed at some length—let's say they have recently left physically abusive partners—this type of sample probably does not require any statistical analysis. The purpose of statistical analysis, you'll remember, is to allow the researcher to take information gathered from many individuals in order to condense and summarize it—for example, to be able to develop a profile of the typical client. Qualitative researchers attempt to understand a phenomenon in-depth, so the quantitative approach to data reduction is not wanted or deemed necessary.

On the other hand, if you are evaluating an intervention that involves gathering quantitative data, then there are several ways to think about sampling as it relates to data analysis. The information in the following table presumes that data meet all the assumptions we discussed previously and are measured at the interval (ratio) level. A good illustration of types of samples and the related statistical procedure is found when the researcher wants to compare the mean of one sample to another. With the t-test procedure, there are three variations depending on the type of sample.

TYPES OF t-TEST	BEST USE
One-sample t-tests	For determining whether a particular sample conforms to the parameters of a specific population
Independent-samples t-tests	For determining whether there are significant differences between two different samples or groups—e.g., between the intervention group and the control group
Paired-sample t-tests	For determining if there are significant changes within the same group of persons, e.g., between pretest and posttest. These are sometimes known as related, or correlated, samples

In some studies, you might use both paired-sample t-tests and independent-samples t-tests. For instance, you might first compare pretest parenting skills with posttest scores (paired-sample t-test) to see if there was any improvement. Then later you might want to compare mothers' scores against fathers' scores (independent-sample t-test). Before using statistical software such as SPSS, the researcher has to have a good understanding of whether the data being analyzed came from independent samples. When we are comparing diverse groups of unrelated individuals (e.g., a control group compared to an intervention group at posttest), independent samples is the type of sampling usually involved. Related samples are those in which only one group is being studied (e.g., pretest-posttest design), or where the subjects are actually related to one another in some fashion (e.g., identical twins, brothers, or sisters); sometimes spouses or partners are presumed to share similar attitudes, knowledge, behavior, and so forth.

As described in Chapter 13, one-sample t-tests are used when population parameters are known and the researcher wants to check to see if a given sample is representative of the population. However, when the variable being tested is categorical and only percentages are known (e.g., the percent of Vietnam vets with post-traumatic stress disorder), then chi-square can be used. The use of chi-square for this purpose is often known as a goodness-of-fit test.

Robustness

A statistical test is considered **robust** when it produces accurate findings, even though its assumptions are violated (e.g., assuming the data are normally distributed when they really aren't). Researchers generally don't plan to disregard the assumptions of normality and so forth; however, sometimes a small sample is all the data that can be obtained. When the N is small and can't be increased, then the researcher wants as robust a statistical test as possible. The following table describes the robustness of three statistical procedures.

PROCEDURE	ROBUSTNESS
t-test	Very robust and virtually unaffected, even when the distribution is not normally distributed
One-way analysis of variance (ANOVA)	Very robust—nonnormality of the data distribution has negligible consequences on the probabilities produced, unless the populations are highly skewed or the sample size is very small (Glass & Hopkins, 1996)
Chi-square	Very robust, even with very small expected frequencies

Assumptions for Multiple Regression

Multiple regression of interval-, or ratio-level data requires the assumption of a normal distribution and requires that the data be linear—that is, the various data points, if plotted, fall in a pattern consistent with a single direction. Data that fit curved paths (e.g., the S-shaped, U-shaped, O-shaped and J-shaped scattergrams mentioned in Chapter 12) are nonlinear data. Further, the data ought to be homoscedastic (having relatively consistent variance). If one of the variables has much greater variance than the other, the data are said to be heteroscedastic, in which case the resulting scatterplot might resemble a fan or funnel shape, where data points are initially clustered close together but then spread out as they get further from the point of origin. Obviously, it makes sense to create scatterplots and visually examine your data in order to determine if they are linear and homoscedastic. Computing multiple regression when the data don't meet these assumptions means, once again, that little confidence can be placed in the findings.

A STATISTICAL GUIDE

As you can see from the discussion so far, numerous factors affect the choice of a procedure to be used for data analysis. Naturally, there are other factors, but we've attempted to summarize some of the more important considerations without overwhelming you with too many decisions. Keep in mind that in any research report or data analysis, it is possible to use more than one statistical procedure. There will be times when chi-squares and ANOVA both will be needed. But if you find yourself planning on doing 15 different t-tests to determine the influence of various socioeconomic variables on the dependent variable, you probably need to consider a multiple regression to avoid multiple comparison error (the chance of obtaining significance even when all the means really are equal, because the more comparisons that are made, the greater the probability of a significant finding).

The following table for parametric (normally distributed) data will help you think about your data and the possible statistical procedures you might want to conduct. Once you have stated your research questions or hypotheses, operationalized all the variables, and formulated a sound methodology for gathering information from clients or research subjects, then you are ready to begin thinking about how you will analyze the resulting data.

Statistical Guide for Parametric Data

CIRCUMSTANCE	ANALYSIS YOU CAN DO
One Variable	
One nominal variable	Examine percentages and frequencies Mode is the appropriate measure of central tendency
One ordinal variable	Examine percentages and frequencies Median is the appropriate measure of central tendency
One interval (ratio) variable	Examine percentages and frequencies Mean is appropriate when the distribution is symmetric; otherwise, use median. Standard deviation and range can also be computed
Two Variables Two nominal variables (One dependent; the other independent)	Chi-square (or Fisher's exact test) examines for significant differences in proportions

Two ordinal variables (One dependent; the other independent)	Chi-square or Fisher's exact test examines for significant differences in proportions Spearman's rho correlation
Two interval variables	Pearson product–moment correlation
Mixed Two Variables **But Only Two Groups** (Dependent variable is interval; independent variable is nominal or ordinal)	*t*-test
More Than Two Groups (Dependent variable is interval; independent variables are nominal or ordinal)	One-way analysis of variance
Multiple Variables (Dependent variable is interval; independent variables are interval)	Multiple regression
(Dependent variable is nominal; independent variables are interval, ordinal, or nominal)	Logistical regression

NONPARAMETRIC STATISTICAL PROCEDURES

When it cannot be assumed that the population is normally distributed (and this assumption cannot be made when the sample is very small), then **nonparametric** techniques may be employed. **Parametric** statistical tests can be easily recognized because they are based on means and standard deviations, whereas, nonparametric procedures may involve ranks (or even signs between pairs). Sometimes nonparametric statistics are known as distribution-free statistical procedures because they do not require the assumption of a normal distribution. However, these techniques still require that observations be independent and that samples are randomly selected. Nonparametric statistical techniques are suited for data measured at the nominal and ordinal level. Often they are used with very small samples. For example, the Wilcoxon sign-ranks needs only seven matched cases, and the Mann-Whitney *U* can be performed with only five cases in each of the experimental and control groups. Nonparametric tests may be useful to you when conducting pilot studies or evaluating your own practice with a small sample of clients. Unlike the parametric procedures described earlier, these statistical tests are not often used or reported in major professional journals.

Quantitatively oriented researchers in the social sciences use parametric tests (e.g., *t*-tests, one-way analysis of variance) whenever possible. Because they do not require interval data, nonparametric procedures are not useful for picking up small differences—either between groups or between pretest and posttest scores. That is, they are not very sensitive to meager differences. Further, parametric tests will give you greater power to decrease the probability of committing a Type II

▪ ▪ ▪ ▪ ▪ ▪

WHEN TO USE NONPARAMETRIC STATISTICAL PROCEDURES

Nonparametric procedures should be used whenever

1. The distribution of values or scores doesn't appear to be normally distributed
   - The data have more than one mode (i.e., they are bimodal or multimodal)
   - The data have multiple outliers

2. Very small samples are being analyzed (e.g., 5 in each group)

3. Dependent variables are ordinal (ranked data) or dichotomous, such as
   - Positive and negative signs are used (e.g., father is older than mother (=+)
   - Nominal categories (e.g., empathetic and nonempathetic) are employed

error (incorrectly accepting a null hypothesis). Power is directly related to sample size, and in some circumstances it may be possible to use a more powerful parametric test by simply increasing sample size. But when the data don't fit, when you have very small samples, or when the assumptions of parametric statistical tests (such as for normal distributions) cannot be met, then the researcher needs to consider nonparametric statistics for analysis.

Although nonparametric tests can be computed by hand, most are easily performed with such statistical software as SPSS. The most common nonparametric procedures are discussed in the following table. However, please note that many more nonparametric statistical techniques exist than are discussed here.

Nonparametric Procedures Recommended According to Level of Data

NOMINAL-LEVEL DATA AND TWO RELATED SAMPLES

- **McNemar's test** is another name for the sign test when the variables being compared are nominal or dichotomous, as in a pretest-posttest research design, where we could have such variables as positive attitudes toward drug use versus negative attitudes toward drug use. Subjects are measured twice on the presence or absence of some characteristic or attitude, and so on. This test can be used to measure the impact of an intervention when the dependent variable is measured at the nominal level.

NOMINAL-LEVEL DATA AND TWO OR MORE INDEPENDENT SAMPLES

- Although chi-square was previously discussed in Chapter 11 for use when the data are presumed to be normally distributed, this statistic is virtually indispensable whenever you have nominal data and independent samples. For this reason, chi-square is often treated as a nonparametric technique. It works well with both very large and very small samples (as long as the expected frequencies for each cell are 5 or larger). SPSS automatically computes a special version of chi-square called Fisher's exact test when you have a 2 × 2 table in which the expected value in one or more cells is small.

NOMINAL-LEVEL DATA AND MULTIPLE RELATED SAMPLES

■ The **Cochran _Q_ test** is very similar to McNemar's test and is useful when there are more than two related samples. For instance, a school social worker might want to check to see if there were significant differences in disciplinary episodes among teens at risk for dropping out of high school. The dependent variable is measured as either the presence (1) or absence (0) of a disciplinary event. Let's assume there are six observations (the last six months of the year) and seven clients in the group. The null hypothesis states that there is no change among the students during the 6 months of intervention.

ORDINAL-LEVEL DATA AND TWO RELATED SAMPLES

■ The **sign test** checks for differences in related samples. Using plus and minus signs, one variable is compared to another based on which one is larger (+) or smaller (−). The procedure counts these signs and tied cases are equal to zero. Typically, subjects' scores come from a pretest/posttest design or from being matched with other subjects who have similar characteristics.

■ The **Wilcoxon matched-pairs test** looks at the rank-ordered differences between matched pairs. It's similar to the sign test, except that the magnitude of the differences is incorporated. As its name implies, the Wilcoxon test is also similar to the paired- (correlated-) samples _t_-test.

ORDINAL-LEVEL DATA AND TWO INDEPENDENT SAMPLES

■ The **Mann-Whitney _U_ test** provides an alternative to the independent-samples _t_-test and is one of the most powerful of nonparametric tests. It is used when two samples are randomly selected, independent, and continuous in nature, and the dependent variable is measured at least at the ordinal level. The distributions for the two groups do not have to be normal, but should have the same shape. The Mann-Whitney _U_ test is used to examine the null hypothesis that the two populations are the same (equivalent population distributions). Unlike the parametric _t_-test, the Mann-Whitney _U_ does not test whether the means are different.

■ The **Wald-Wolfowitz runs test** allows the researcher to test whether two samples have been drawn from the same population by picking up differences in continuous variables in terms of central tendency, concentration of values, skewness, and so forth. When there is one sample, the Wald-Wolfowitz runs test enables the researcher to determine whether a sequence of values is random.

ORDINAL-LEVEL DATA AND MULTIPLE INDEPENDENT SAMPLES

■ The **Kruskal-Wallis test** is an alternative to one-way analysis of variance; it tests whether the population distributions for several groups are similar by comparing the sum of ranks. Like the Mann-Whitney _U_ procedure, the Kruskal-Wallis requires only that the scores are measured at least at the ordinal level, the scores are obtained from independent groups randomly selected, and the dependent variable has a continuous distribution. Additionally, there should be at least five cases, or research subjects, in each group.

■ ■ ■ ■ ■

AN EXAMPLE OF THE MANN-WHITNEY *U* TEST

Theo is the director of a halfway house for men returning to the community from prison. He has noted that those who seem the least motivated to get additional education (either obtain their GED or take some classes at a nearby college) seem to return to prison more often than those with motivation for education. Theo had a friend, Brooke, from graduate school who worked at a halfway house for women. She agreed with Theo's observation, but wondered if women parolees were more motivated than men. Together they decided to test the null hypothesis that women parolees were no more motivated than men to further their educations.

Both Brooke and Theo rated all of the former residents of their facilities for the past two years in terms of motivation to acquire education using a simple 10-point scale (0 = no interest in education). From the list of their residents, Brooke and Theo randomly drew out 10 names and ranked the residents from the highest (1) to the lowest (10) in motivation for education.

This is what the data looked like:

BROOKE'S RESIDENTS	MOTIVATIONAL LEVEL	RANK	THEO'S RESIDENTS	MOTIVATIONAL LEVEL	RANK
Female A	9	2	Male A	10	1
Female B	5	6	Male B	8	3
Female C	7	4	Male C	4	7
Female D	3	10	Male D	3	8
Female E	2	5	Male E	2	9

The Mann-Whitney *U* was an appropriate nonparametric test to use because of the ordinal (ranked) data and small samples. Using SPSS, Brooke entered in the 10 rankings and created a variable to indicate her residents were in group 1 and Theo's were in group 2. She then chose from the ANALYZE menu NONPARAMETRIC TESTS, and from there selected TWO INDEPENDENT SAMPLES and MANN-WHITNEY *U*.

SPSS computed the mean ranking of the female residents to be 5.4. Although this was slightly lower than the men's ranking of 5.6, it was not a statistically significant difference ($p > .05$). Brooke and Theo concluded that, based on these two samples of halfway house residents, there wasn't any difference by gender in motivation for education.

For further reading on nonparametric procedures, see the classic work by Sidney Siegel, *Nonparametric Statistics for the Behavioral Sciences* (1956). You might also find Norusis' *SPSS: 9.0 Guide to Data Analysis* (1999) helpful.

TERMS TO KNOW

Cochran Q test (p. 289)   Parametric data (p. 287)
Kruskal-Wallis test (p. 289)   Robust (p. 285)
Mann-Whitney U test (p. 289)   Sign test (p. 289)
McNemar's test (p. 288)   Wald-Wolfowitz runs test (p. 289)
Nonparametric data (p. 287)   Wilcoxon matched-pairs test (p. 289)

REVIEW PROBLEMS

The situation: Robin and James have designed a questionnaire to collect information from social work students on their preferences for how they want to be graded on their practicums. These are the data they collected:

	FEMALES	MALES
In favor of pass/fail	10	7
In favor of letter grades	25	8
Totals	35	15

1. What is the appropriate statistic to help Robin and James decide if there are differences by gender?

2. Calculate the necessary statistical test. What do you conclude?

3. Robin and James look through the completed survey forms and discover that they have both interviewed nine of the same students. In order for them to meet the condition of _____, they decide to throw out duplicate surveys from the same individuals.

4. Using the unduplicated data that follow, would Robin and James reach a different conclusion?

	FEMALES	MALES
In favor of pass/fail	8	8
In favor of letter grades	20	5
Total	28	13

5. Lynn has collected over 400 surveys from clients who received intervention from his agency. Every case manager participated in randomly sampling 20 clients from his or her caseload. Should Lynn be concerned that the data might violate the assumptions of normal distribution?

6. True or false—like parametric statistical procedures, nonparametric techniques are most appropriately used with large samples.

7. Sue wants to compare the success of her Saturday morning psycho-education group with a control group of clients who received a standard treatment regimen. Because she has used an instrument which provides interval-level data on clients' life satisfaction, Sue is planning to use the paired-samples *t*-test. Is she correct?

8. Sue's supervisor asks her to include the data from a third group of clients, those who dropped out after the first month. Sue is now looking to see if there are significant differences among the three groups of clients, so which statistical procedure should she use?

REFERENCES

Glass, G. V., & Hopkins, K. D. (1996). *Statistical methods in education and psychology.* Boston: Allyn & Bacon.

Norusis, M. J. (1999). *SPSS 9.0 guide to data analysis.* Upper Saddle River, NJ: Prentice-Hall.

Siegel, S. (1956). *Nonparametric statistics for the behavioral sciences.* New York: McGraw-Hill.

ANSWERS TO REVIEW QUESTIONS

CHAPTER 1

1. Yes. Bob has defined adolescent as persons 13 to 18—not 12 to 17 or 13 to 19.

2. The 50 case records constitute a small sample from the population of 900 adolescents admitted to the agency in the past year.

3. Yes, although it is not formally stated as one. He could have said, "I have a hypothesis that, of the clients admitted to the treatment center, teens who have dropped out of school will show higher levels of depression than students who are still attending."

4. School attendance is an independent variable used to understand the dependent variable of depression.

5. Bob is right. The raw data constitute the information actually used in the study.

6. Age, school status (dropped out or still attending regularly), and level of depression.

7. This term might be operationalized several different ways depending on the researcher's interests: (a) a young person who has been arrested on more than one occasion, (b) anyone under the age of 18 who is charged with and found guilty of breaking a law, (c) any teen who commits a felony.

8. Descriptive statistics.

CHAPTER 2

1. The informed consent should contain such information as the following:
    - Who is responsible for conducting the study and who can answer questions about it
    - The purpose of the study
    - Where and when the study will take place, and the amount of time involved
    - What subjects will be asked to do (e.g., what procedures)
    - Any risks or possible harm, and any potential benefits
    - Any incentives
    - Statement that research subjects may drop out or stop participating at any time without losing benefits or privileges to which they are entitled

2. The guidelines for conducting ethical research typically include the following:
    - Research participant must freely volunteer (no coercion is allowed).
    - Sufficient information about the study must be provided.
    - No harm shall result as a consequence of participation.
    - Sensitive information must be protected.

3. The correct term is *confidentiality.* Since George knows the subjects he is collecting data from, they are not anonymous. Whether they are his friends or not, professional ethics require that George not repeat or share any information that could identify individuals in the group of college students he interviewed.

4. Yes. Information about cheating practices and the amount of cheating one has done is very sensitive information that could harm one's current reputation.

5. Pam was unethical on two counts: First, because she didn't read the materials given to her, she wasn't in a position to be knowledgeable about the risks and benefits associated with participants taking the new drug. Not only would she have been unable to answer questions, she also wasn't able to alert subjects to possible risks, contra-indications, or interaction effects with other medicines. There's a potential problem if some subjects might have thought there was no danger and signed the consent form when the medication did have real risks attached to it.

    Second, telling patients that Dr. Osgood would not be happy with their lack of participation is an implied threat. Patients may have felt they were being coerced into participation or they would lose their doctor. The fear of losing a doctor familiar with a long-standing or tricky medical problem is a very real fear for many adults with chronic difficulties.

CHAPTER 3

1. Nominal.

2. Interval/ratio.

3. Ordinal.

4. Yes, because the increments of months and years are intervals of equal width and predictable.

5. Yes. Each director, representing each mental health agency, can be considered a case, or subject.

6. Answers vary, but here are some examples: male/female, voter/nonvoter, full-time employee/part-time employee.

7. Here are some examples: height (when measured in inches or centimeters), years of education, days absent from school, hours of overtime worked, number of crying spells in the last 30 days, number of angry outbursts in the last 7 days.

8. The lowest ranking would be those with little or no knowledge of parenting, followed by those with some knowledge, and the top ranking could be good knowledge of parenting. Other answers are possible—for instance, moderate could be another way of saying some. These are often subjective decisions.

CHAPTER 4

1. Boys' self-esteem scores = 6, 6, 8, 9, 11, 11, 12, 14, 14, 17

2.
BOYS' SCORES	FREQUENCY (*f*)	
6	//	2
8	/	1
9	/	1
11	//	2
12	/	1
14	//	2
17	/	1
Total:		10

3. **Absolute and Cumulative Frequencies and Percentages: Self-Esteem Scores for Participants in Boys' Friendship Group**

SELF-ESTEEM SCORES	FREQUENCY (*f*)	CUMULATIVE FREQUENCY (*Cf*)	PERCENT (%)	CUMULATIVE PERCENT (%)
6	2	2	20	20
8	1	3	10	30
9	1	4	10	40
11	2	6	20	60
12	1	7	10	70
14	2	9	20	90
17	1	10	10	100
	N = 10		100	

4. Girls = 3; Boys = 0

5. 40%

6. Since 50% scored 10 or lower, 100% − 50% = 50%

7. It's generally a good idea to report the underlying frequencies when presenting percentages—this is especially critical when dealing with small sample sizes like Amber's.

8. Percentages are not only familiar to most of us, but they're also more intuitively meaningful. Specifically, it's easier to talk in terms of number per 100 than parts of a whole (or 1). Although the decimals associated with proportions are descriptive, they're awkward to discuss and interpret.

9. Answers will vary. One option might center around basic needs, such as food, clothing, and shelter. Another might target social services' roles—advocacy, counseling, and case management. Still another might sort by targeted client systems—individual, family, group, and community.

CHAPTER 5

1. A histogram or frequency polygon could be used to display the clients' age data, since age has been measured at an interval/ratio level. Given the nominal nature of the race and gender data, Chelsie could use a pie or bar graph to display these variables.

2. Histograms are appropriate for displaying data measured at an interval or ratio level. They can also be used to depict ordinal-level data—especially when the categories associated with the variable represent interval-, or ratio-level data that have been collapsed (i.e., they can be considered inherently interval/ratio).

3. Answers will vary. If the data remain uncollapsed, students are likely to present a histogram or frequency polygon, given the interval/ratio nature of the client age data reported. Note: The inclusion of an age of zero poses an interesting dilemma. Developing a category labeled *less than one year* is one solution.

4. In terms of appearance, Figure 5.9 is horizontal in perspective, whereas Figure 5.18 is vertical. The category labels differ from figure to figure. Labels are included in the histogram and omitted from the stem-and-leaf diagram. Two differences of special note are that (1) one can glean more information from the stem-and-leaf display because it includes actual scores, and (2) the differences in frequency have been exaggerated slightly in the histogram, due to the truncation of the vertical axis, or *y*-axis. The most striking similarity is the comparable pattern in the overall distribution of scores that is communicated. Interestingly, this occurs despite the distortion we created by truncating the *y*-axis used in the histogram.

5. Based on an examination of the data presented in this histogram (Figure 5.6), it appears that the agency is indeed serving clients of different ages. Note, however, the relatively low number of individuals being served between the ages of 1 to 10 and 61 to 70. Census data would be helpful in discerning whether the proportion of clients being served within these (and other age groups for that matter) reflect the age distribution that actually exists within the targeted service community.

CHAPTER 6

1. The central tendency figures for 1998 are
   Mode   = 10
   Median = 10 (simple) or 10.55 (50th percentile)
   Mean   = 10.13

   The central tendency figures for 1999 are
   Mode   = 5
   Median = 5 (simple) or 5.44 (50th percentile)
   Mean   = 13.33

2. The modal category dropped in half over the 2-year period from a caseload size of 10 to 5. The median dropped the same amount. Meanwhile, a slight increase in the mean caseload size occurred, from 10.13 in 1998 to 13.33 in 1999. Overall, the modes and medians suggest a substantial reduction in caseload size during this 2-year period. The means, however, suggest an average increase in caseload of 3.

3. Given the similar values calculated for all three measures for 1998, the mean appears to be a reasonably good indicator of what's typical. For 1999, however, the mean is over twice as large as the mode or the median, suggesting a rather skewed distribution. In such cases, the median is usually more representative of what's typical than the mean. In light of the unusual distribution presented for 1999, though, it's difficult to say a caseload of 5 is typical.

4. No one indicator of central tendency clearly communicates what's been happening with the size of these workers' caseloads. It's probably wise, therefore, to report the mode, median, and mean for both distributions. Inclusion of a frequency table or histogram would help tell the story, too!

5. Potential answers will vary. However, the need to reach better equity in caseload distribution among these workers seems clear.

CHAPTER 7

1. The observed scores for the outpatient group have a high of 10 and a low of 0. The range of observed scores for the clients being served as outpatients, therefore, is 10 (10 − 0 = 10). There are no observations of 0, 1, 9, or 10 for the inpatient group, which leaves us with a high of 8 and a low of 2. The range of observed scores for this group, then, is 6 (8 − 2 = 6).

2. The value that contains the 1st quartile is 4, and the 3rd quartile is located within the score of 6. Therefore, the interquartile range is 2 (6 − 4 = 2).

3. The boxplot indicates that the medians of the two groups are the same, and that there is greater variability in the scores obtained by the group being served on an outpatient basis. Additionally, there are no scores for either group that have been identified as either outliers or extreme scores.

   Answers will vary for the second part of the question. One possible explanation is that the combination of treatment effects (e.g., regulated stimulation, medication, therapy) prompt a certain level of homogeneity in anxiety levels among people receiving inpatient services.

4. The completed table should look like the following table:

Ages of Group Members over the Previous 3 Months, by Age

	Children's Group			Adult Group	
NUMBER OF SESSIONS ATTENDED (X)	DEVIATION (d_1) $(X - \bar{X}_1)$	SQUARED DEVIATION $(d_1)^2$ $(X - \bar{X}_1)^2$	NUMBER OF SESSIONS ATTENDED (X)	DEVIATION (d_2) $(X - \bar{X}_2)$	SQUARED DEVIATION $(d_2)^2$ $(X - \bar{X}_2)^2$
6	−4	16	5	−5	25
11	1	1	5	−5	25
14	4	16	16	6	36
10	0	0	16	6	36
5	−5	25	6	−4	16
10	0	0	15	5	25
9	−1	1	13	3	9
15	5	25	4	−6	36
12	2	4	6	−4	16
8	−2	4	14	4	16
$\bar{X}_1 = 10$	Sum = 0	Sum = 92	$\bar{X}_2 = 10$	Sum = 0	Sum = 240

The standard deviation for the adult group is 5.164 = ($\sqrt{240/9}$).

CHAPTER 8

1. **a.** Typically, income is positively skewed, meaning that most people's earnings cluster along the lower to center values of the wage continuum. Outliers will consist of those relatively few people who earn from a hundred thousand to millions of dollars annually. Graphically, income distributions tend to look like the poor policy test scores depicted in Figure 8.1—with the tail pointing to the right.

   b. In a positively skewed distribution, outliers lie on the right, or positive side, of the number line. Because the mean is pulled in the direction of these outliers, we'll find it lying to the right of the median. Alternatively, we can say the median will be smaller in value than the mean and, therefore, will lie to its left.

   c. Because of its resistance to outliers, the median is the best indicator of "average" in a skewed distribution. When in doubt, it's best to report all indicators of central tendency (i.e., mean, median, and mode).

2. **a.** Skewness for the data on length of time in foster care was reported as –0.115. This value is well within acceptable limits, indicating the data are fairly normally distributed around the mean. The skewness measure divided by its standard error produces a value of 0.6686—much less than the cutoff of 2.0 for "markedly skewed."

   b. Kurtosis for our data on length of time in foster care is –1.20. Because the value is lower than –1, the distribution would be described as platykurtic, or somewhat flatter than the standard bell-shaped curve. Dividing the kurtosis measure by its standard error produces a value of 3.5—much more than the 2.0 guideline for a normal distribution.

3. In a normal distribution, we can expect to find 95.44% of scores within ± 2 standard deviations of the mean (34.13 + 34.13 + 13.59 + 13.59 = 95.44).

4. The standard normal curve is a unimodal, symmetrical (skewness = 0), bell-shaped (kurtosis = 0), asymptotic curve with a mean, median, and mode of 0 and a standard deviation of 1.

5. Maggie's score of 38 on this depression scale would yield a z-score of 1.6 [(38 – 30) / 5 = 1.6]. This converts to a percentile ranking of approximately 95 (50 + 44.52 = 94.52). In other words, Maggie is quite depressed and definitely is in need of intervention.

CHAPTER 9

1. Sorting the data into ascending order, by length of time sober, we have the following:

CLIENT	JOHNS	JONES	KRANTZ	QUINN	SIMMS	CROSS	HALL	CAGE	MACK	HOSE
Length of Time Sober (Months)	4	5	6	7	10	11	12	13	16	18

The probability that the client you select will have at least 1 year of sobriety is 4/10, or 40%.

P (Hall or Cage or Mack or Hose)
$$= 1/10 + 1/10 + 1/10 + 1/10 = 4/10$$

The probability that the client you select will have at least 1½ years of sobriety is 1/10, or 10%.

P (Hose) $= 1/10$

The probability that the client you select will have less than 1 year of sobriety is 6/10, or 60%.

P (Johns or Jones or Krantz or Quinn or Simms or Cross)
$$= 1/10 + 1/10 + 1/10 + 1/10 + 1/10 + 1/10 = 6/10$$

Alternatively, this can be calculated using the complement rule, where

[P (not Hall or Cage or Mack or Hose) $= 1 - P$ (Hall or Cage or Mack or Hose) $= 1 - 4/10 = 6/10$]

The probability that the client you select will have less than 6 months of sobriety is 2/10, or 20%.

P (Johns or Jones) $= 1/10 + 1/10 = 2/10$

The probability you'll select the 2 clients who reported the longest periods of sobriety (i.e., Mack *and* Hose) is pretty slim—1/100 or 1%.

[P (Mack *and* Hose) $= 1/10 \times 1/10 = 1/100$]

2. The information associated with a 99% confidence interval is shown in the following graph:

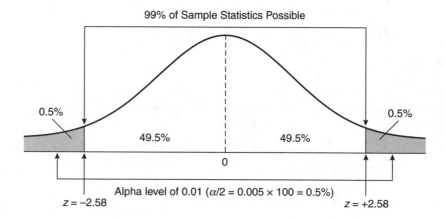

99% of Sample Statistics Possible

0.5%   0.5%

49.5%   49.5%

0

Alpha level of 0.01 ($\alpha/2 = 0.005 \times 100 = 0.5\%$)

$z = -2.58$ $z = +2.58$

3. The first step in constructing the 99% confidence interval would be to calculate the standard error $(s/\sqrt{n})$, which comes out to 1.49. To construct the confidence interval, we multiply this standard error by the relevant z-score of 2.58, which yields a product of 3.84. To complete the construction of the confidence interval, we subtract and then add this figure to the mean score of 10.2, generating an interval that ranges from 6.36 to 14.04.

CHAPTER 10

1. Wording will vary. The null hypothesis conveys the notion that there is no relationship between flexible hours and the frequency of successful case outcomes. The research hypothesis can convey the logical opposite of the null hypothesis in one of two ways: (1) The research hypothesis may argue that there is a relationship between flexible hours and the frequency of positive case outcomes, or (2) given the empirical data described, the research hypothesis may suggest a negative relationship between flexible hours and the frequency of positive case outcomes.

   In choosing an appropriate α level, consider (a) the consequences associated with finding a relationship between the variables when in fact there isn't one (i.e., committing a Type I error), or (b) the consequences of not detecting a relationship that does exist (i.e., committing a Type II error). In the first case (a), if the concern is centered around prematurely revoking a policy that employees have found beneficial, you may want to set a more stringent α level (such as 0.01) to minimize the likelihood of attributing the declining success rate to this policy in error. Alternately (b), if your goal is to identify factors that are potentially having a negative impact on successful case outcomes, you would want to set a less stringent α level (such as 0.10) to minimize the possibility of overlooking a meaningful relationship. Of course, you may opt to follow standard protocol and set your α level at 0.05.

2. The null hypothesis would state that there is no difference between the two treatment strategies (treatment A and treatment B) with respect to reducing anxiety. The research hypothesis would state that there is a difference between the two treatment strategies, and it may predict the direction or nature of that relationship. With respect to the possibility of committing a Type II error, you can breathe a sigh of relief—Type II error can be committed only when the decision is made *not* to reject H_0.

3. The choices that constitute statistical hypotheses are (c) $\mu = 8$ and (e) $\sigma = 4.3$. The other options are omitted because they specify numerical values for statistics, rather than parameters.

CHAPTER 11

1. Calculating the percentages in the columns does give the impression that persons with obvious handicaps have higher self-esteem (see Table 1). Thirty-three percent of students with obvious handicaps are at the highest level of self-esteem, compared with only 25% of those falling within the invisibly handicapped category. Similarly, about 42% of those with invisible handicaps are in the lowest self-esteem category, compared with just 28% of those with obvious handicaps.

2. The computed chi-square is 1.558 with two degrees of freedom, and this is not statistically significant ($p = .46$). If you calculated the chi-square manually and didn't arrive at the same conclusion, you might want to check your expected frequencies against those in Table 2 (p. 305).

3. Examples of possible control variables are
   gender, race, age group (18 to 24/25 or older)
   length of time with the disability (less than a year, 1 to 5 years, more than 5 years)
   etiology (congenital or accident)
   severity (severe, moderate, slight)

4. The correct answer is (c)—a weak relationship.

1. Self-Esteem and Disability Type Cross-Tabulation

		DISABILITY TYPE		
SELF-ESTEEM		Invisible	Obvious	TOTAL
Lowest	Count	15	11	26
	% within disability type	41.7%	28.2%	34.7%
Moderate	Count	12	15	27
	% within disability type	33.3%	38.5%	36.0%
Highest	Count	9	13	22
	% within disability type	25.0%	33.3%	29.3%
Total	Count	36	39	75
	% within disability type	100.0%	100.0%	100.0%

2. Self-Esteem and Disability Type Cross-Tabulation

SELF-ESTEEM		DISABILITY TYPE		
		Invisible	Obvious	TOTAL
Lowest	Count	15	11	26
	Expected count	12.5	13.5	26.0
	% within disability type	41.7%	28.2%	34.7%
Moderate	Count	12	15	27
	Expected count	13.0	14.0	27.0
	% within disability type	33.3%	38.5%	36.0%
Highest	Count	9	13	22
	Expected count	10.6	11.4	22.0
	% within disability type	25.0%	33.3%	29.3%
Total	Count	36	39	75
	Expected count	36.0	39.0	75.0
	% within disability type	100.0%	100.0%	100.0%

CHAPTER 12

1. True.

2. Yes, because both variables are increasing.

3. In the last case, an individual has reported being in drug treatment 676 times. This is an outlier because it is so vastly different from what is reported by the others. We'd probably exclude this data because it seems pretty unlikely that anyone would enter treatment on that many occasions.

4. The coefficient of determination is .19 (19%).

5. Curvilinear data exist if you can detect any curves in the scattergram (e.g., U-, S-, or J-shaped data) or if you find it difficult to see a linear direction (e.g., the data moving from the bottom left of the graph to the top right on a diagonal) and can't easily fit a narrow band or envelope around the data points outlining a single direction.

6. False. They can use different interval scales.

7. False.

8. Rho = .79

9. There are no inverse correlations displayed in the correlation matrix.

10. The data are heteroscedastic.

CHAPTER 13

1. Interval.

2. Treatment group mean = .20 re-arrests. Control group mean = .7308 re-arrests.

3. Independent-samples t-test

4. There are significant differences between the two groups; $p = .04$.

5. $t(32.77) = -2.178$, $p = .04$. (The degrees of freedom is not 44 because the variances were not equal.)

6. ANOVA.

7. The jailed group (mean = .92).

8. The differences among the three groups are not significantly different, $p = .07$.

9. $F(2, 68) = 2.77$, $p = .07$.

10. True; it would be a paired-samples t-test.

11. No; the mean of 16.5 months (13 cases) is not statistically significant. The $t = -.339$ (12 df), $p = .74$.

CHAPTER 14

1. Answers may vary. It appears that together, age and income explain about 25% of the variance observed in the burden scores obtained. Furthermore, given the probability value reported, the likelihood of getting this finding by chance is quite slim (i.e., 1 in 1,000).

2. Age was found to be a significant predictor of caregiver burden ($\beta = -.28, p < .003$). The relationship, however, is negative, suggesting that younger caregivers experience greater burden. At the same time, a significant positive relationship was observed between income and burden ($\beta = .37, p < .003$). That is, those earning more tended to experience greater burden.

   With regard to the age/burden finding, it has been observed that older family caregivers also tend to be the care recipients' spouses. This relationship and its concurrent role expectations seem to render caregiving less burdensome for older, caregiving spouses. Initially, students may find the positive relationship between income and burden somewhat puzzling. After all, if you have sufficient funds, can't you hire someone to assist with the more burdensome aspects of caregiving? Although this makes sense, it has also been observed that caregivers who are employed report higher levels of burden. If we equate income with employment status, then the positive relationship between income and burden tends to make more sense.

3.a.

GENDER	TREATMENT				ROW MEANS
	Outpatient	Methadone	Residential	Dropouts	
Male	$M = 4.14$	$M = 12.47$	$M = 1.71$	$M = 16.77$	$M = 8.78$
Female	$M = 12.50$	$M = 17.60$	$M = 4.81$	$M = 15.33$	$M = 12.56$
Difference	−8.36	−5.13	−3.1	1.44	
COLUMN MEANS:	$M = 8.38$	$M = 15.03$	$M = 3.27$	$M = 16.05$	

Any number of observations regarding these data can be made. For example, the row means tell us that, as a group, women used drugs more often during the past 30 days than their male counterparts did. Furthermore, this pattern held across three of the four treatment conditions. The only exception involved female dropouts who tended to do slightly better (used drugs less frequently on average) than the males who dropped out of the program. Comparisons involving the column means suggest that clients involved in the residential treatment program used drugs less frequently during the past 30 days than any other group. Those in the outpatient group did better than the methadone or dropout conditions. On average, men who participated in the residential treatment program used drugs less often than any other group.

---

3. **b.** DIFFERENCE: −8.36   −5.13   −3.1   1.44

The differences noted between rows are not identical from column to column. It appears, therefore, that there is interaction between gender and treatment.

3. **c.** H_{01} There is no actual difference in the mean substance-use patterns observed among the four treatment groups.

H_{02} There is no actual difference in the mean substance-use patterns observed between men and women.

H_{03} There is no actual difference in the mean substance-use patterns observed among the four treatment groups, whether the treatments are used with men or women (i.e., there is no differential impact).

3. **d.** Tiffinea can tell Ms. Collins that, as before, a significant main effect was found for both treatments. Specifically, the mean substance-use patterns obtained for those in the residential and outpatient treatment conditions were notably lower than those observed for the methadone and treatment groups. A significant main effect was found for gender, as well. In particular, the data suggest that women participating in these treatments seem to be less successful (i.e., report a higher average substance-use rate) than their male counterparts. Although an interaction between gender and treatment was observed, it was not found to be significant.

CHAPTER 15

1. Chi-square.

2. There were no significant differences by gender (chi-square $= 1.53, p = .22$).

3. Independence.

4. Yes, the results are now statistically significant (chi-square $= 4.056, p = .044$). When the duplicated students are removed from the sample, 71% of the females are in favor of letter grades, but less than 40% of the males are in favor of them.

5. No. This large sample obtained by random sampling should conform to a normal distribution. The normal distribution can usually be assumed as long as the data are not known to be biased in some way.

6. False. Usually they are used with small samples.

7. No. Sue should use the independent-samples t-test because she is comparing two different groups of individuals.

8. With one independent variable (type of treatment received) producing three different groups and the interval-level dependent variable, Sue should use one-way analysis of variance (ANOVA).